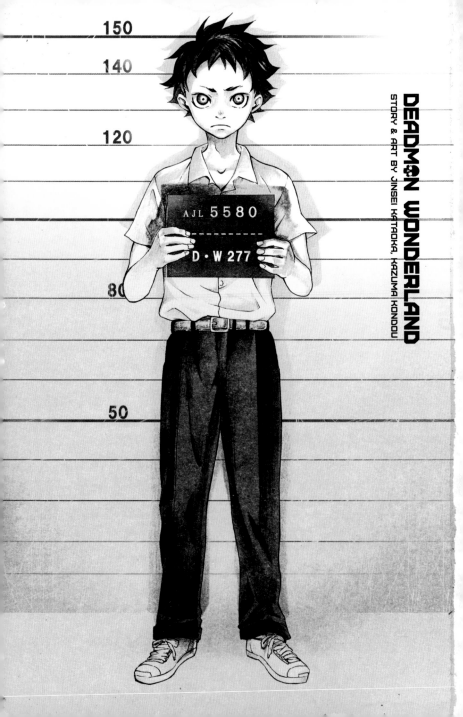

AJL 5580

D · W 277

# DEADMAN WONDERLAND

STORY & ART BY JINSEI KATAOKA, KAZUMA KONDOU

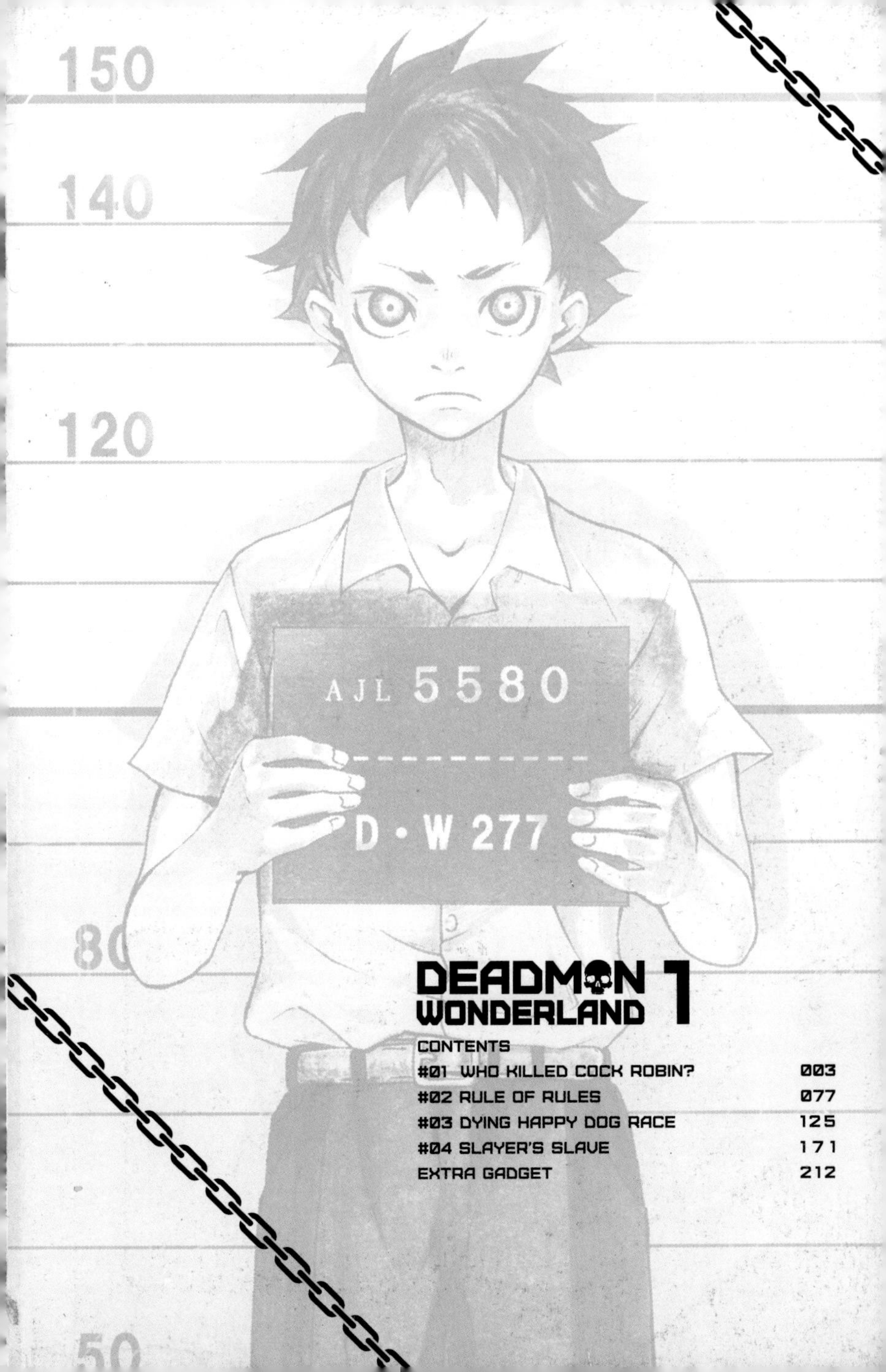
150
140
120
80
50
AJL 5580
D • W 277

# DEADMAN WONDERLAND 1

CONTENTS

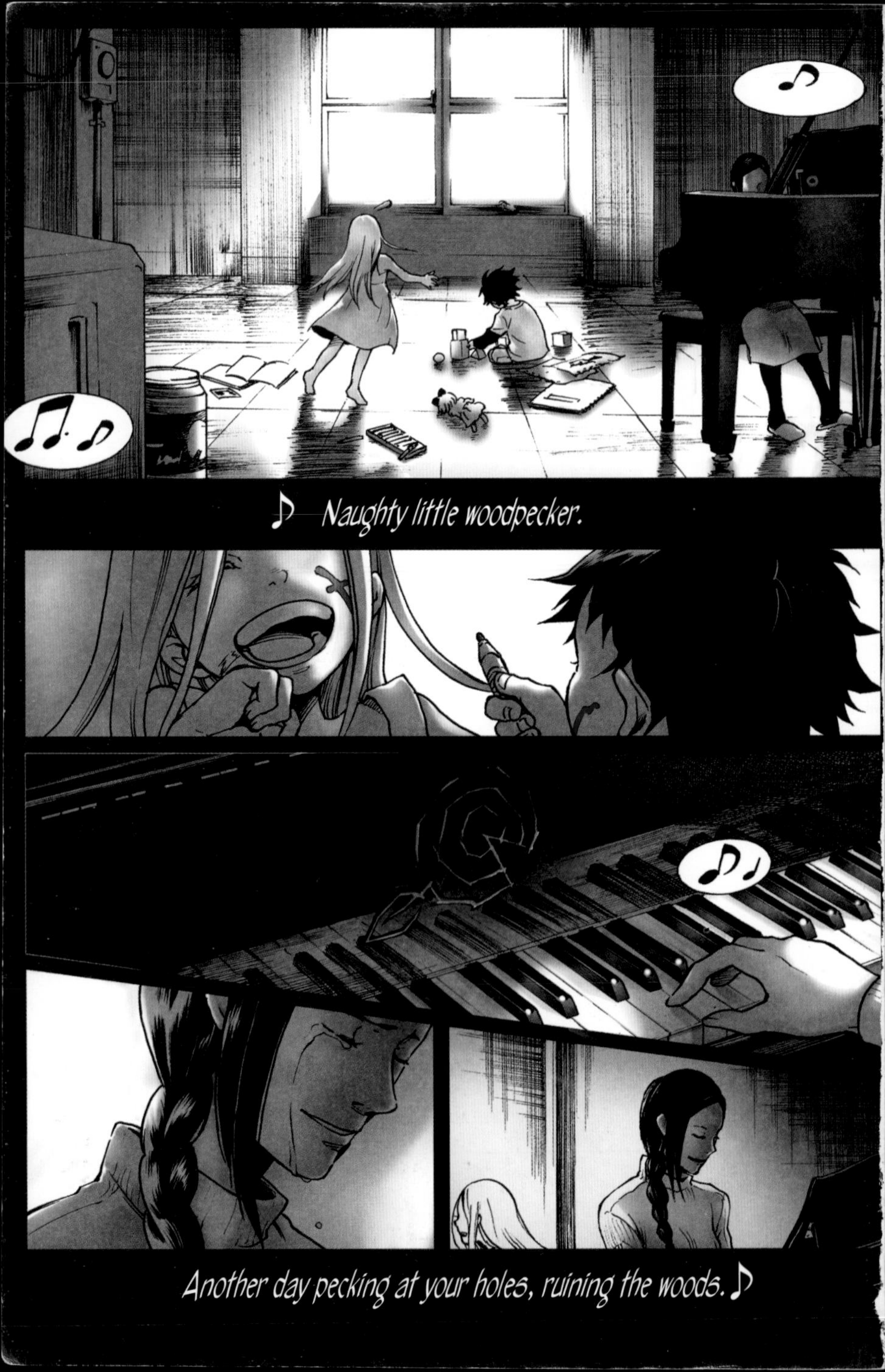
♪ Naughty little woodpecker.
Another day pecking at your holes, ruining the woods. ♪

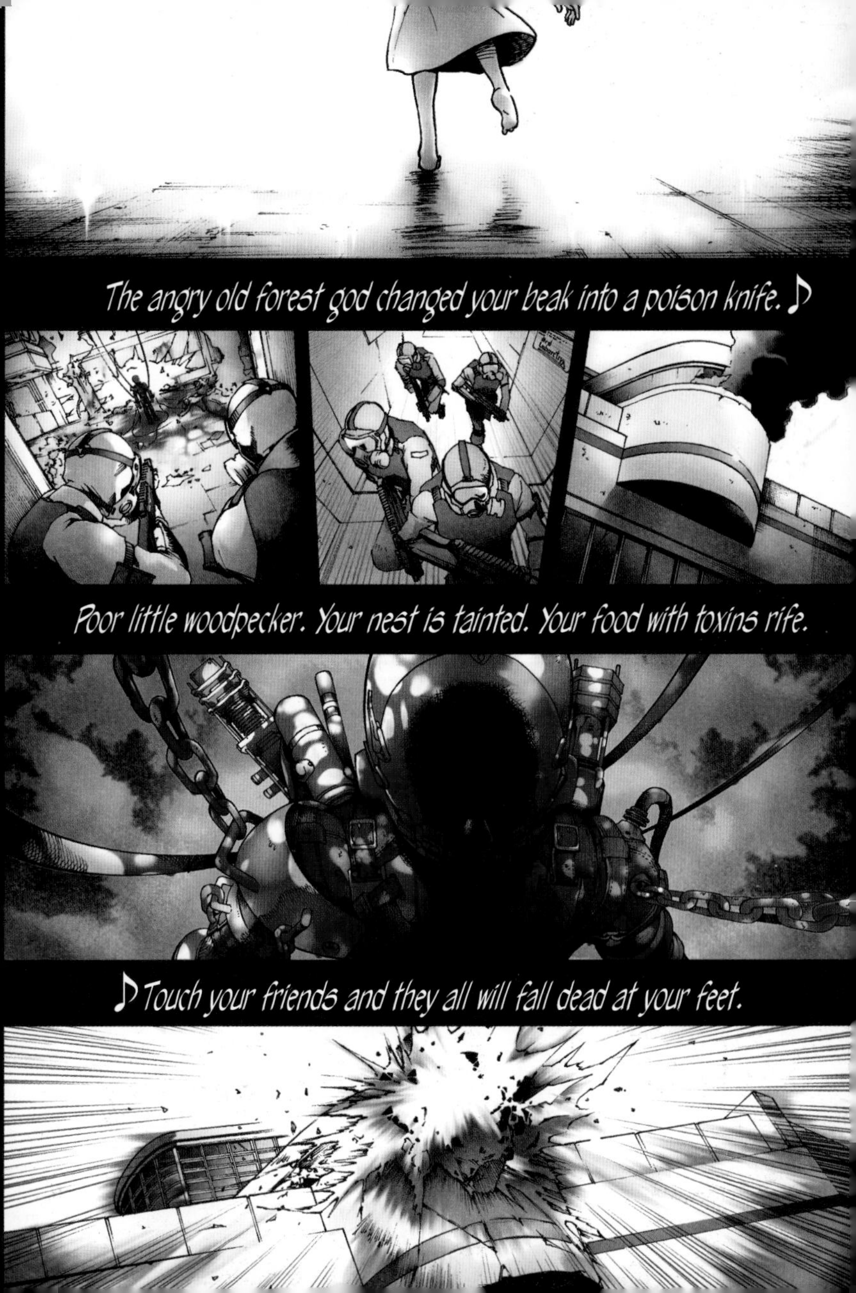
The angry old forest god changed your beak into a poison knife. ♪
Poor little woodpecker. Your nest is tainted. Your food with toxins rife.
♪ Touch your friends and they all will fall dead at your feet.

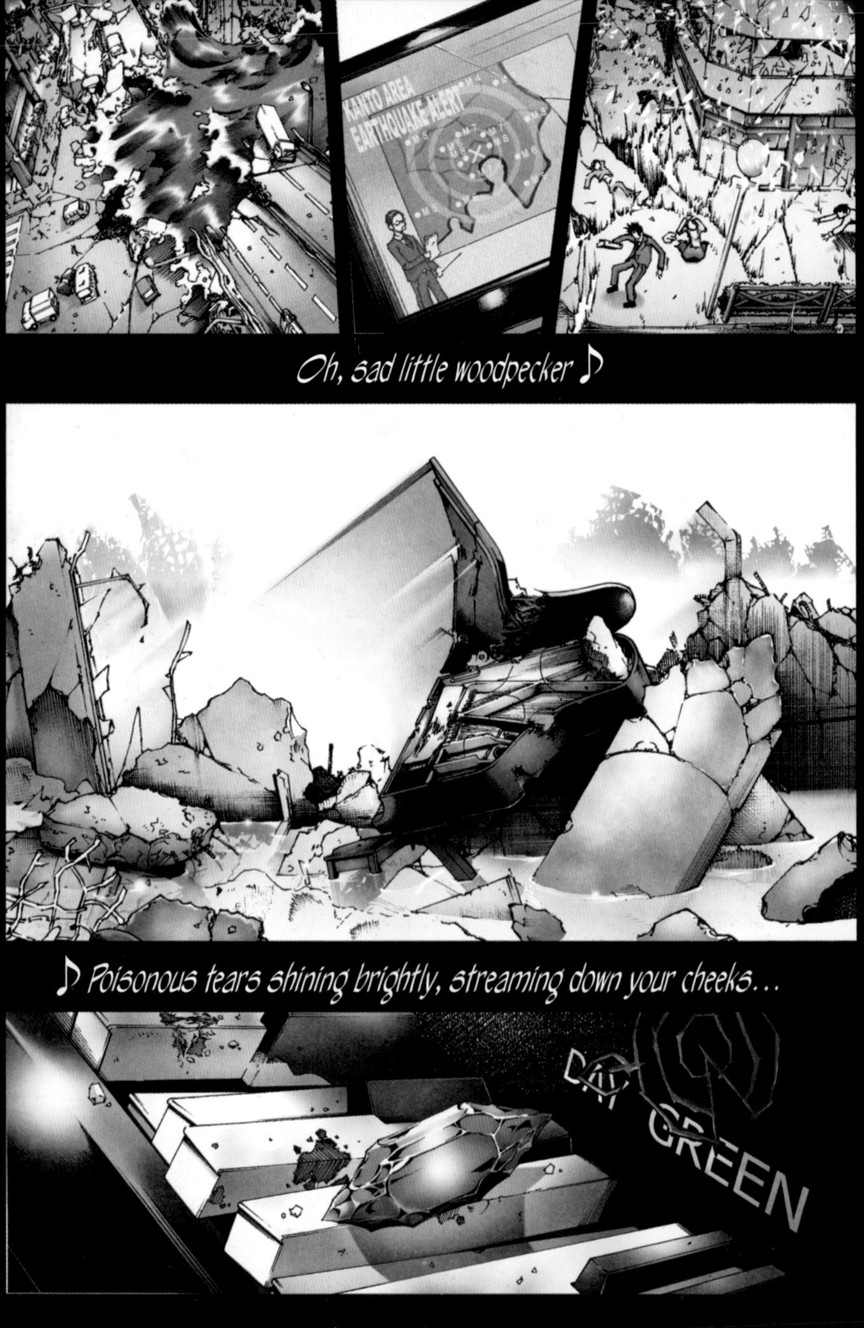
KANTO AREA
EARTHQUAKE ALERT
Oh, sad little woodpecker ♪
♪ Poisonous tears shining brightly, streaming down your cheeks...
GREEN

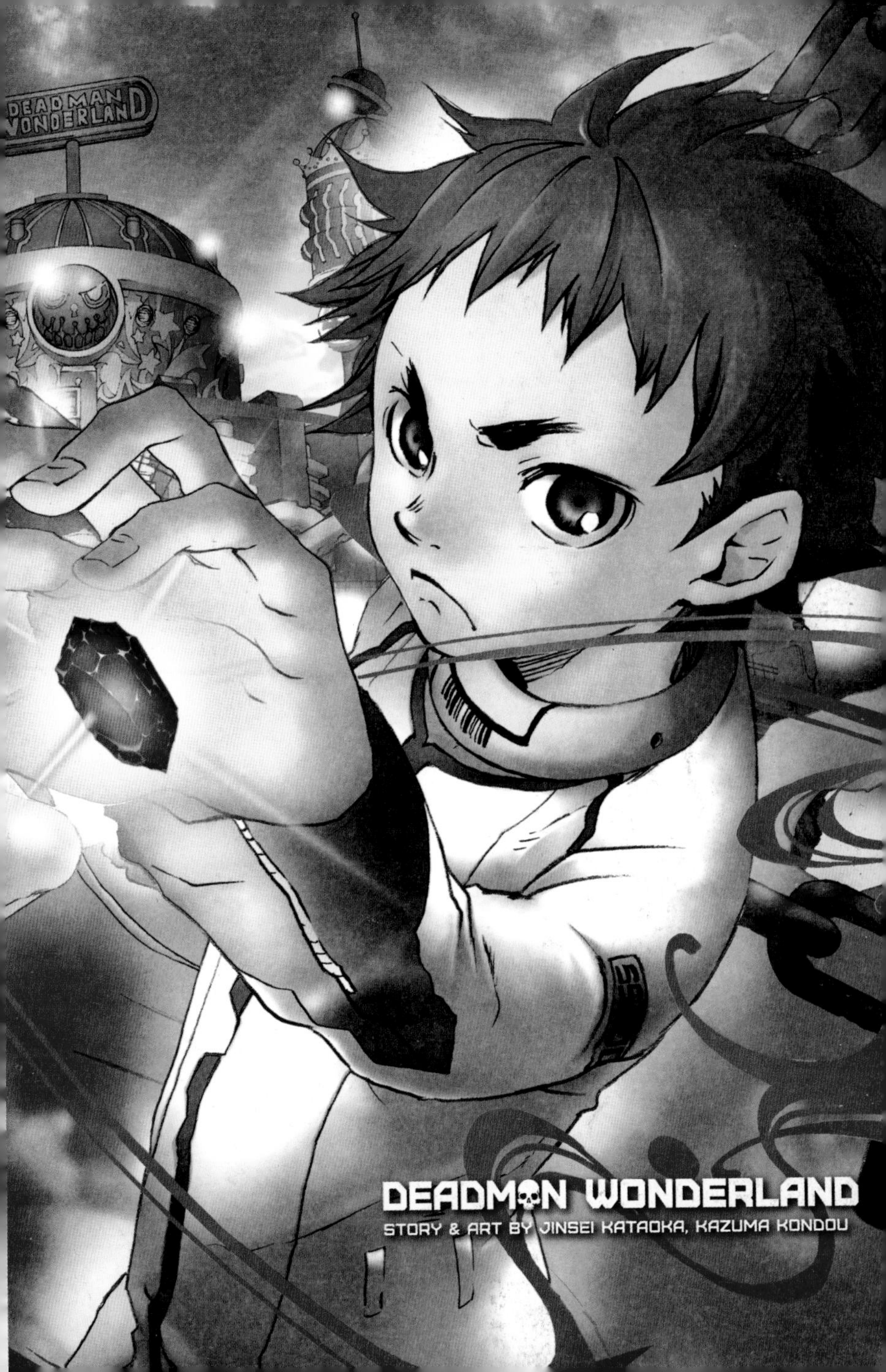
DEADMAN WONDERLAND
DEADMAN WONDERLAND
STORY & ART BY JINSEI KATAOKA, KAZUMA KONDOU

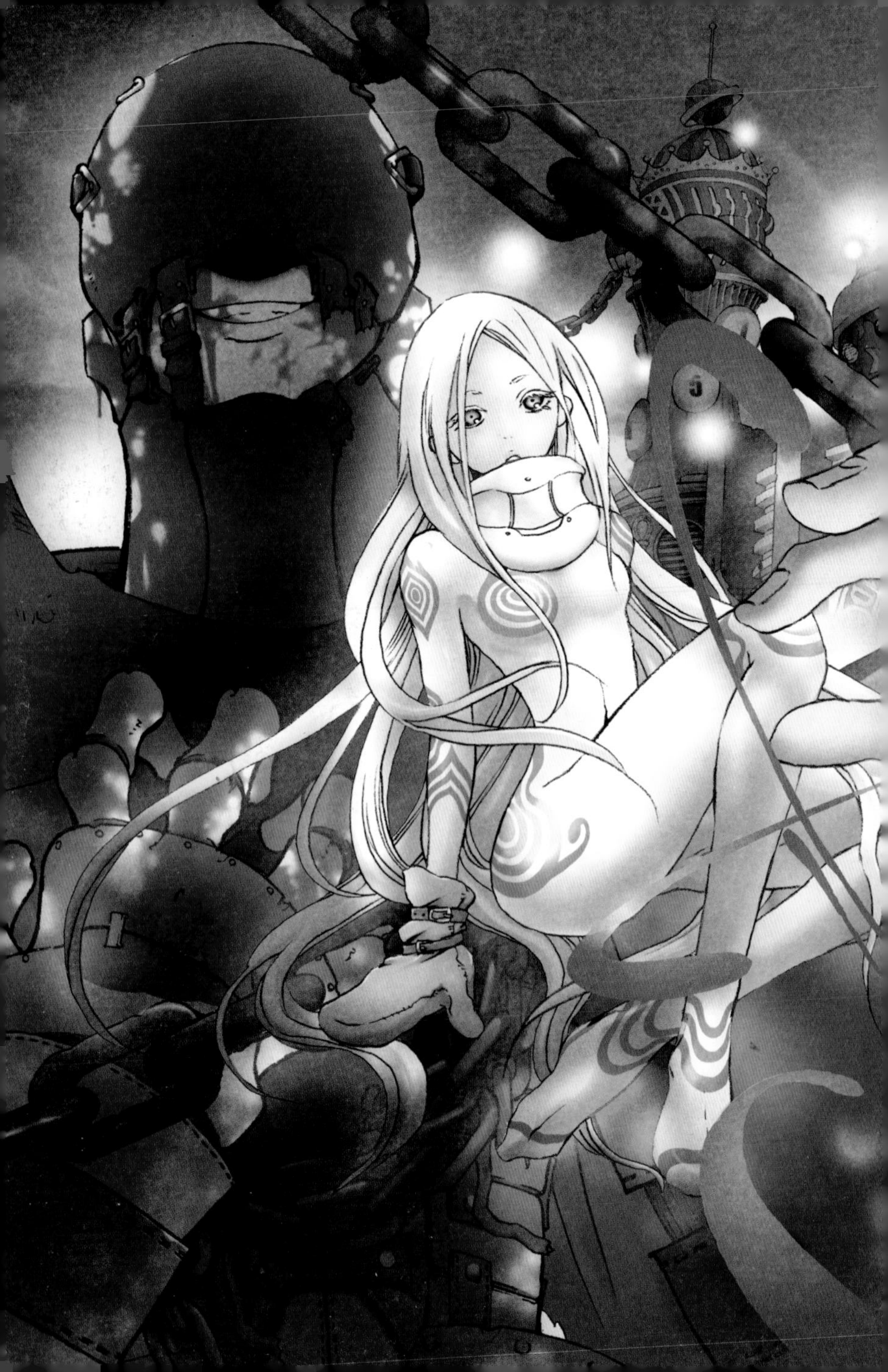

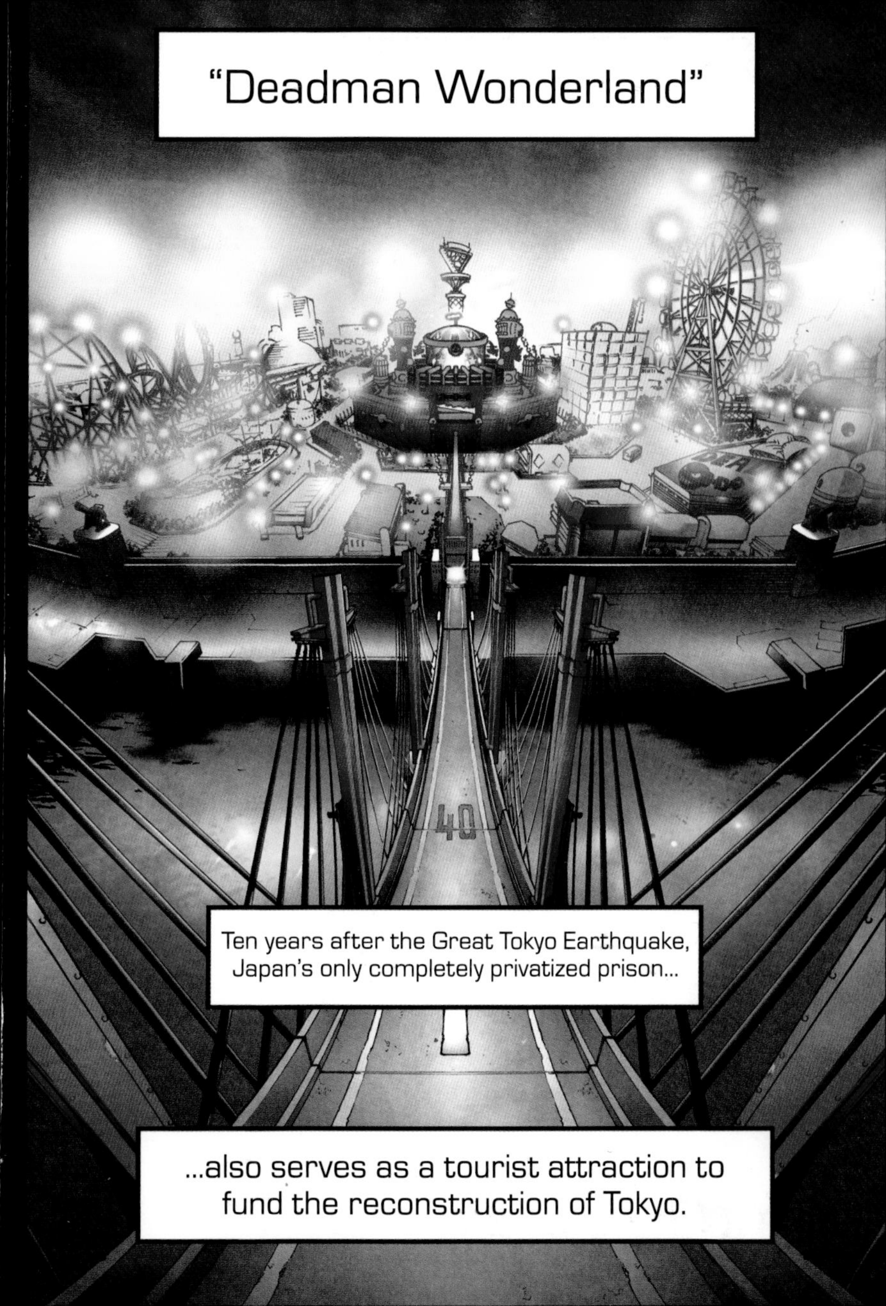
"Deadman Wonderland"
40
Ten years after the Great Tokyo Earthquake, Japan's only completely privatized prison...
...also serves as a tourist attraction to fund the reconstruction of Tokyo.

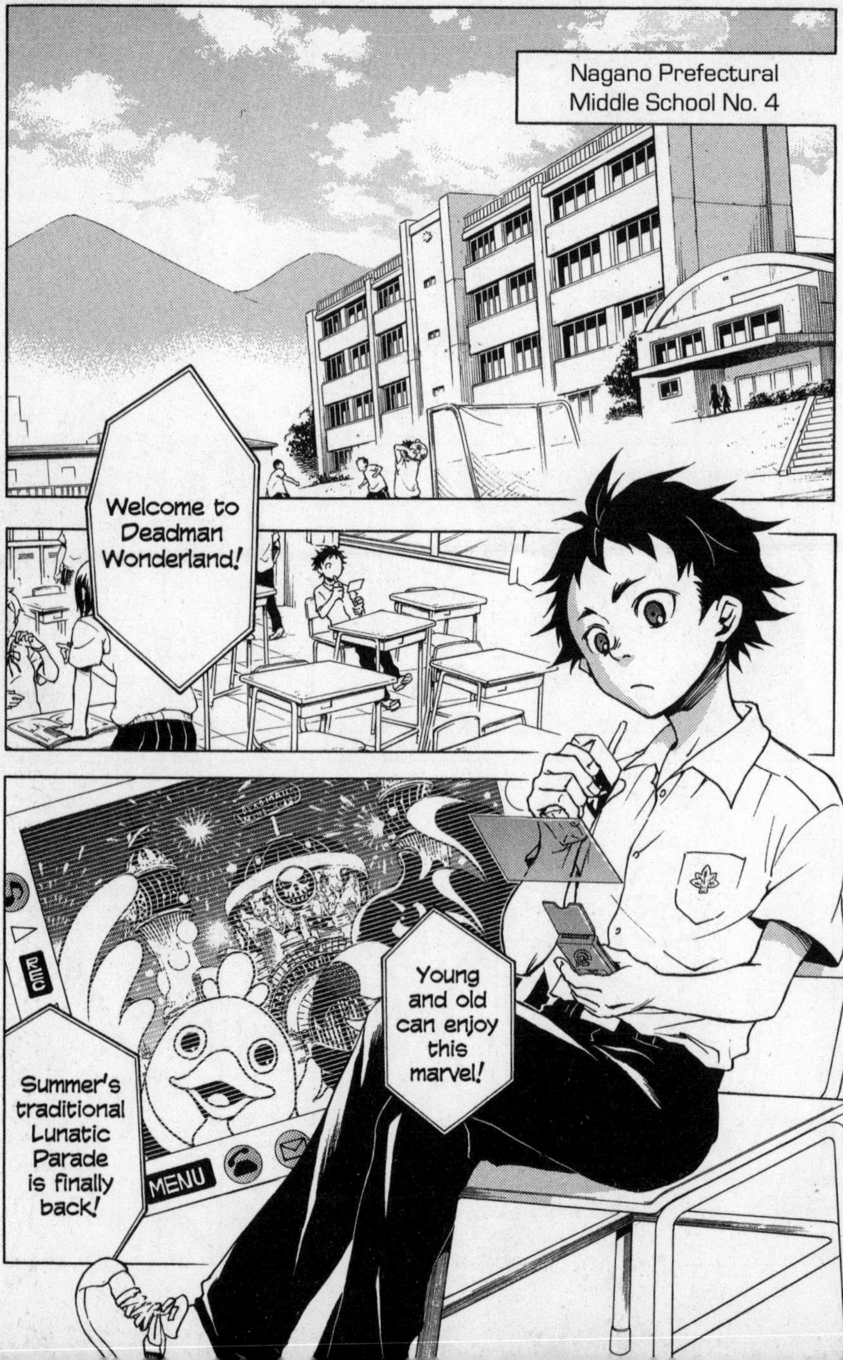
Nagano Prefectural Middle School No. 4
Welcome to Deadman Wonderland!
Young and old can enjoy this marvel!
REC
Summer's traditional Lunatic Parade is finally back!
MENU

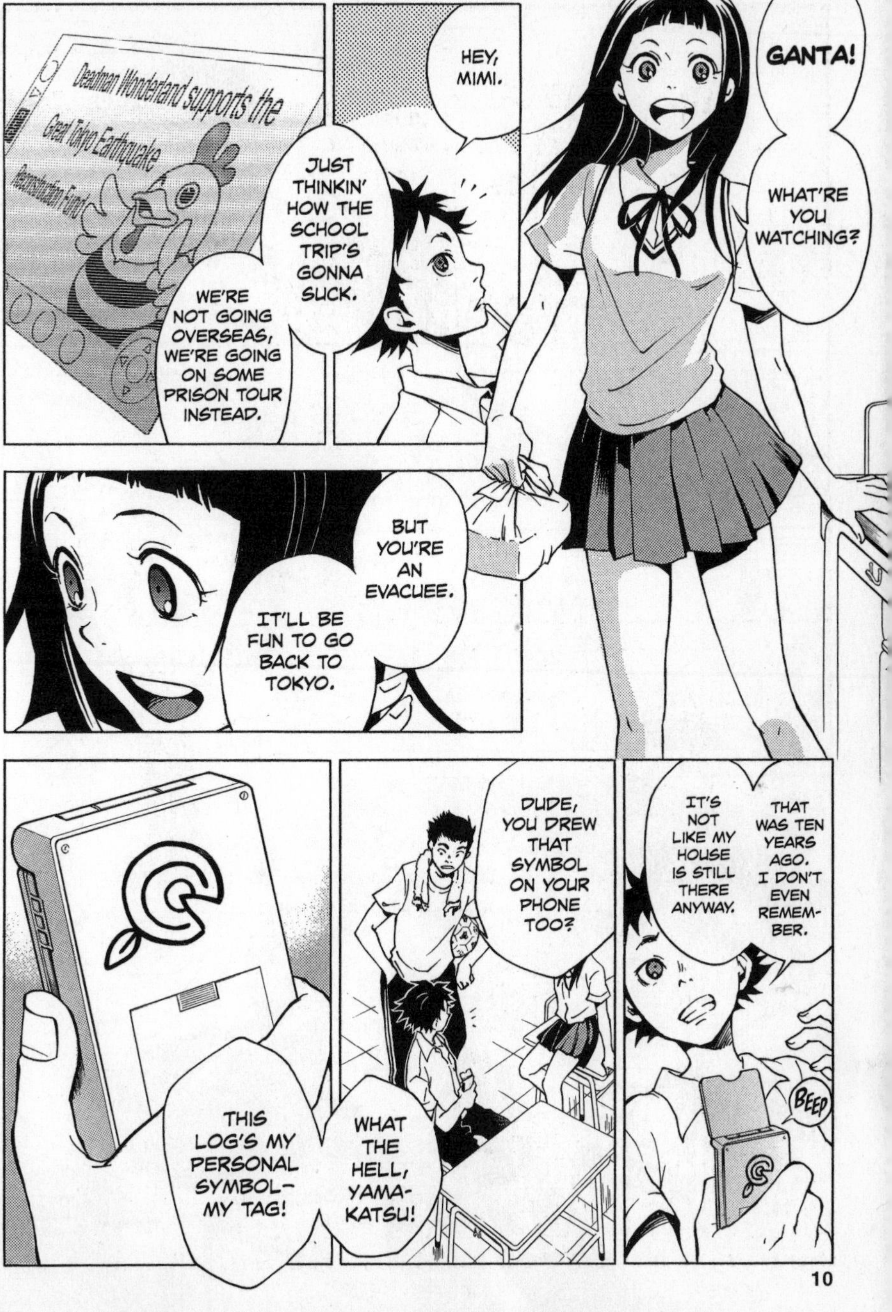
GANTA!
WHAT'RE YOU WATCHING?
HEY, MIMI.
JUST THINKIN' HOW THE SCHOOL TRIP'S GONNA SUCK.
Deadman Wonderland supports the Great Tokyo Earthquake Reconstruction Fund
WE'RE NOT GOING OVERSEAS, WE'RE GOING ON SOME PRISON TOUR INSTEAD.
BUT YOU'RE AN EVACUEE.
IT'LL BE FUN TO GO BACK TO TOKYO.
THAT WAS TEN YEARS AGO. I DON'T EVEN REMEM-BER.
IT'S NOT LIKE MY HOUSE IS STILL THERE ANYWAY.
BEEP
DUDE, YOU DREW THAT SYMBOL ON YOUR PHONE TOO?
WHAT THE HELL, YAMA-KATSU!
THIS LOG'S MY PERSONAL SYMBOL- MY TAG!

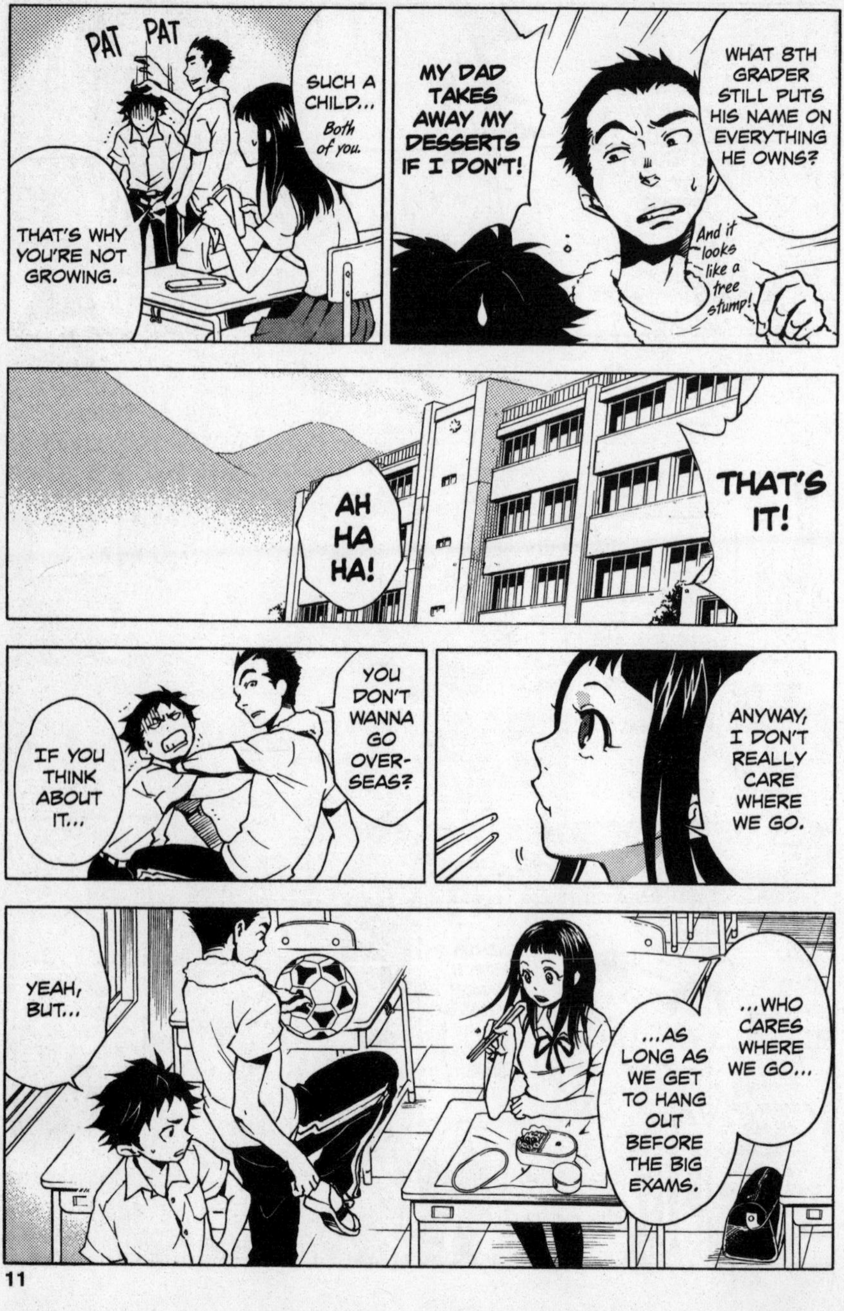
WHAT 8TH GRADER STILL PUTS HIS NAME ON EVERYTHING HE OWNS?
And it looks like a tree stump!
MY DAD TAKES AWAY MY DESSERTS IF I DON'T!
SUCH A CHILD... Both of you.
PAT PAT
THAT'S WHY YOU'RE NOT GROWING.
THAT'S IT!
AH HA HA!
ANYWAY, I DON'T REALLY CARE WHERE WE GO.
YOU DON'T WANNA GO OVER-SEAS?
IF YOU THINK ABOUT IT...
...WHO CARES WHERE WE GO...
...AS LONG AS WE GET TO HANG OUT BEFORE THE BIG EXAMS.
YEAH, BUT...

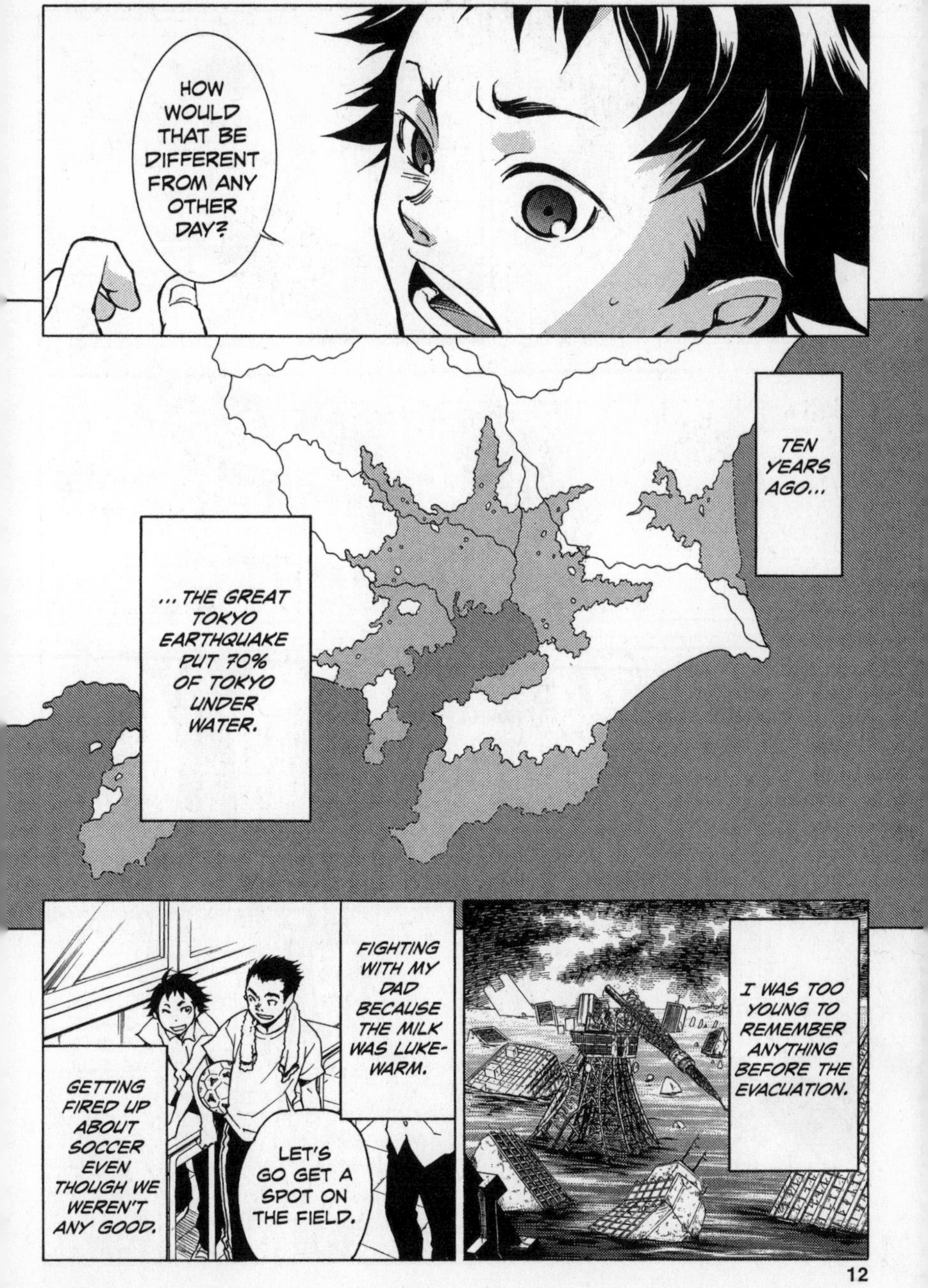
HOW WOULD THAT BE DIFFERENT FROM ANY OTHER DAY?
TEN YEARS AGO...
...THE GREAT TOKYO EARTHQUAKE PUT 70% OF TOKYO UNDER WATER.
I WAS TOO YOUNG TO REMEMBER ANYTHING BEFORE THE EVACUATION.
FIGHTING WITH MY DAD BECAUSE THE MILK WAS LUKE-WARM.
GETTING FIRED UP ABOUT SOCCER EVEN THOUGH WE WEREN'T ANY GOOD.
LET'S GO GET A SPOT ON THE FIELD.

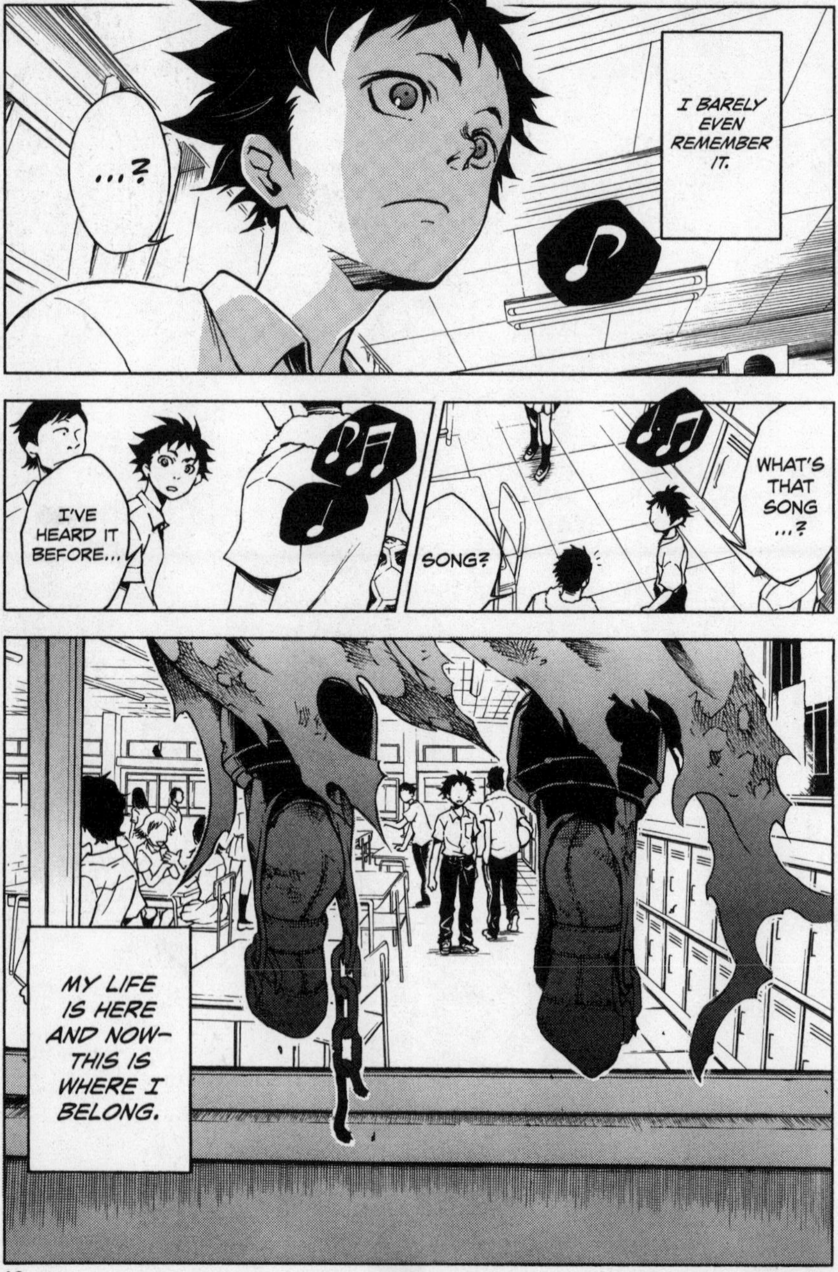
I BARELY EVEN REMEMBER IT.
...?
WHAT'S THAT SONG ...?
SONG?
I'VE HEARD IT BEFORE...
MY LIFE IS HERE AND NOW— THIS IS WHERE I BELONG.

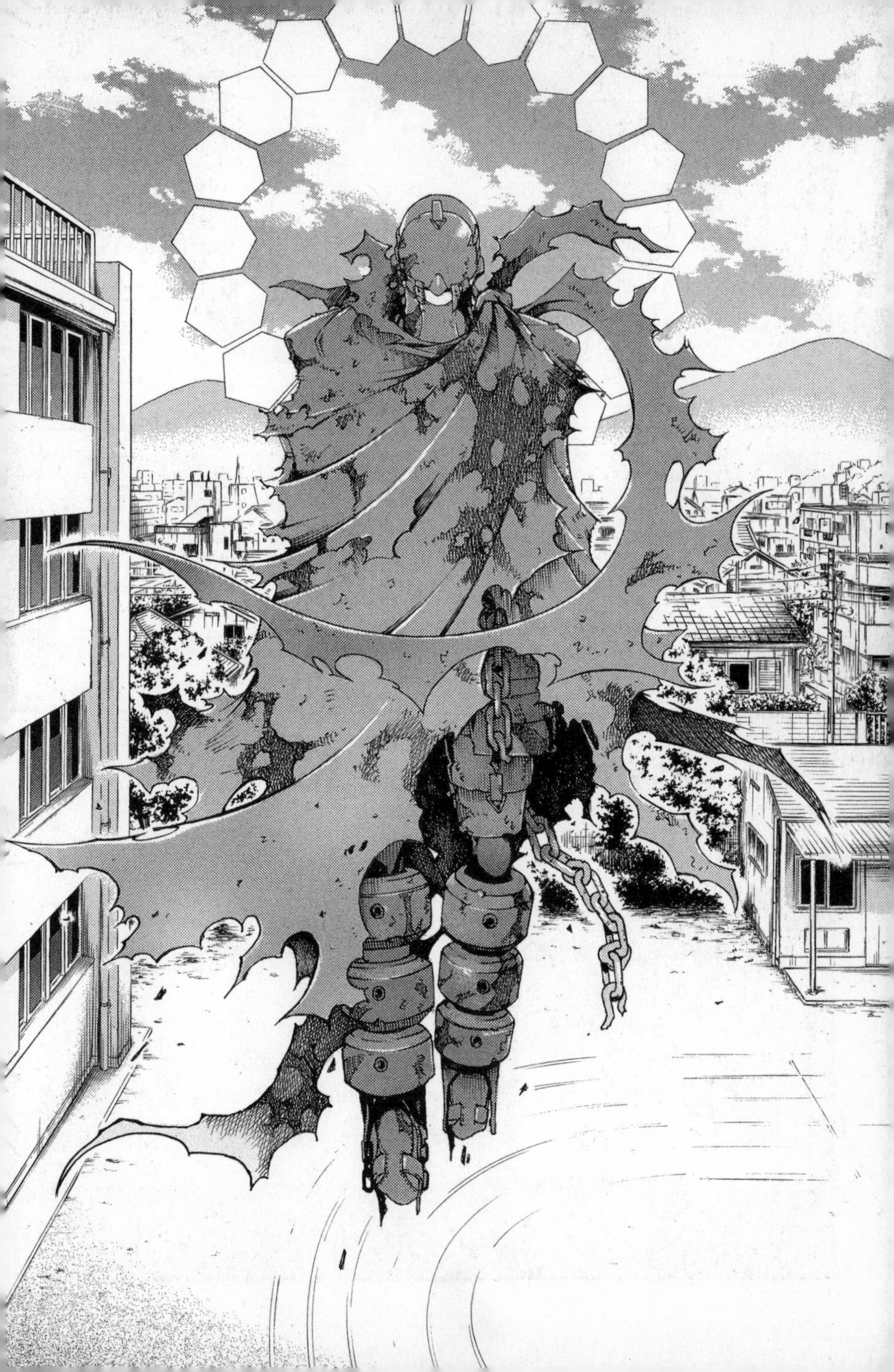

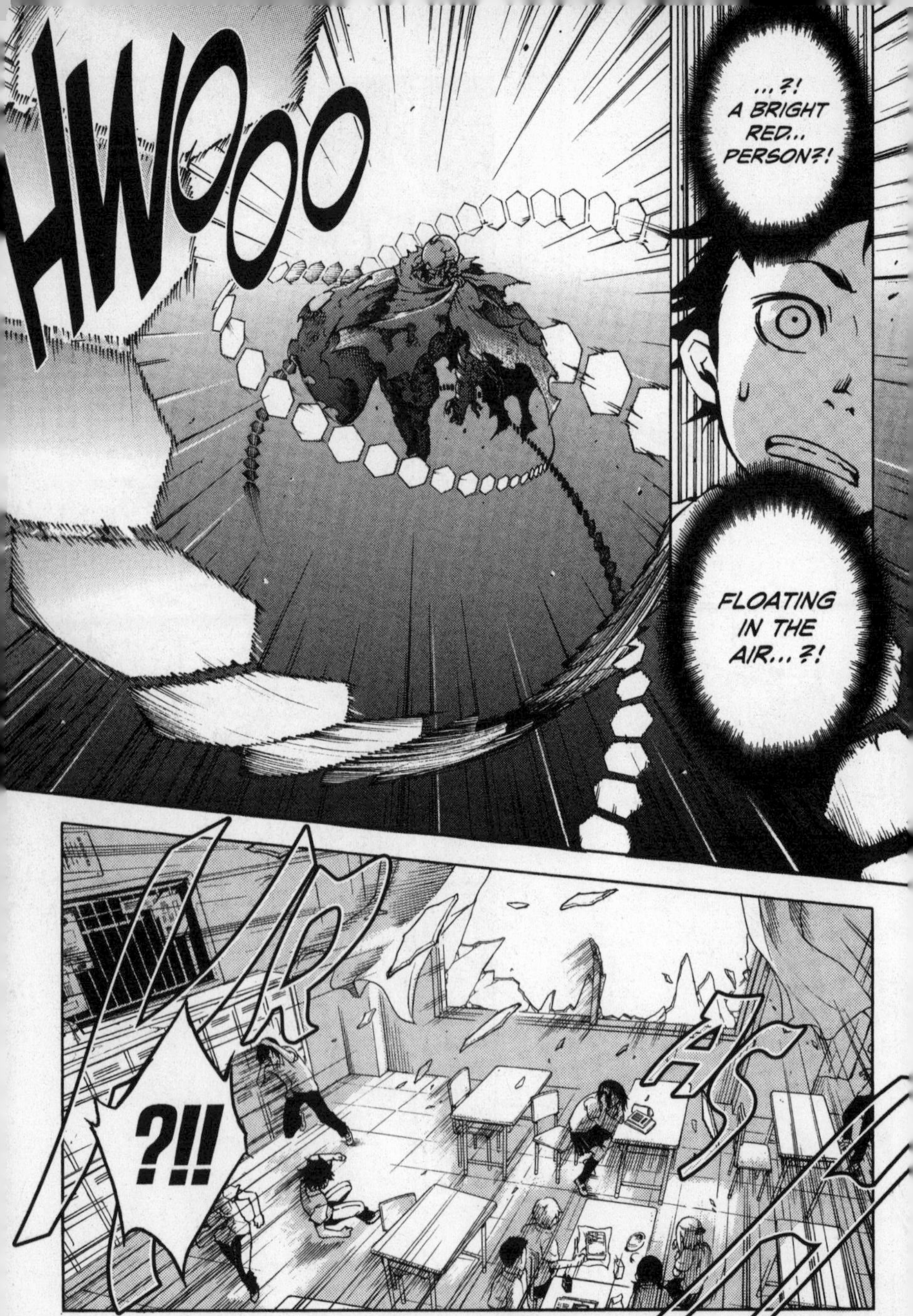

...?! A BRIGHT RED... PERSON?!
FLOATING IN THE AIR...?!
HWOOO
?!!

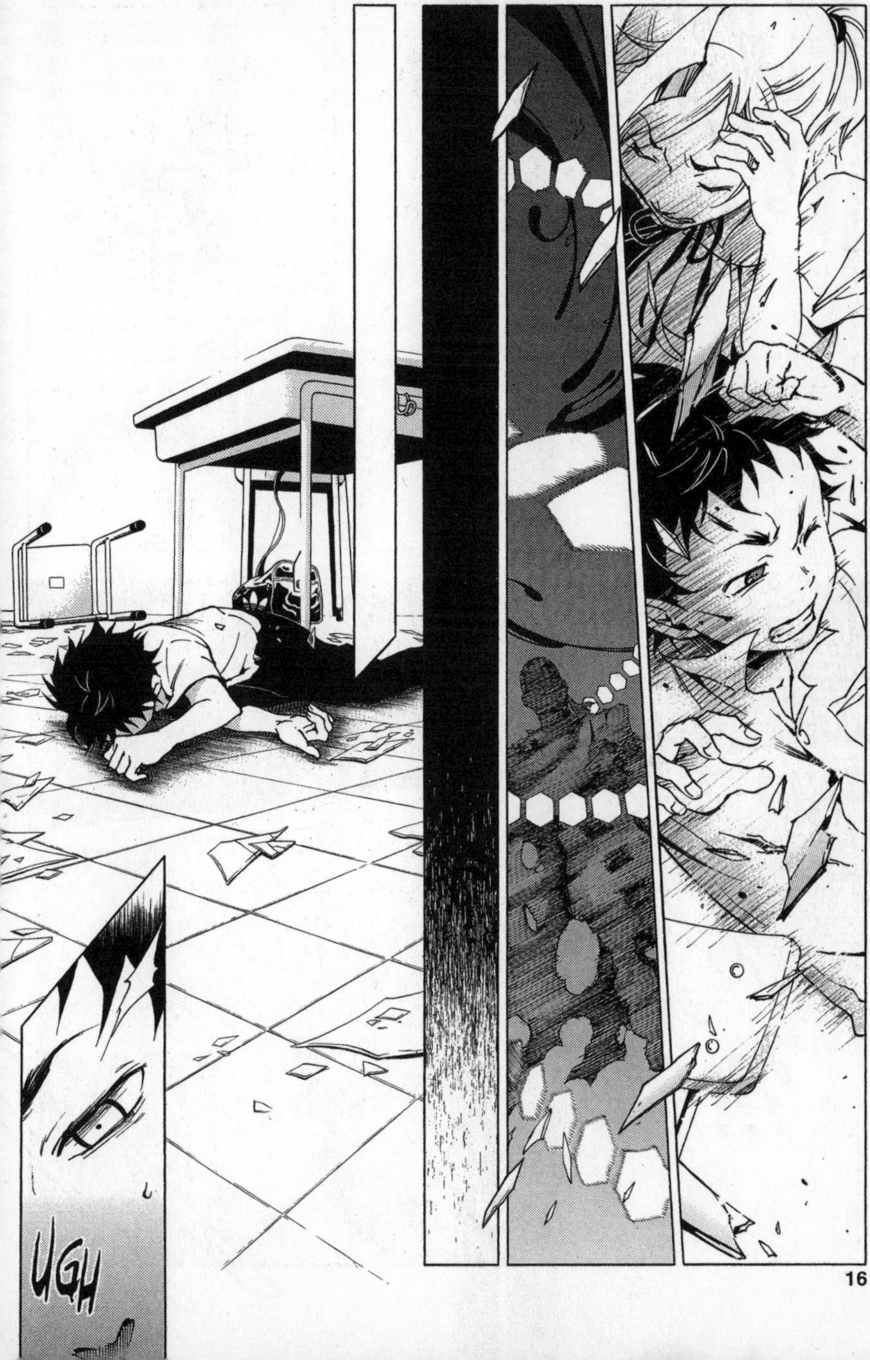
UGH

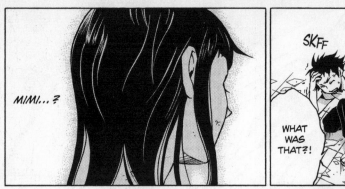

MIMI...?

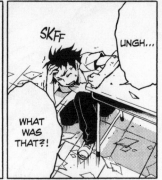

SKFF

UNGH...

WHAT WAS THAT?!

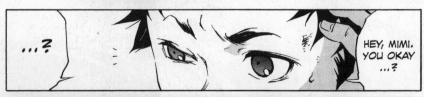

...?

HEY, MIMI. YOU OKAY ...?

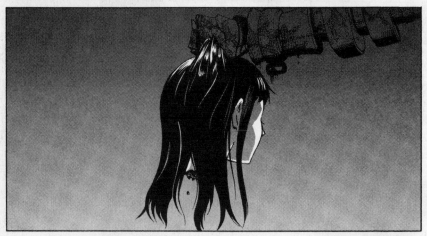

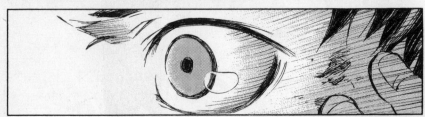

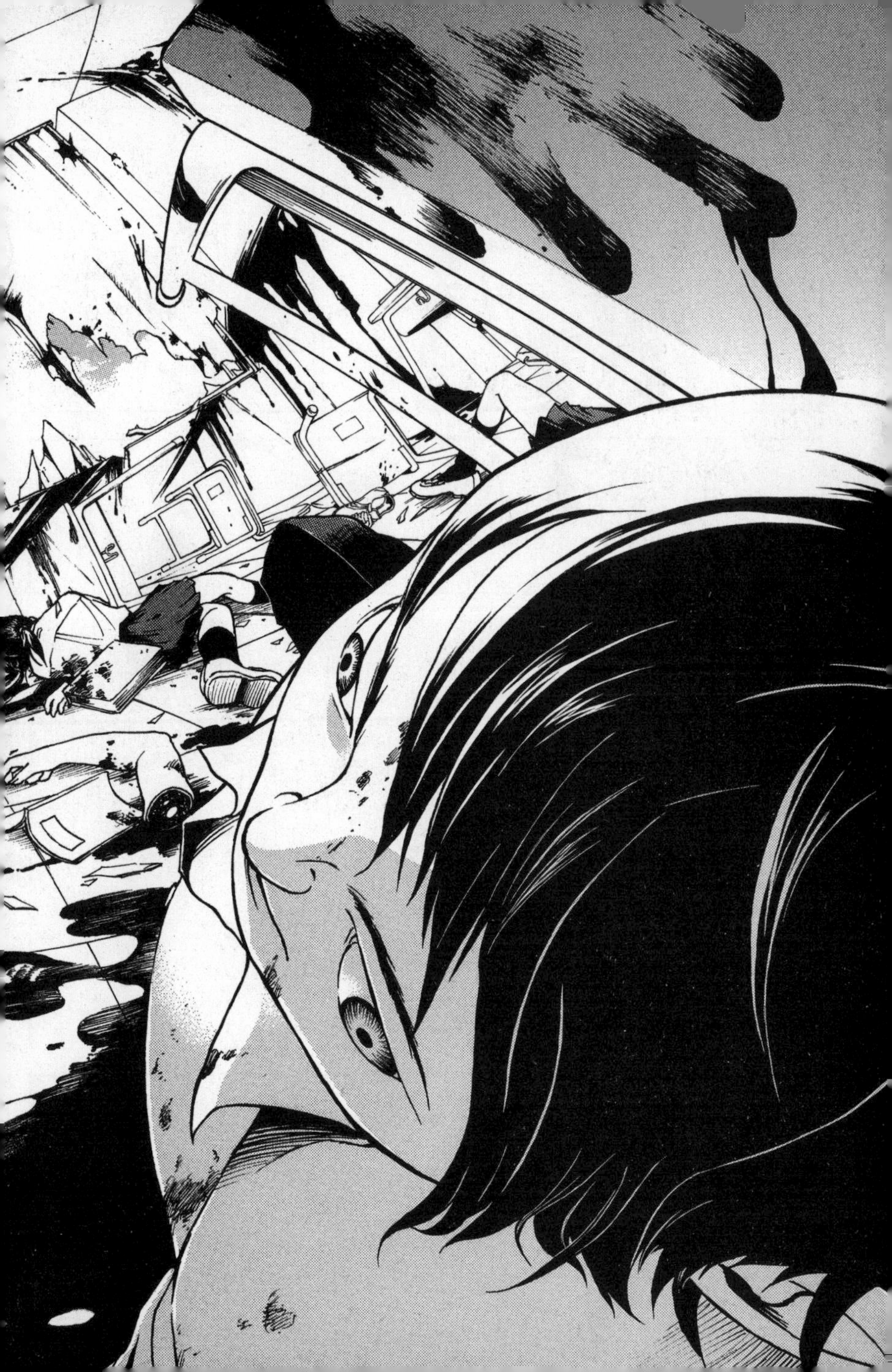

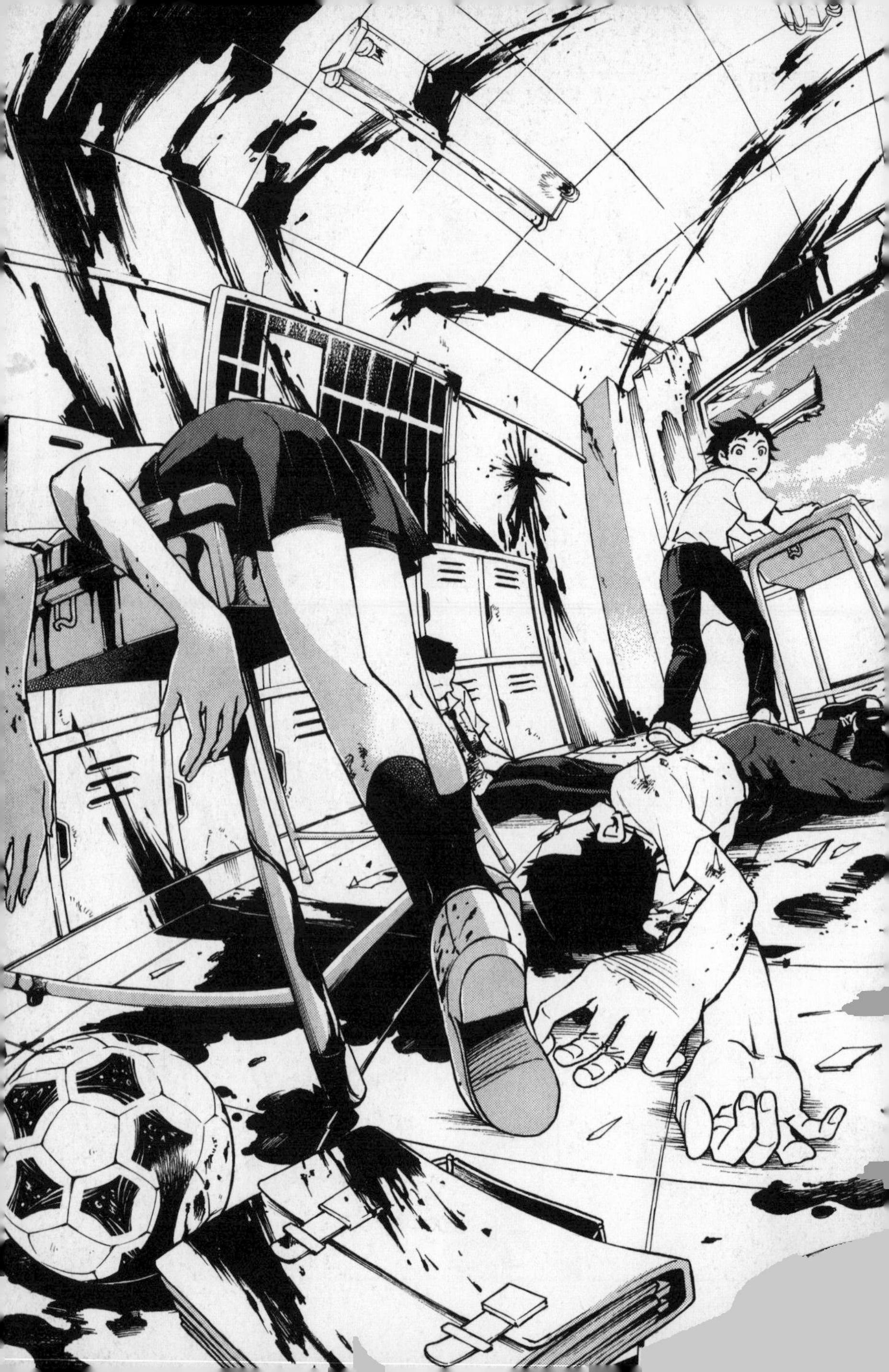

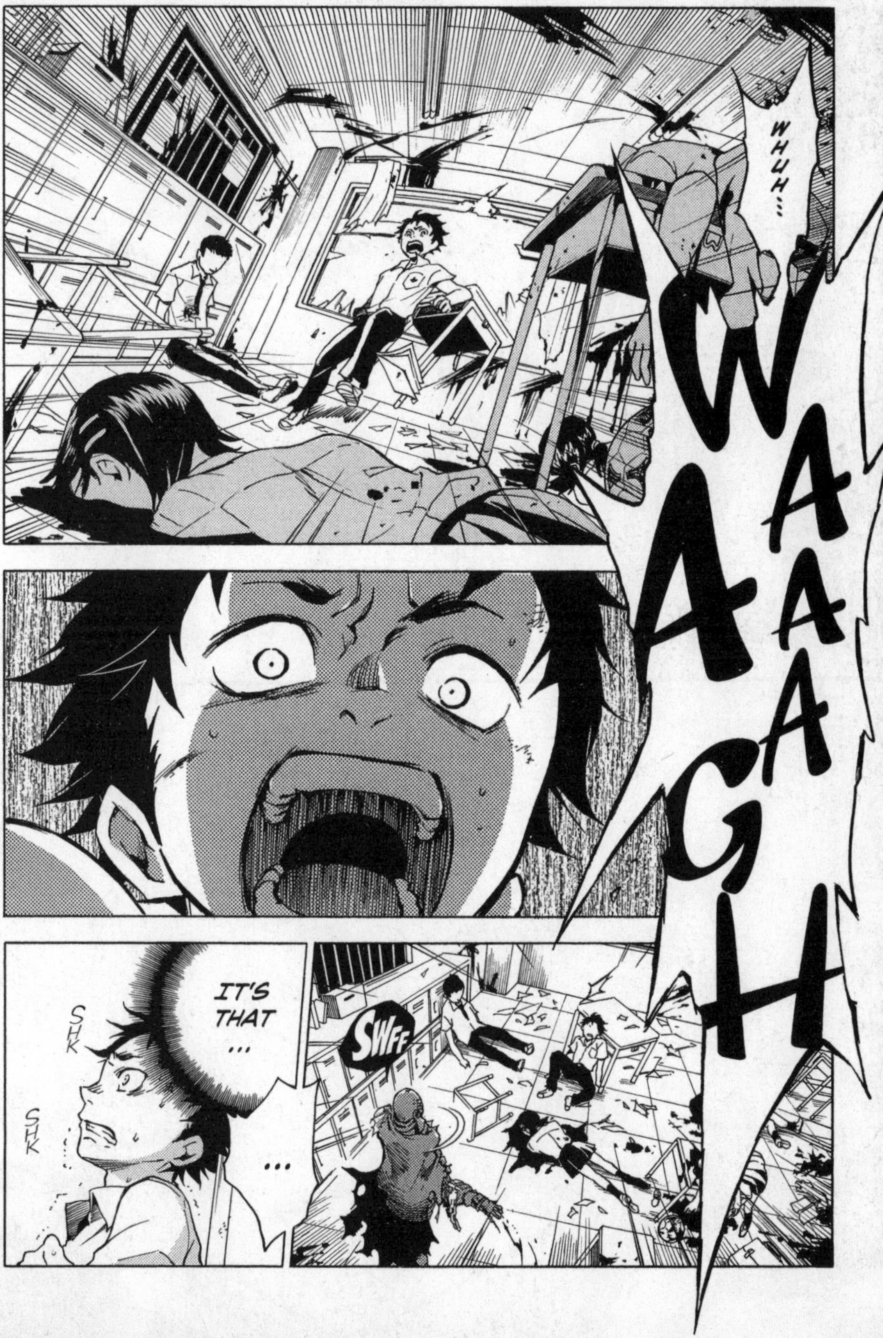
WHUH...
WAAAAAGH
SWFF
IT'S THAT ...
SHK
SHK
...

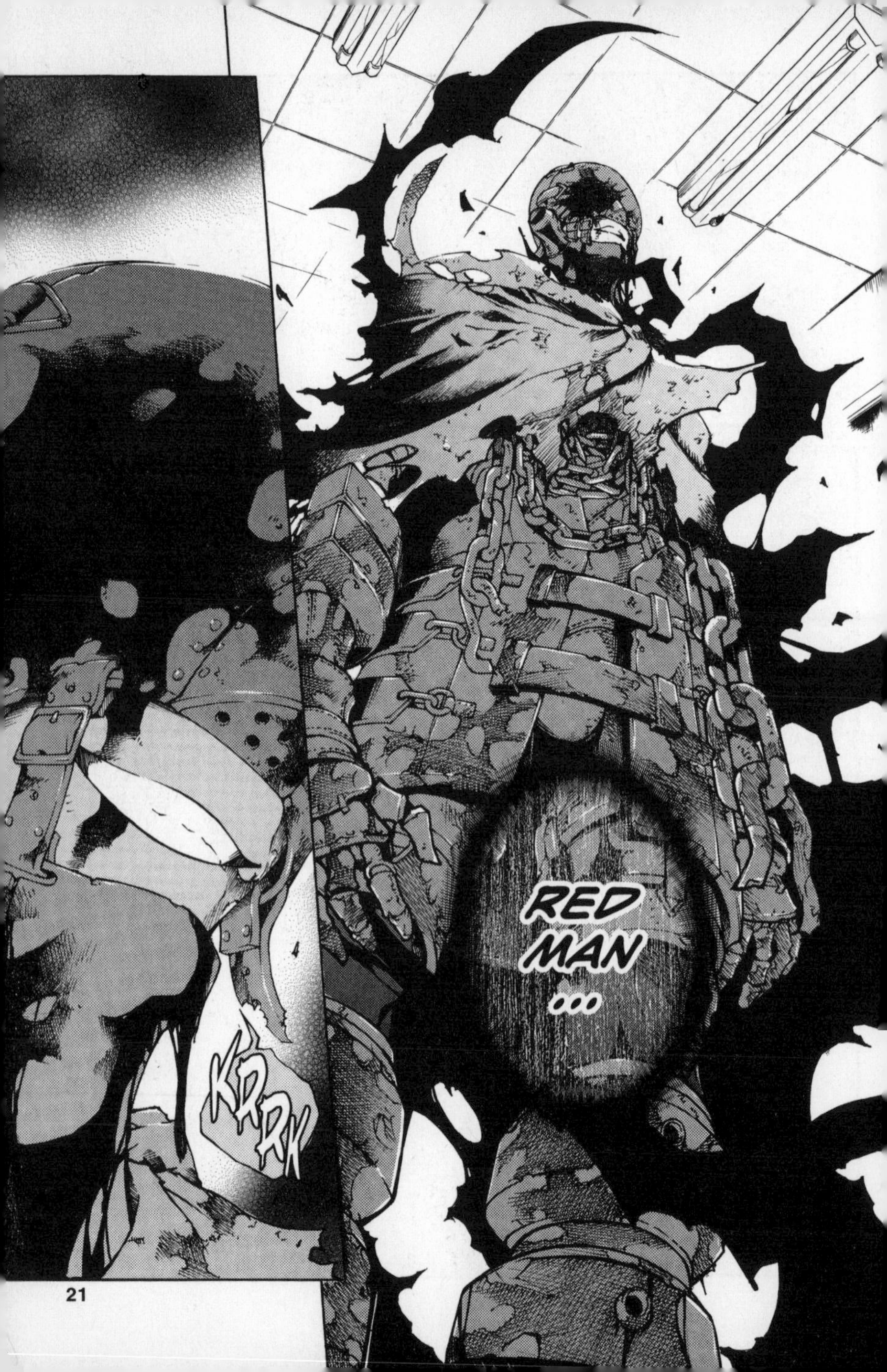
RED MAN ...
KDRK

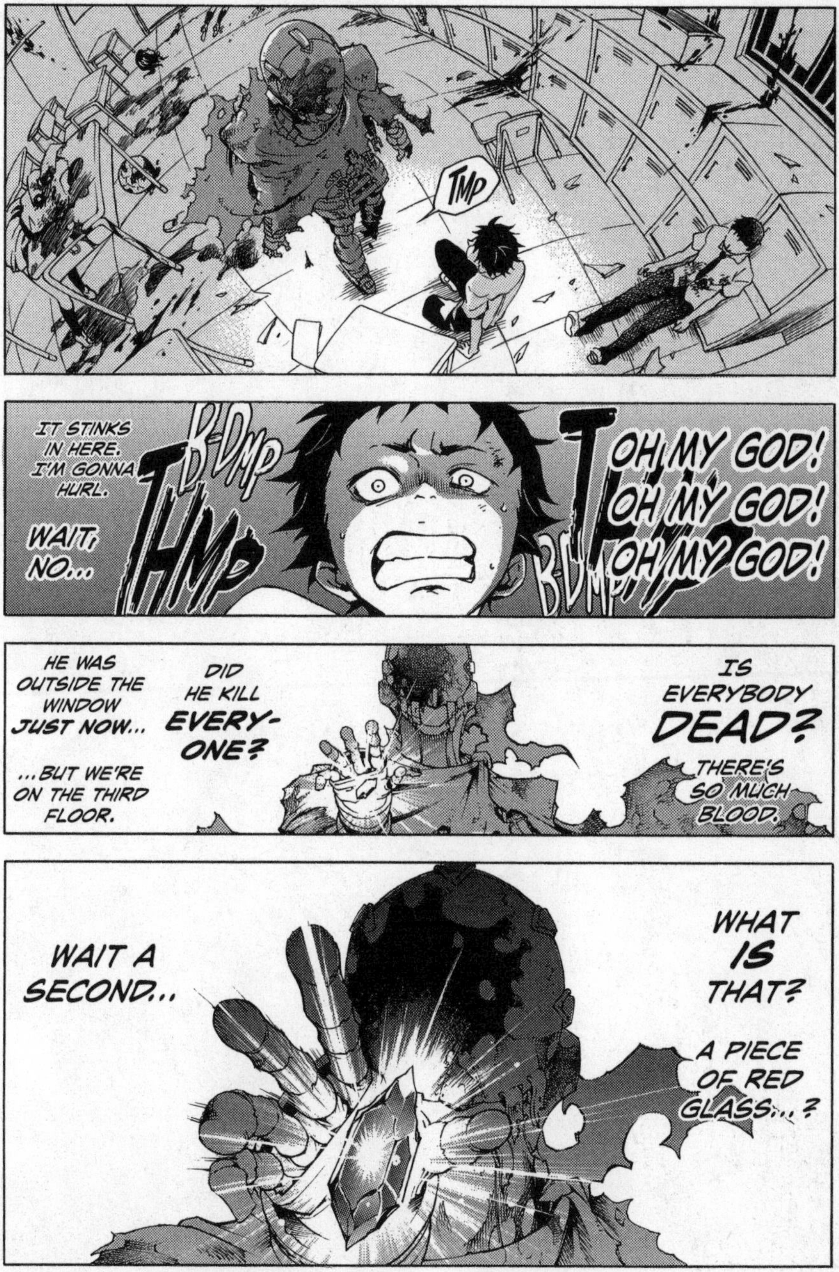

TMP
OH MY GOD! OH MY GOD! OH MY GOD!
BDMP
THMP
BDMP
THMP
IT STINKS IN HERE. I'M GONNA HURL.
WAIT, NO...
IS EVERYBODY DEAD?
THERE'S SO MUCH BLOOD.
DID HE KILL EVERY-ONE?
HE WAS OUTSIDE THE WINDOW JUST NOW...
...BUT WE'RE ON THE THIRD FLOOR.
WHAT IS THAT?
A PIECE OF RED GLASS...?
WAIT A SECOND...

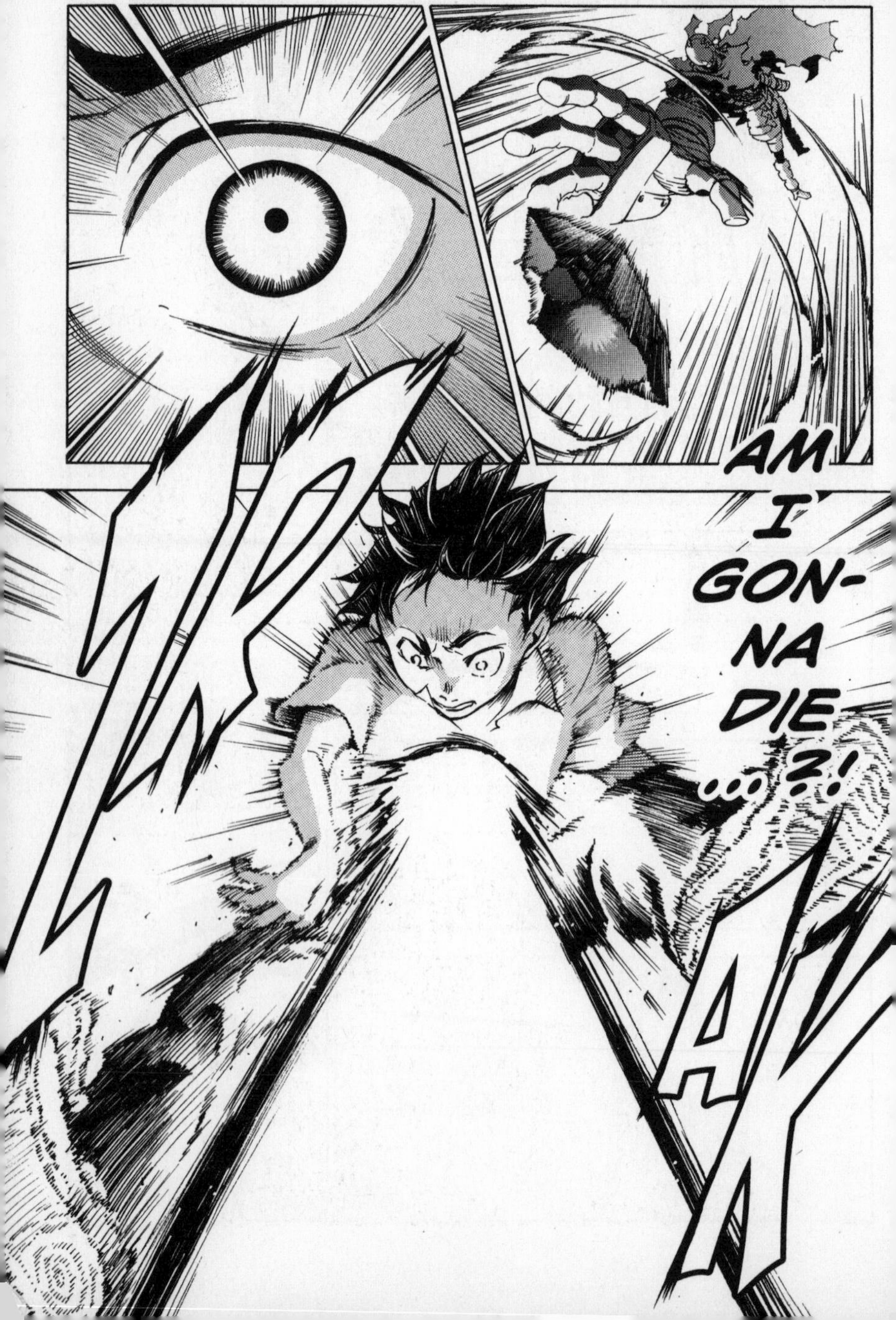
AM I GON-NA DIE ...?!

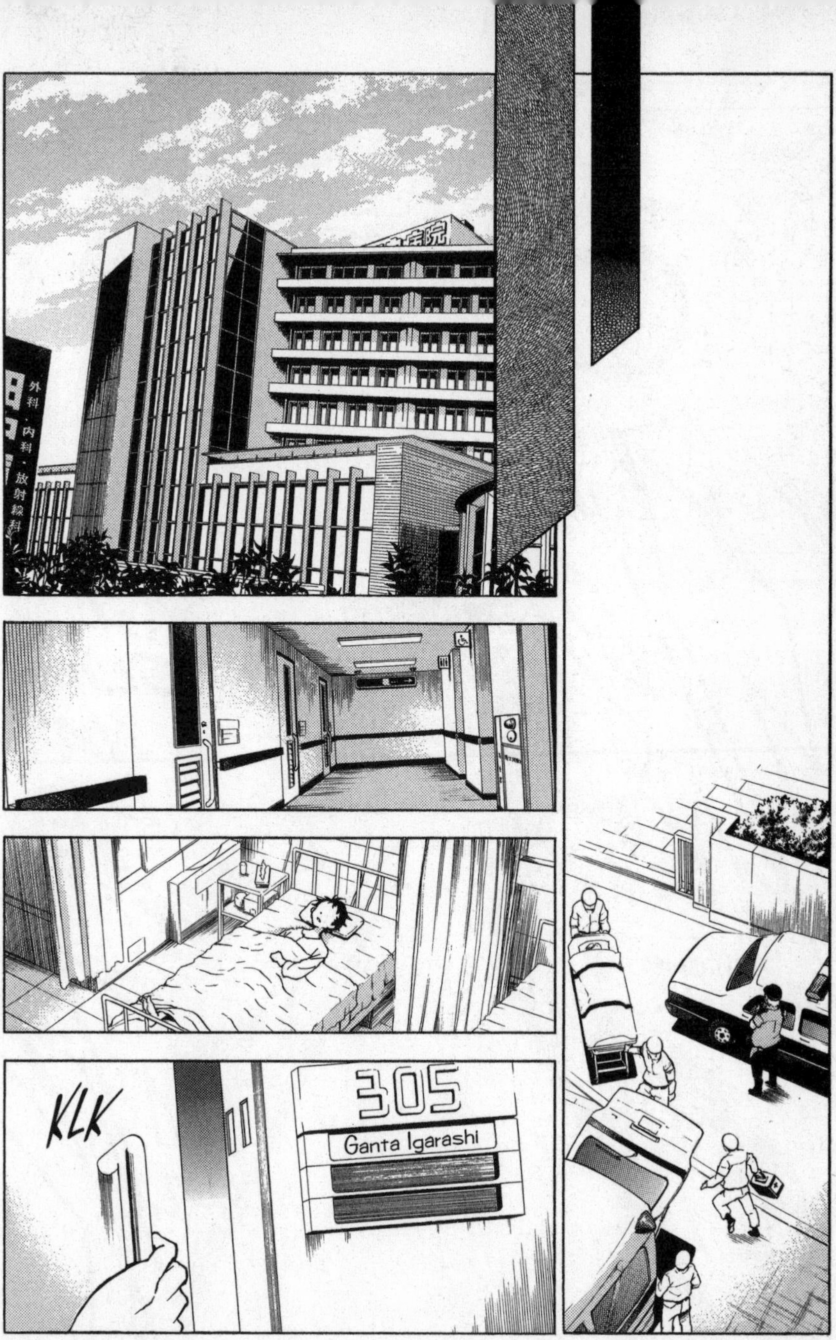
外科・内科・放射線科
305
Ganta Igarashi
KLK

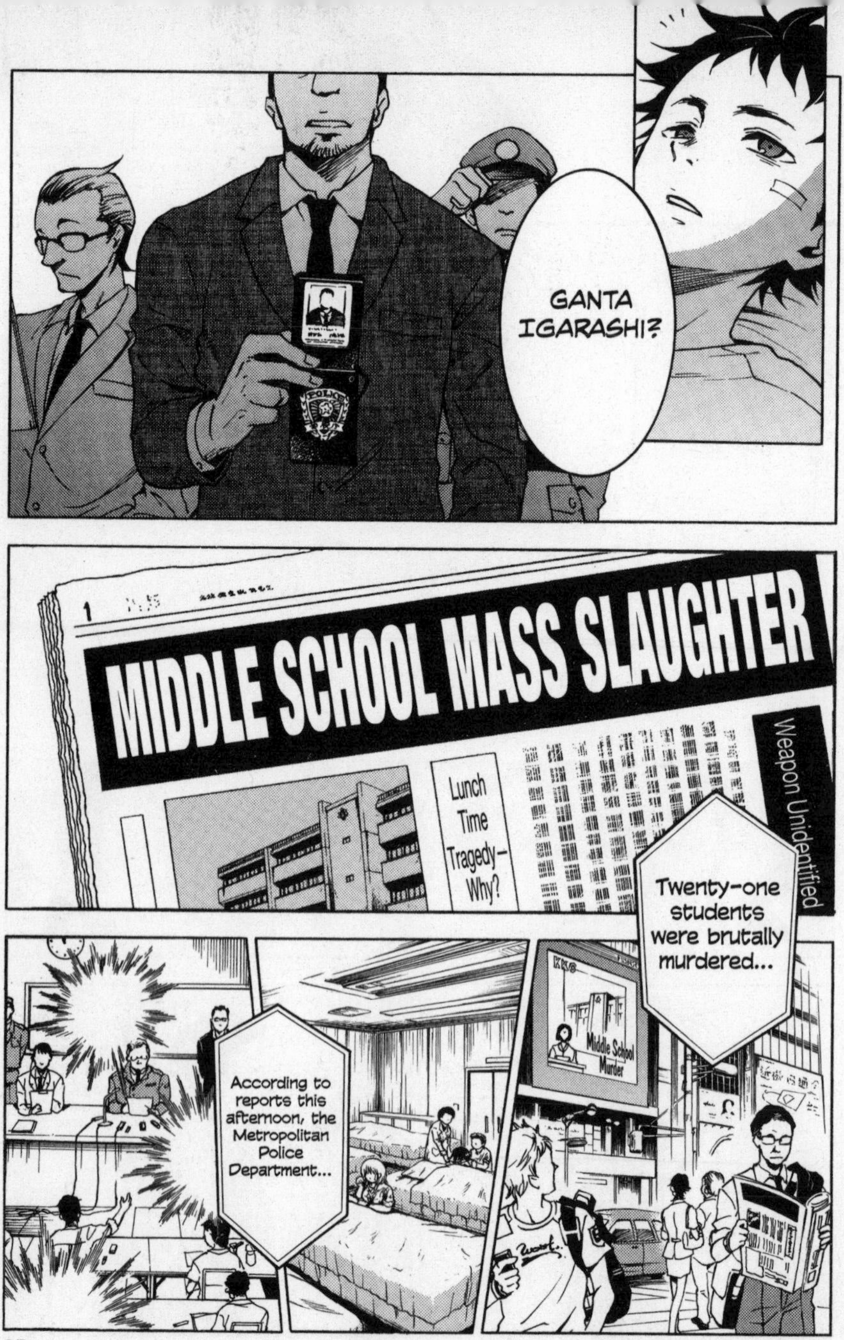
GANTA IGARASHI?
MIDDLE SCHOOL MASS SLAUGHTER
Weapon Unidentified
Lunch Time Tragedy—Why?
Twenty-one students were brutally murdered...
Middle School Murder
According to reports this afternoon, the Metropolitan Police Department...

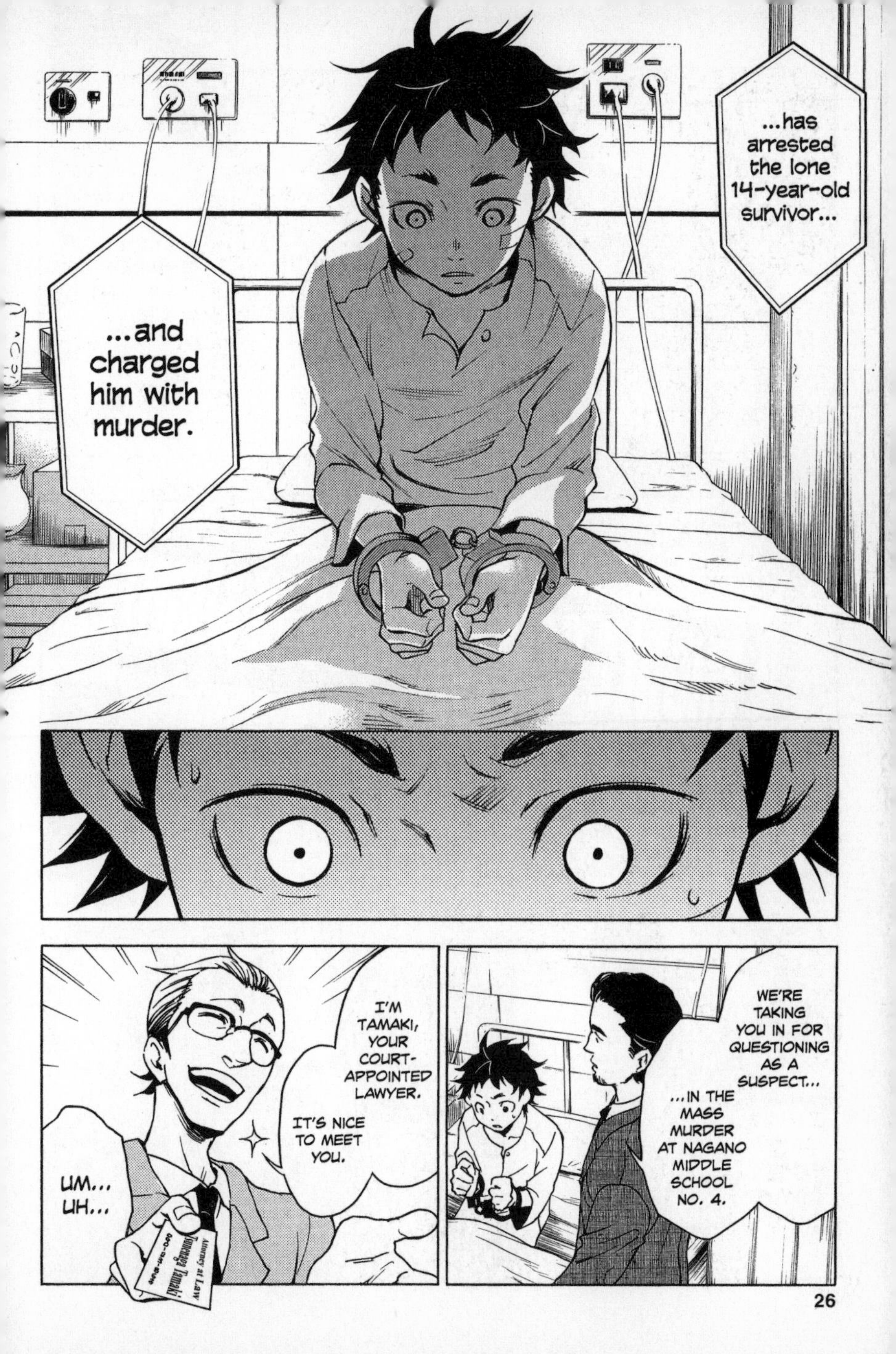
...has arrested the lone 14-year-old survivor...
...and charged him with murder.
WE'RE TAKING YOU IN FOR QUESTIONING AS A SUSPECT...
...IN THE MASS MURDER AT NAGANO MIDDLE SCHOOL NO. 4.
I'M TAMAKI, YOUR COURT-APPOINTED LAWYER.
IT'S NICE TO MEET YOU.
UM... UH...

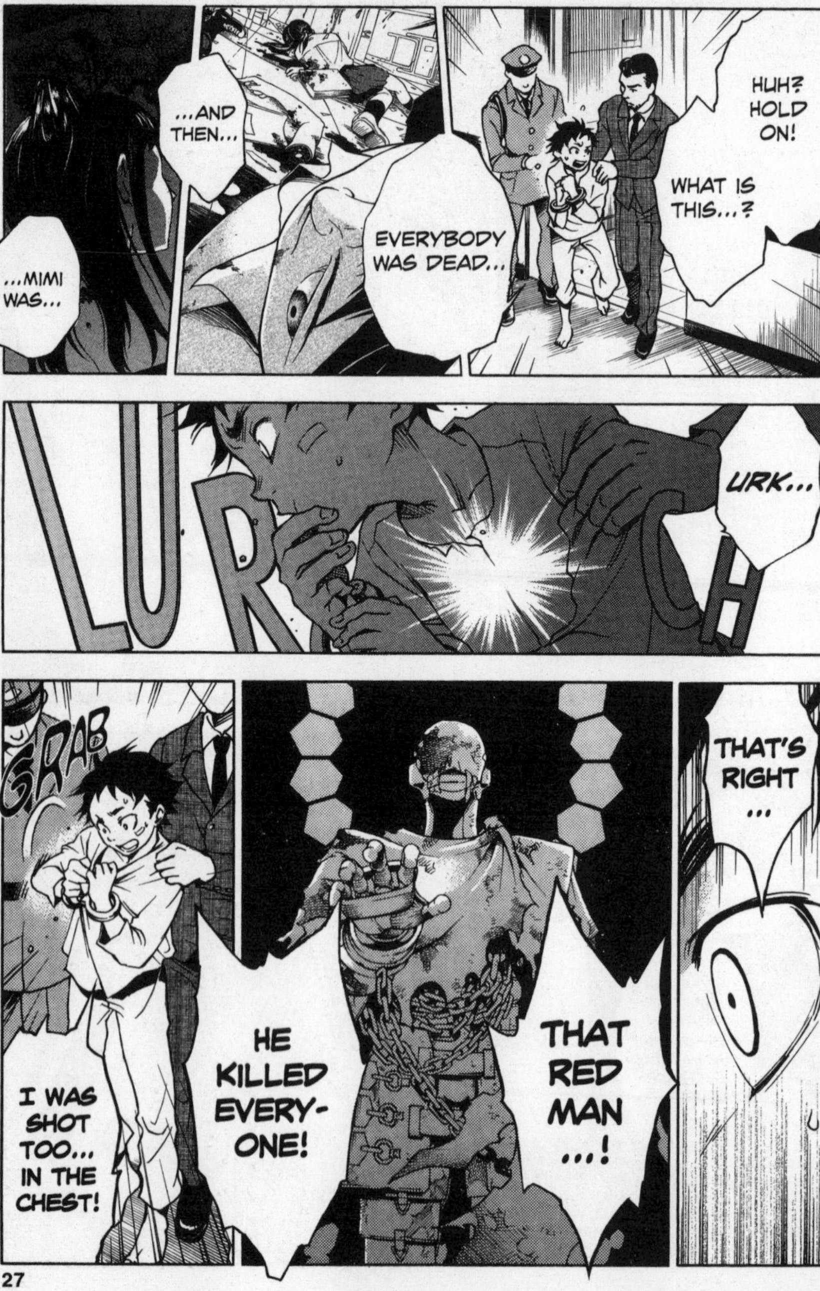
HUH? HOLD ON!
WHAT IS THIS...?
...AND THEN...
EVERYBODY WAS DEAD...
...MIMI WAS...
URK...
LURCH
THAT'S RIGHT ...
THAT RED MAN ...!
HE KILLED EVERY-ONE!
GRAB
I WAS SHOT TOO... IN THE CHEST!

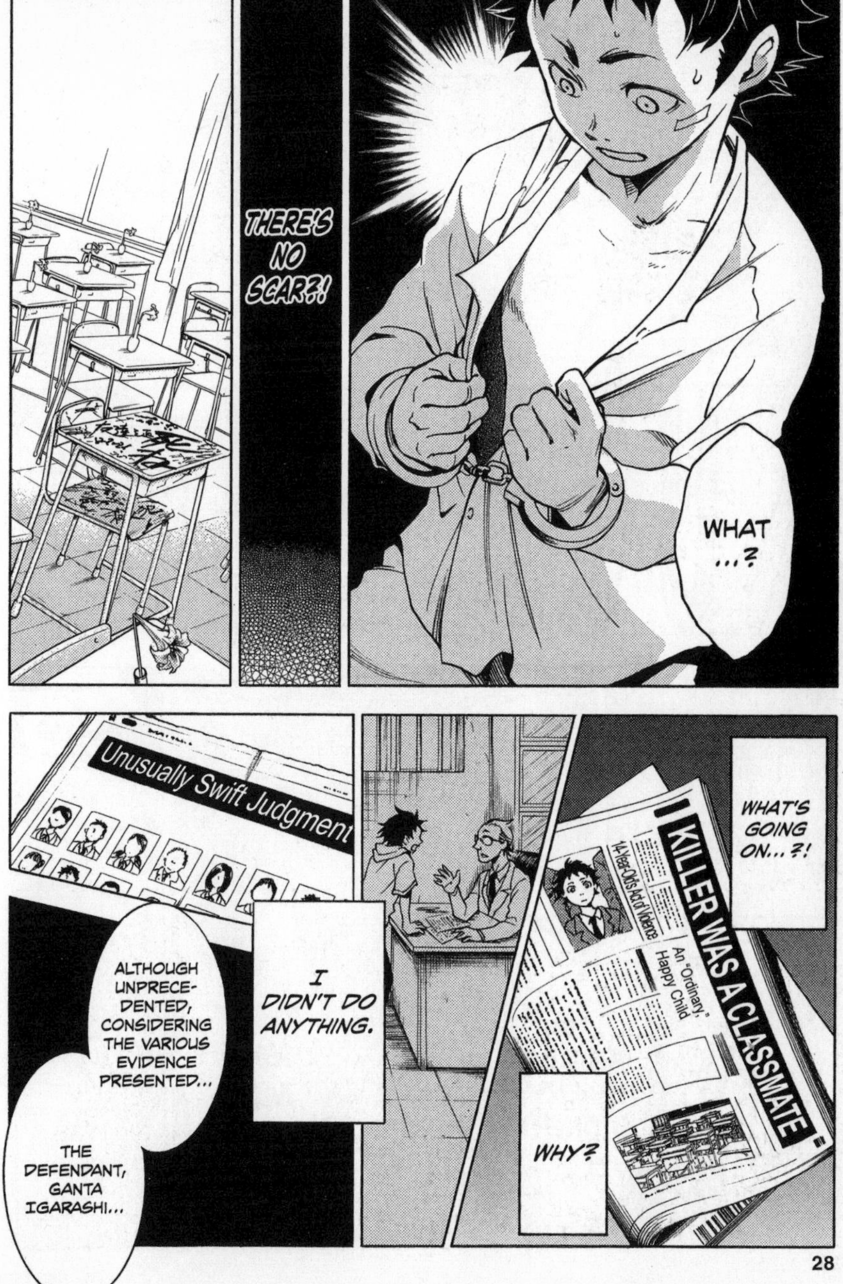
WHAT ...?
THERE'S NO SCAR?!
WHAT'S GOING ON...?!
KILLER WAS A CLASSMATE
14-Year-Old's Act of Violence
An "Ordinary," Happy Child
WHY?
I DIDN'T DO ANYTHING.
Unusually Swift Judgment
ALTHOUGH UNPRECE-DENTED, CONSIDERING THE VARIOUS EVIDENCE PRESENTED...
THE DEFENDANT, GANTA IGARASHI...

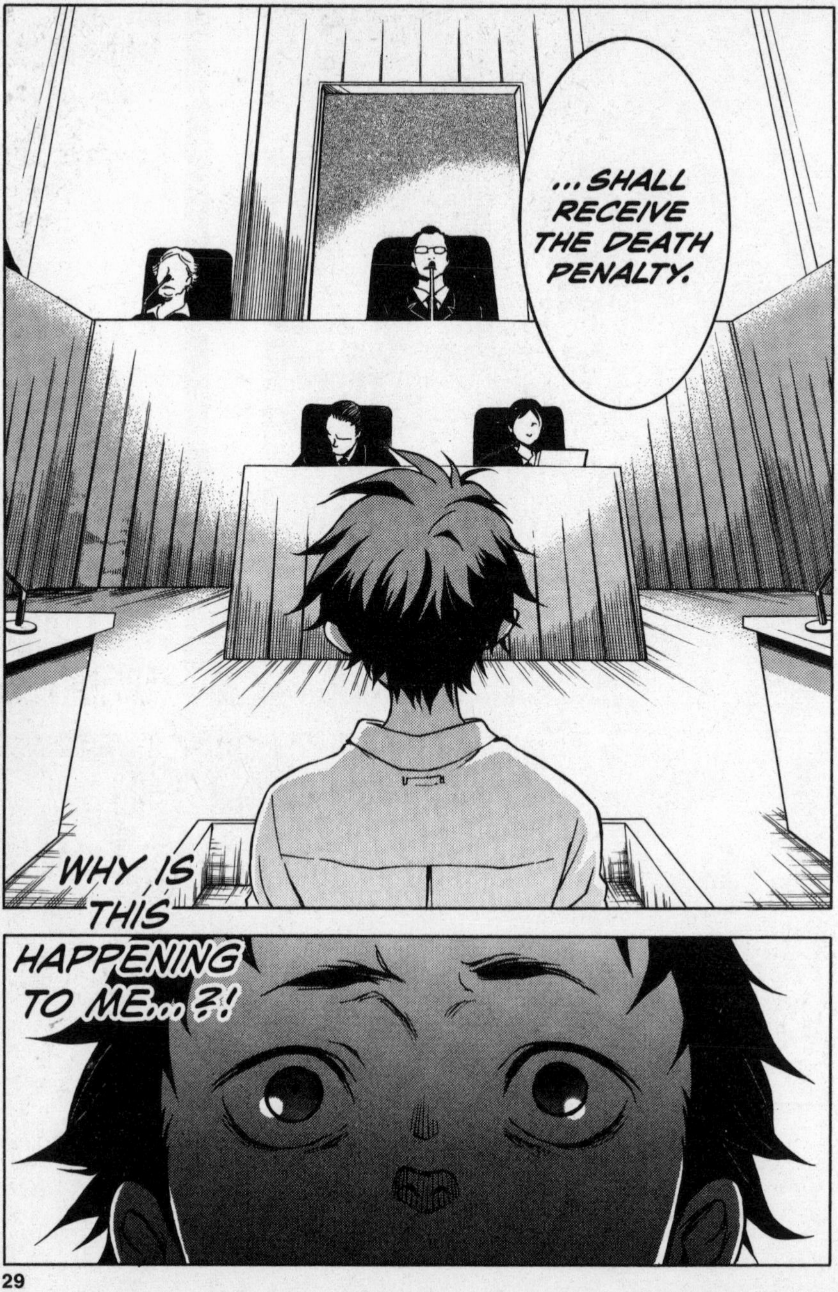
...SHALL RECEIVE THE DEATH PENALTY.
WHY IS THIS HAPPENING TO ME...?!

THIS IS A JOKE... RIGHT...?

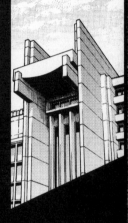

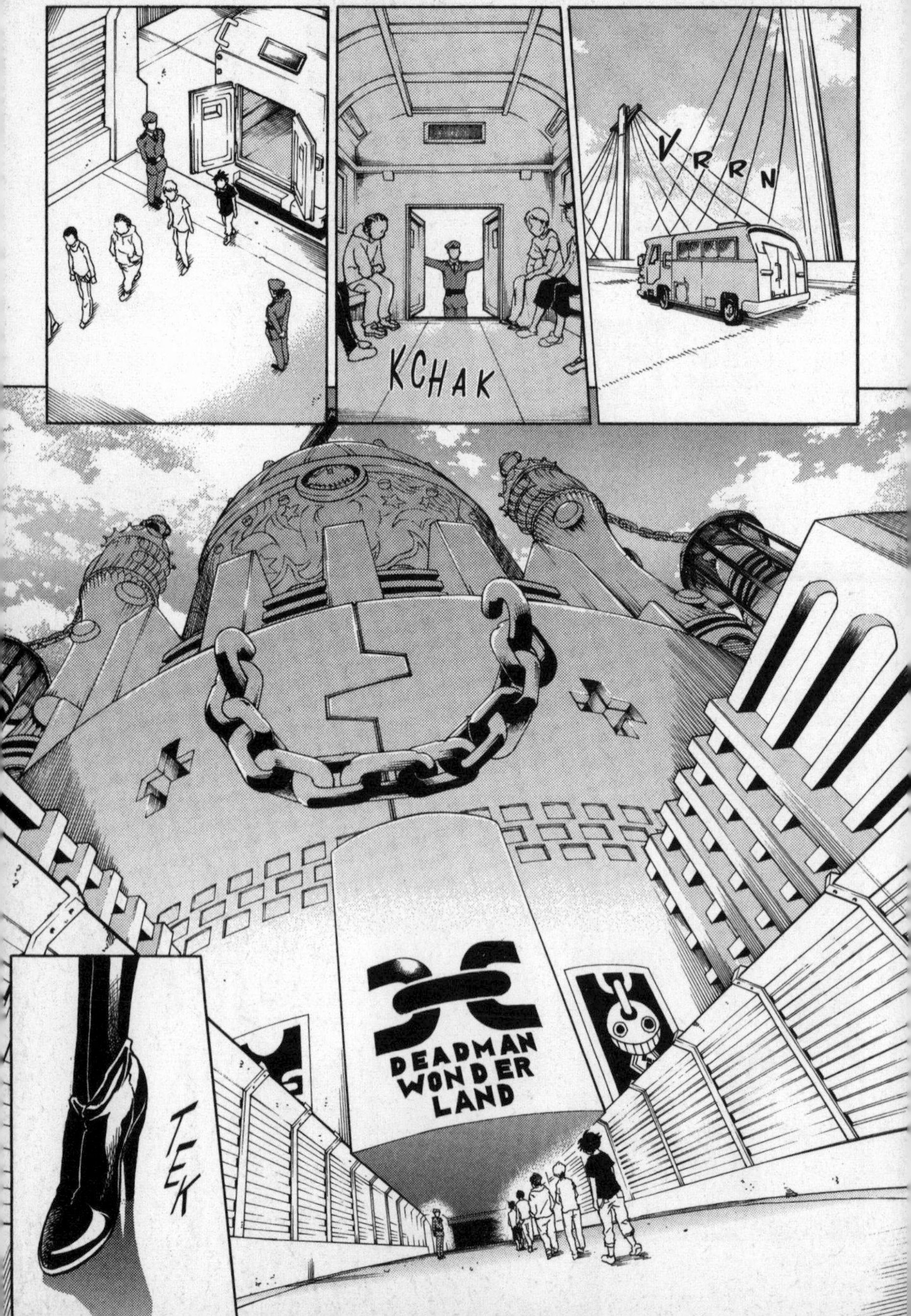
VRRN
KCHAK
DEADMAN WONDER LAND
TEK

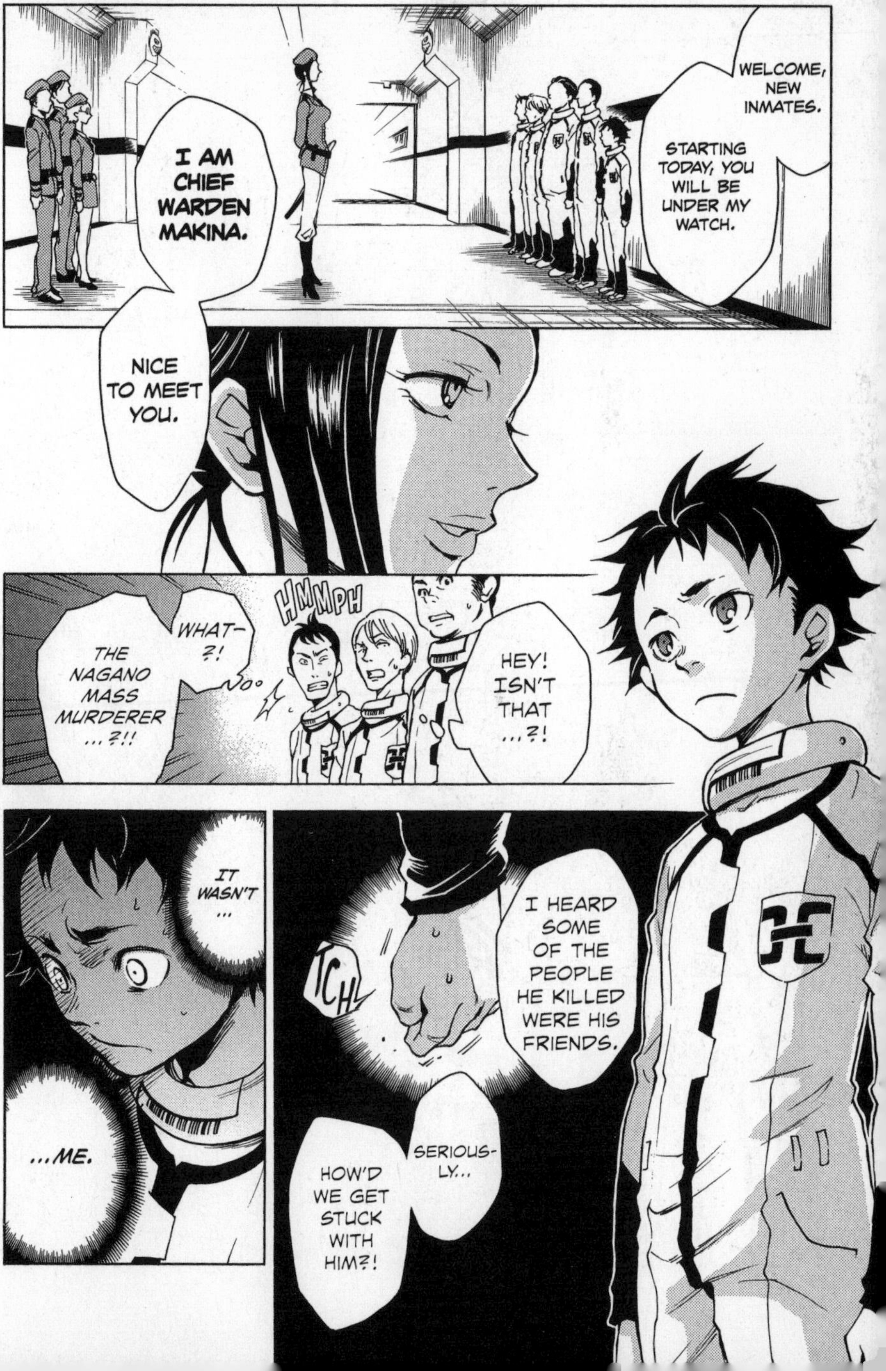
WELCOME, NEW INMATES.
STARTING TODAY, YOU WILL BE UNDER MY WATCH.
I AM CHIEF WARDEN MAKINA.
NICE TO MEET YOU.
HEY! ISN'T THAT ...?!
HMMPH
WHAT—?!
THE NAGANO MASS MURDERER ...?!!
I HEARD SOME OF THE PEOPLE HE KILLED WERE HIS FRIENDS.
TCH
SERIOUS-LY...
HOW'D WE GET STUCK WITH HIM?!
IT WASN'T ...
...ME.

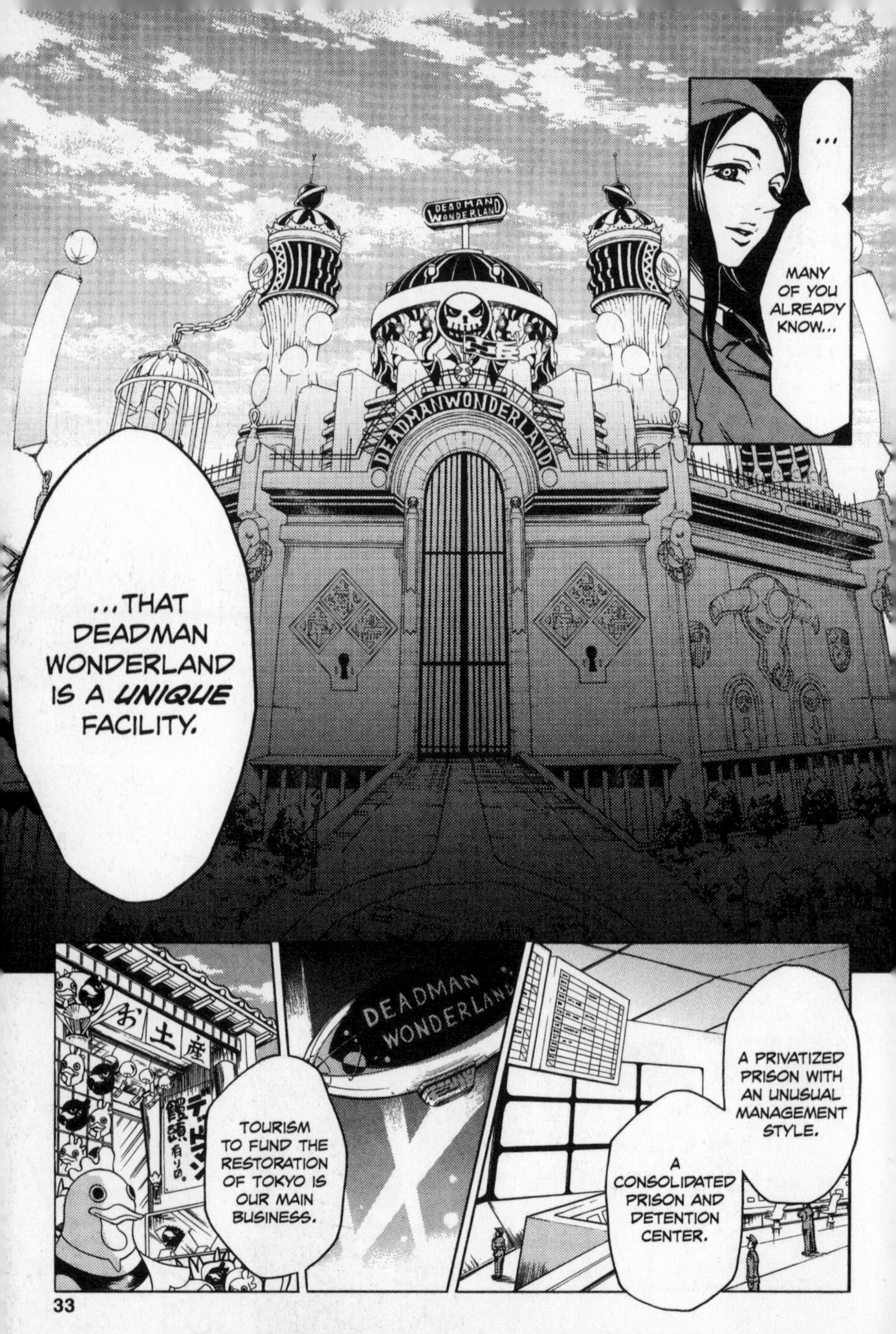
...
MANY OF YOU ALREADY KNOW...
DEADMAN WONDERLAND
DEADMANWONDERLAND
...THAT DEADMAN WONDERLAND IS A *UNIQUE* FACILITY.
A PRIVATIZED PRISON WITH AN UNUSUAL MANAGEMENT STYLE.
A CONSOLIDATED PRISON AND DETENTION CENTER.
DEADMAN WONDERLAND
TOURISM TO FUND THE RESTORATION OF TOKYO IS OUR MAIN BUSINESS.
お土産

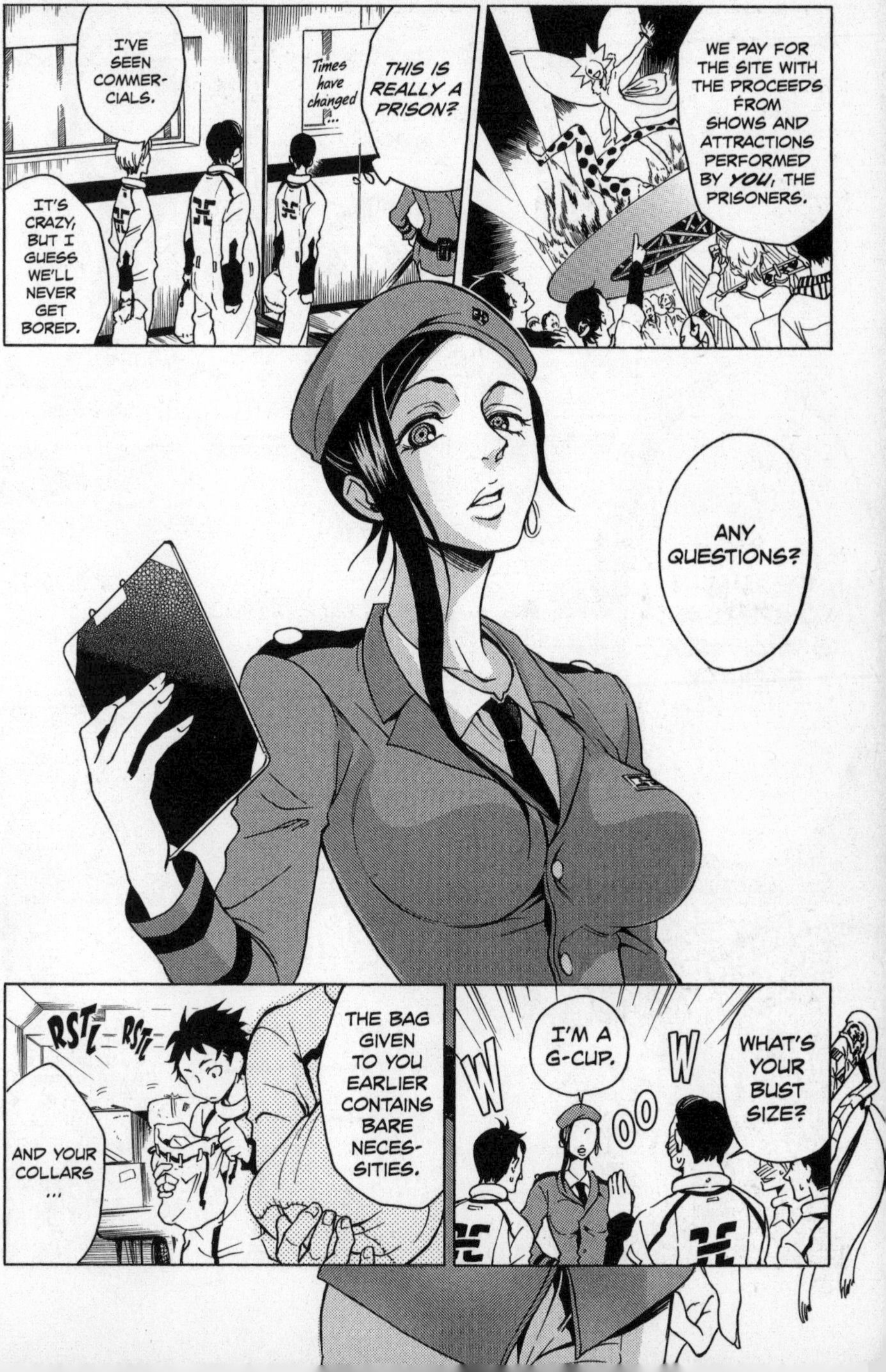
WE PAY FOR THE SITE WITH THE PROCEEDS FROM SHOWS AND ATTRACTIONS PERFORMED BY *YOU*, THE PRISONERS.
*THIS IS REALLY A PRISON?*
*Times have changed ...*
I'VE SEEN COMMER-CIALS.
IT'S CRAZY, BUT I GUESS WE'LL NEVER GET BORED.
ANY QUESTIONS?
WHAT'S YOUR BUST SIZE?
W
I'M A G-CUP.
W
OO
THE BAG GIVEN TO YOU EARLIER CONTAINS BARE NECES-SITIES.
RSTL RSTL
AND YOUR COLLARS ...

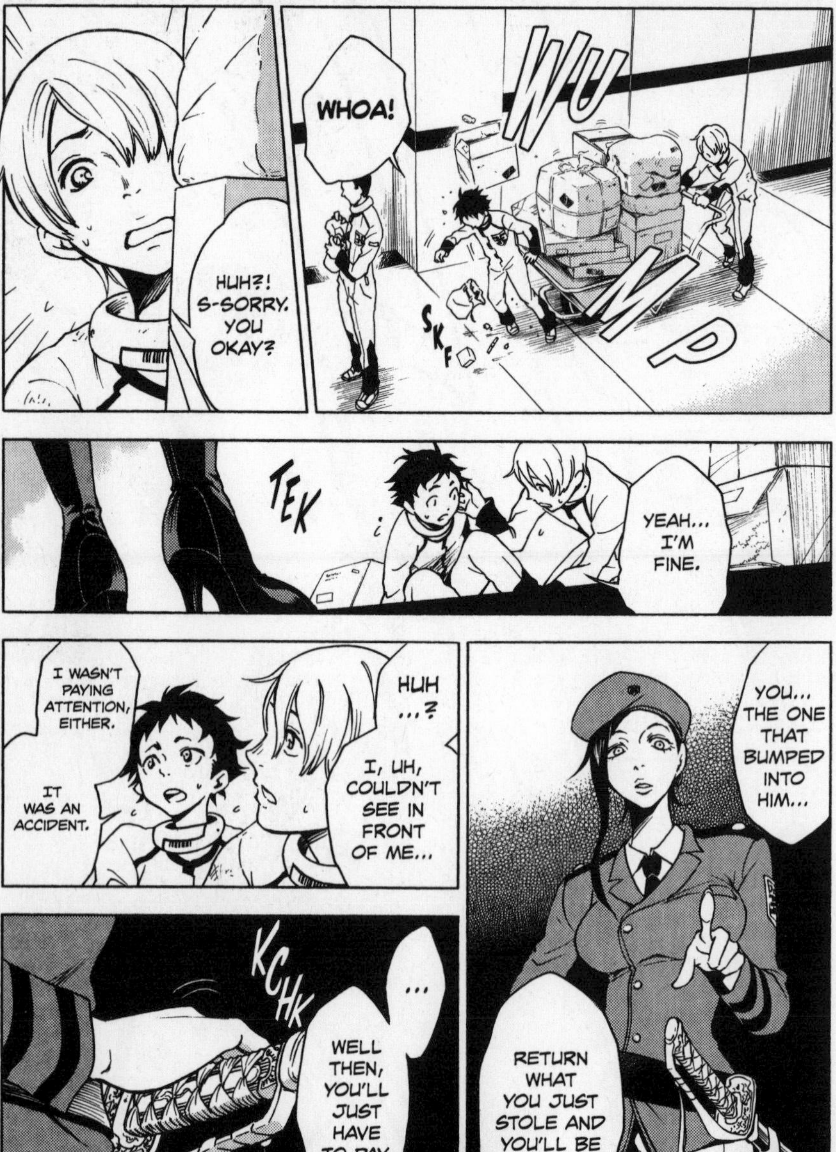
WHOA!
WUMP
SKF
HUH?! S-SORRY. YOU OKAY?
TEK
YEAH... I'M FINE.
YOU... THE ONE THAT BUMPED INTO HIM...
RETURN WHAT YOU JUST STOLE AND YOU'LL BE FORGIVEN.
HUH ...?
I, UH, COULDN'T SEE IN FRONT OF ME...
I WASN'T PAYING ATTENTION, EITHER.
IT WAS AN ACCIDENT.
KCHK
...
WELL THEN, YOU'LL JUST HAVE TO PAY.

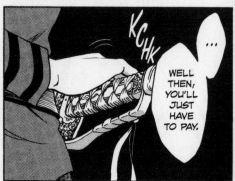

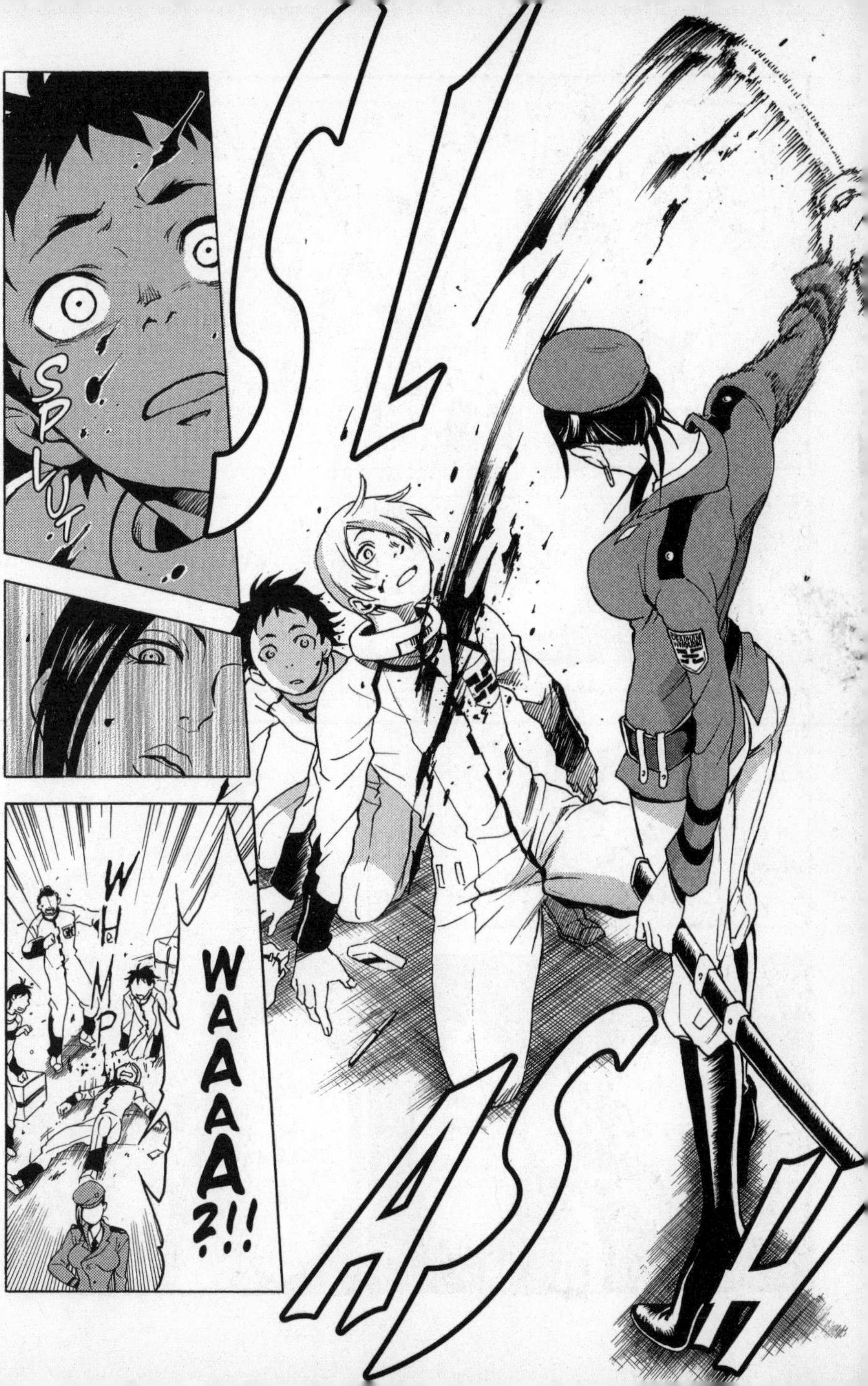
SLASH
SPLUT
WHeMP
WAAAAA?!!

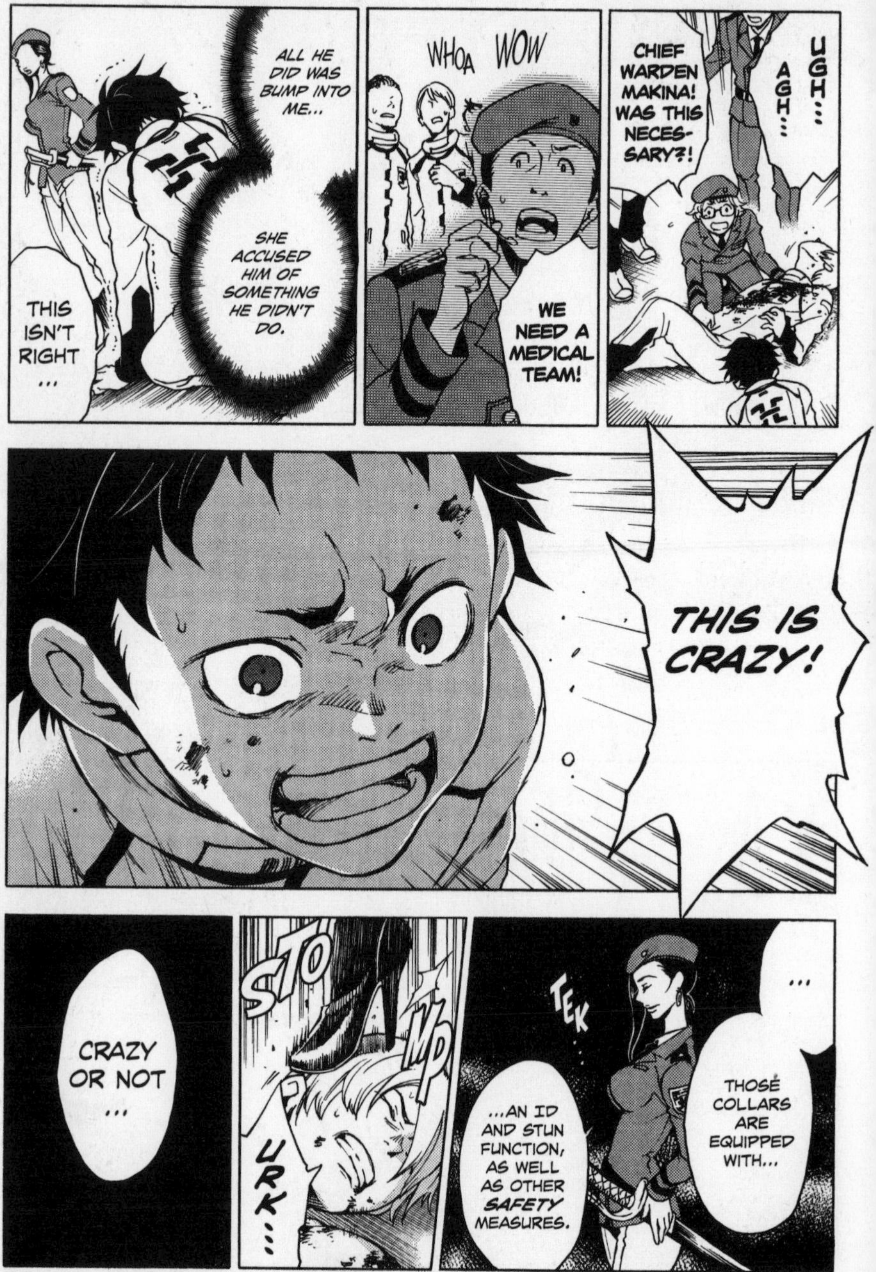
UGH...
AGH...
CHIEF WARDEN MAKINA! WAS THIS NECES-SARY?!
WOW
WHOA
WE NEED A MEDICAL TEAM!
ALL HE DID WAS BUMP INTO ME...
SHE ACCUSED HIM OF SOMETHING HE DIDN'T DO.
THIS ISN'T RIGHT...
THIS IS CRAZY!
...
THOSE COLLARS ARE EQUIPPED WITH...
TEK...
...AN ID AND STUN FUNCTION, AS WELL AS OTHER SAFETY MEASURES.
STOMP
URK...
CRAZY OR NOT...

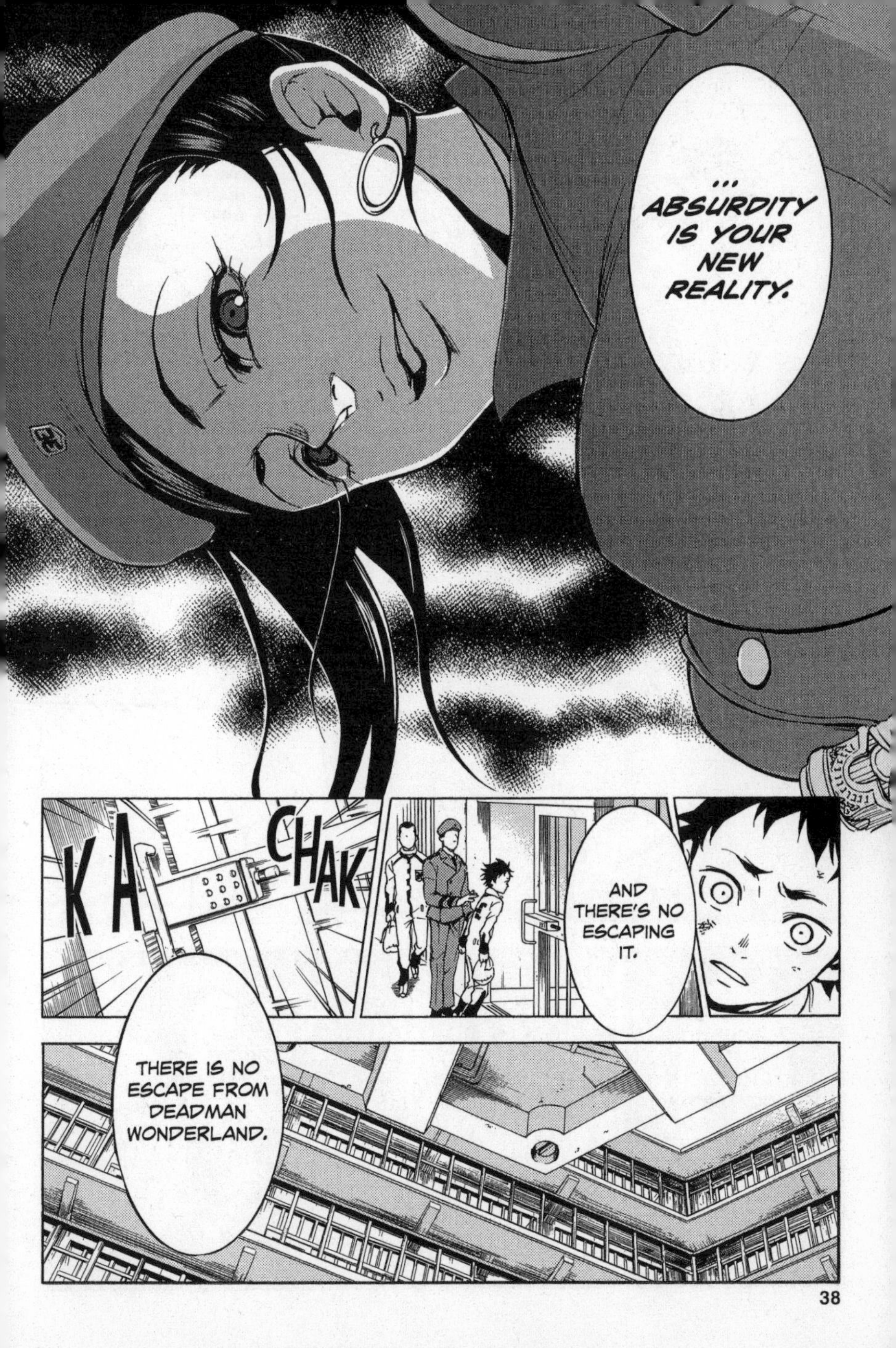
...ABSURDITY IS YOUR NEW REALITY.
AND THERE'S NO ESCAPING IT.
KA CHAK
THERE IS NO ESCAPE FROM DEADMAN WONDERLAND.

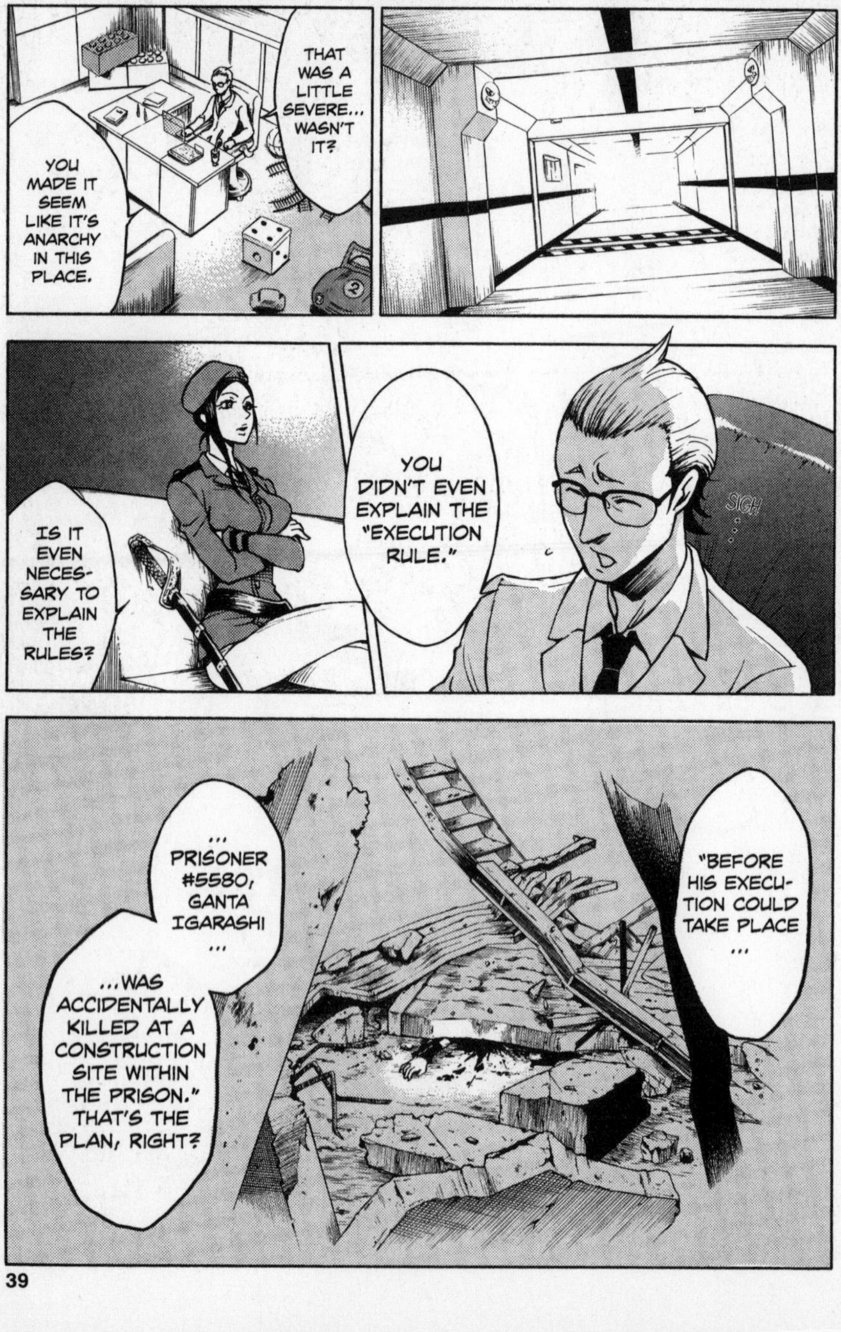
THAT WAS A LITTLE SEVERE... WASN'T IT?
YOU MADE IT SEEM LIKE IT'S ANARCHY IN THIS PLACE.
YOU DIDN'T EVEN EXPLAIN THE "EXECUTION RULE."
SIGH
IS IT EVEN NECES-SARY TO EXPLAIN THE RULES?
"BEFORE HIS EXECU-TION COULD TAKE PLACE ...
... PRISONER #5580, GANTA IGARASHI ...
...WAS ACCIDENTALLY KILLED AT A CONSTRUCTION SITE WITHIN THE PRISON." THAT'S THE PLAN, RIGHT?

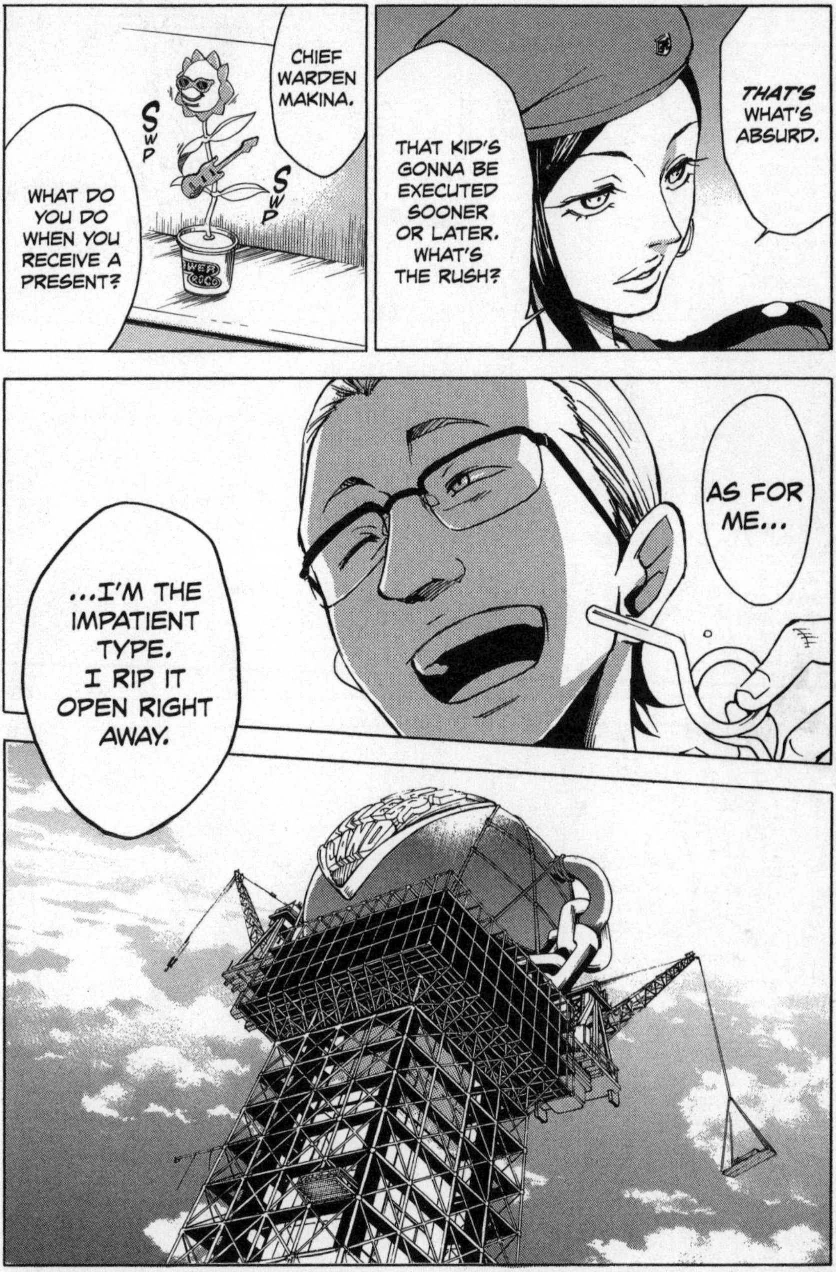
THAT'S WHAT'S ABSURD.
THAT KID'S GONNA BE EXECUTED SOONER OR LATER. WHAT'S THE RUSH?
CHIEF WARDEN MAKINA.
SWP
SWP
WHAT DO YOU DO WHEN YOU RECEIVE A PRESENT?
AS FOR ME...
...I'M THE IMPATIENT TYPE. I RIP IT OPEN RIGHT AWAY.

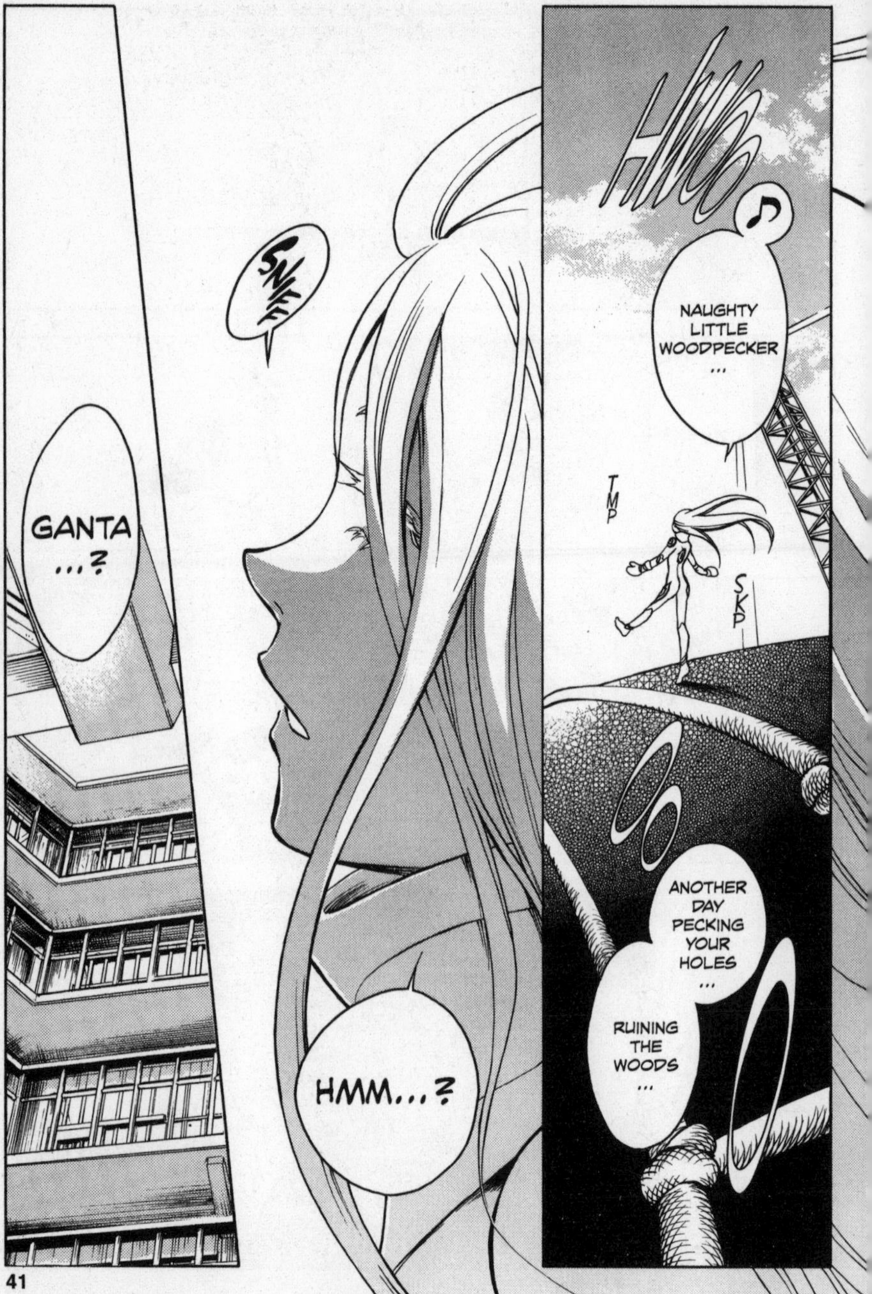
HWOO ♪
NAUGHTY LITTLE WOODPECKER...
TMP
SKP
ANOTHER DAY PECKING YOUR HOLES...
RUINING THE WOODS...
SNIFF
HMM...?
GANTA...?

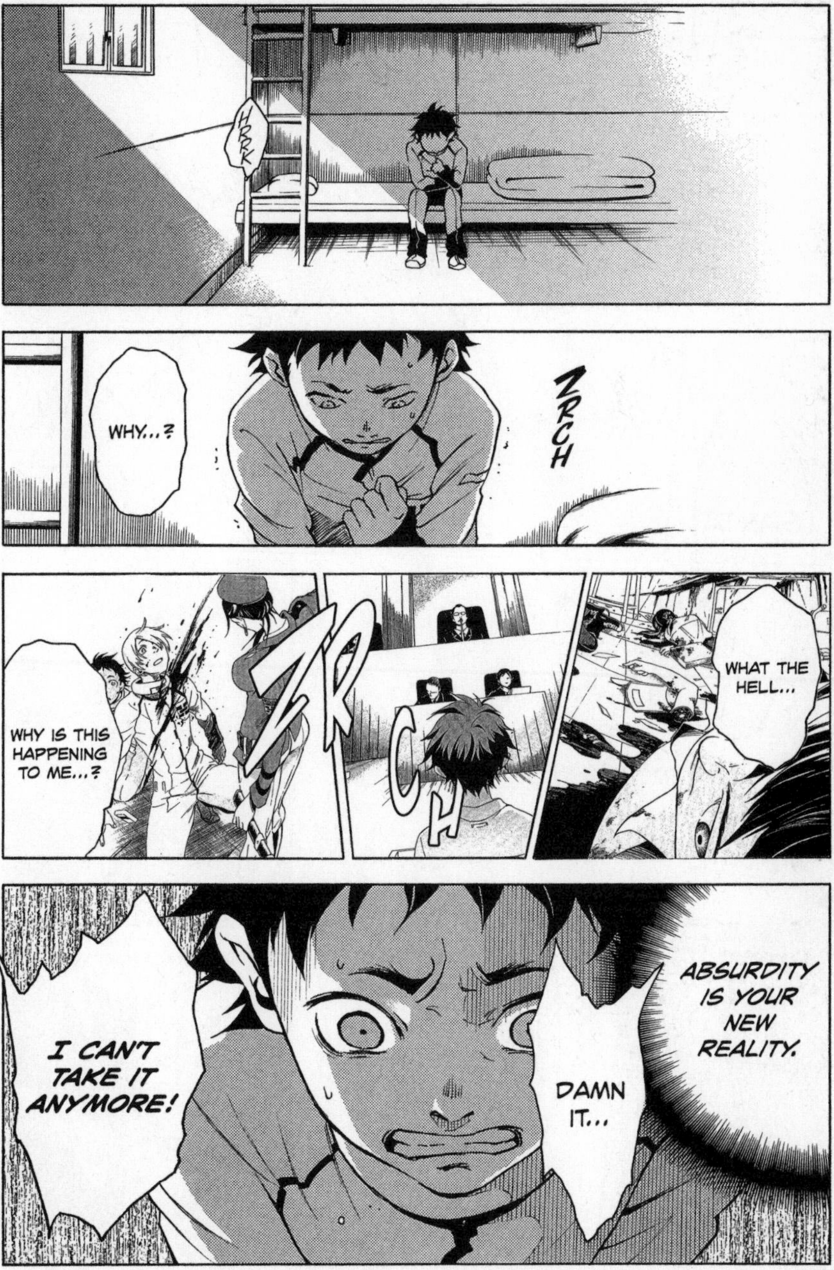
HRRK
ZRCH
WHY...?
WHAT THE HELL...
ZRCH
WHY IS THIS HAPPENING TO ME...?
ABSURDITY IS YOUR NEW REALITY.
DAMN IT...
I CAN'T TAKE IT ANYMORE!

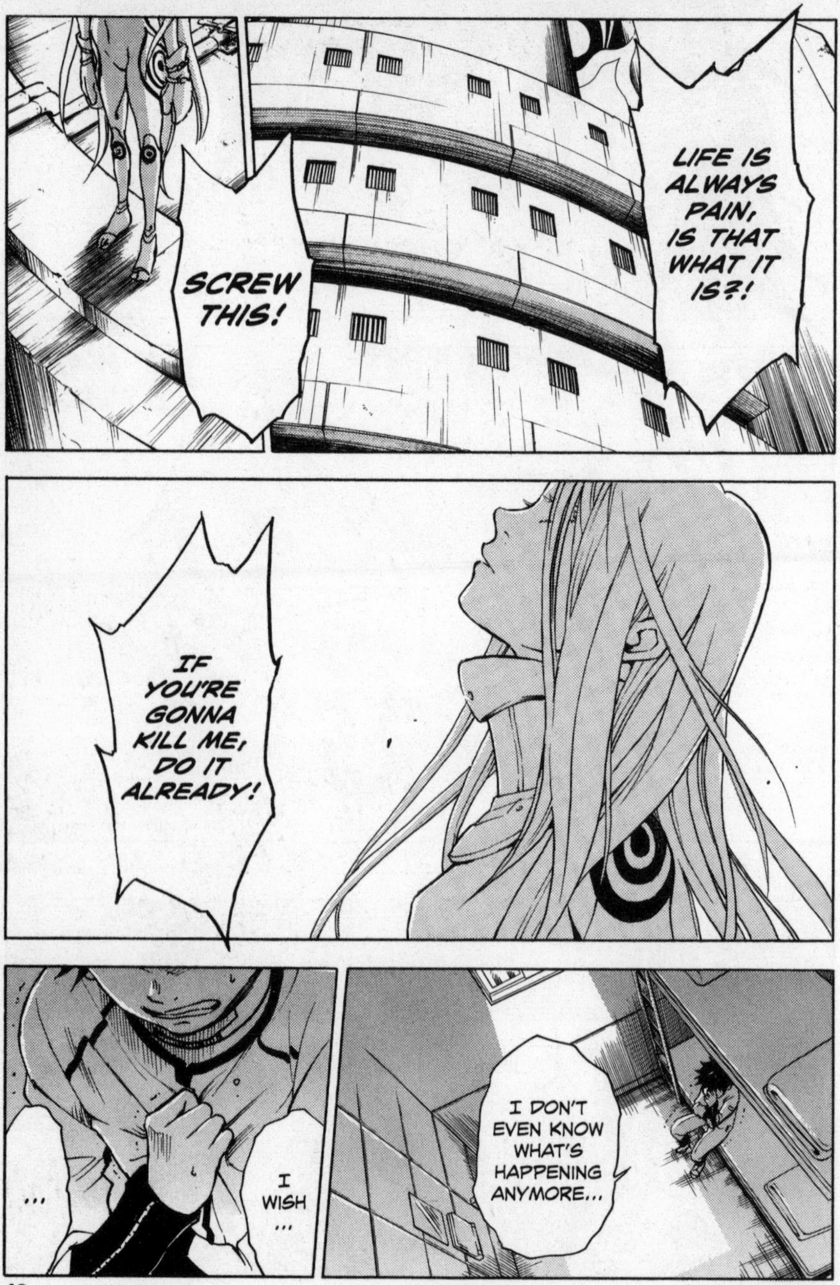
LIFE IS ALWAYS PAIN, IS THAT WHAT IT IS?!
SCREW THIS!
IF YOU'RE GONNA KILL ME, DO IT ALREADY!
I DON'T EVEN KNOW WHAT'S HAPPENING ANYMORE...
I WISH ...
...

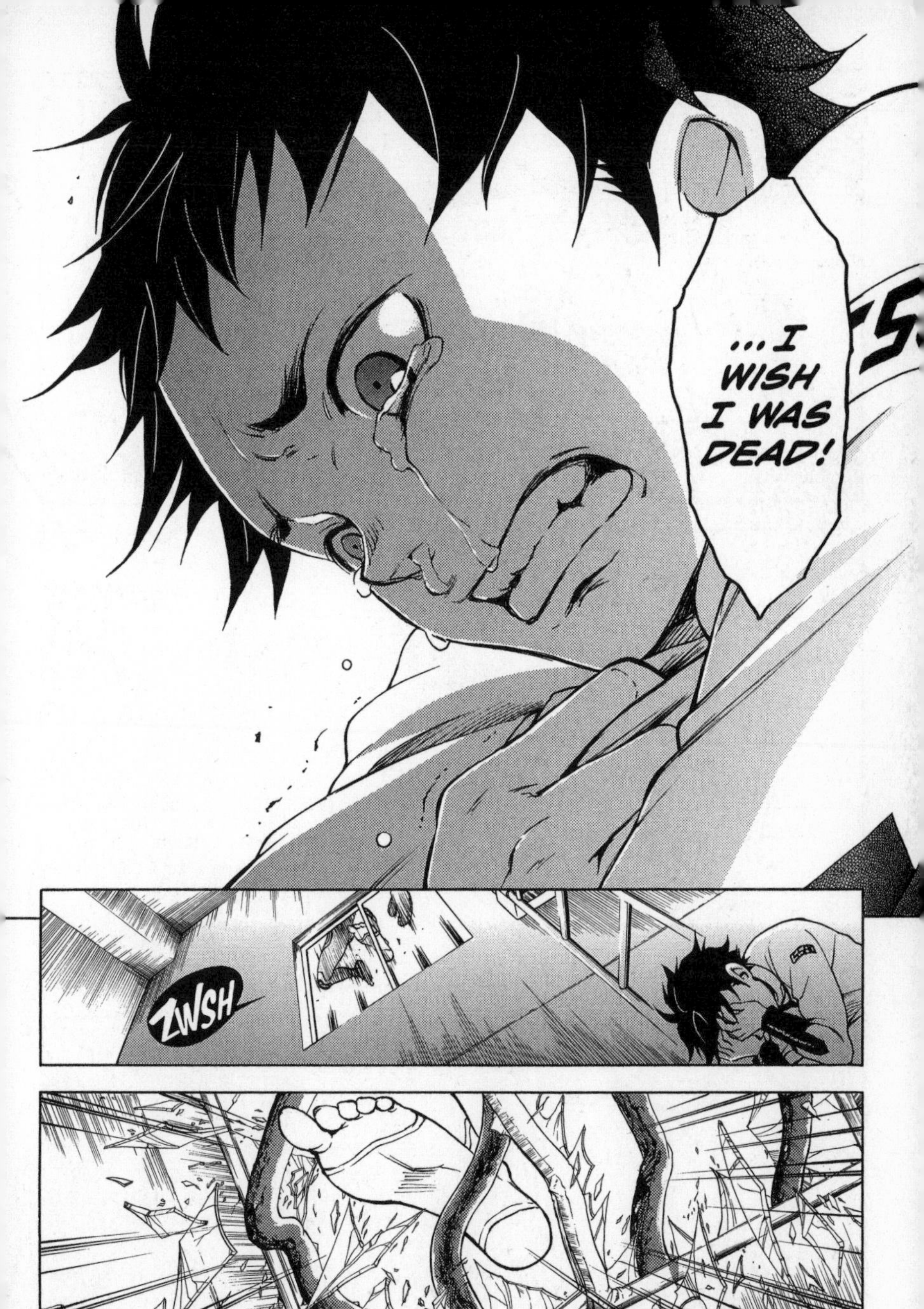
...I WISH I WAS DEAD!
ZWSH

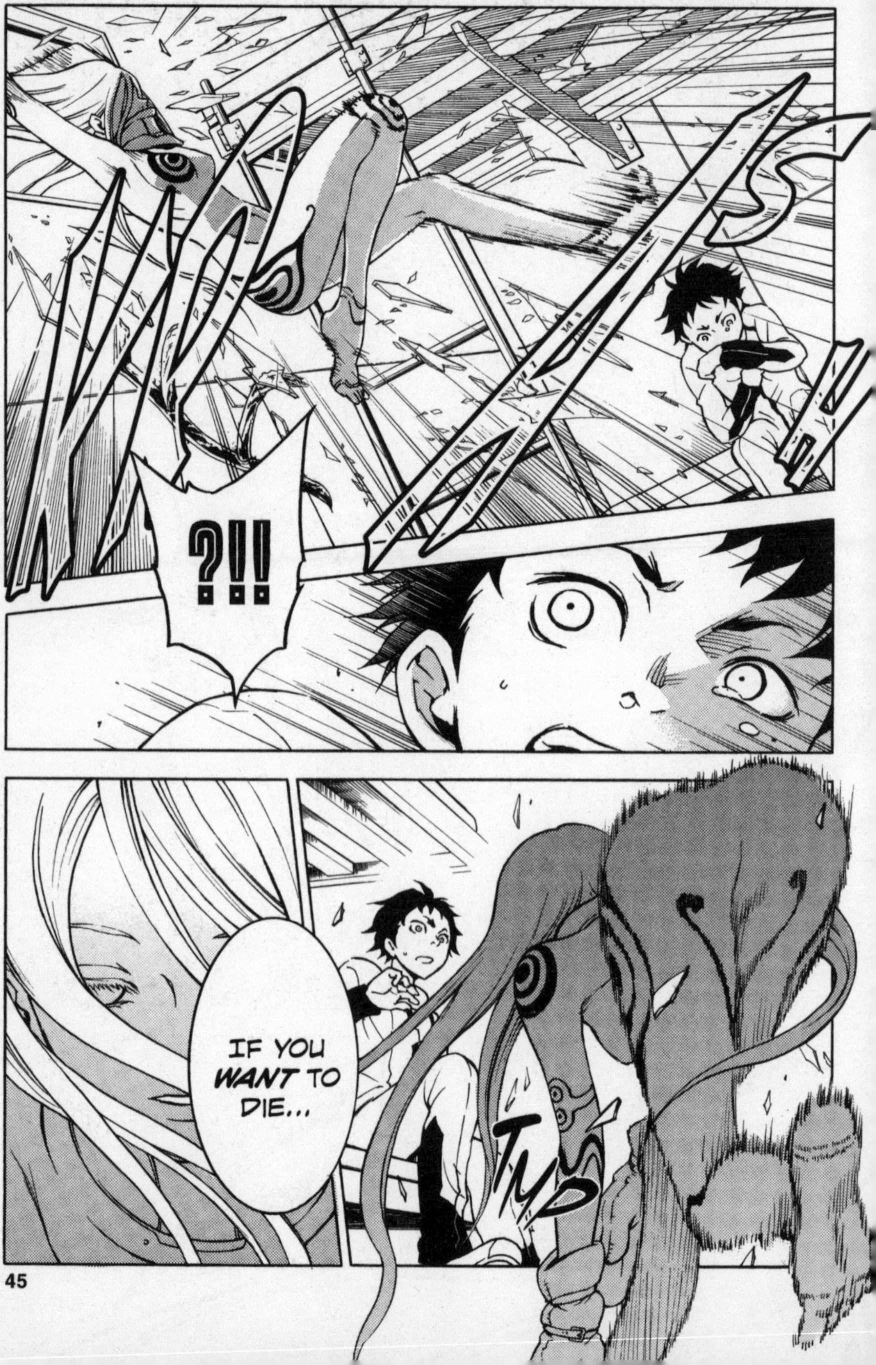
?!!
IF YOU *WANT* TO DIE...
TMP

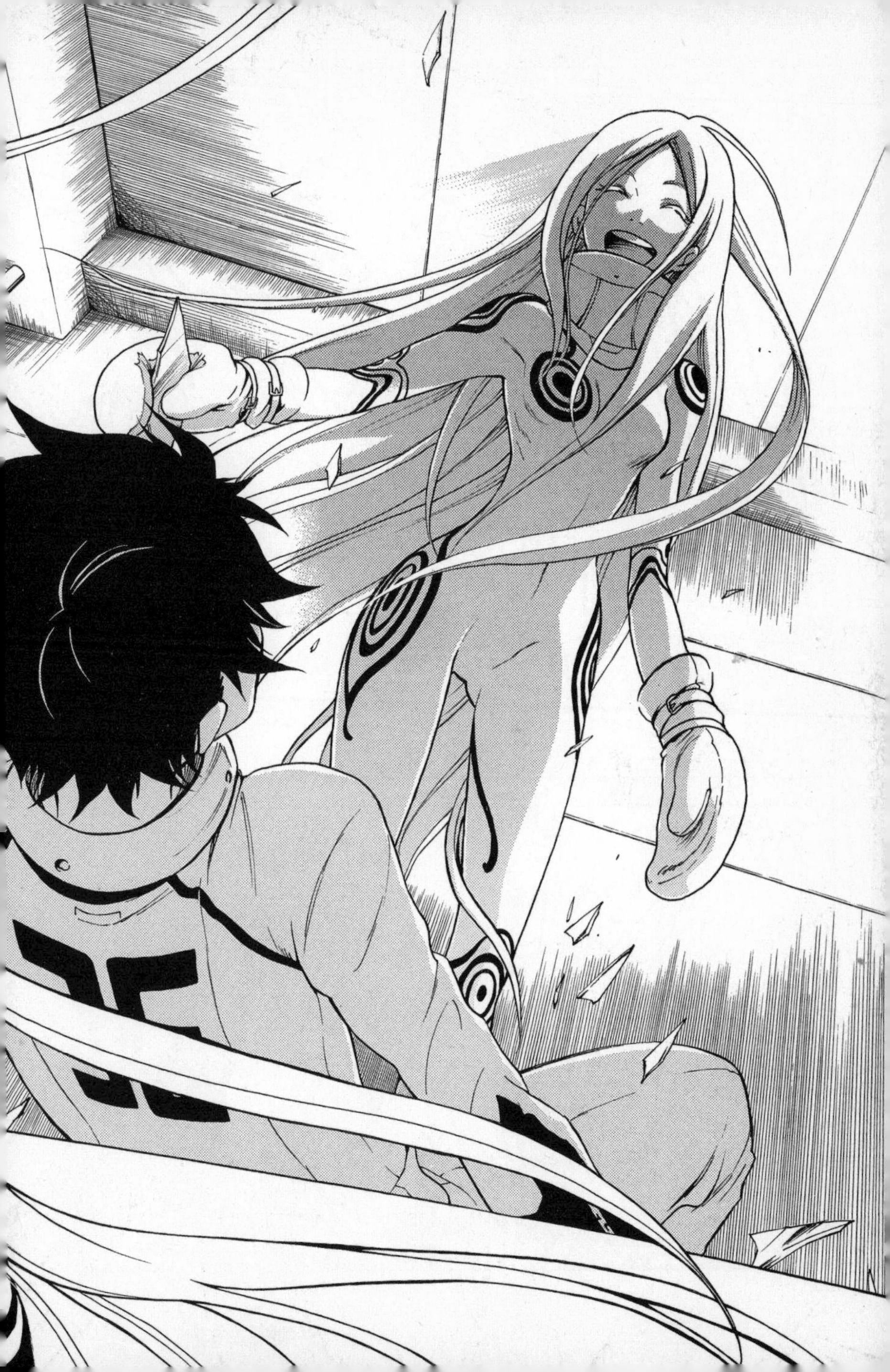

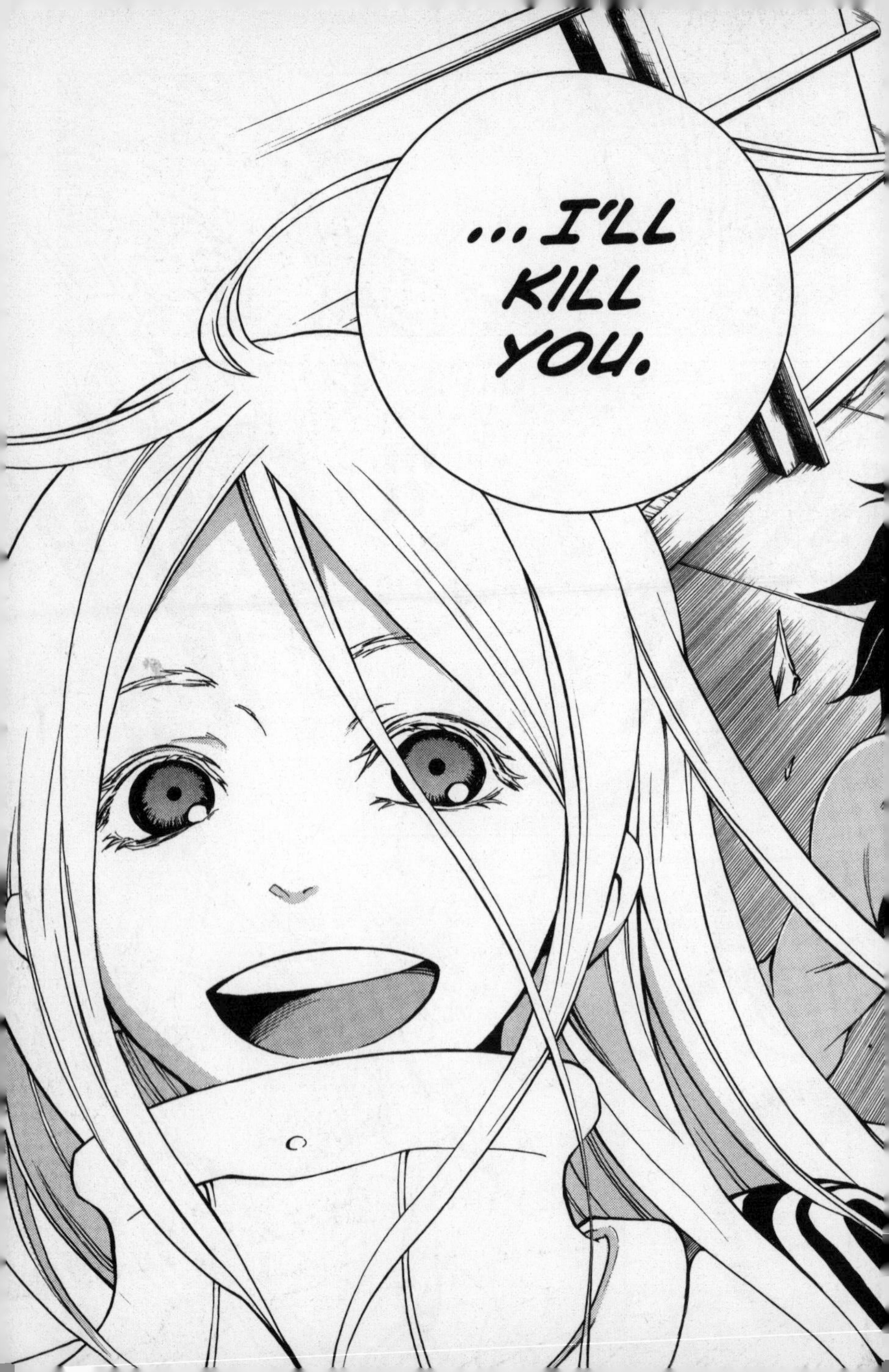
...I'LL KILL YOU.

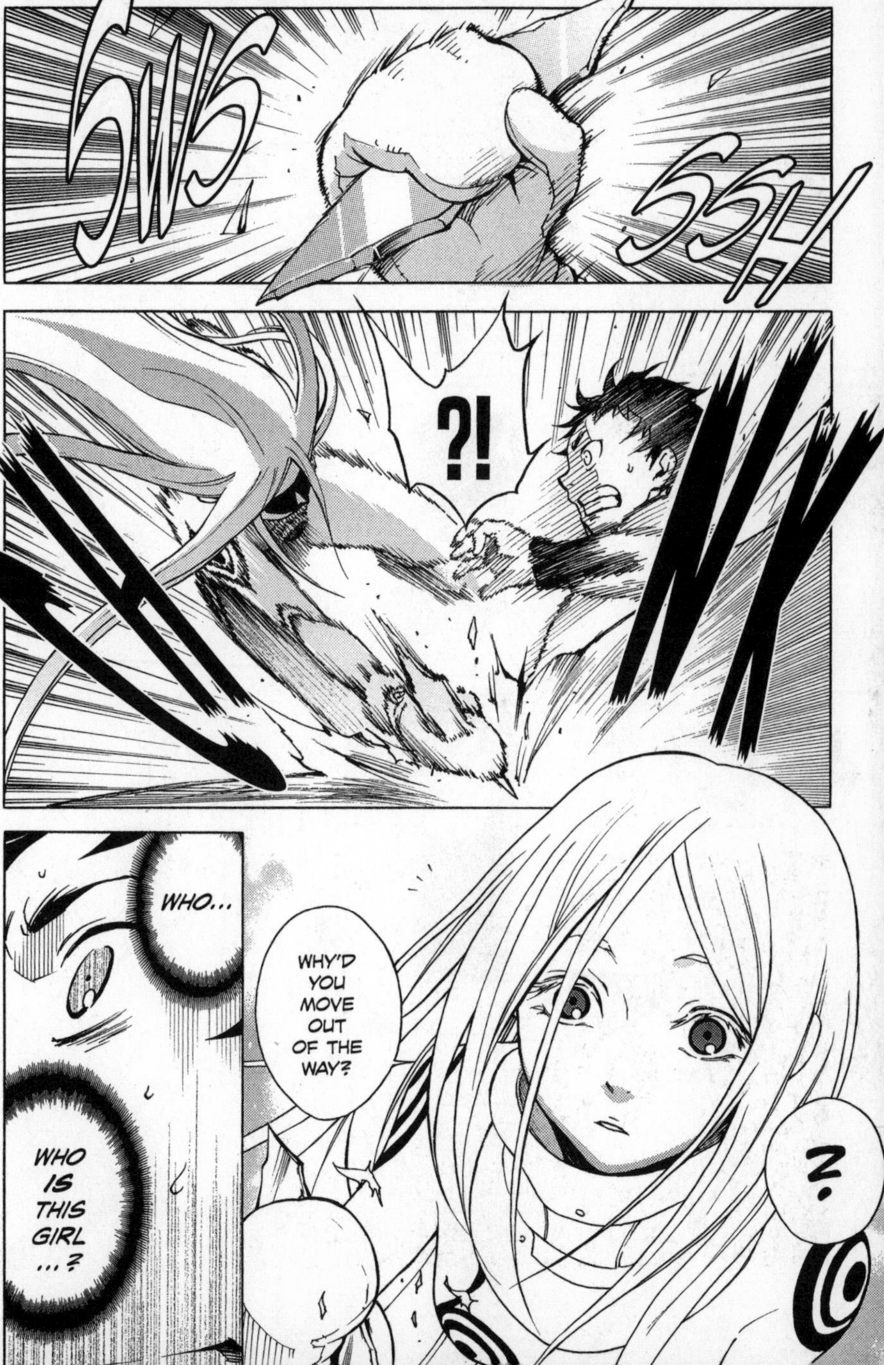
SWS
SSH
?!
WHY'D YOU MOVE OUT OF THE WAY?
?
WHO...
WHO IS THIS GIRL...?

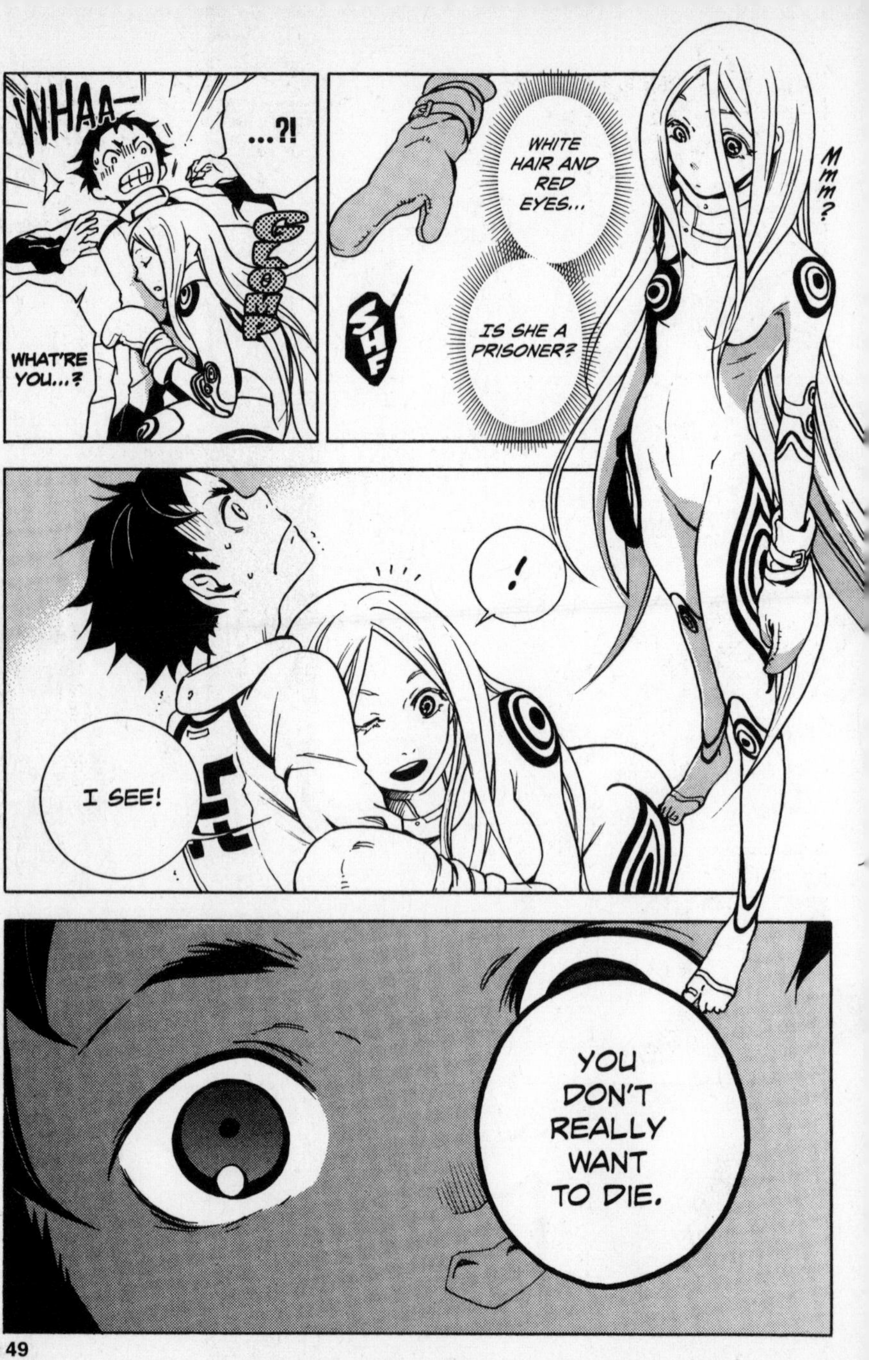

Mmm?
WHITE HAIR AND RED EYES...
IS SHE A PRISONER?
SHF
...?!
WHAA—
CLOMP
WHAT'RE YOU...?
!
I SEE!
YOU DON'T REALLY WANT TO DIE.

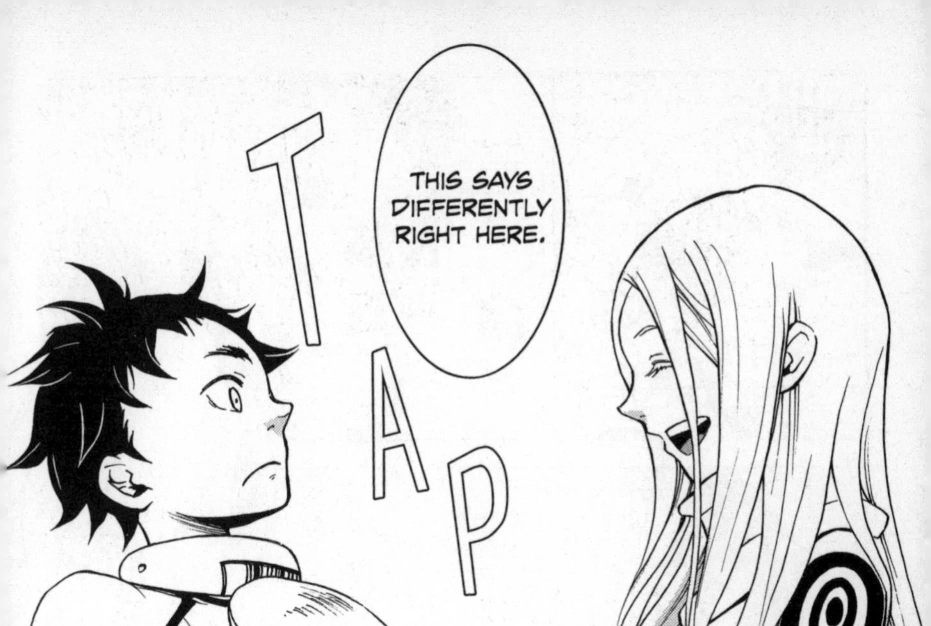
THIS SAYS DIFFERENTLY RIGHT HERE.
TAP

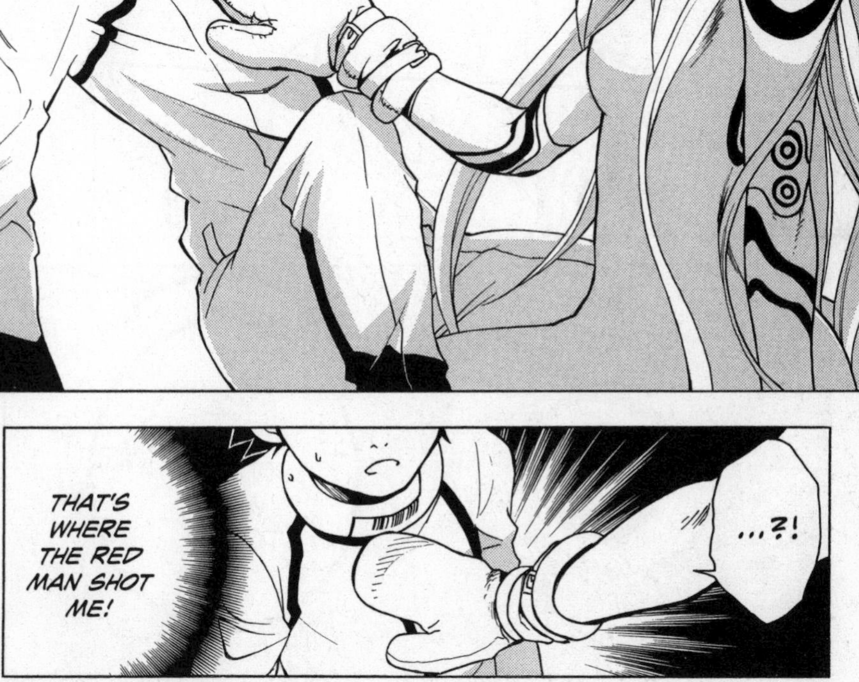
...?!
THAT'S WHERE THE RED MAN SHOT ME!

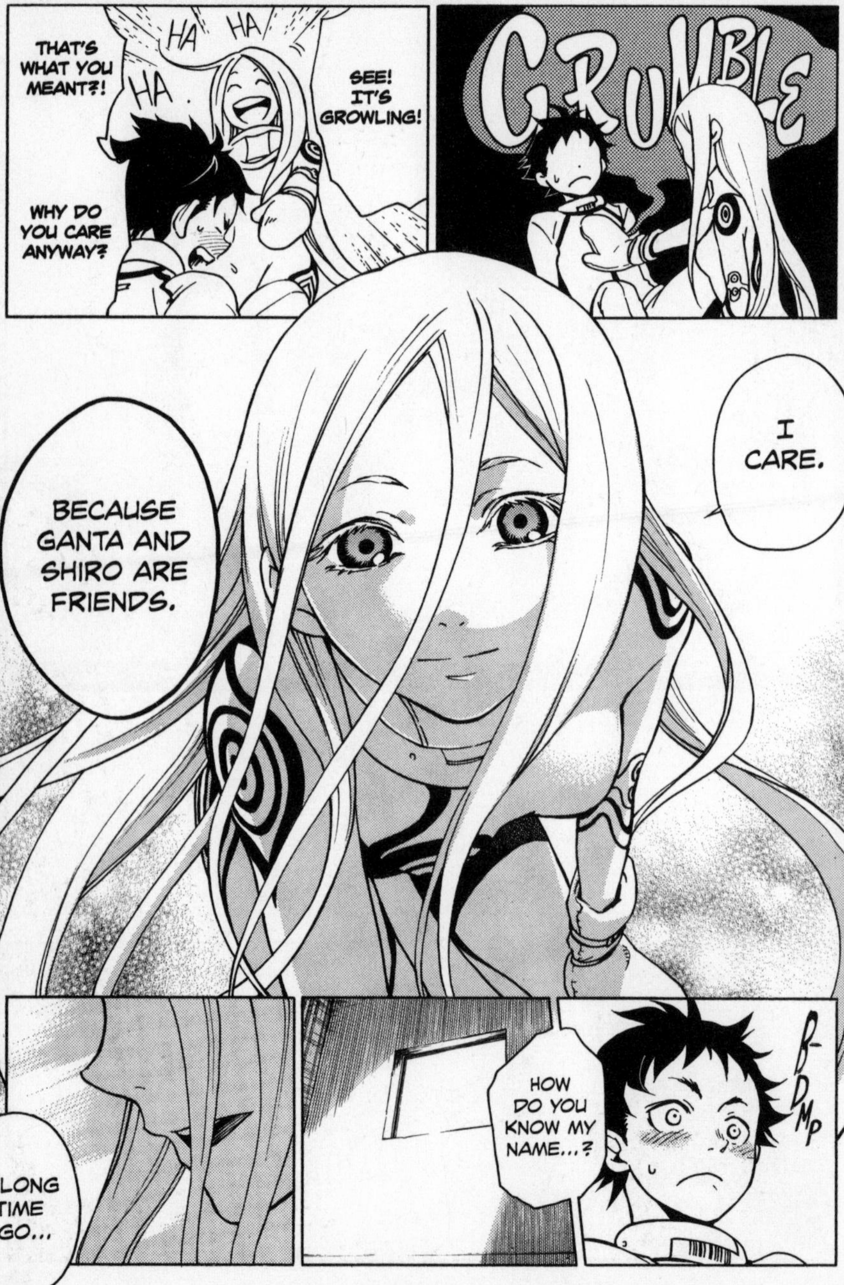
GRUMBLE
SEE! IT'S GROWLING!
HA HA HA
THAT'S WHAT YOU MEANT?!
WHY DO YOU CARE ANYWAY?
I CARE.
BECAUSE GANTA AND SHIRO ARE FRIENDS.
B-DMP
HOW DO YOU KNOW MY NAME...?
A LONG TIME AGO...

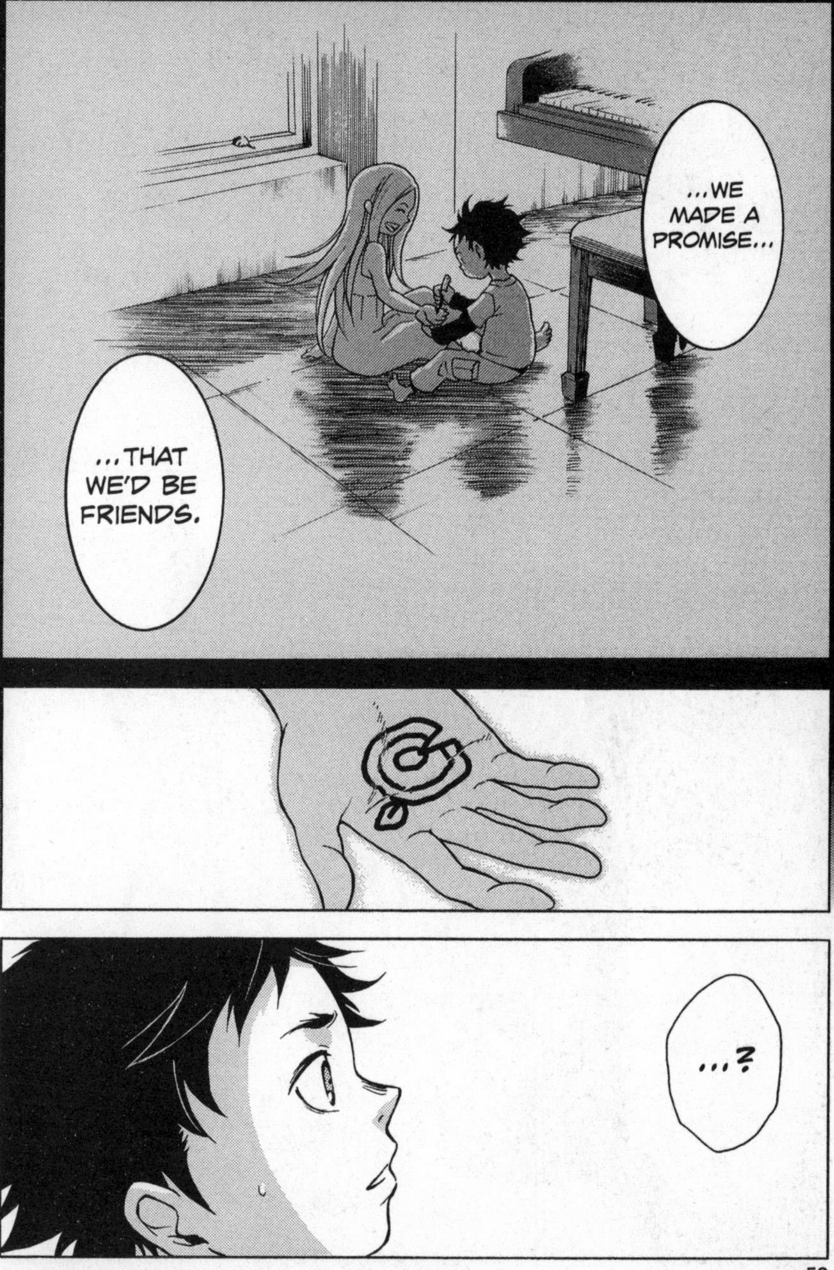
...WE MADE A PROMISE...
...THAT WE'D BE FRIENDS.
...?

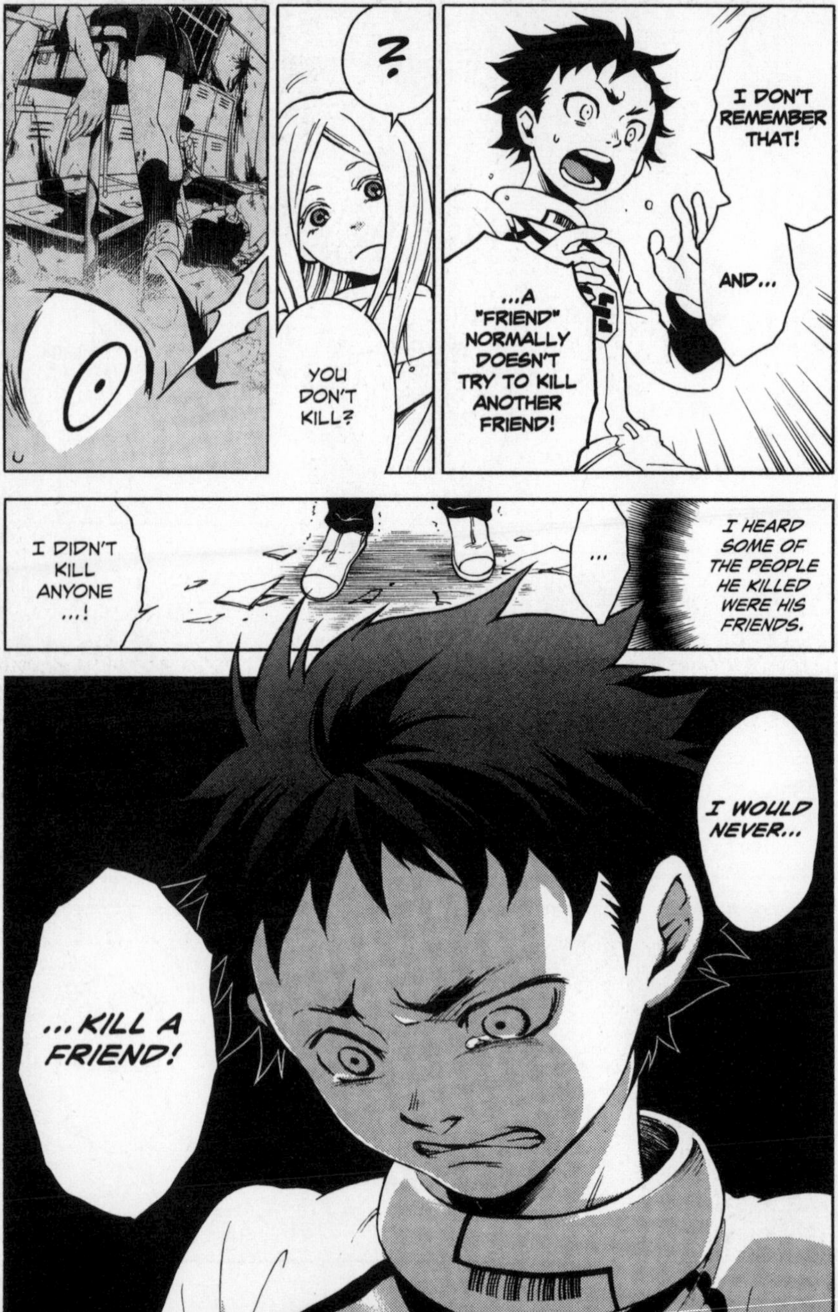
I DON'T REMEMBER THAT!
AND...
...A "FRIEND" NORMALLY DOESN'T TRY TO KILL ANOTHER FRIEND!
?
YOU DON'T KILL?
I HEARD SOME OF THE PEOPLE HE KILLED WERE HIS FRIENDS.
...
I DIDN'T KILL ANYONE ...!
I WOULD NEVER...
...KILL A FRIEND!

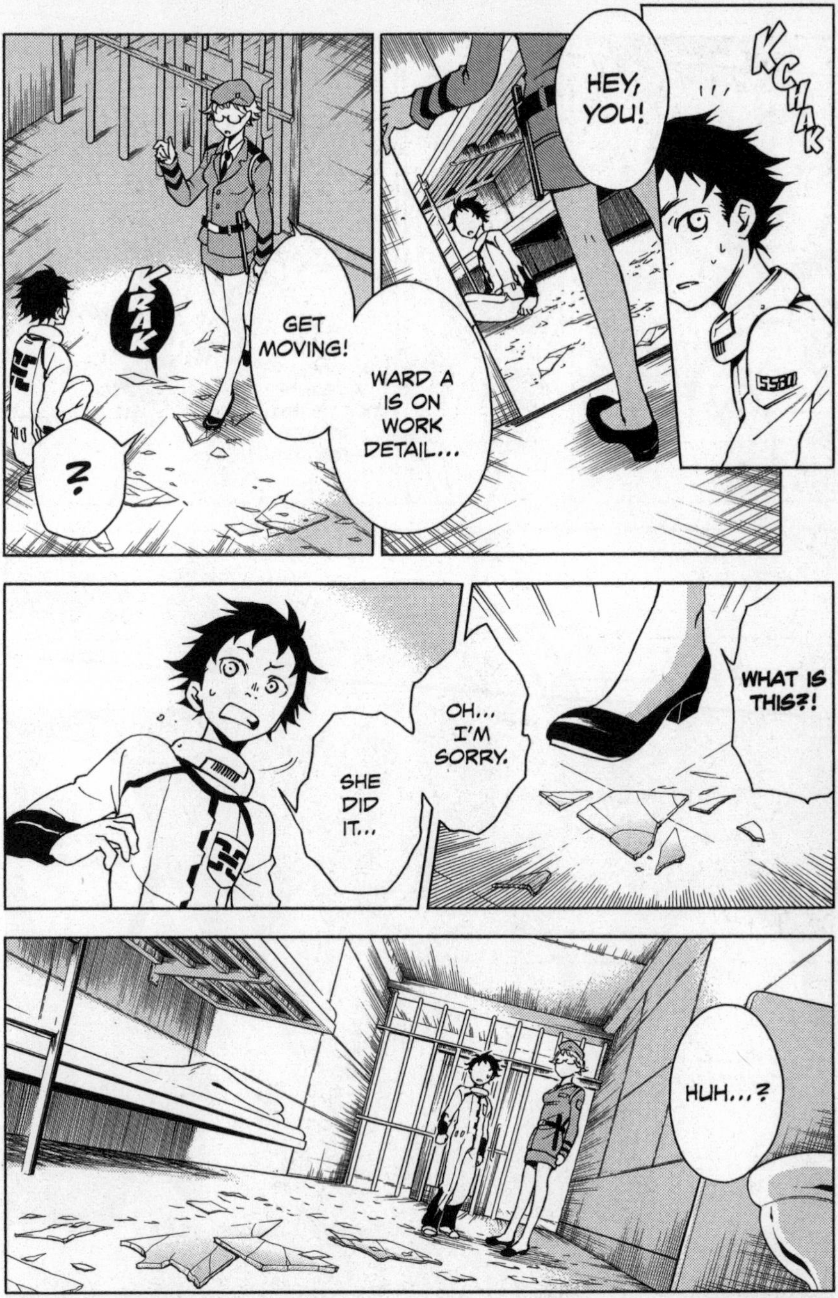
KCHAK
HEY, YOU!
GET MOVING!
WARD A IS ON WORK DETAIL...
KRAK
?
WHAT IS THIS?!
OH... I'M SORRY.
SHE DID IT...
HUH...?

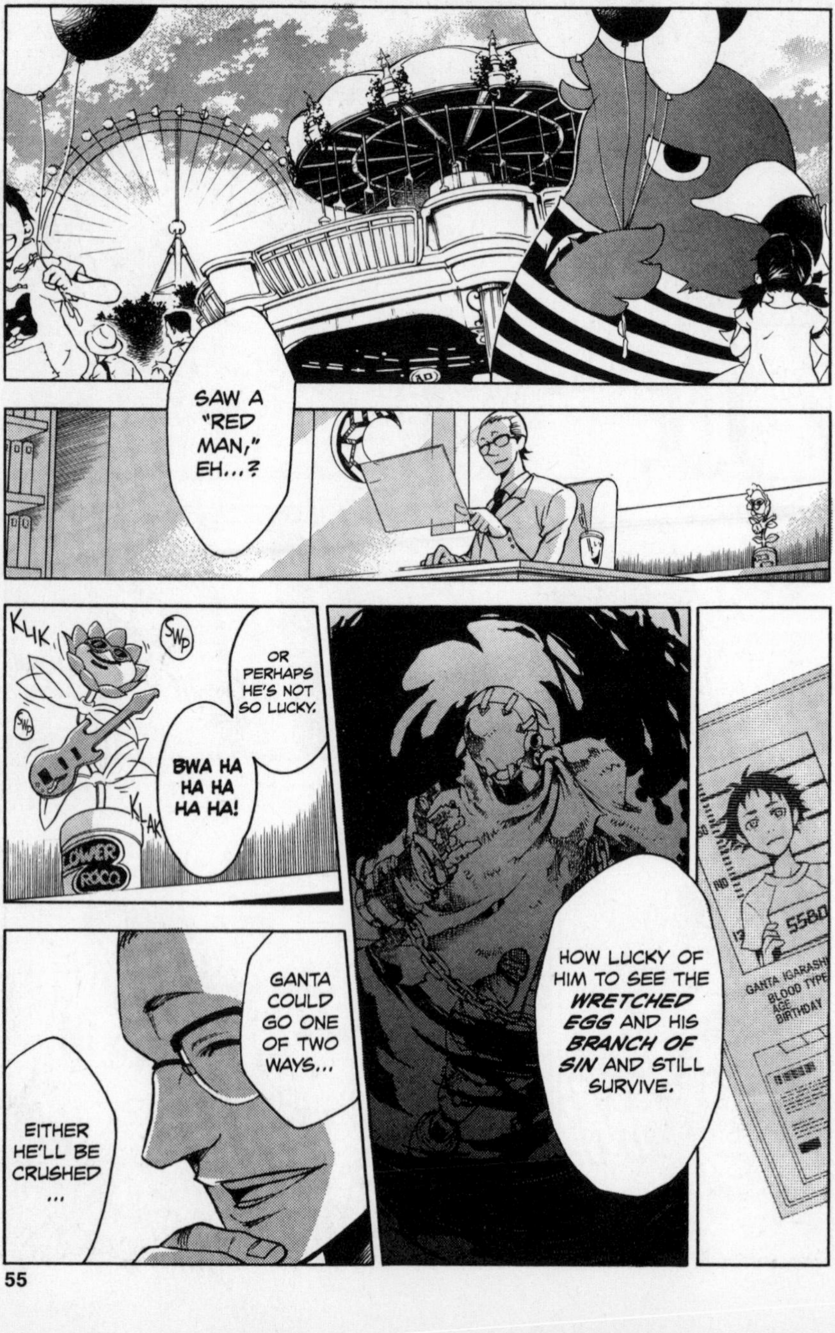
SAW A "RED MAN," EH...?
HOW LUCKY OF HIM TO SEE THE *WRETCHED EGG* AND HIS *BRANCH OF SIN* AND STILL SURVIVE.
5580
GANTA IGARASHI
BLOOD TYPE
AGE
BIRTHDAY
OR PERHAPS HE'S NOT SO LUCKY.
BWA HA HA HA HA HA!
SWP
KUK
SWP
KLAK
GANTA COULD GO ONE OF TWO WAYS...
EITHER HE'LL BE CRUSHED ...

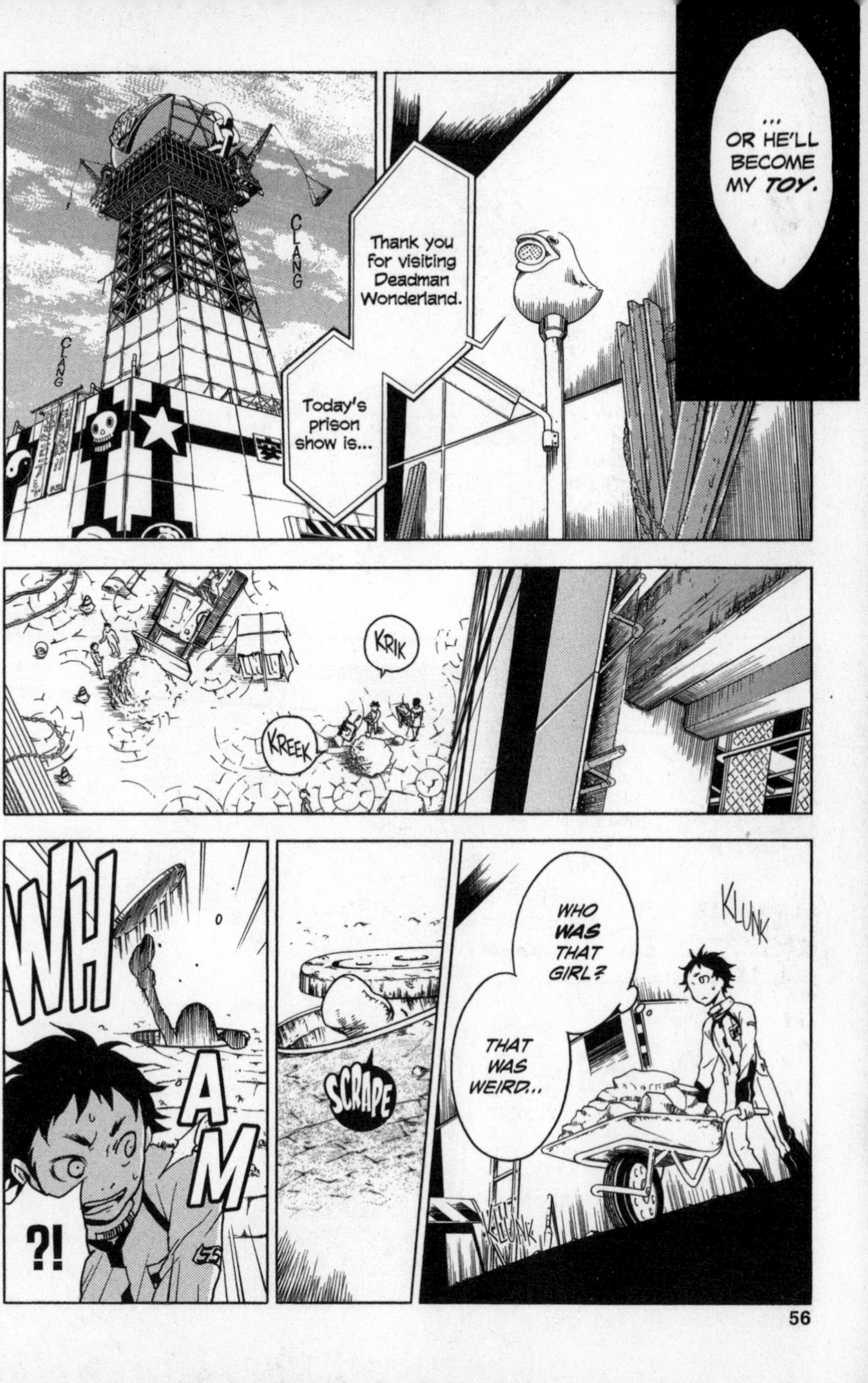
... OR HE'LL BECOME MY *TOY*.
Thank you for visiting Deadman Wonderland.
Today's prison show is...
CLANG
CLANG
KRIK
KREEK
KLUNK
WHO WAS THAT GIRL?
THAT WAS WEIRD...
KLUNK
SCRAPE
WHAM
?!

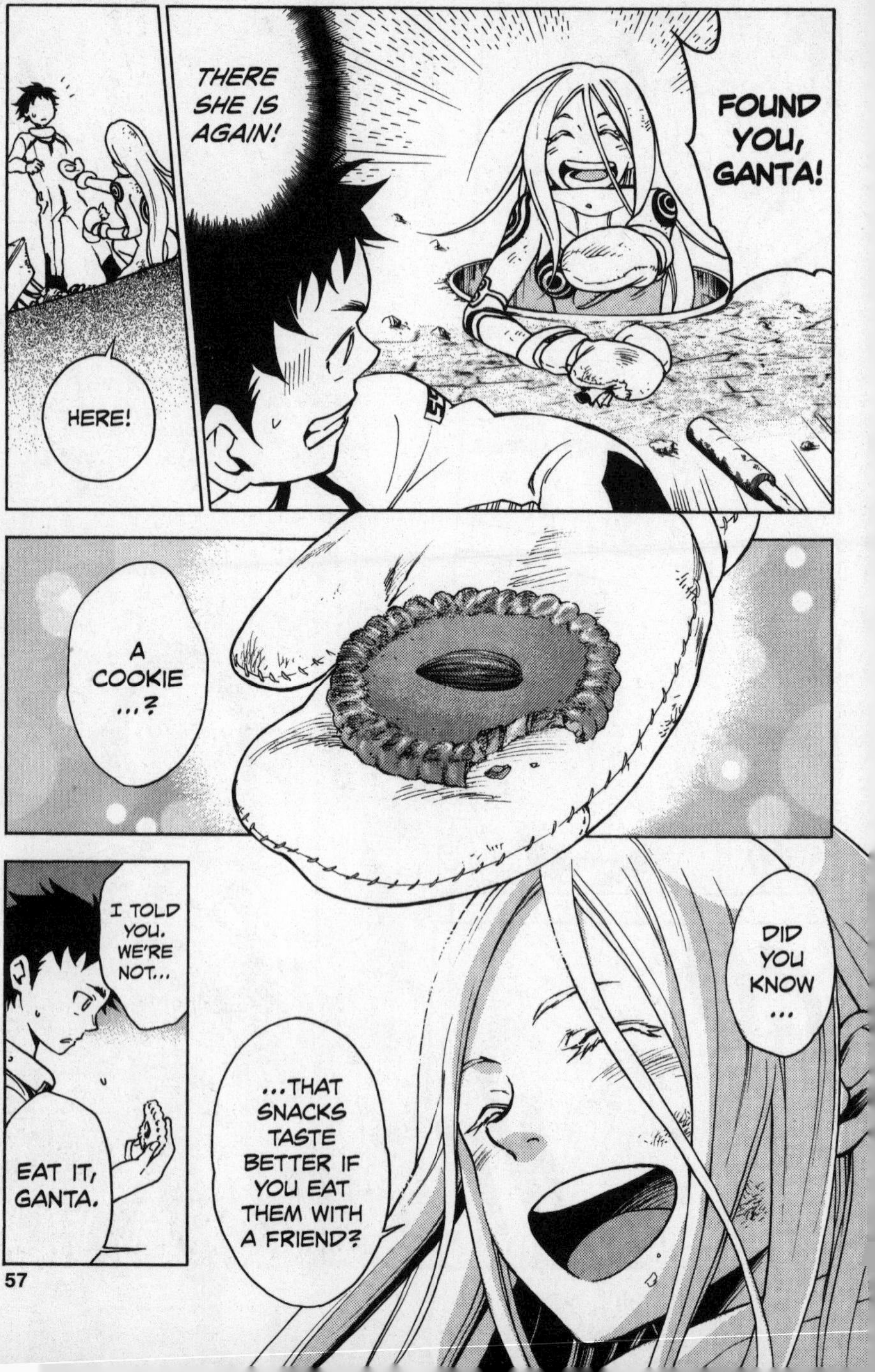
FOUND YOU, GANTA!
THERE SHE IS AGAIN!
HERE!
A COOKIE ...?
DID YOU KNOW ...
...THAT SNACKS TASTE BETTER IF YOU EAT THEM WITH A FRIEND?
I TOLD YOU. WE'RE NOT...
EAT IT, GANTA.

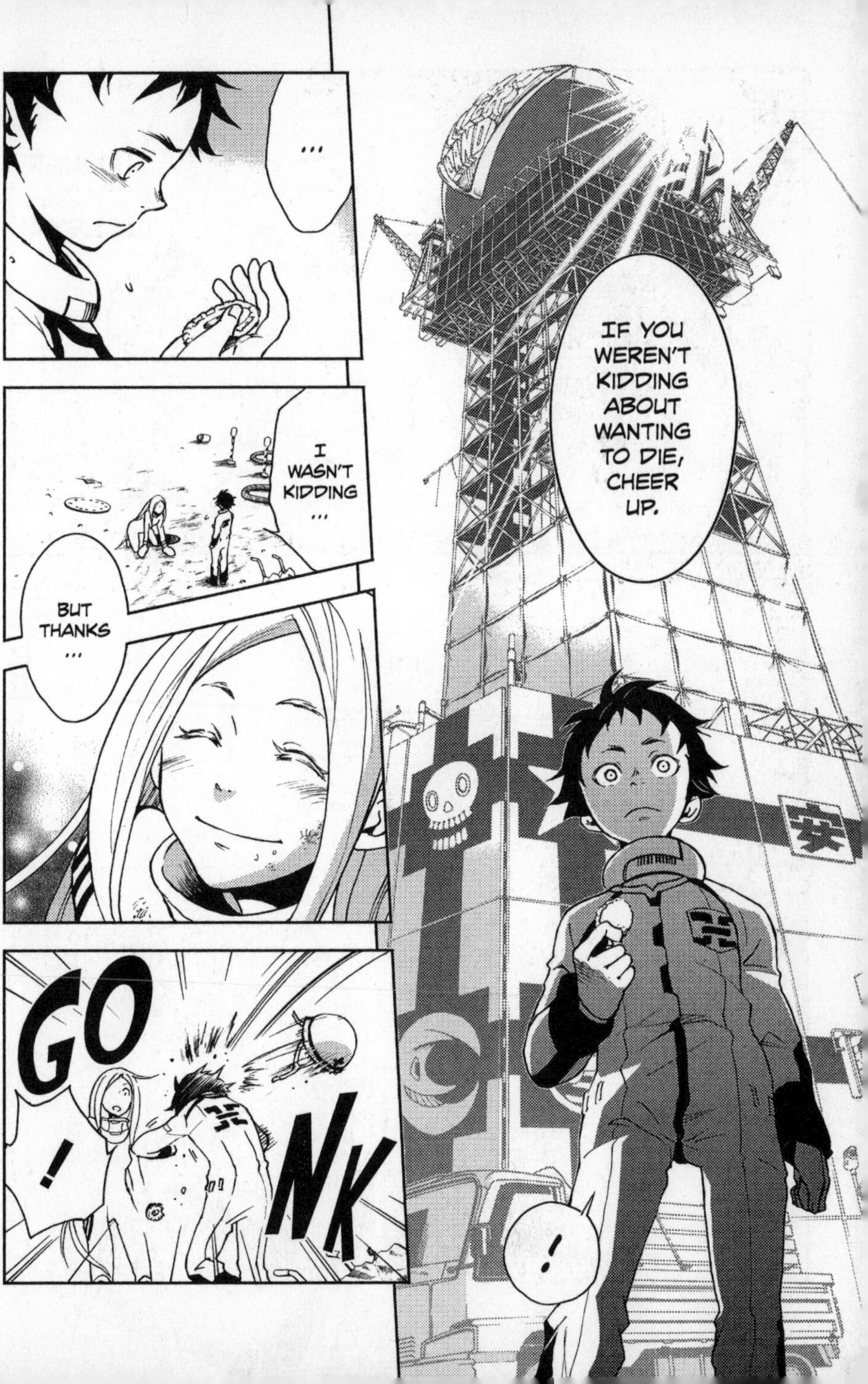
IF YOU WEREN'T KIDDING ABOUT WANTING TO DIE, CHEER UP.
!
...
I WASN'T KIDDING ...
BUT THANKS ...
GONK
!

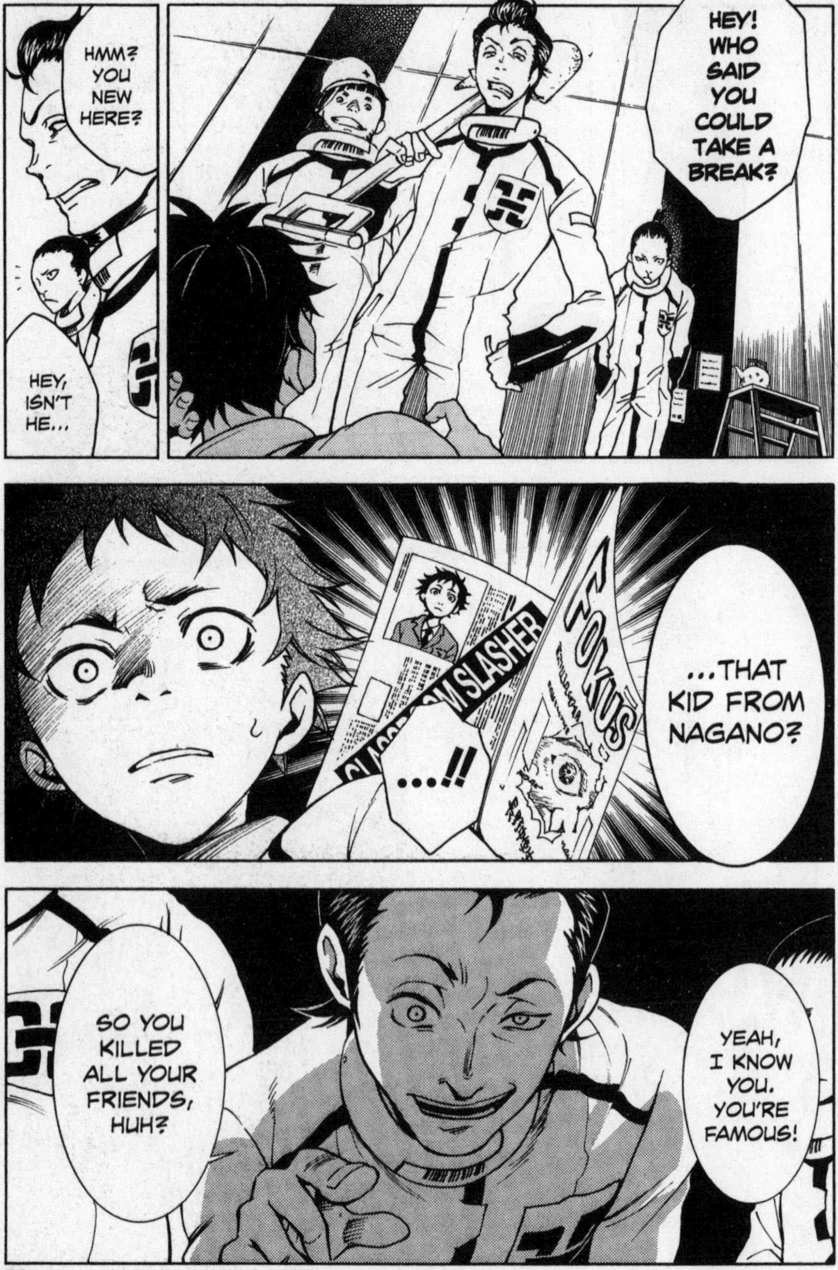
HEY! WHO SAID YOU COULD TAKE A BREAK?
HMM? YOU NEW HERE?
HEY, ISN'T HE...
...THAT KID FROM NAGANO?
FOKUS
SLASHER
...!!
YEAH, I KNOW YOU. YOU'RE FAMOUS!
SO YOU KILLED ALL YOUR FRIENDS, HUH?

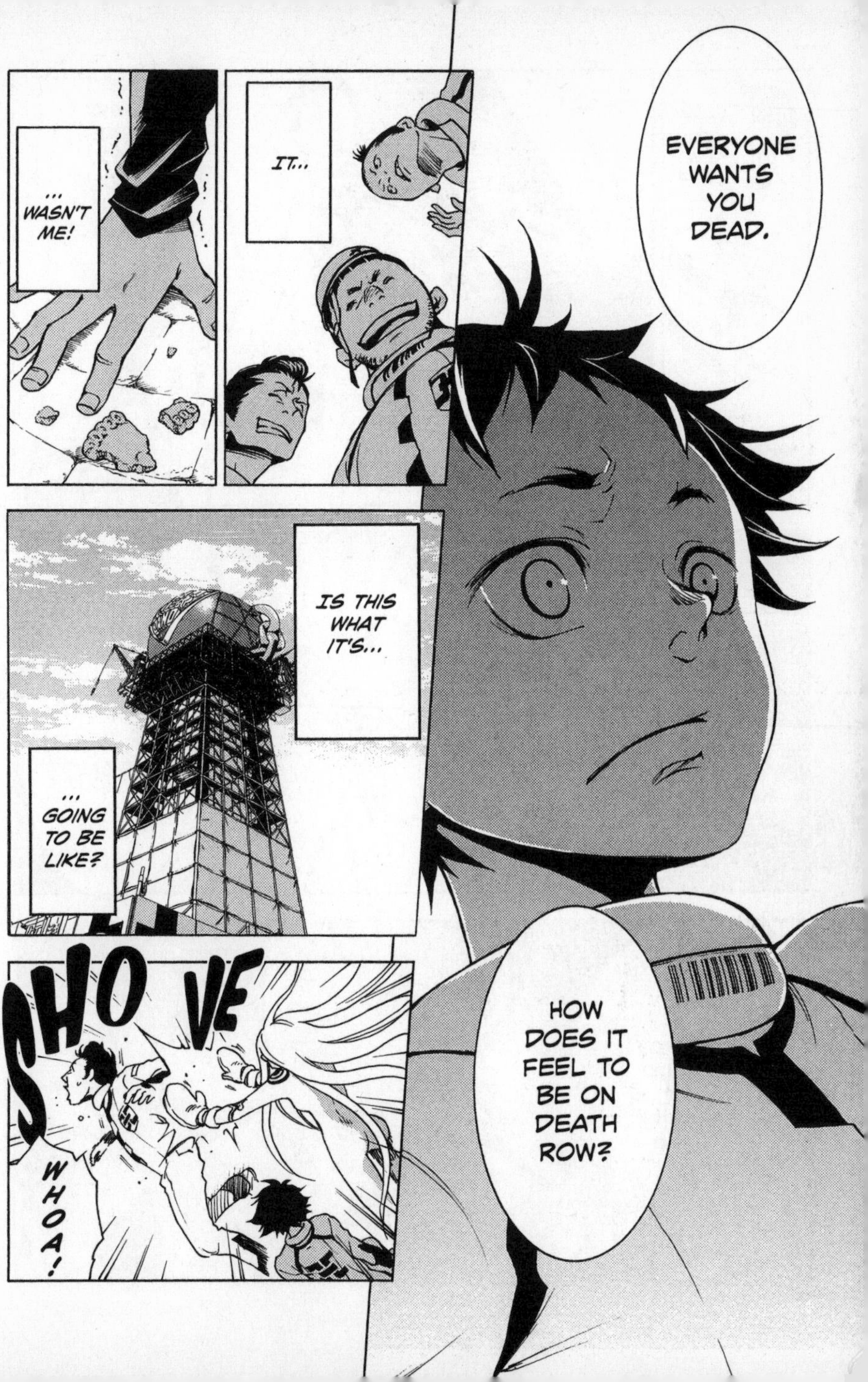
EVERYONE WANTS YOU DEAD.
HOW DOES IT FEEL TO BE ON DEATH ROW?
IT...
...WASN'T ME!
IS THIS WHAT IT'S...
...GOING TO BE LIKE?
SHOVE
WHOA!

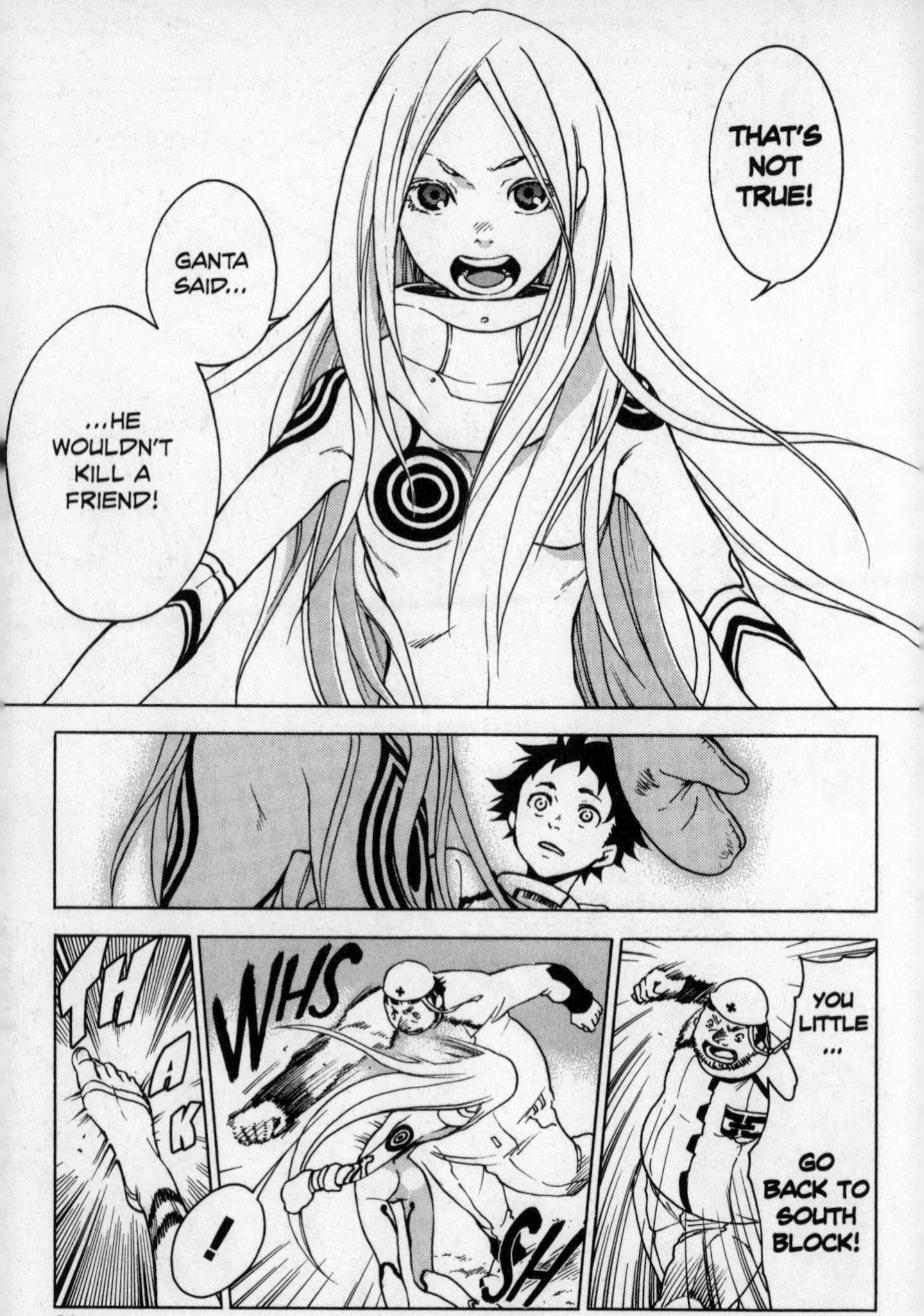
THAT'S NOT TRUE!
GANTA SAID...
...HE WOULDN'T KILL A FRIEND!
YOU LITTLE ...
GO BACK TO SOUTH BLOCK!
WHS
SH
THAK
!

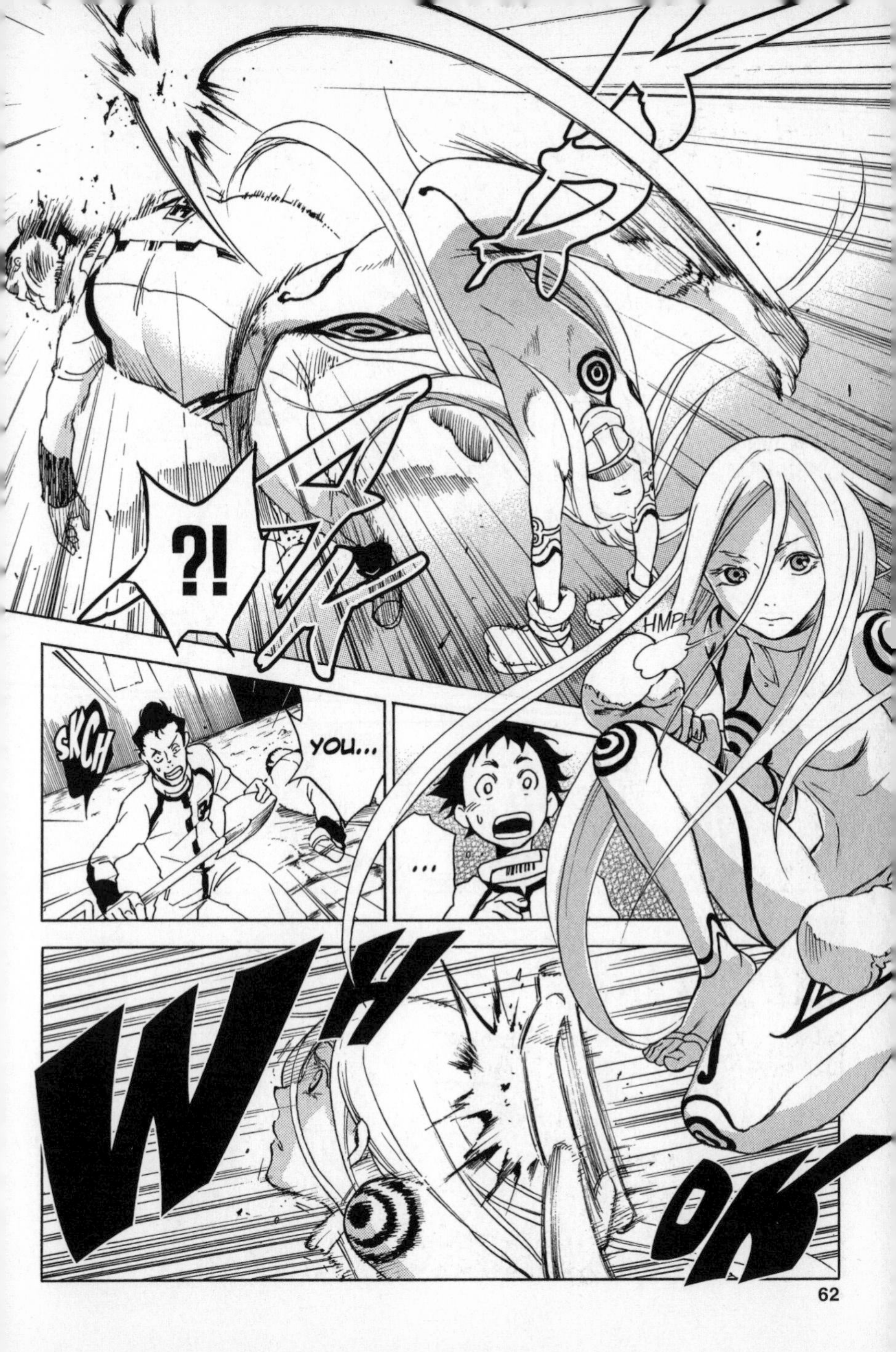
?!
HMPH
...
YOU...
SKCH
WHOK

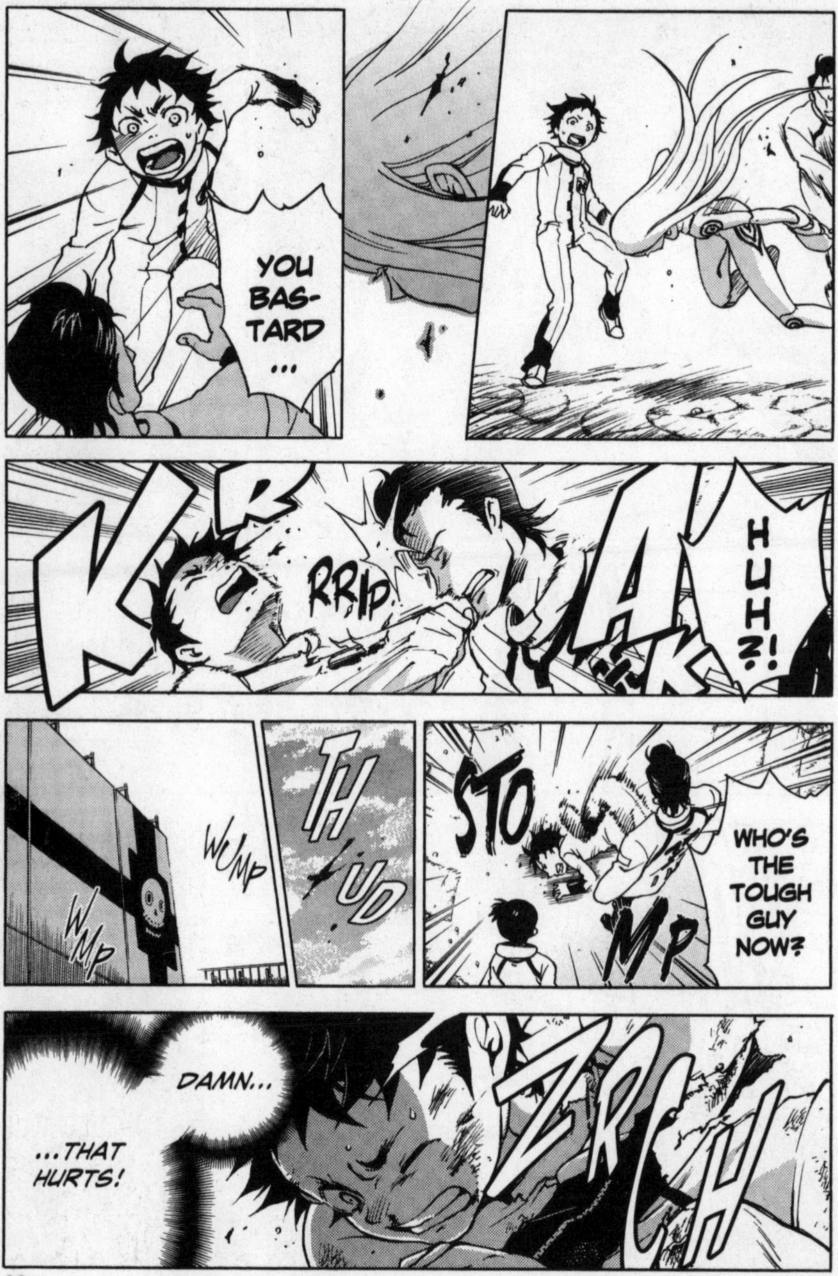
YOU BAS-TARD ...
HUH?!
KRAK
RRIP
WHO'S THE TOUGH GUY NOW?
STOMP
THUD
WUMP
WMP
ZRCH
DAMN...
...THAT HURTS!

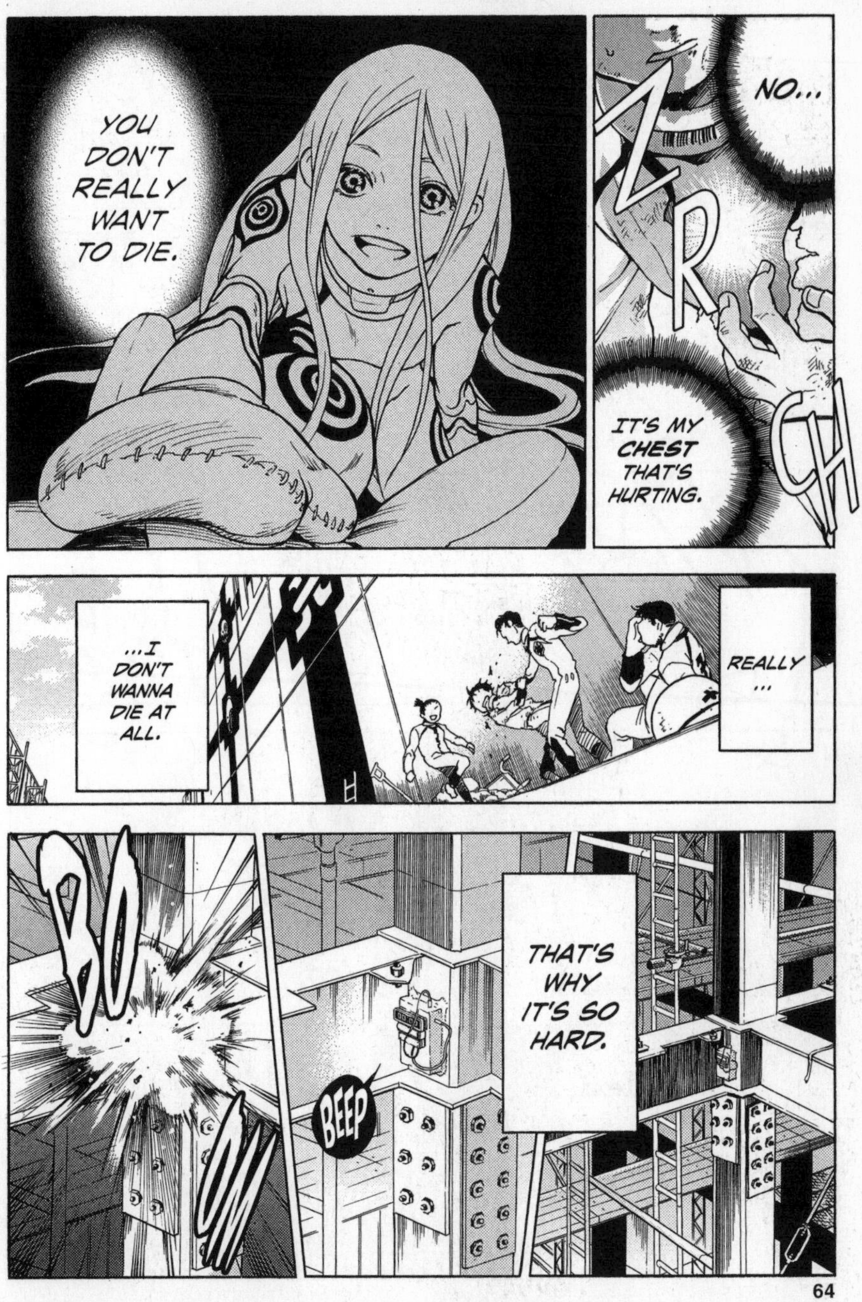
NO...
ZRCH
IT'S MY CHEST THAT'S HURTING.
YOU DON'T REALLY WANT TO DIE.
REALLY ...
...I DON'T WANNA DIE AT ALL.
THAT'S WHY IT'S SO HARD.
BEEP
BOOM

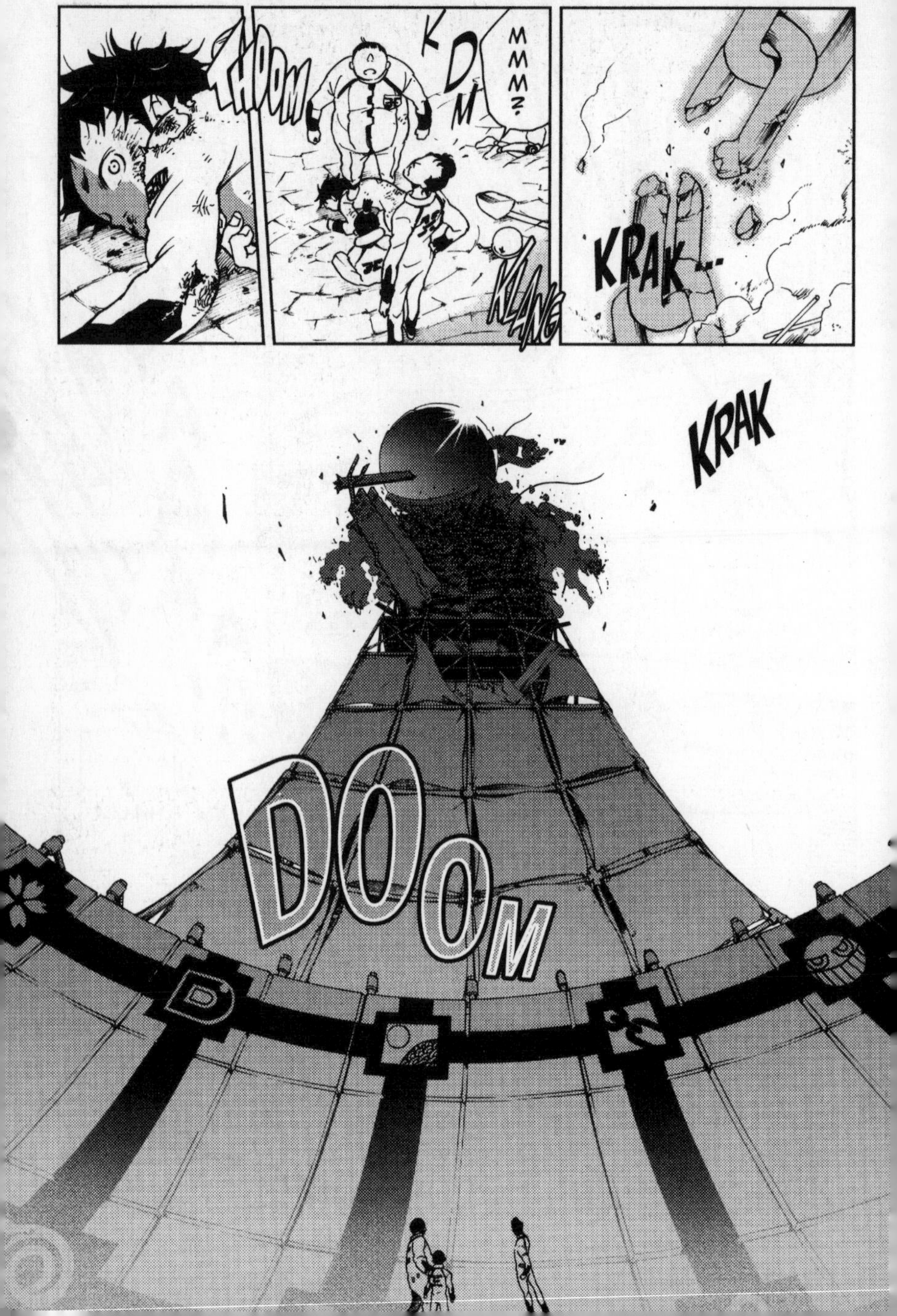
KRAK...
MMMM?
KDM
KLANG
THOOM
KRAK
DOOOM

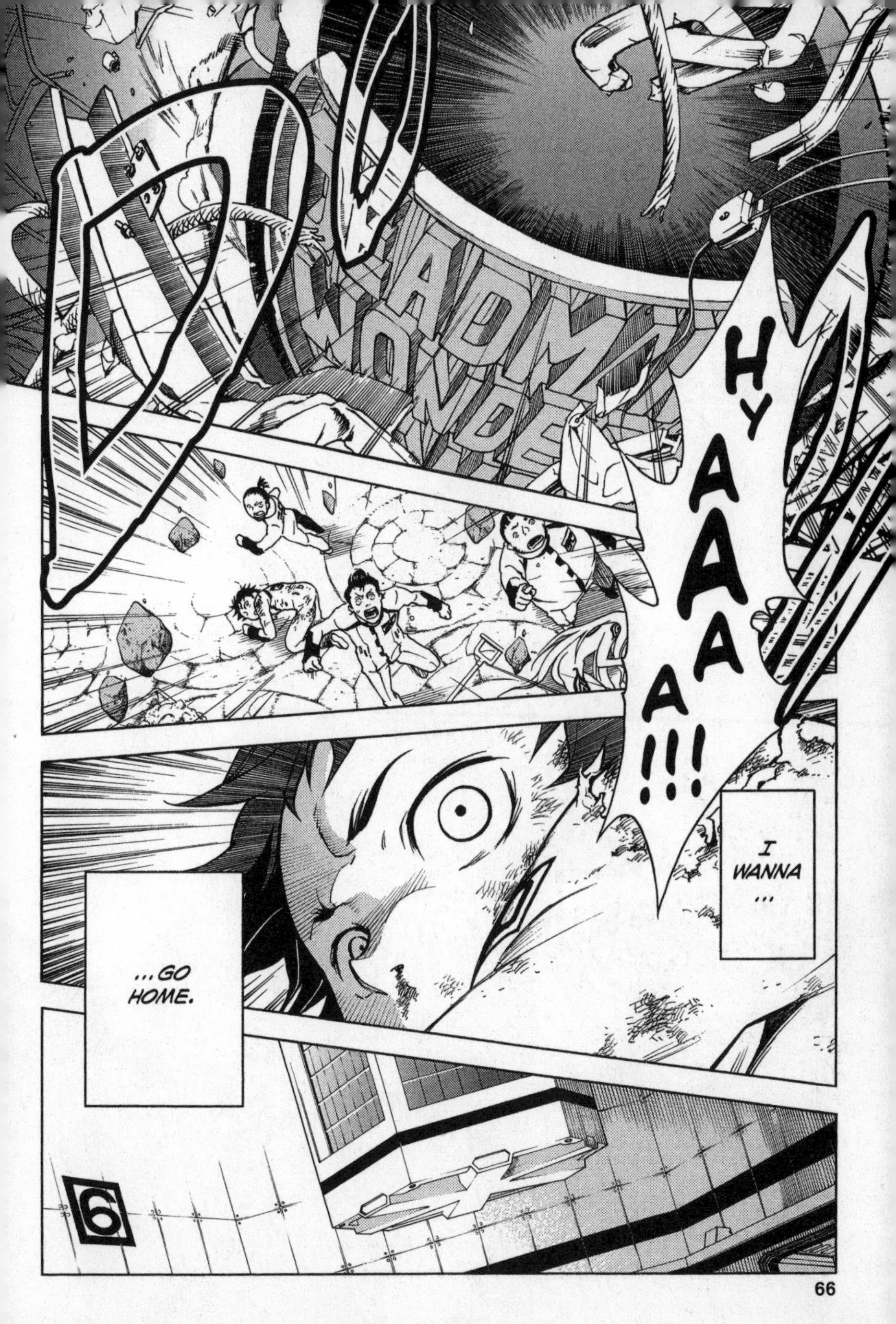
HYAAAAA!!!
I WANNA ...
...GO HOME.
6

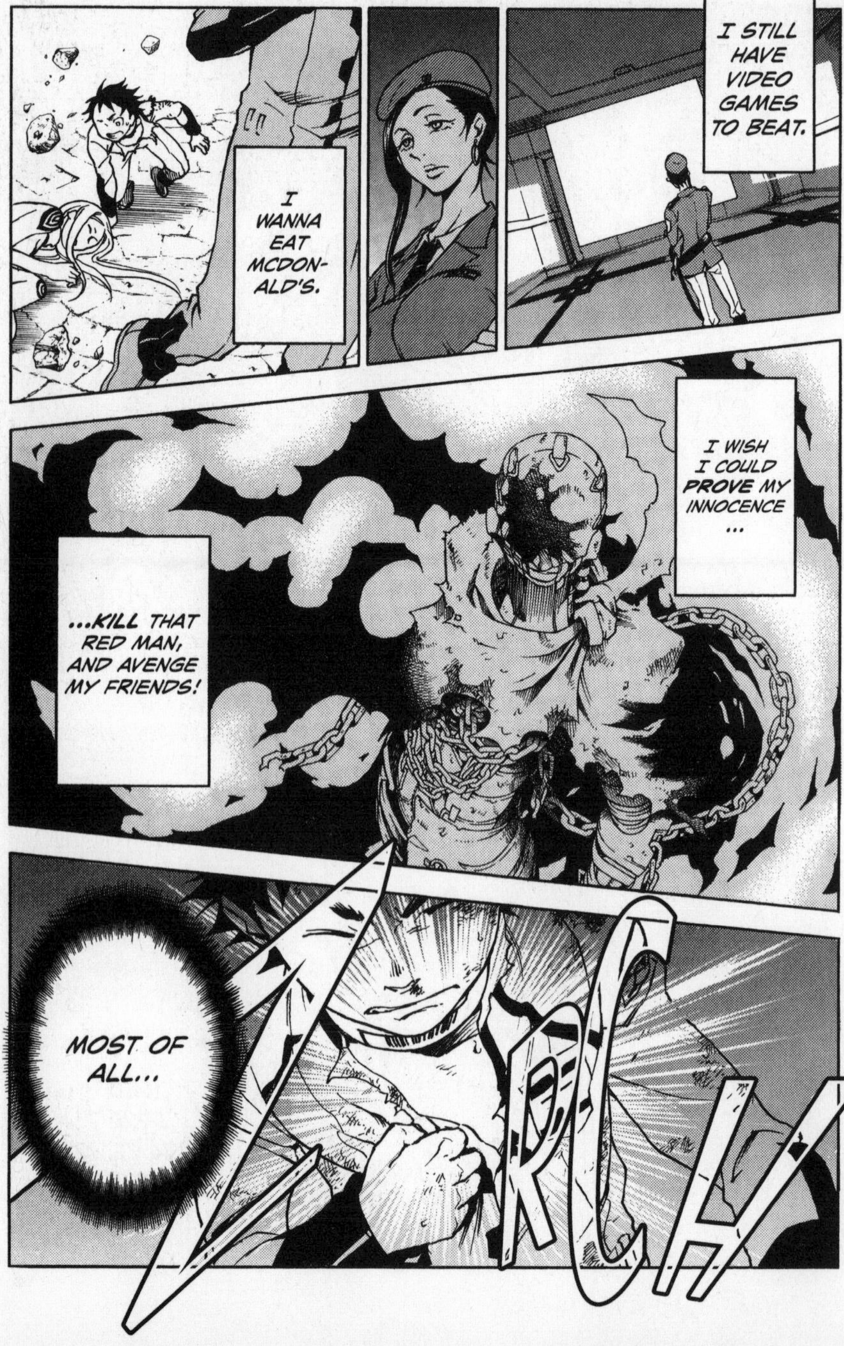
I STILL HAVE VIDEO GAMES TO BEAT.
I WANNA EAT MCDON-ALD'S.
I WISH I COULD PROVE MY INNOCENCE...
...KILL THAT RED MAN, AND AVENGE MY FRIENDS!
MOST OF ALL...
ZRCH

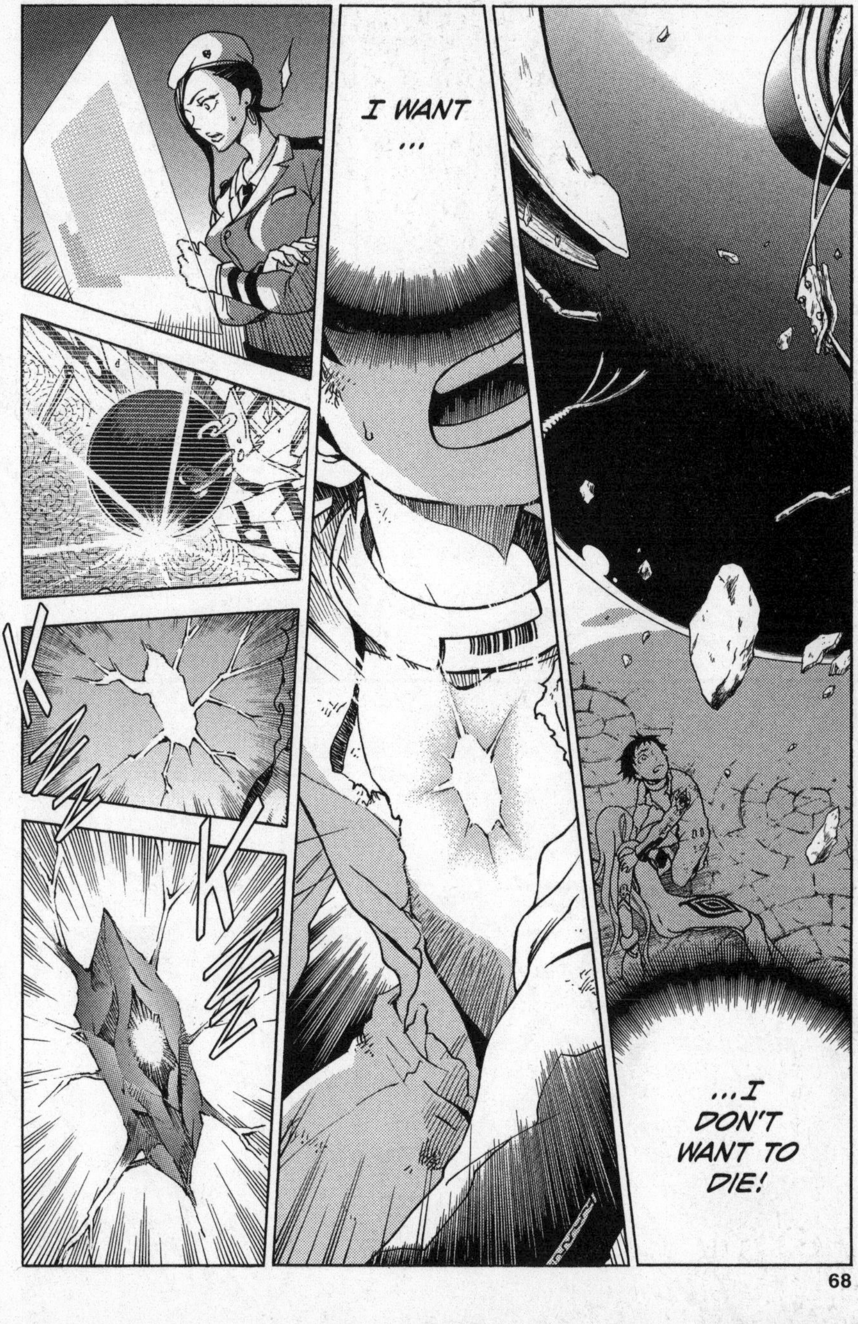
...I DON'T WANT TO DIE!
I WANT ...
KNN
KNNN

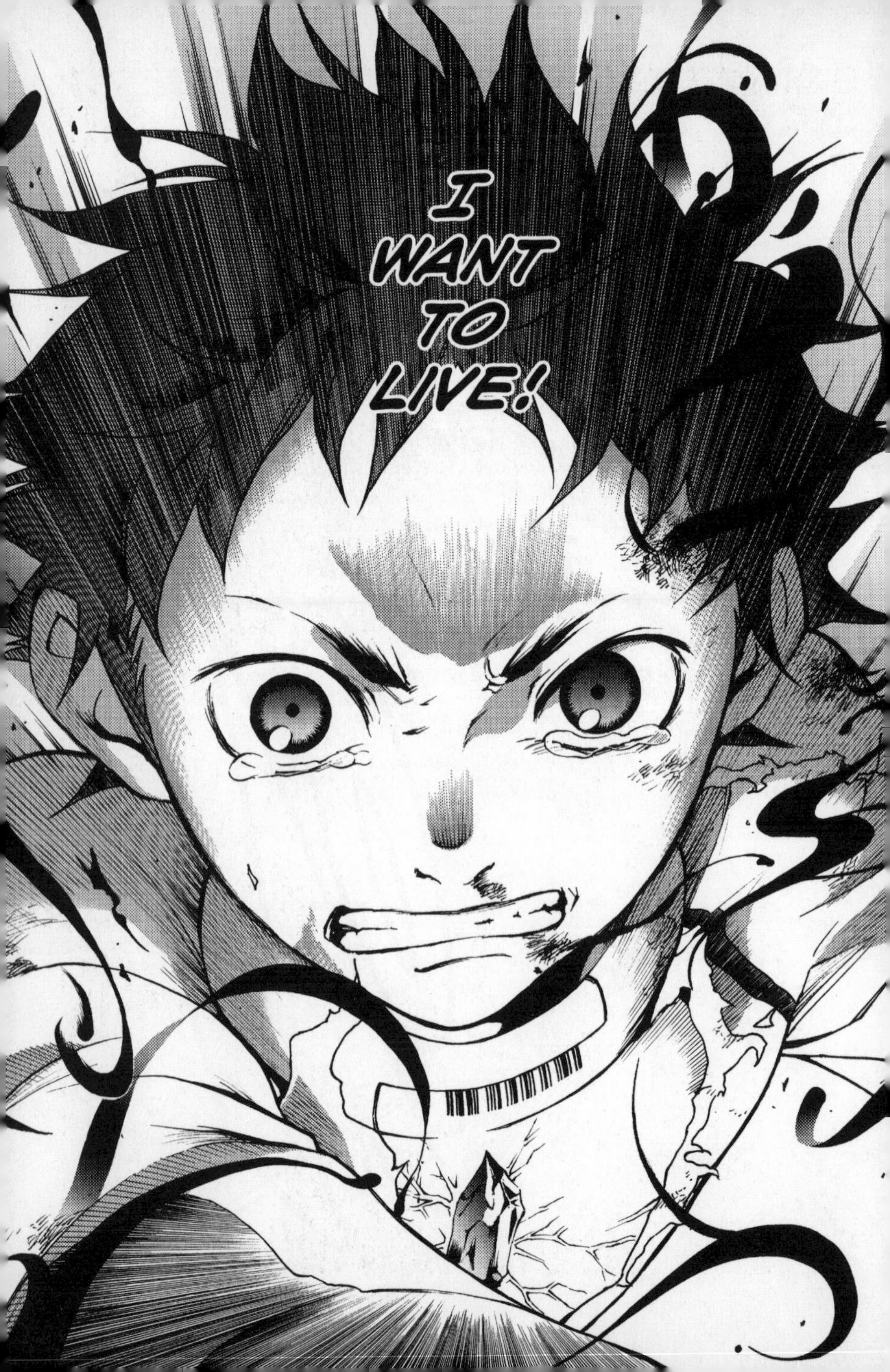
I WANT TO LIVE!

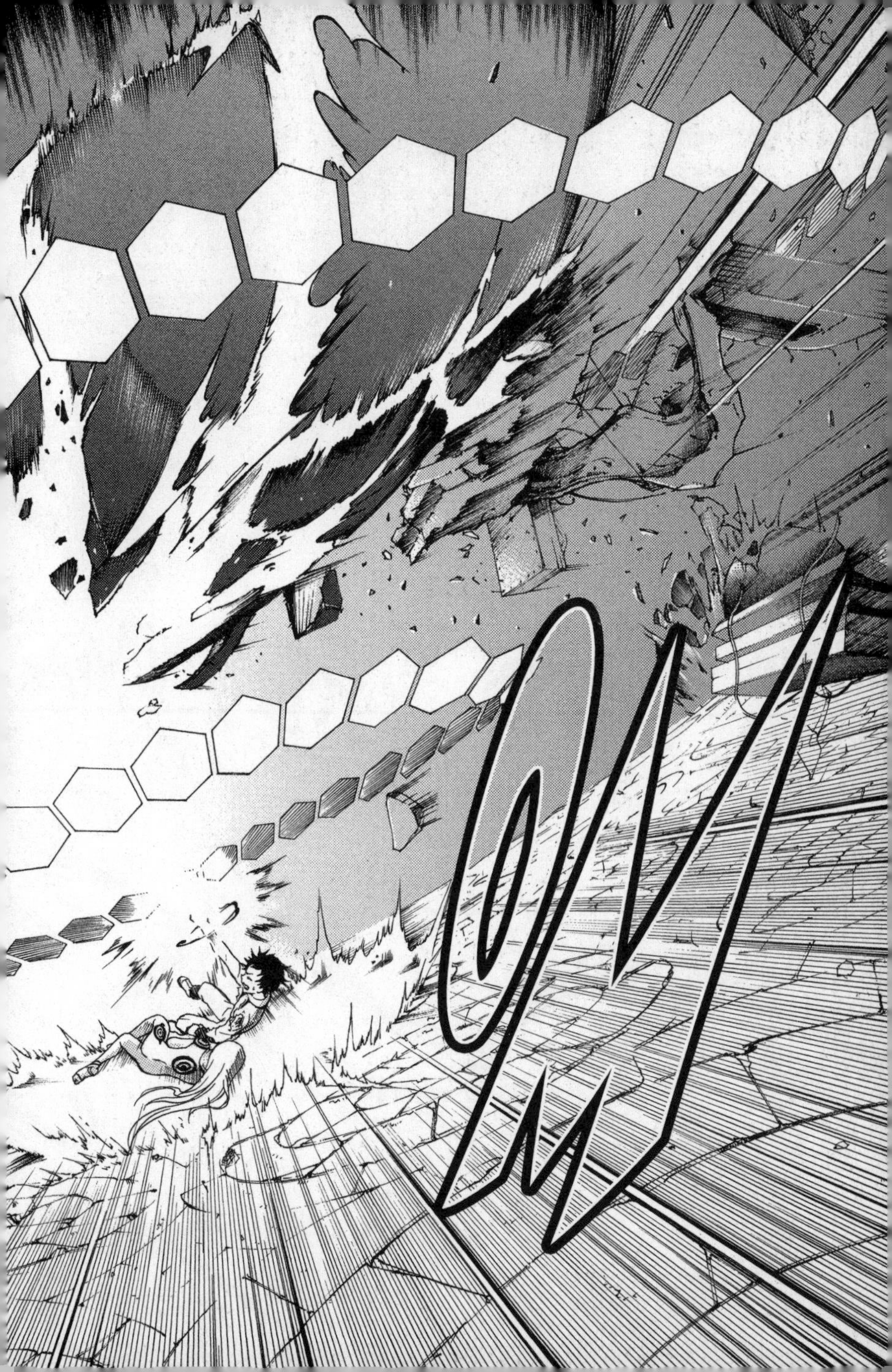

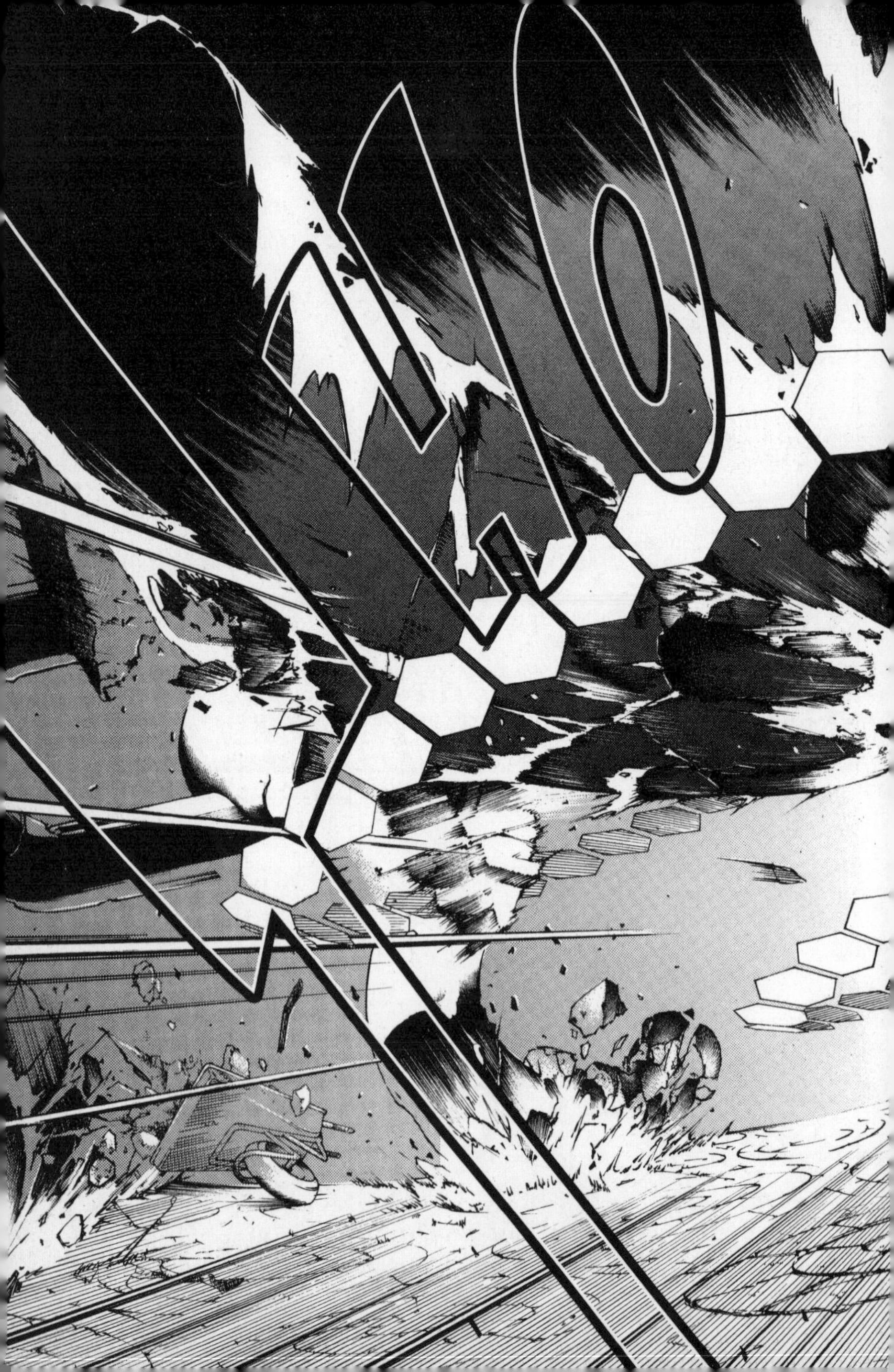

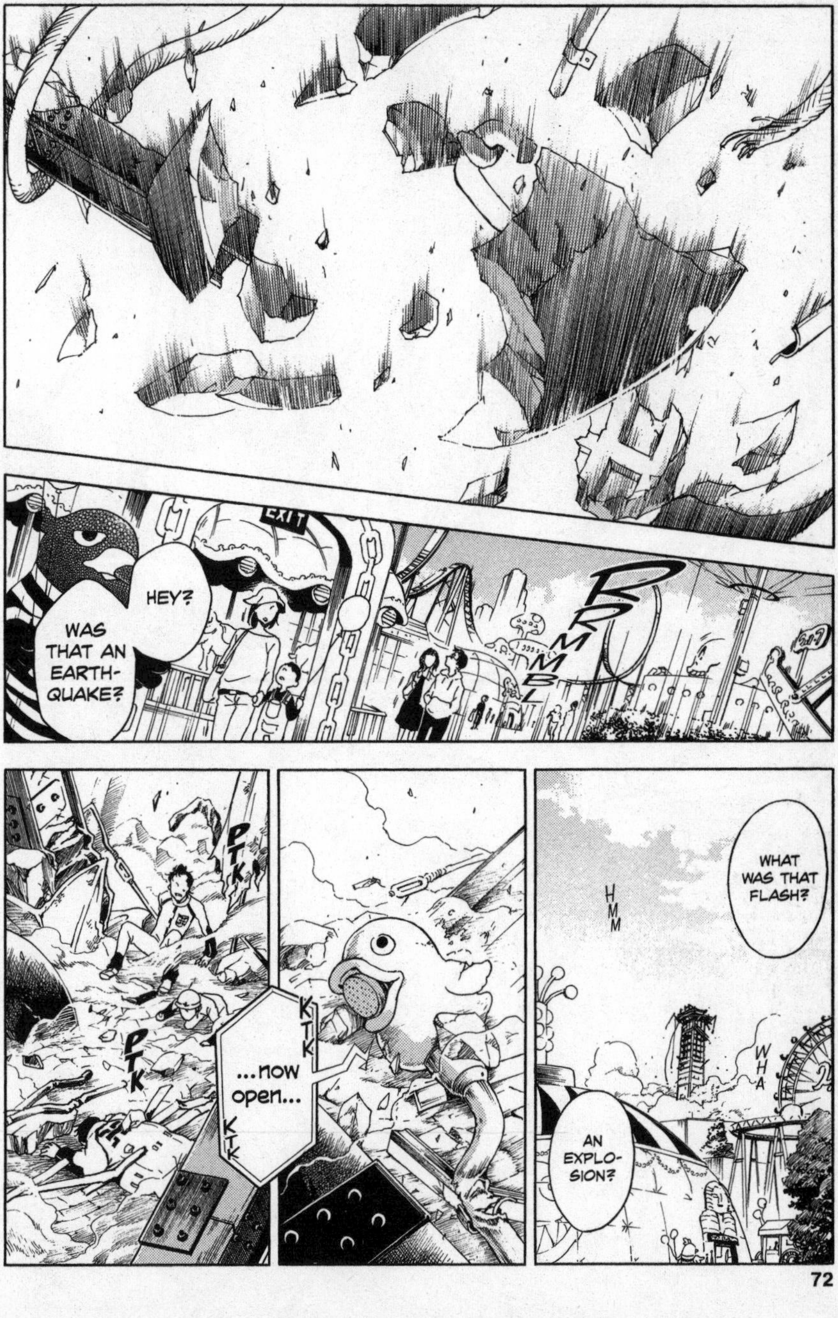
RRMMBL
HEY?
WAS THAT AN EARTH-QUAKE?
WHAT WAS THAT FLASH?
HMM
WHA
AN EXPLO-SION?
KTK
...now open...
KTK
PTK
PTK

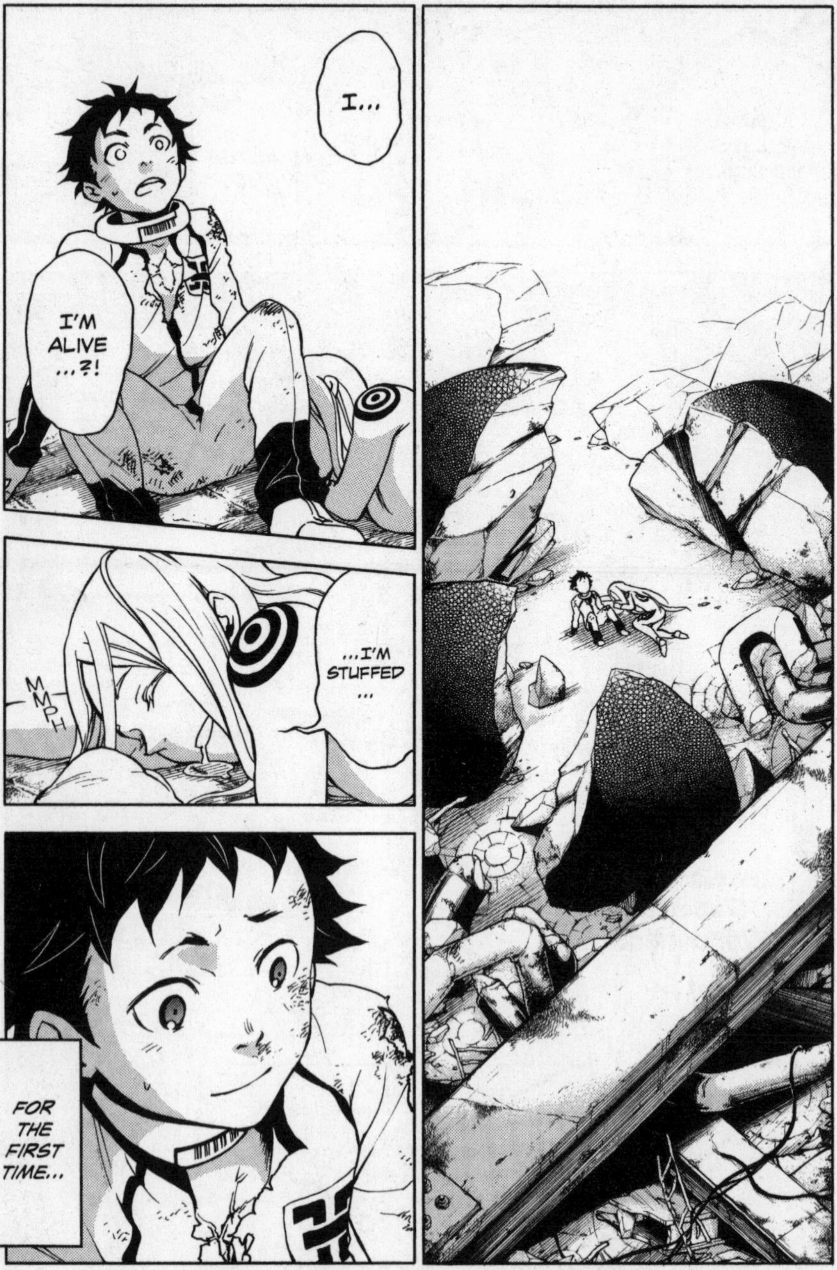
I...
I'M ALIVE ...?!
...I'M STUFFED ...
MMPH
FOR THE FIRST TIME...

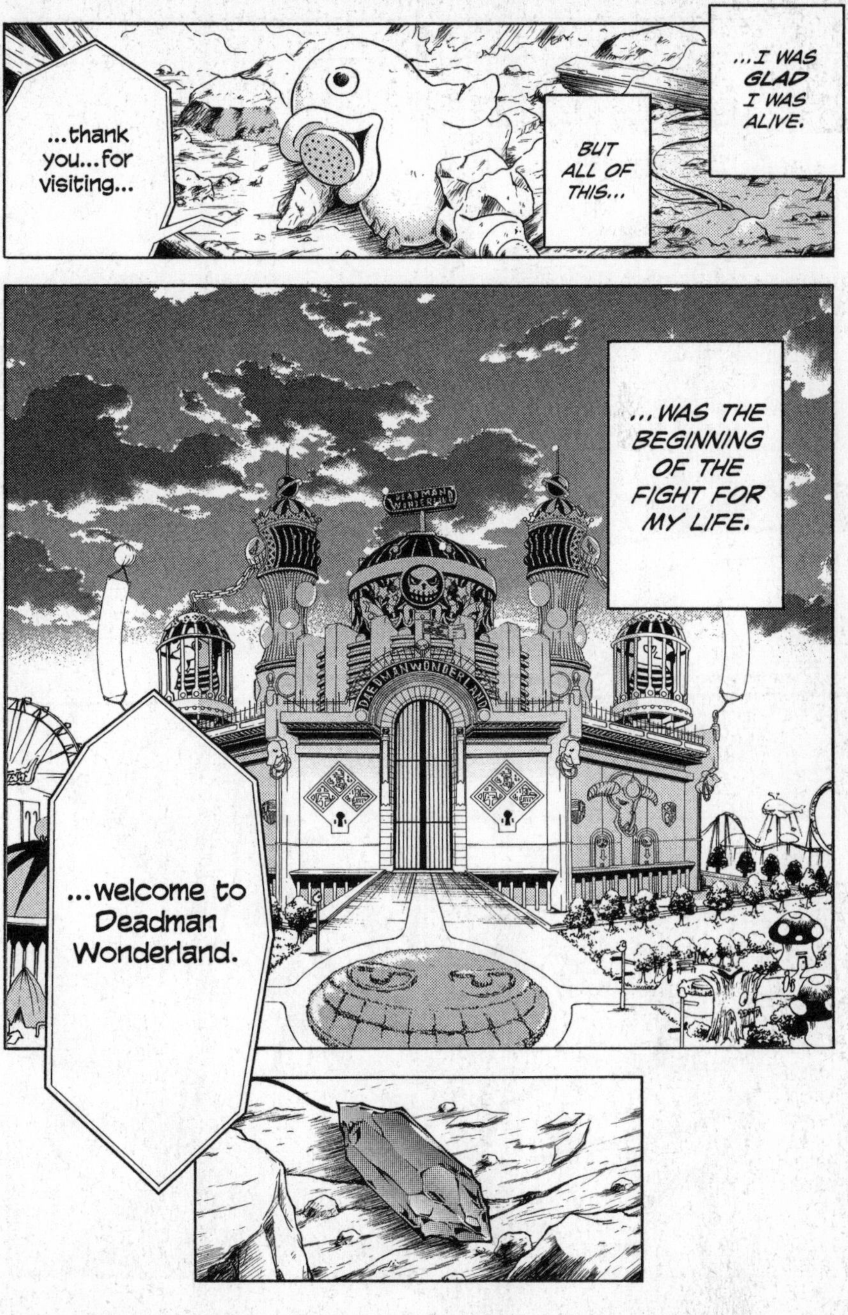
...I WAS GLAD I WAS ALIVE.
BUT ALL OF THIS...
...thank you...for visiting...
...WAS THE BEGINNING OF THE FIGHT FOR MY LIFE.
...welcome to Deadman Wonderland.

# DEADMAN WONDERLAND

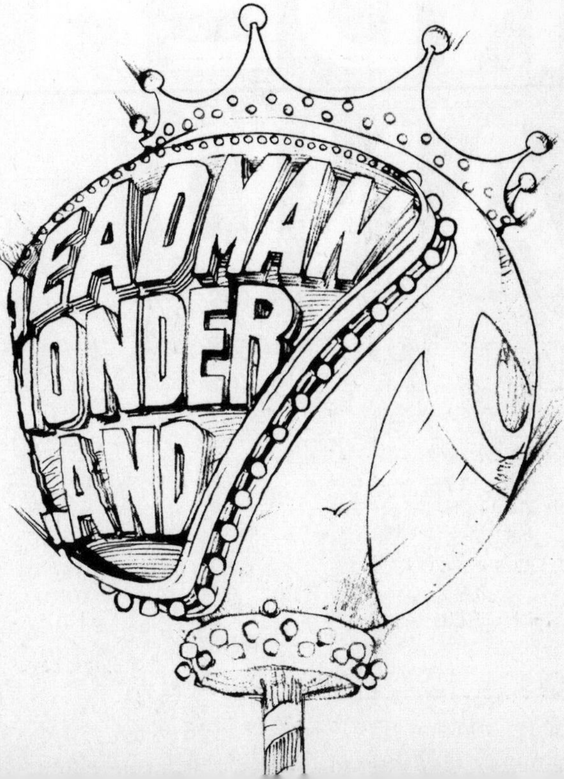
EADMAN
ONDER
AND

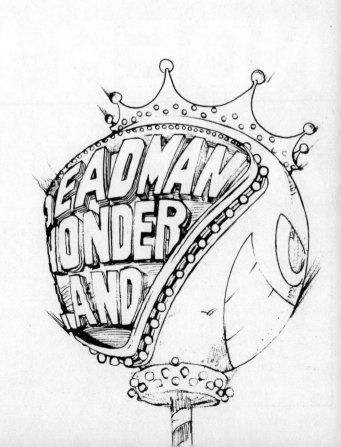

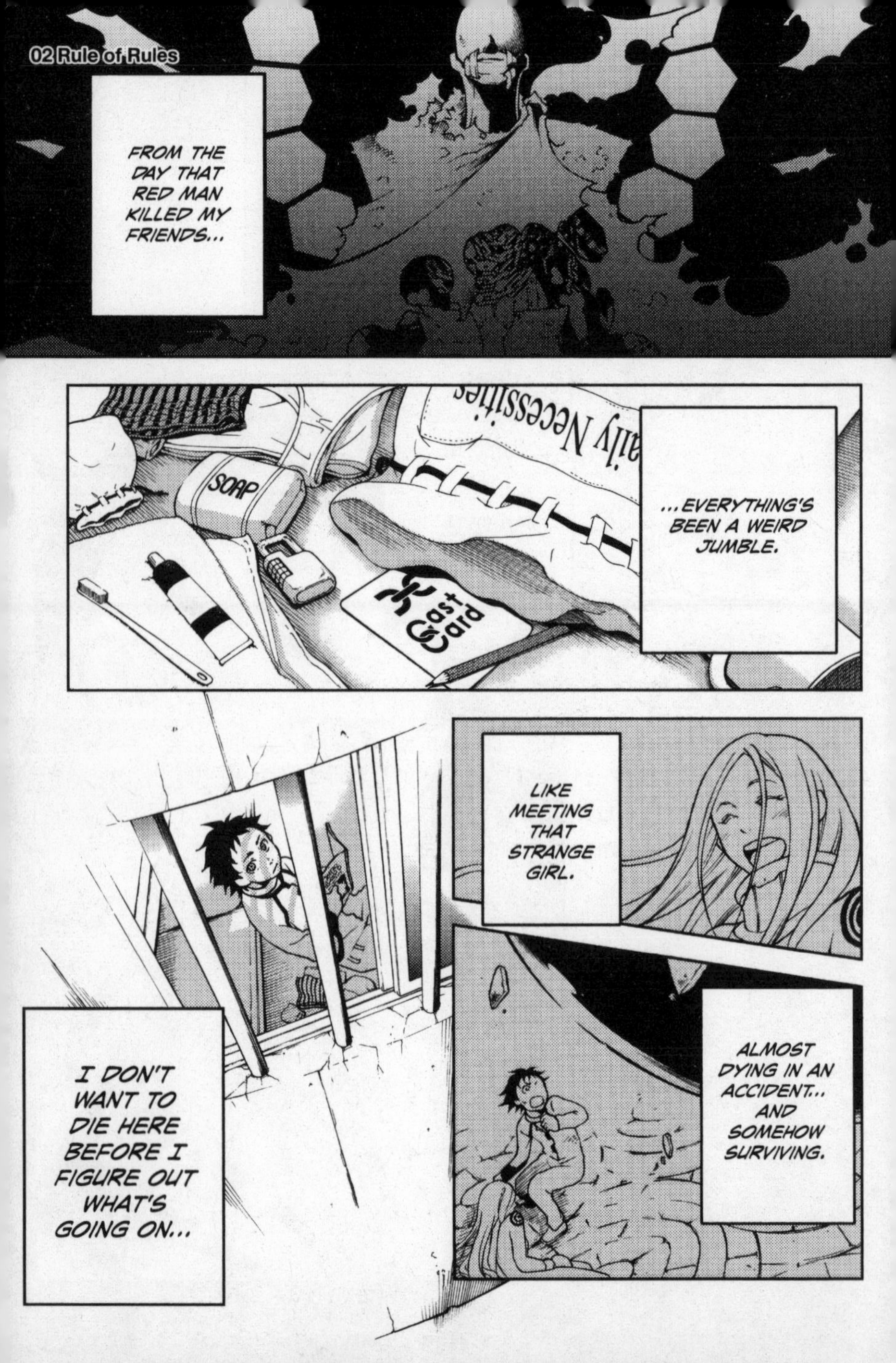
FROM THE DAY THAT RED MAN KILLED MY FRIENDS...
...EVERYTHING'S BEEN A WEIRD JUMBLE.
SOAP
Cast Card
LIKE MEETING THAT STRANGE GIRL.
ALMOST DYING IN AN ACCIDENT... AND SOMEHOW SURVIVING.
I DON'T WANT TO DIE HERE BEFORE I FIGURE OUT WHAT'S GOING ON...

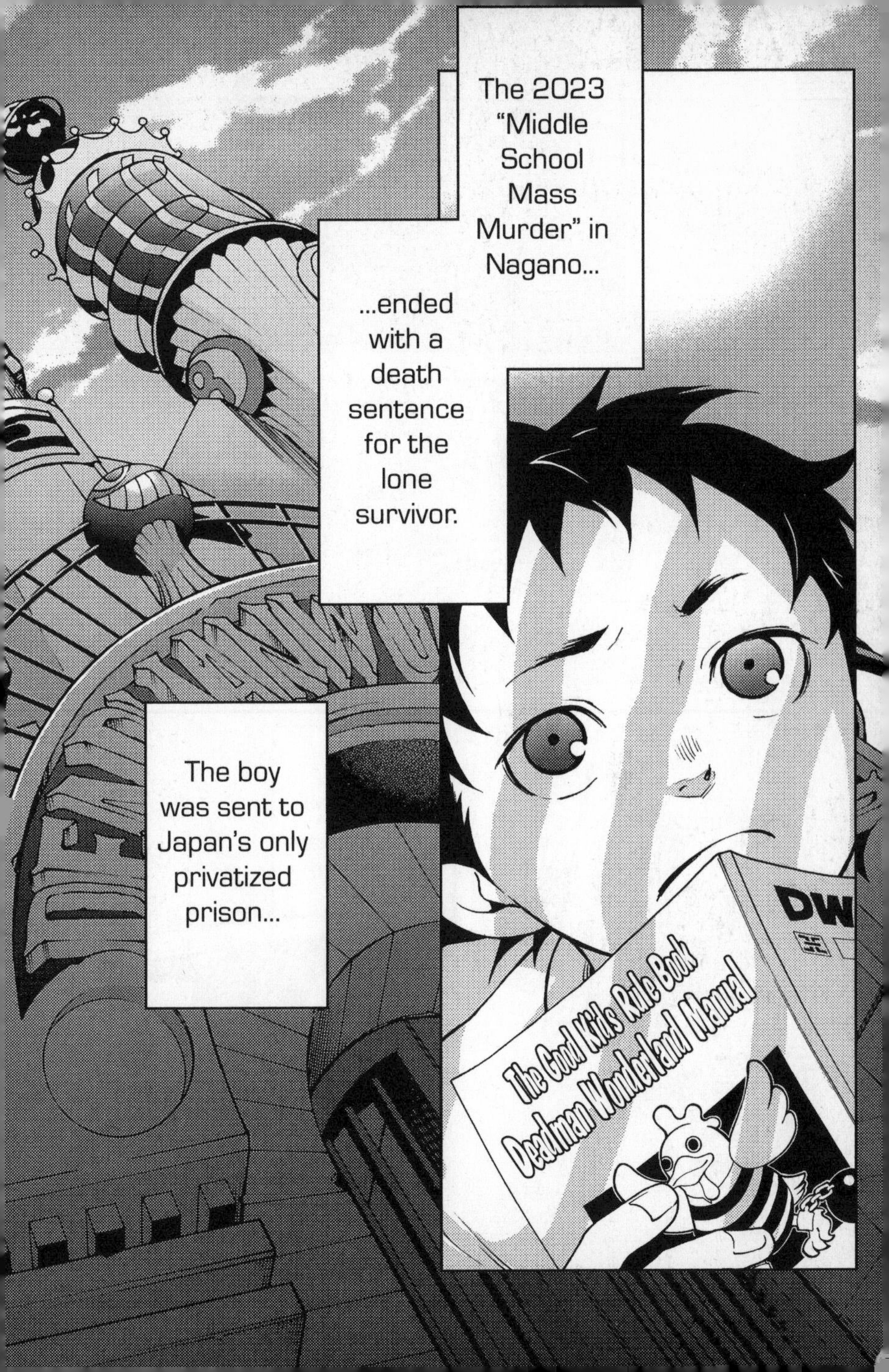
The 2023 "Middle School Mass Murder" in Nagano...
...ended with a death sentence for the lone survivor.
DW
The Good Kids Rule Book
Deadman Wonderland Manual
The boy was sent to Japan's only privatized prison...

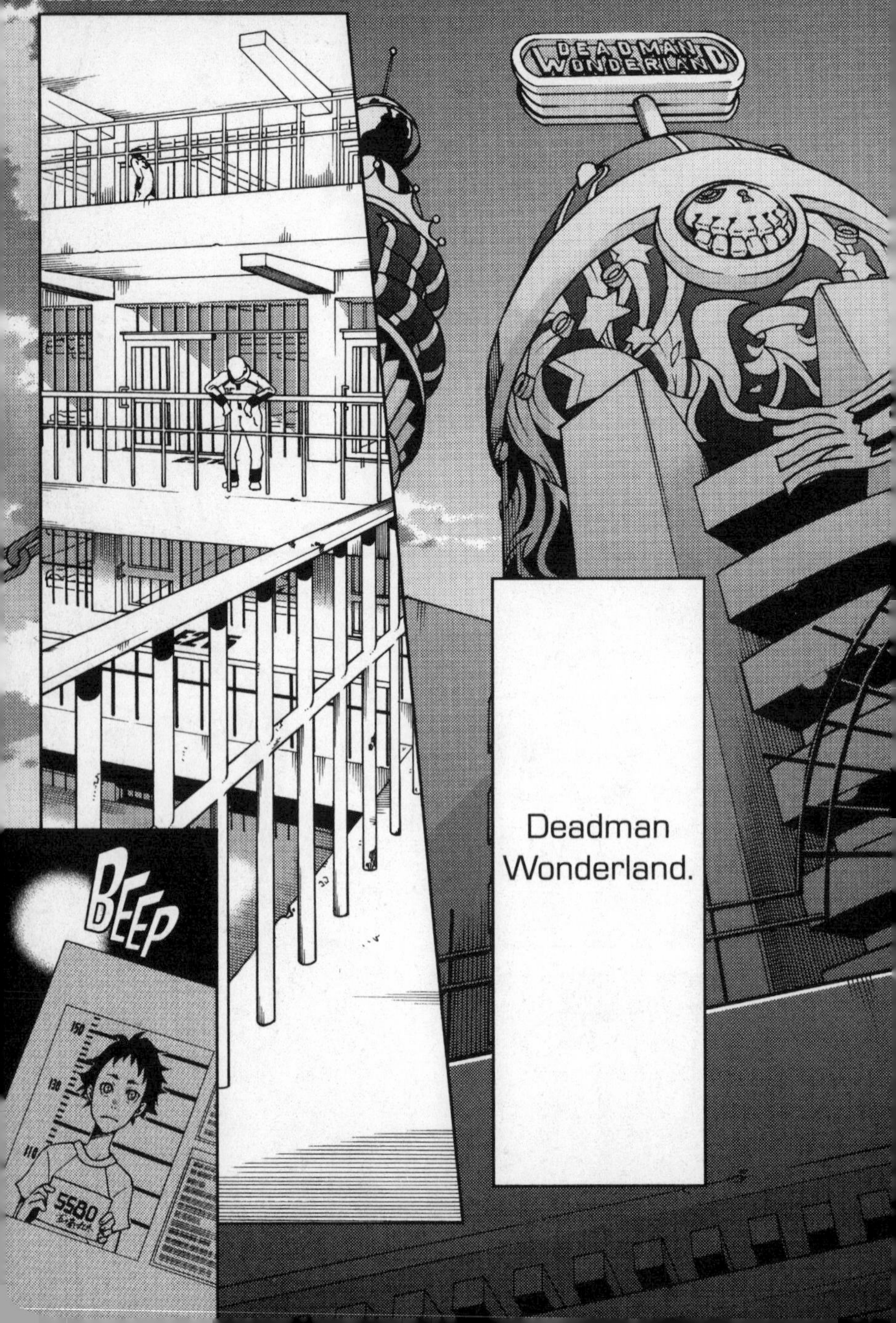
DEADMAN WONDERLAND
Deadman Wonderland.
BEEP
150
130
110
5580

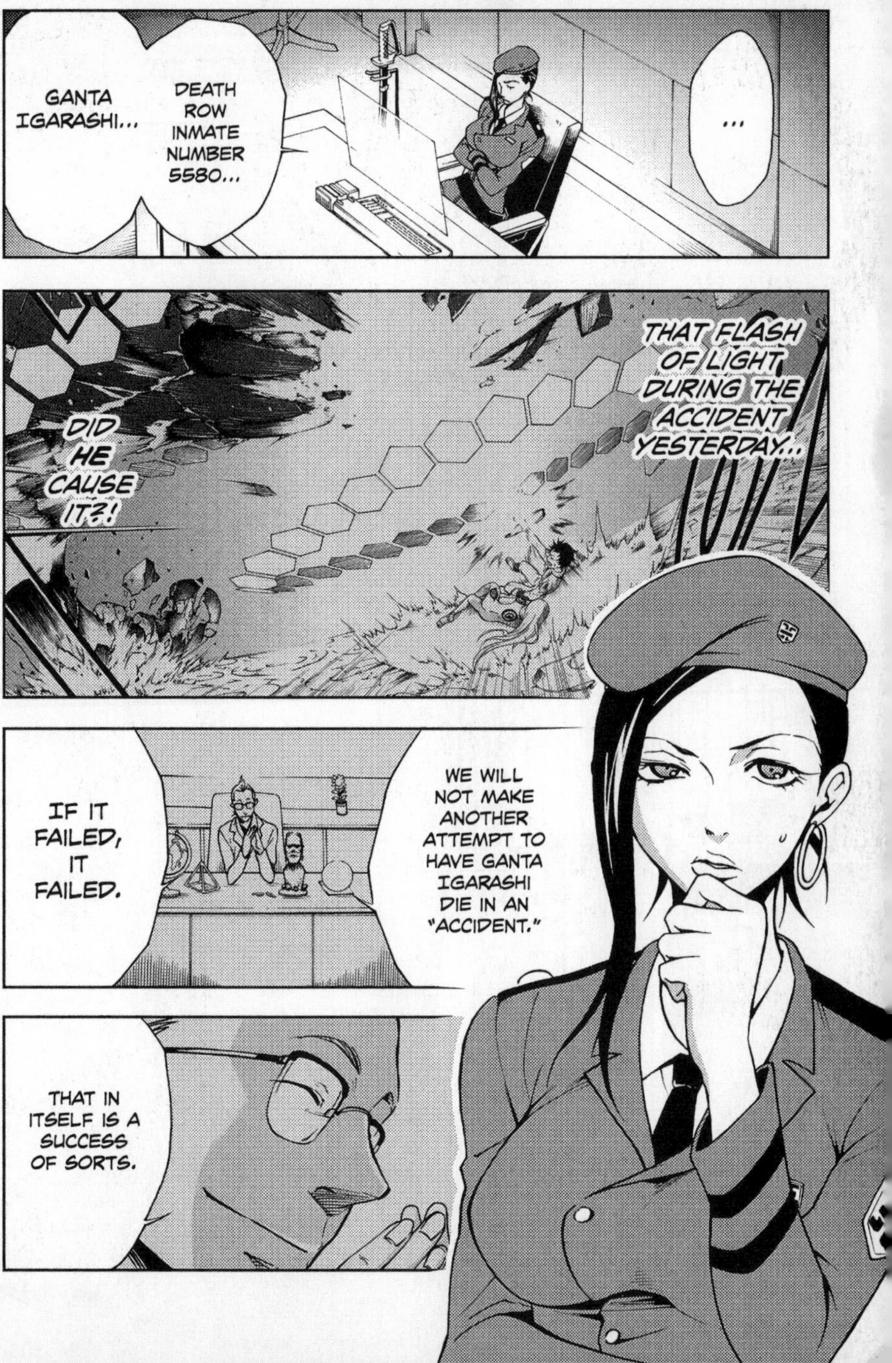
...
DEATH ROW INMATE NUMBER 5580...
GANTA IGARASHI...
THAT FLASH OF LIGHT DURING THE ACCIDENT YESTERDAY...
DID HE CAUSE IT?!
WE WILL NOT MAKE ANOTHER ATTEMPT TO HAVE GANTA IGARASHI DIE IN AN "ACCIDENT."
IF IT FAILED, IT FAILED.
THAT IN ITSELF IS A SUCCESS OF SORTS.

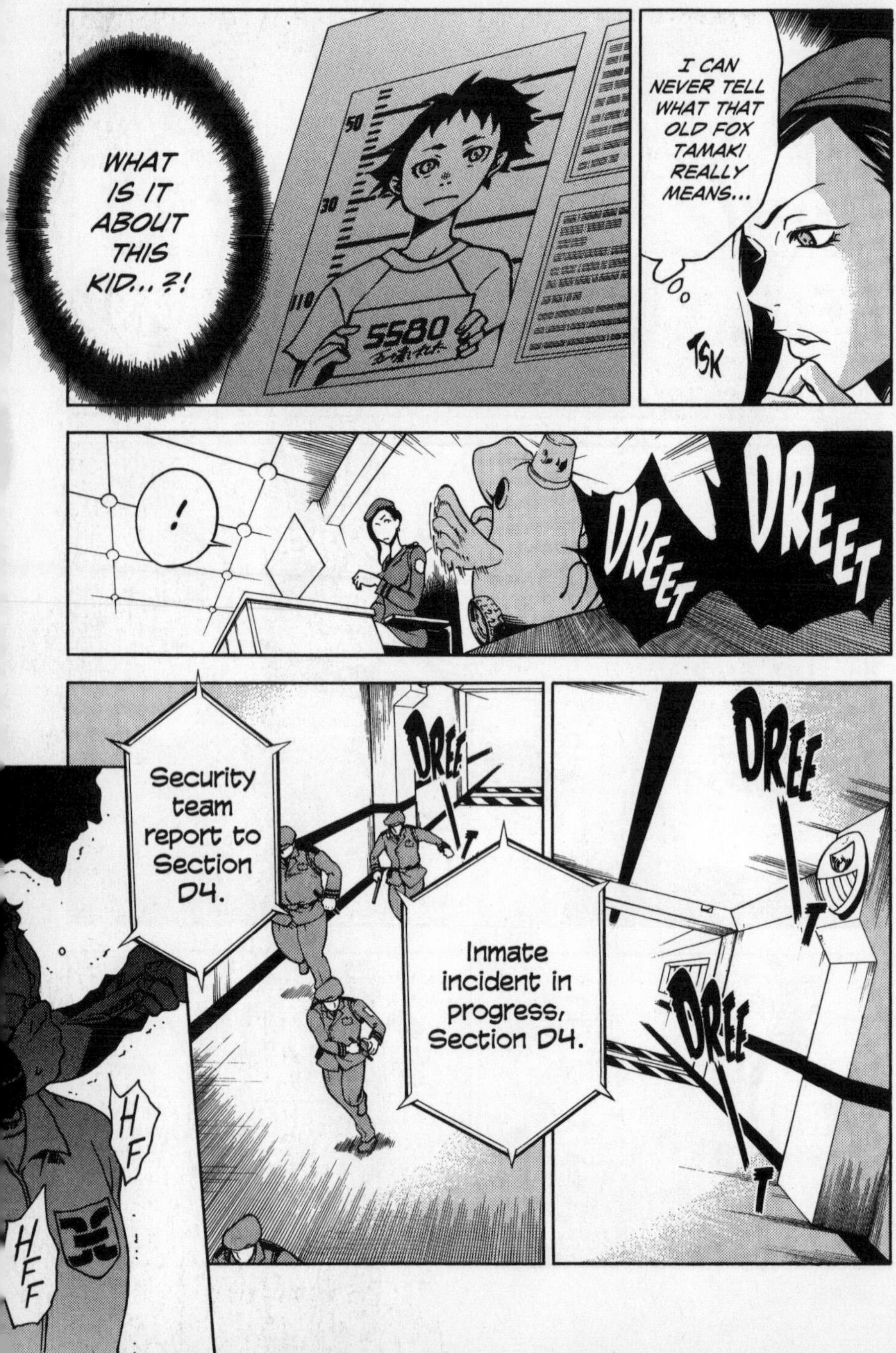

I CAN NEVER TELL WHAT THAT OLD FOX TAMAKI REALLY MEANS...
TSK
WHAT IS IT ABOUT THIS KID...?!
5580
DREET DREET
DREET
!
DREET
DREET
DREET
Security team report to Section D4.
Inmate incident in progress, Section D4.
HF
HFF

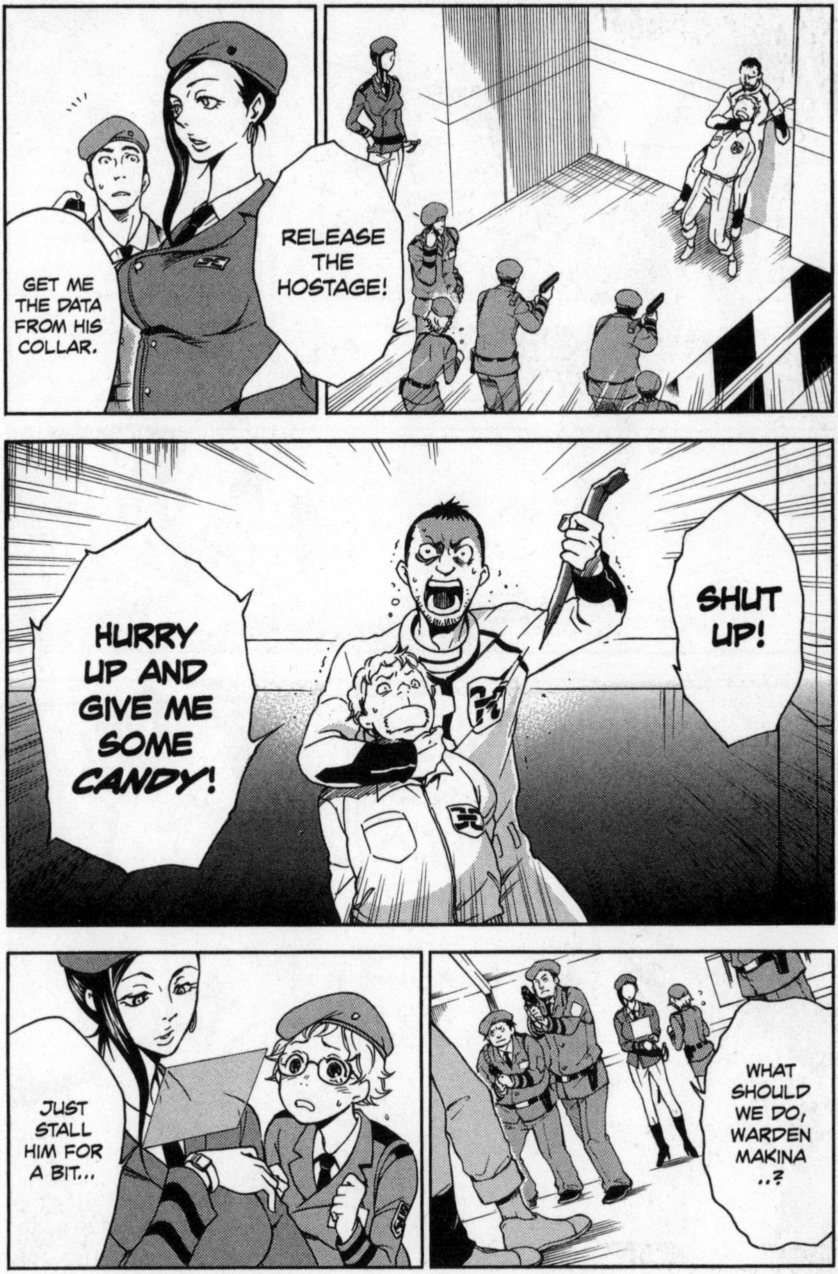
RELEASE THE HOSTAGE!
GET ME THE DATA FROM HIS COLLAR.
SHUT UP!
HURRY UP AND GIVE ME SOME CANDY!
WHAT SHOULD WE DO, WARDEN MAKINA ..?
JUST STALL HIM FOR A BIT...

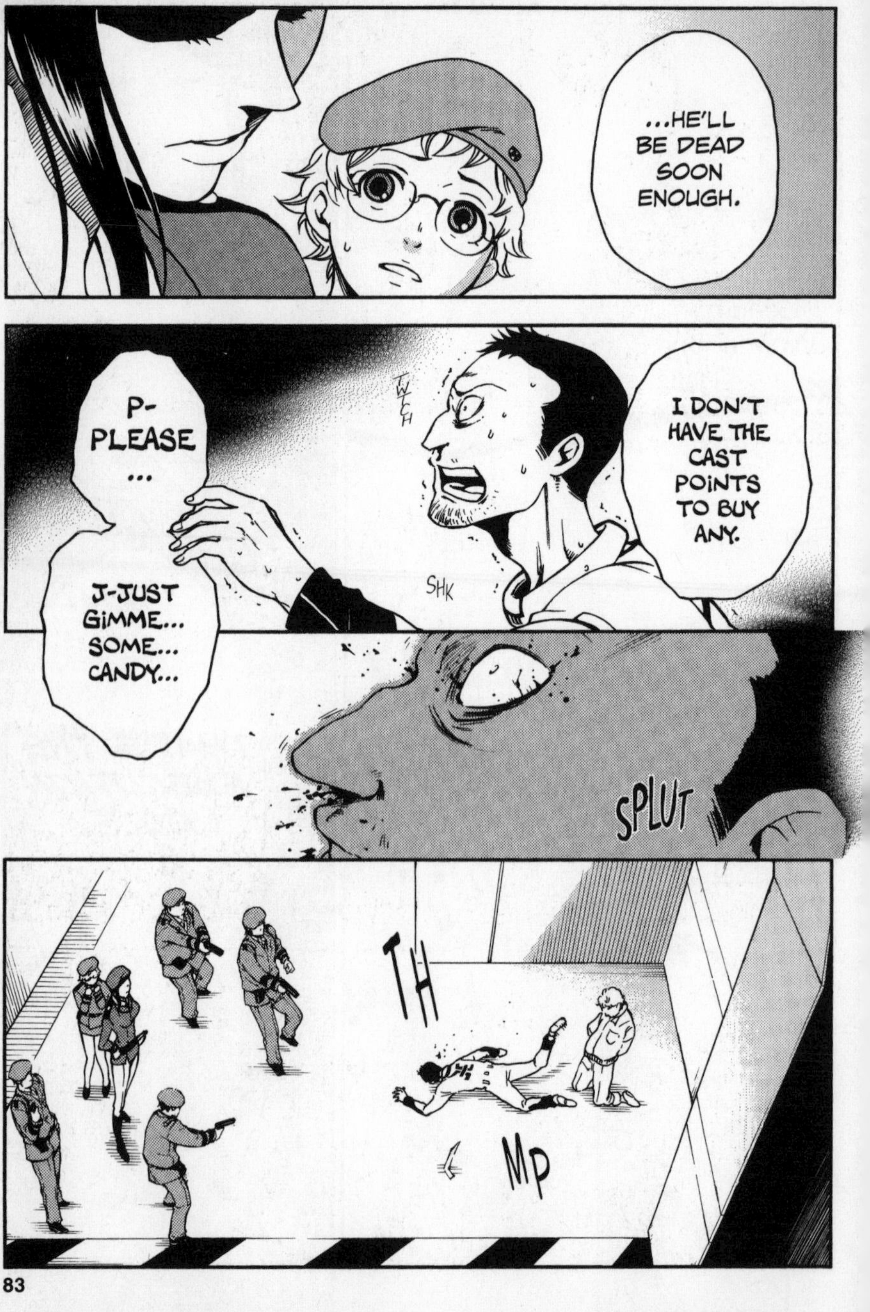
...HE'LL BE DEAD SOON ENOUGH.
I DON'T HAVE THE CAST POINTS TO BUY ANY.
P-PLEASE...
SHK
J-JUST GIMME... SOME... CANDY...
SPLUT
TH
Mp

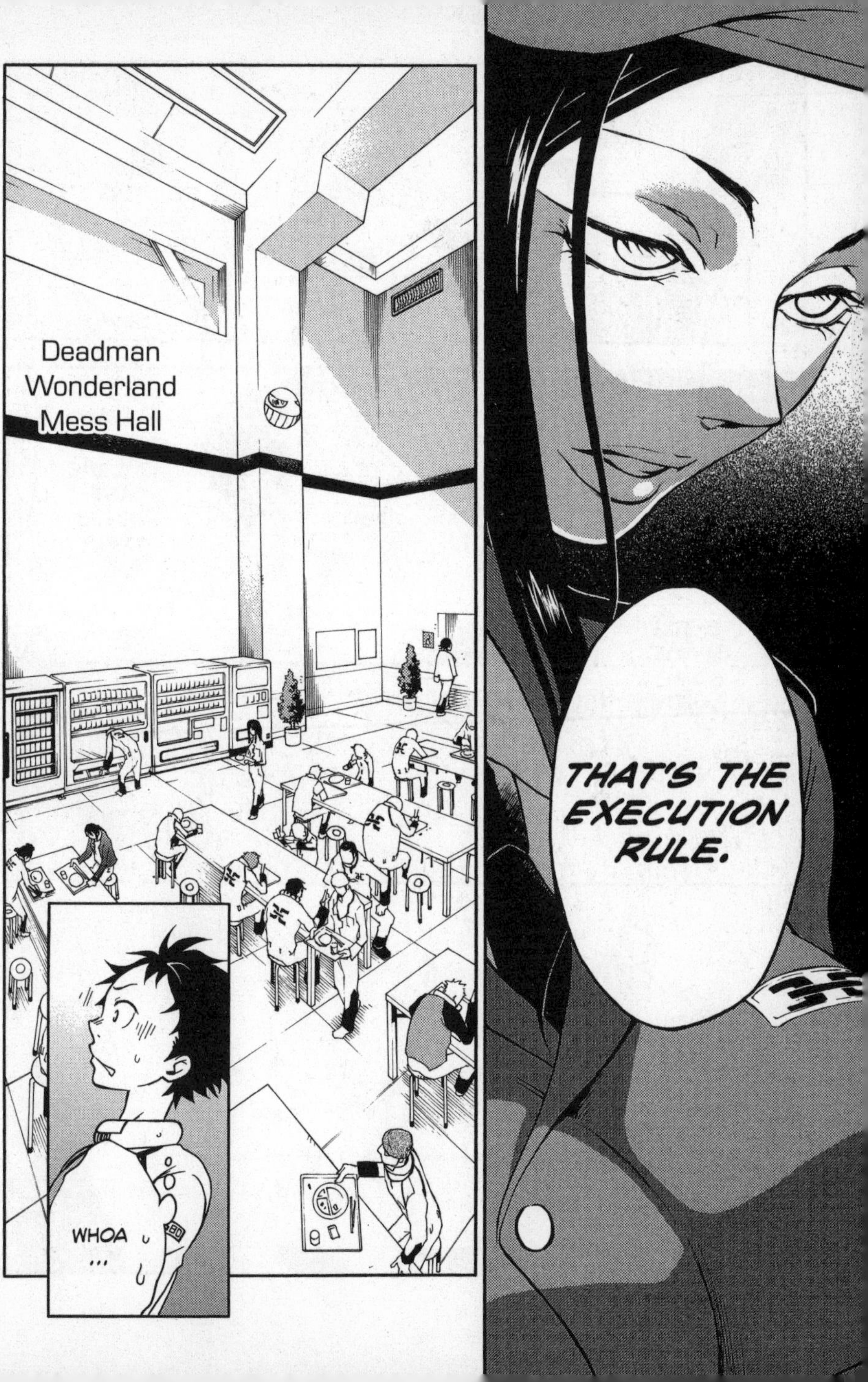
THAT'S THE EXECUTION RULE.
Deadman Wonderland Mess Hall
WHOA ...

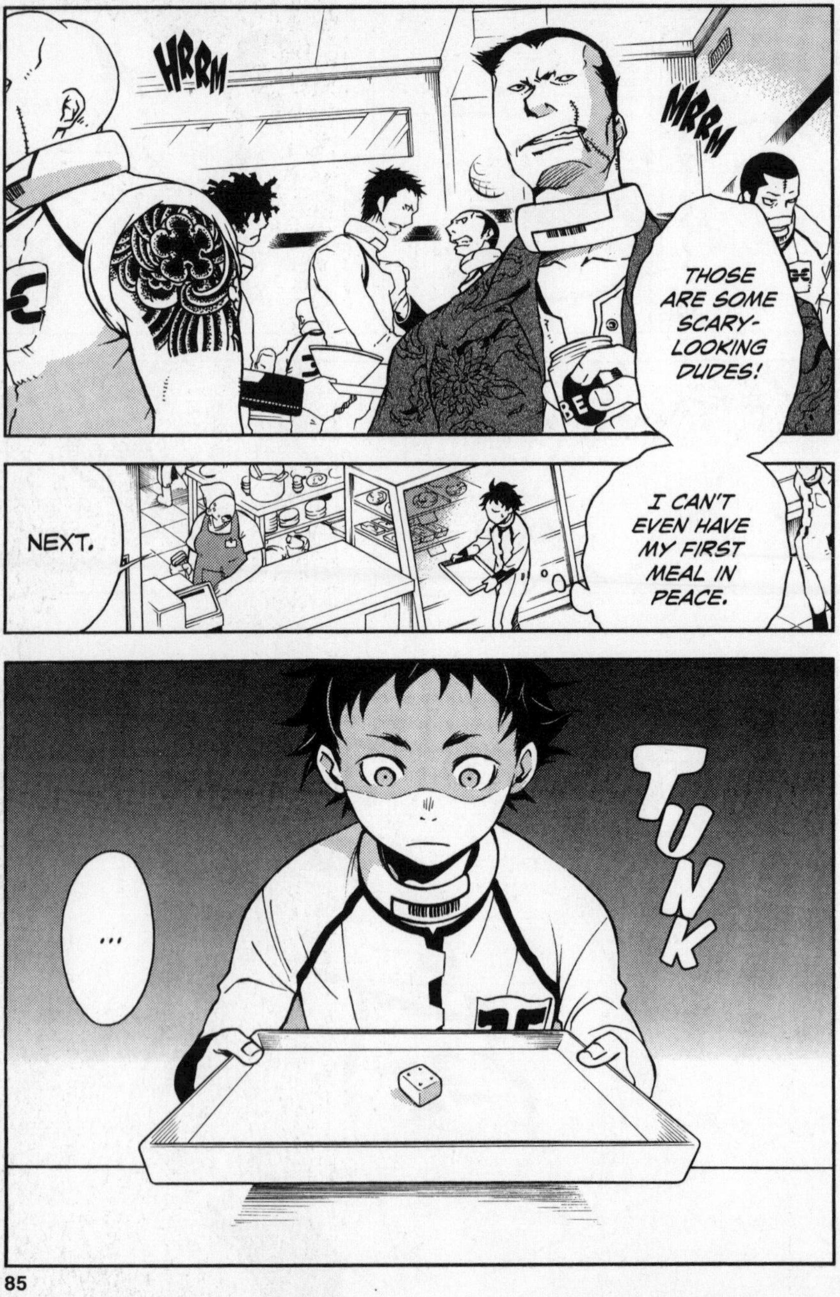
MRRM
HRRM
THOSE ARE SOME SCARY-LOOKING DUDES!
I CAN'T EVEN HAVE MY FIRST MEAL IN PEACE.
NEXT.
TUNK
...

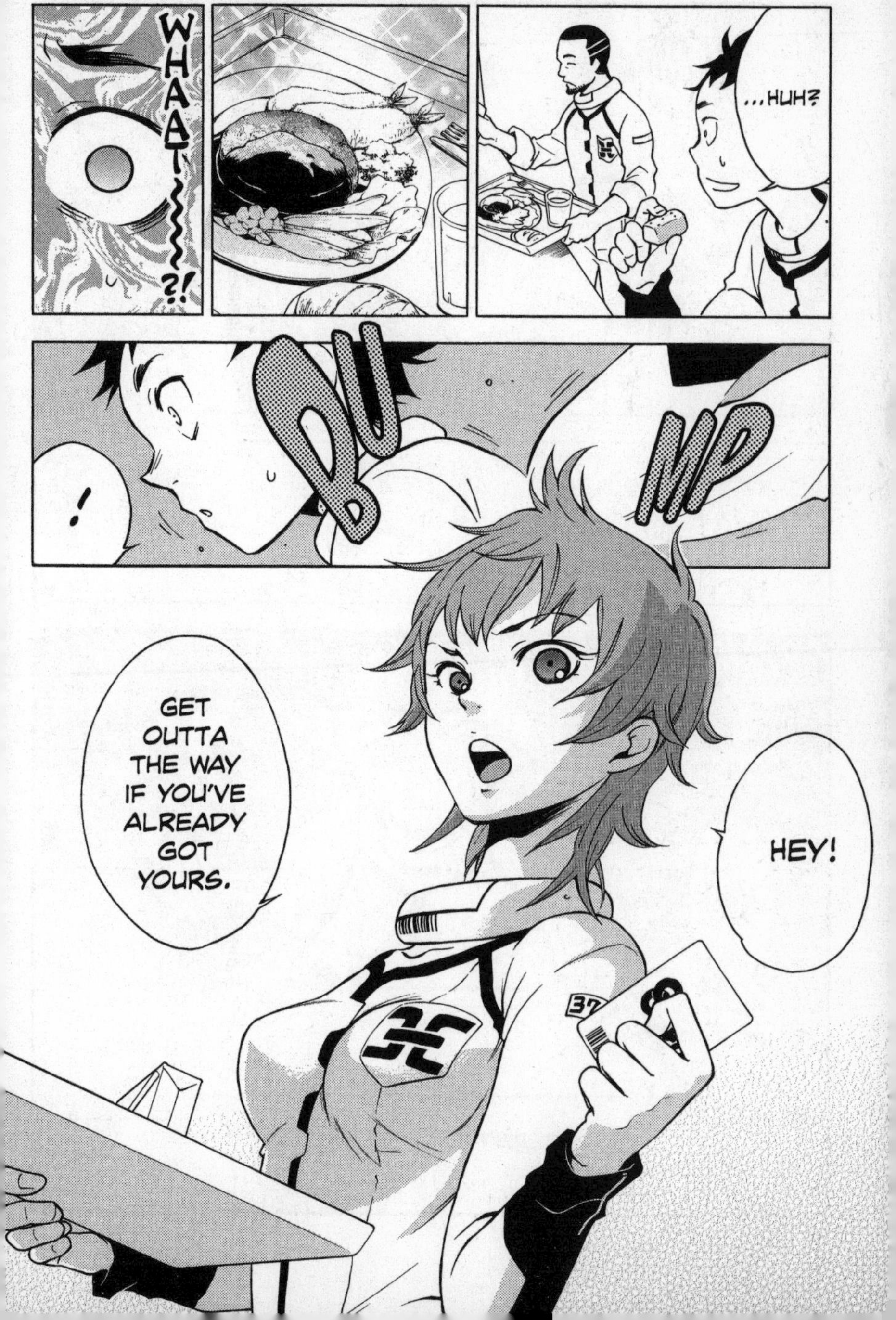
...HUH?
WHAAT~~~?!
!
BUMP
HEY!
GET OUTTA THE WAY IF YOU'VE ALREADY GOT YOURS.

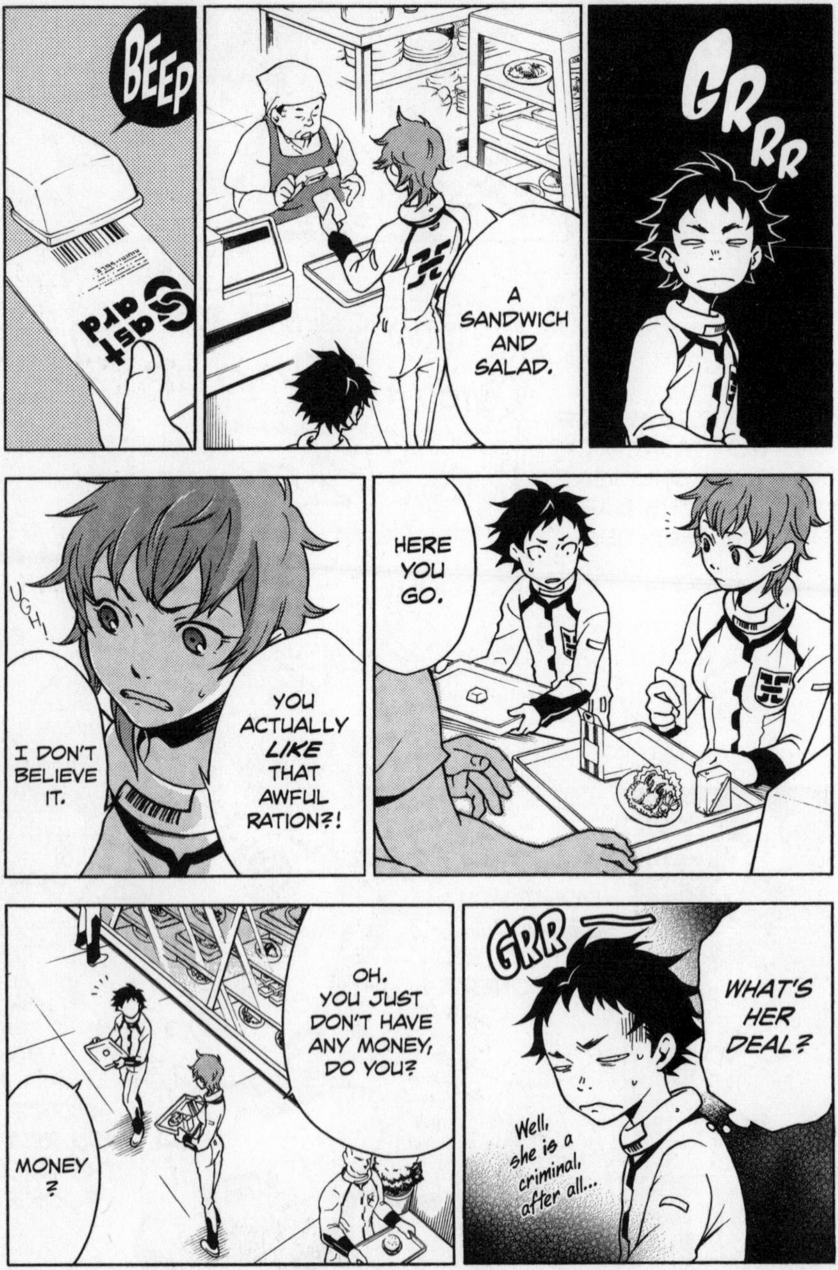
GRRRR
A SANDWICH AND SALAD.
BEEP
HERE YOU GO.
YOU ACTUALLY *LIKE* THAT AWFUL RATION?!
UGH!
I DON'T BELIEVE IT.
GRR—
WHAT'S HER DEAL?
Well, she is a criminal, after all...
OH. YOU JUST DON'T HAVE ANY MONEY, DO YOU?
MONEY?

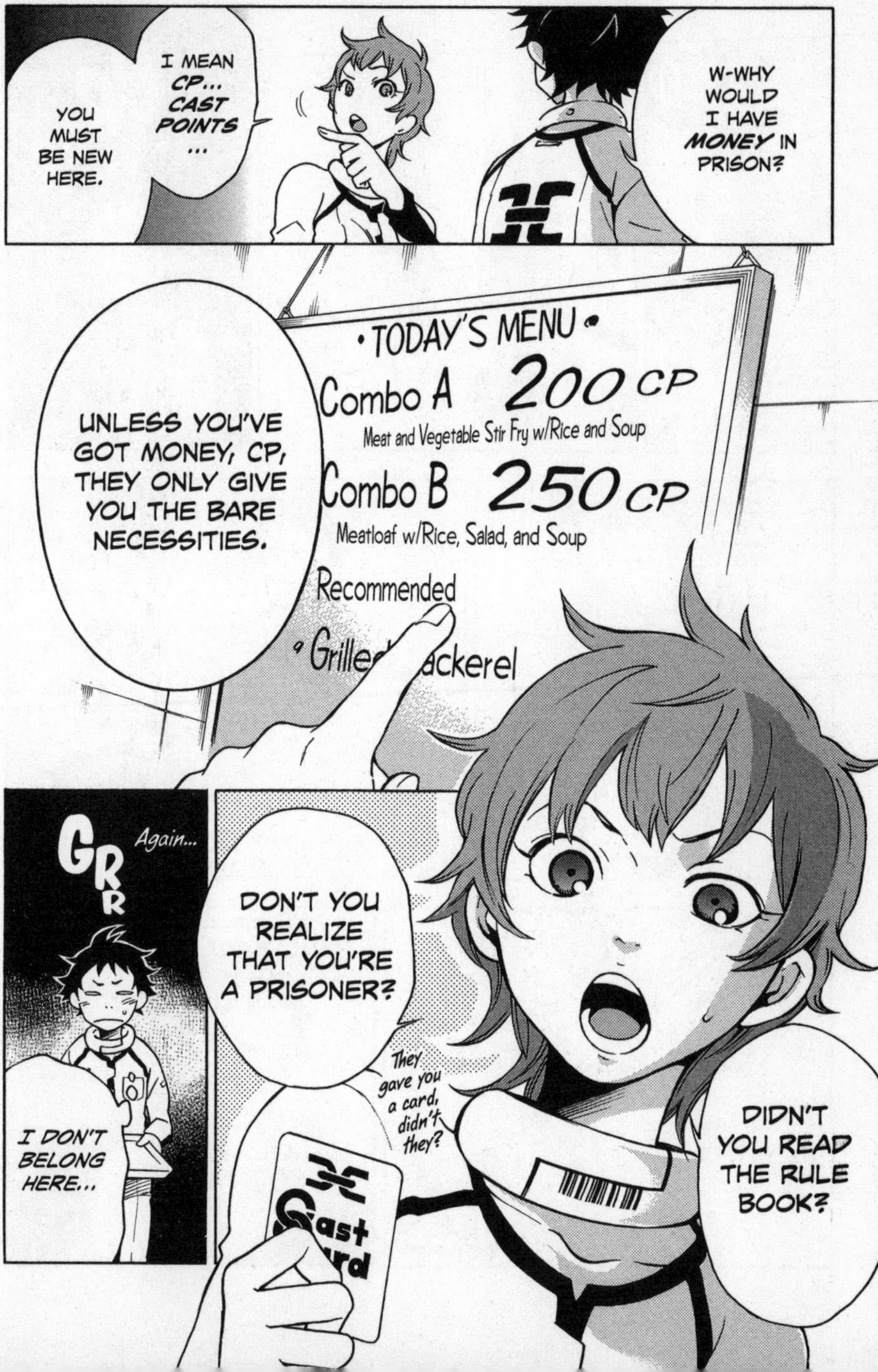
W-WHY WOULD I HAVE MONEY IN PRISON?
I MEAN CP... CAST POINTS...
YOU MUST BE NEW HERE.
•TODAY'S MENU•
Combo A 200 CP
Meat and Vegetable Stir Fry w/Rice and Soup
Combo B 250 CP
Meatloaf w/Rice, Salad, and Soup
Recommended
UNLESS YOU'VE GOT MONEY, CP, THEY ONLY GIVE YOU THE BARE NECESSITIES.
DIDN'T YOU READ THE RULE BOOK?
They gave you a card, didn't they?
DON'T YOU REALIZE THAT YOU'RE A PRISONER?
GRR
Again...
I DON'T BELONG HERE...

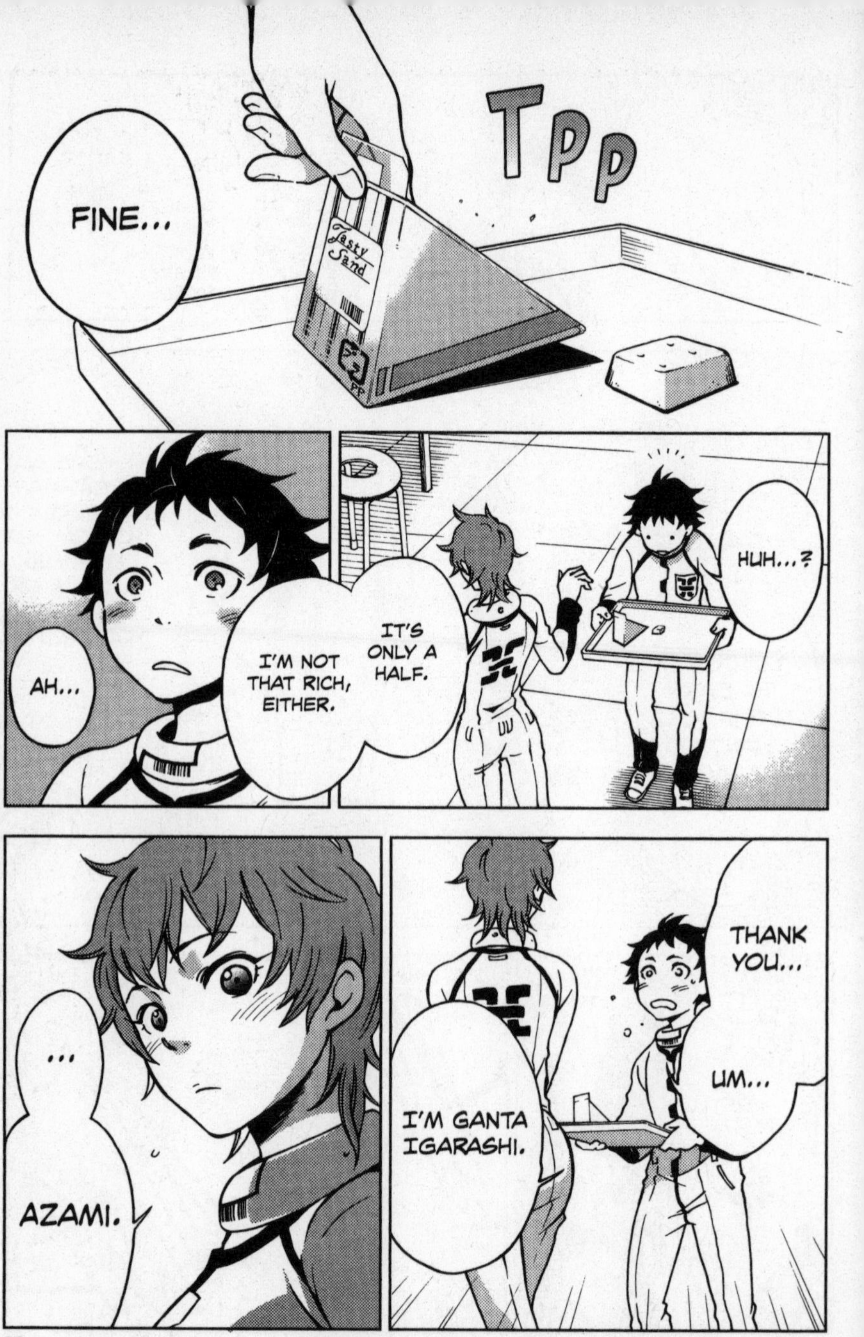
TPP
Tasty Sand
FINE...
HUH...?
IT'S ONLY A HALF.
I'M NOT THAT RICH, EITHER.
AH...
THANK YOU...
UM...
I'M GANTA IGARASHI.
...
AZAMI.

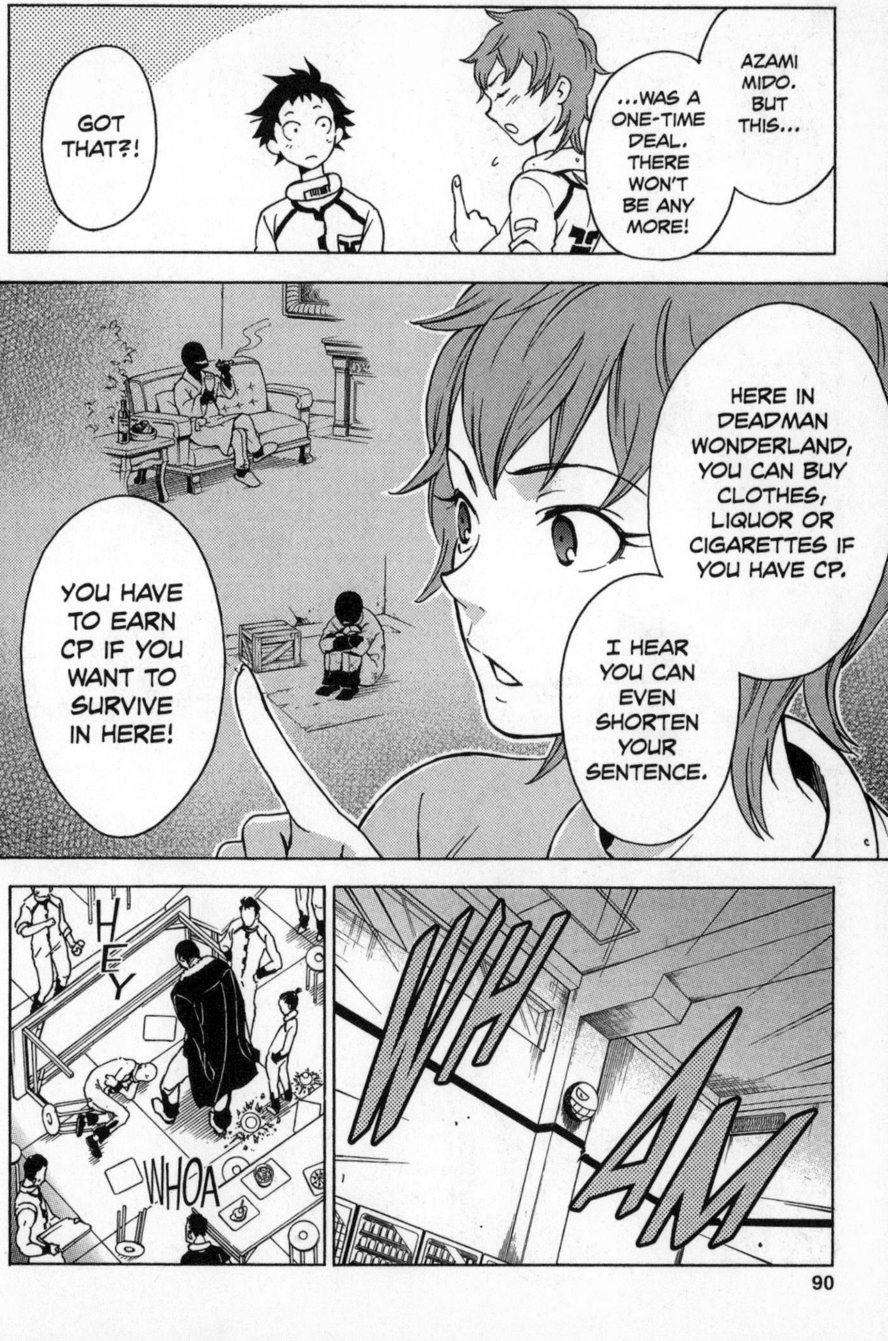
AZAMI MIDO. BUT THIS...
...WAS A ONE-TIME DEAL. THERE WON'T BE ANY MORE!
GOT THAT?!
HERE IN DEADMAN WONDERLAND, YOU CAN BUY CLOTHES, LIQUOR OR CIGARETTES IF YOU HAVE CP.
I HEAR YOU CAN EVEN SHORTEN YOUR SENTENCE.
YOU HAVE TO EARN CP IF YOU WANT TO SURVIVE IN HERE!
WHAM
HEY
WHOA

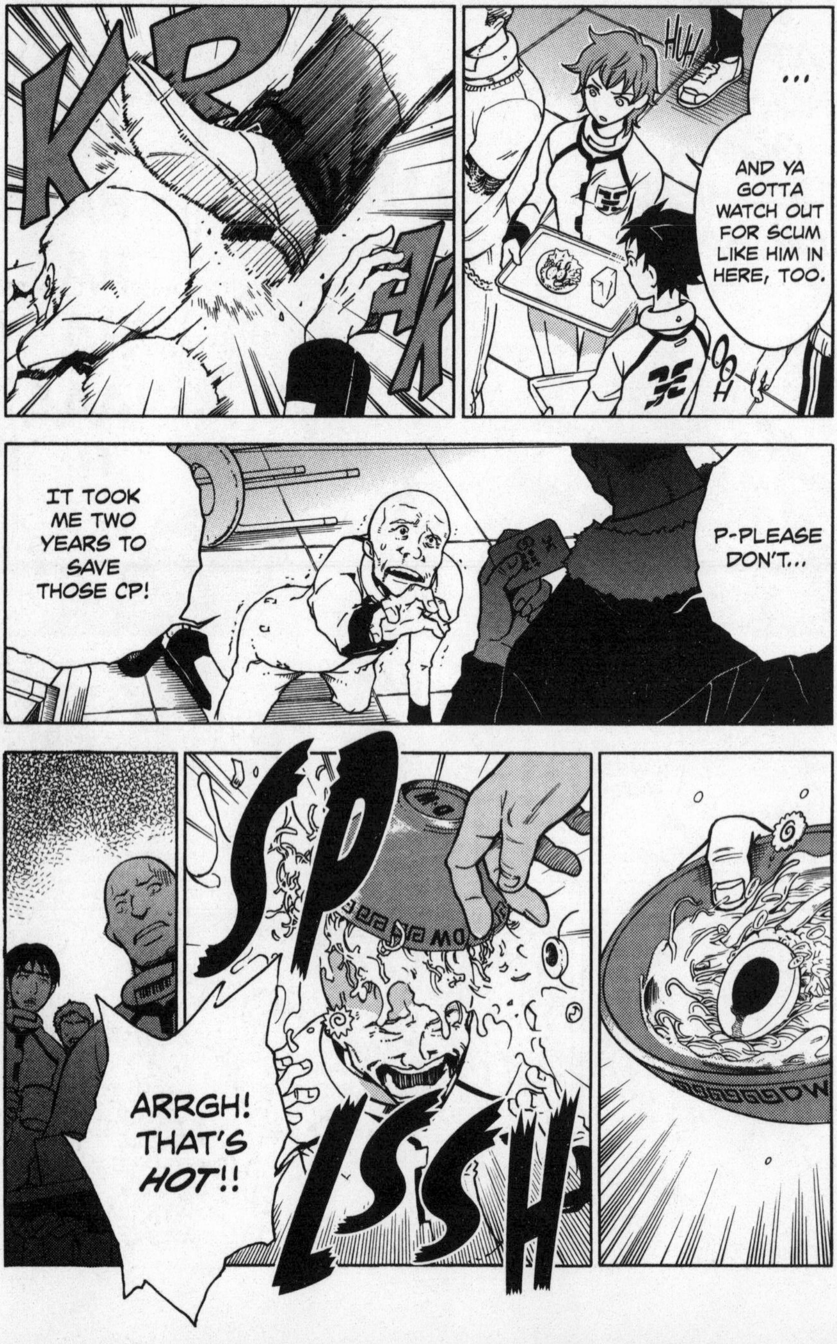
HUH
...
AND YA GOTTA WATCH OUT FOR SCUM LIKE HIM IN HERE, TOO.
OOH
KRAK
P-PLEASE DON'T...
IT TOOK ME TWO YEARS TO SAVE THOSE CP!
SPLISSH
ARRGH! THAT'S *HOT*!!

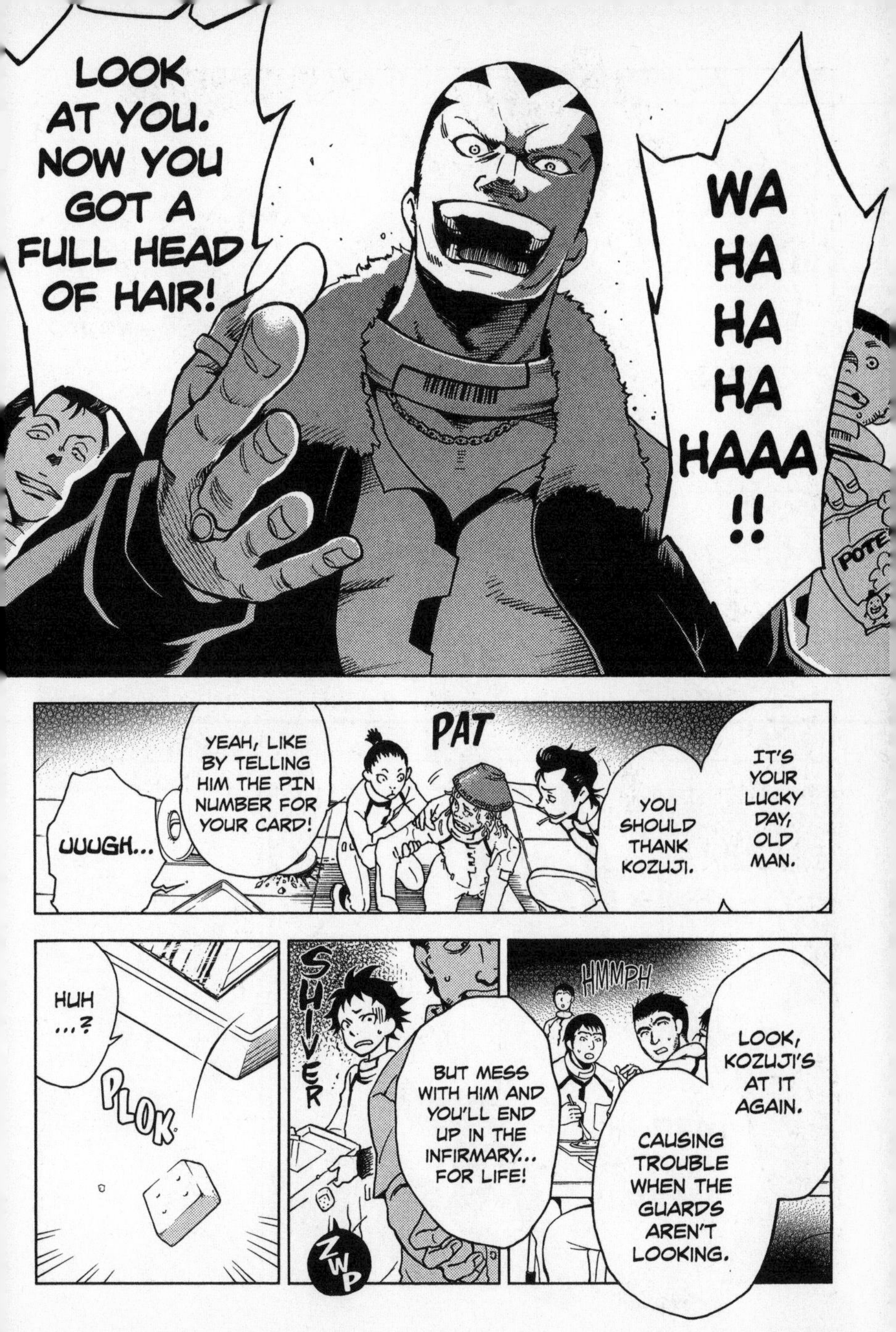
WA HA HA HA HAAAA!!
LOOK AT YOU. NOW YOU GOT A FULL HEAD OF HAIR!
POTE
IT'S YOUR LUCKY DAY, OLD MAN.
YOU SHOULD THANK KOZUJI.
PAT
YEAH, LIKE BY TELLING HIM THE PIN NUMBER FOR YOUR CARD!
UUUGH...
HMMPH
LOOK, KOZUJI'S AT IT AGAIN.
CAUSING TROUBLE WHEN THE GUARDS AREN'T LOOKING.
SHIVER
BUT MESS WITH HIM AND YOU'LL END UP IN THE INFIRMARY... FOR LIFE!
ZWP
HUH ...?
PLOK

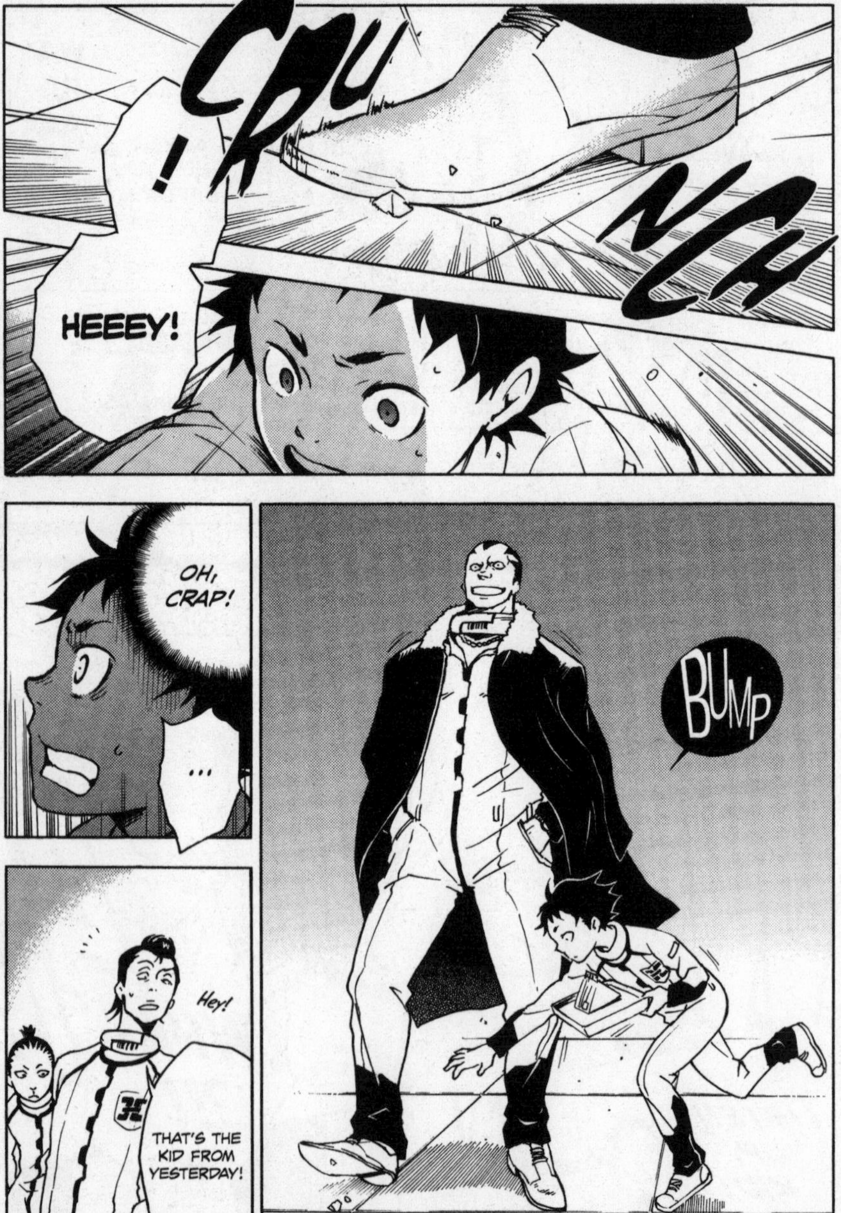
CRUNCH
!
HEEEY!
BUMP
OH, CRAP!
...
Hey!
THAT'S THE KID FROM YESTERDAY!

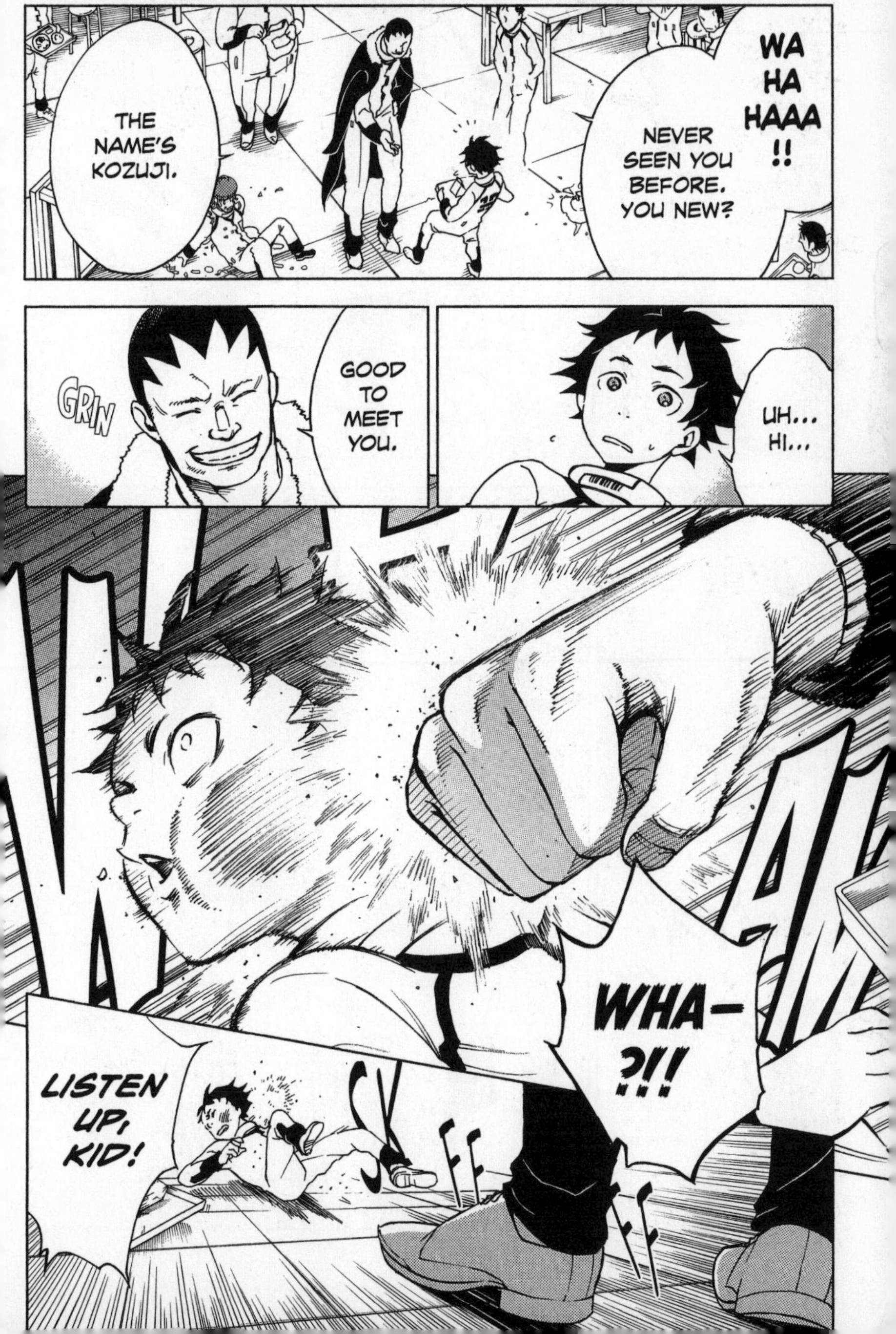
WA HA HAAA!!
NEVER SEEN YOU BEFORE. YOU NEW?
THE NAME'S KOZUJI.
UH... HI...
GOOD TO MEET YOU.
GRIN
WHA- ?!!
LISTEN UP, KID!

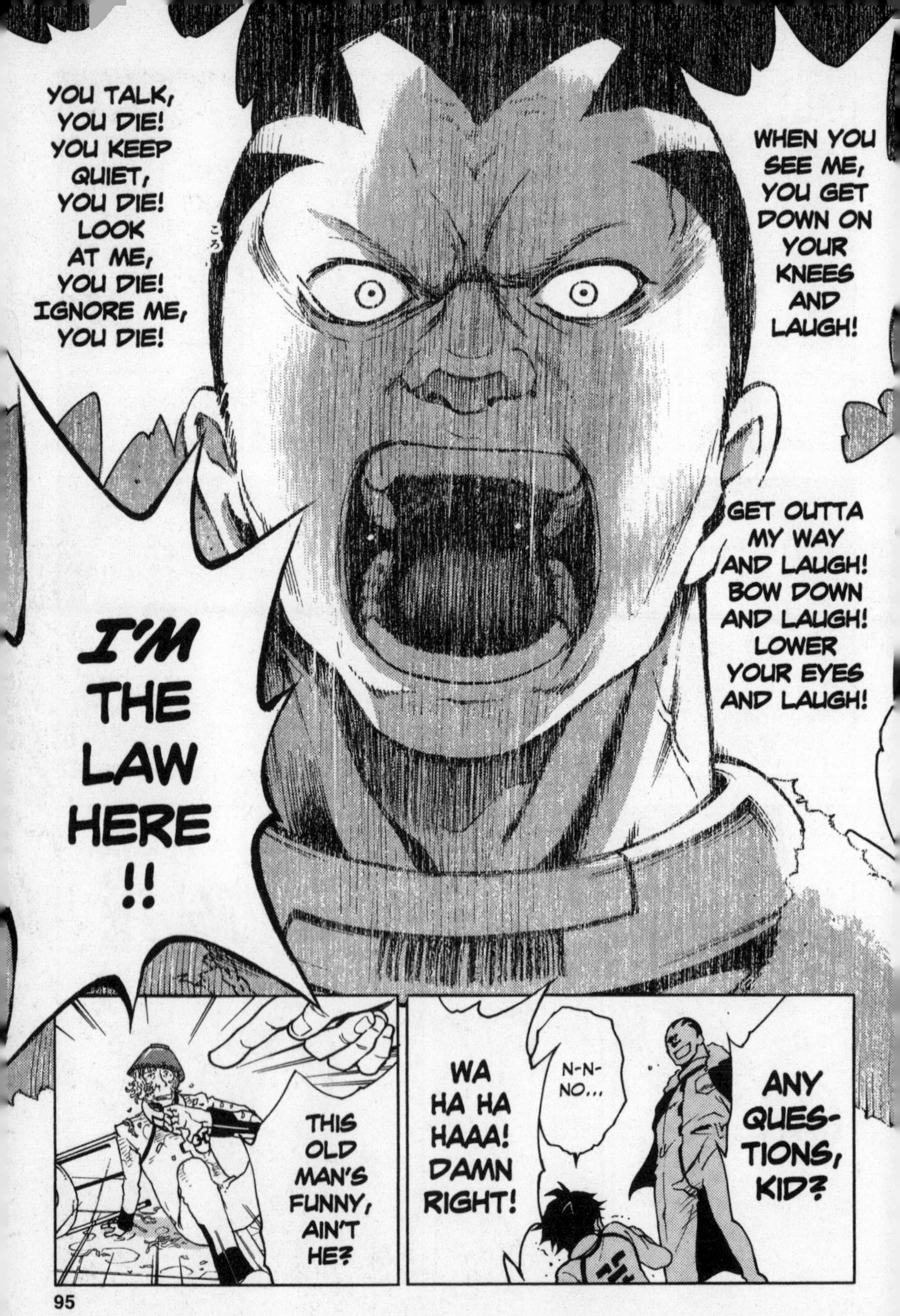
WHEN YOU SEE ME, YOU GET DOWN ON YOUR KNEES AND LAUGH!
YOU TALK, YOU DIE! YOU KEEP QUIET, YOU DIE! LOOK AT ME, YOU DIE! IGNORE ME, YOU DIE!
GET OUTTA MY WAY AND LAUGH! BOW DOWN AND LAUGH! LOWER YOUR EYES AND LAUGH!
I'M THE LAW HERE!!
ANY QUES-TIONS, KID?
N-N-NO...
WA HA HA HAAA! DAMN RIGHT!
THIS OLD MAN'S FUNNY, AIN'T HE?

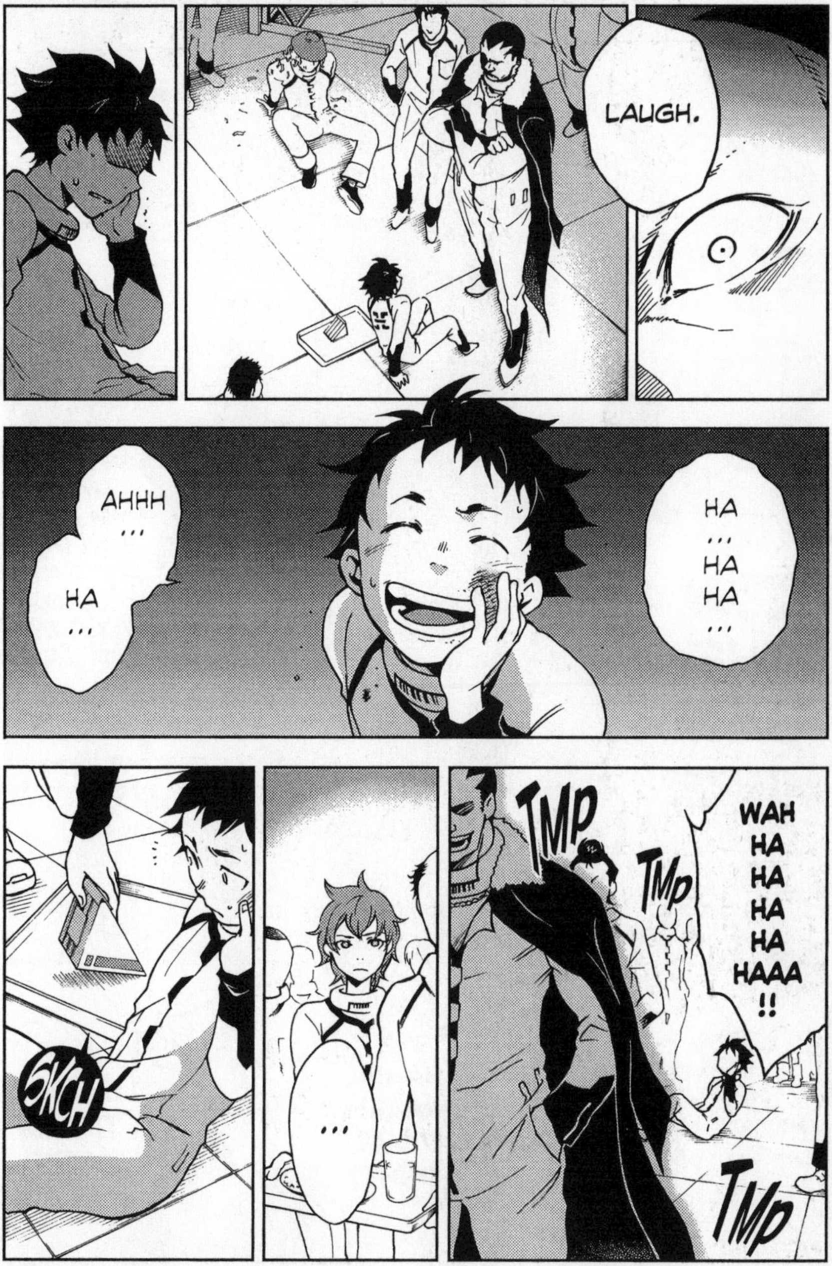
LAUGH.
HA ... HA HA ...
AHHH ... HA ...
WAH HA HA HA HA HA HAAA!!
TMP
TMP
TMP
...
SKCH

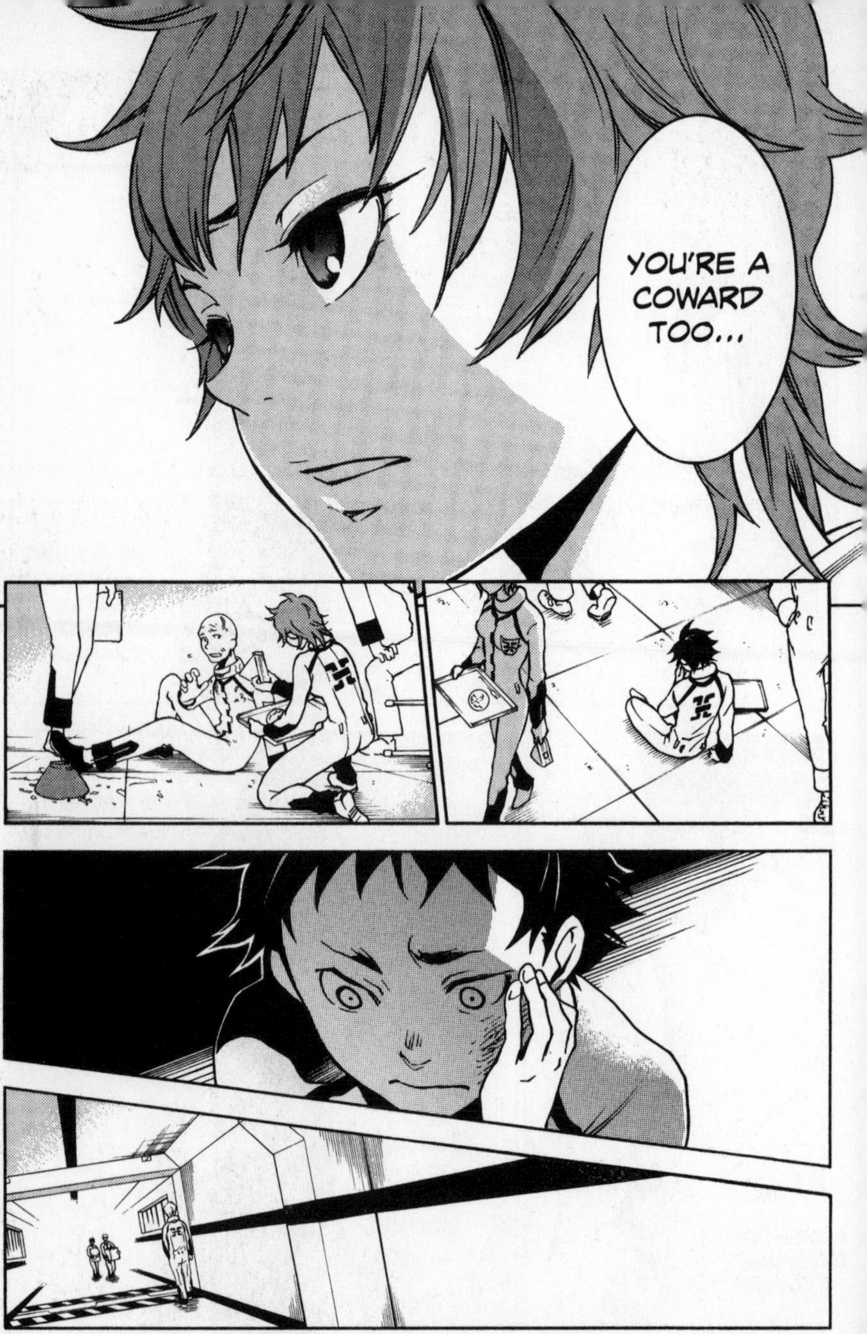
YOU'RE A COWARD TOO...

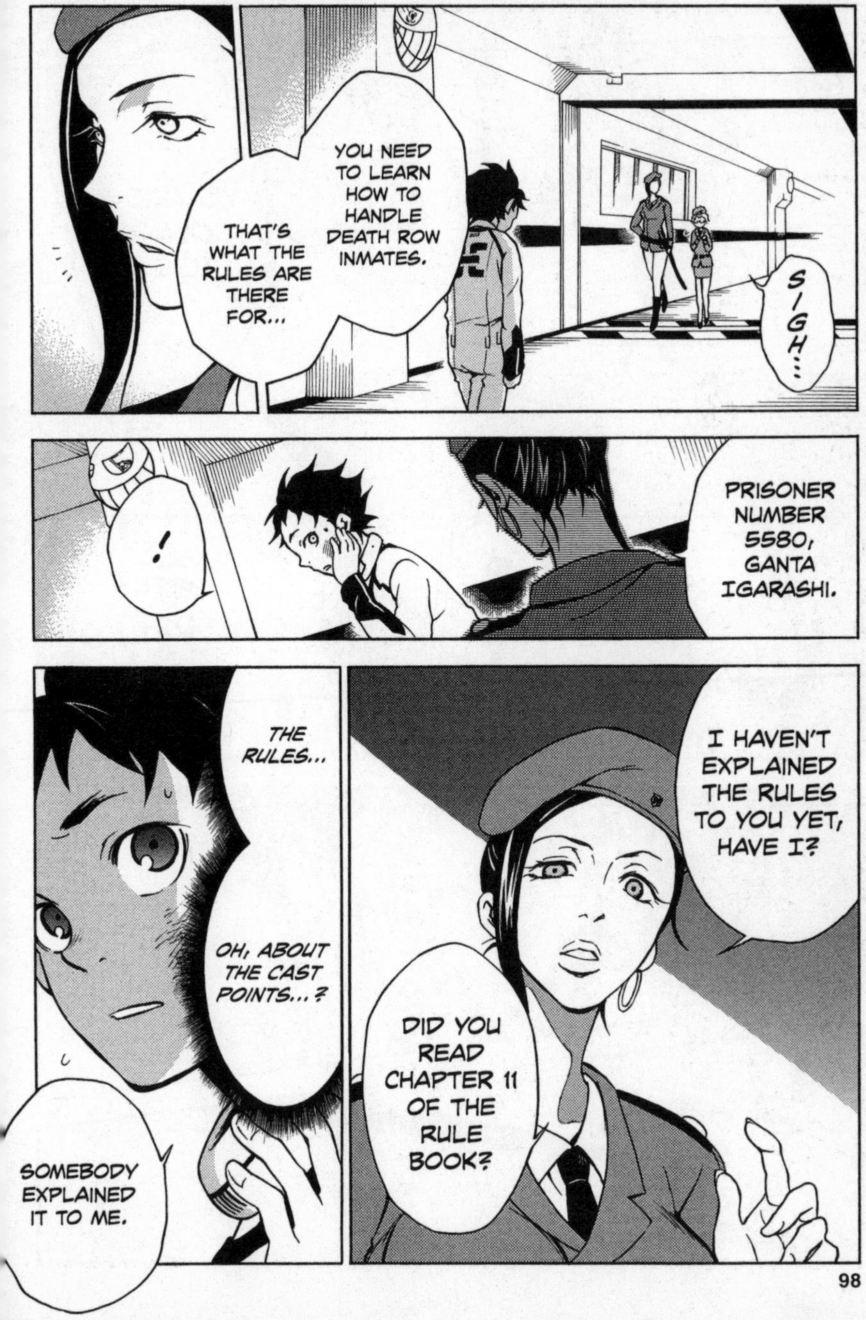
SIGH...
YOU NEED TO LEARN HOW TO HANDLE DEATH ROW INMATES.
THAT'S WHAT THE RULES ARE THERE FOR...
PRISONER NUMBER 5580, GANTA IGARASHI.
!
I HAVEN'T EXPLAINED THE RULES TO YOU YET, HAVE I?
DID YOU READ CHAPTER 11 OF THE RULE BOOK?
THE RULES...
OH, ABOUT THE CAST POINTS...?
SOMEBODY EXPLAINED IT TO ME.

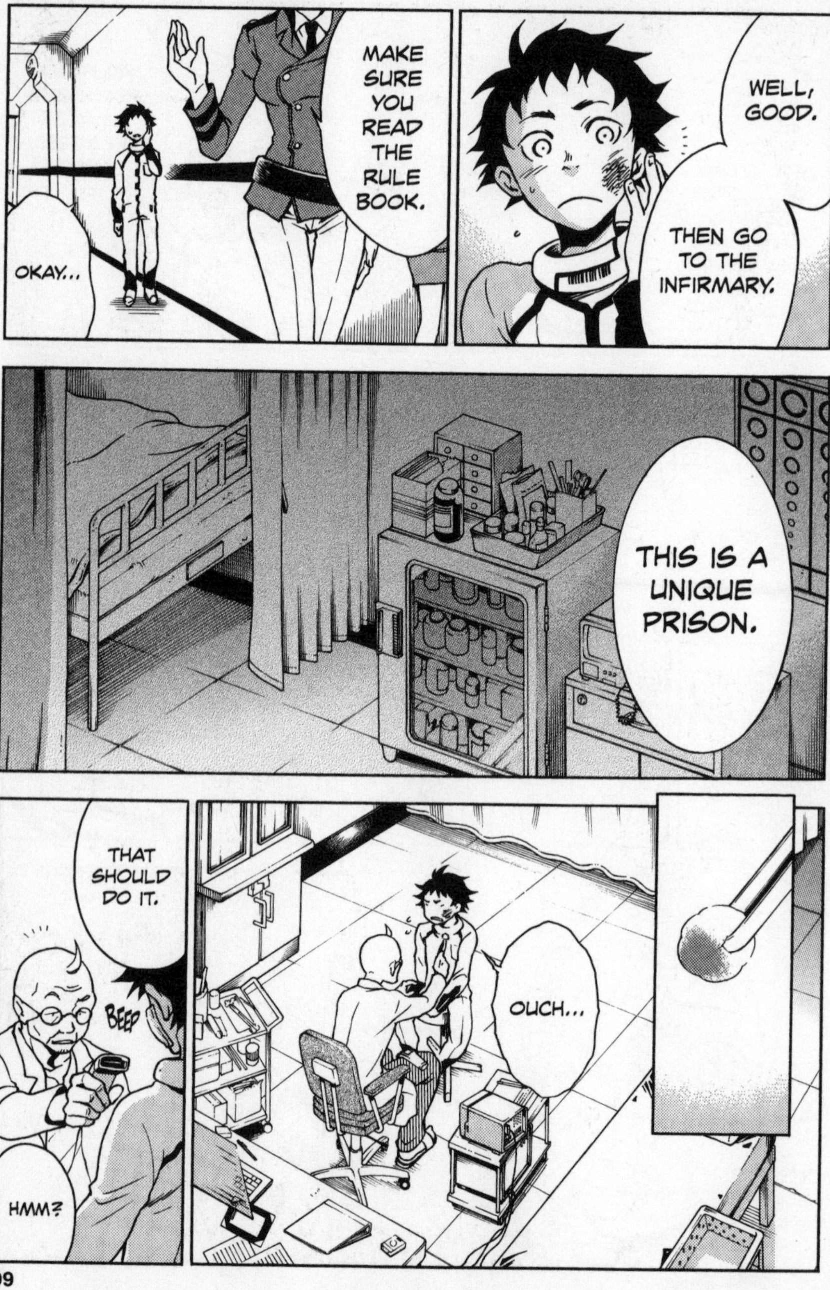
WELL, GOOD.
THEN GO TO THE INFIRMARY.
MAKE SURE YOU READ THE RULE BOOK.
OKAY...
THIS IS A UNIQUE PRISON.
OUCH...
THAT SHOULD DO IT.
BEEP
HMM?

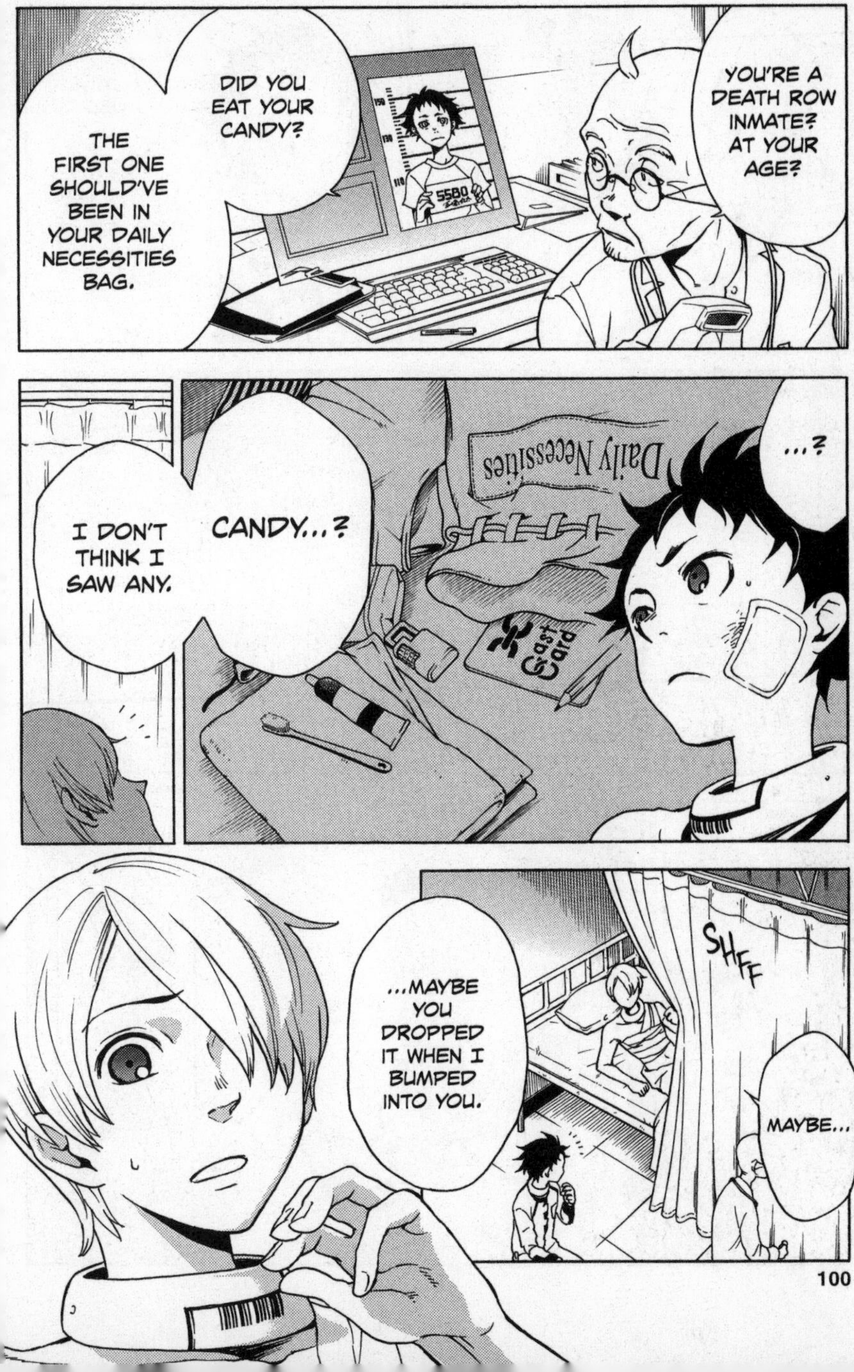
YOU'RE A DEATH ROW INMATE? AT YOUR AGE?
5580
DID YOU EAT YOUR CANDY?
THE FIRST ONE SHOULD'VE BEEN IN YOUR DAILY NECESSITIES BAG.
...?
Daily Necessities
CANDY...?
I DON'T THINK I SAW ANY.
SHFF
MAYBE...
...MAYBE YOU DROPPED IT WHEN I BUMPED INTO YOU.

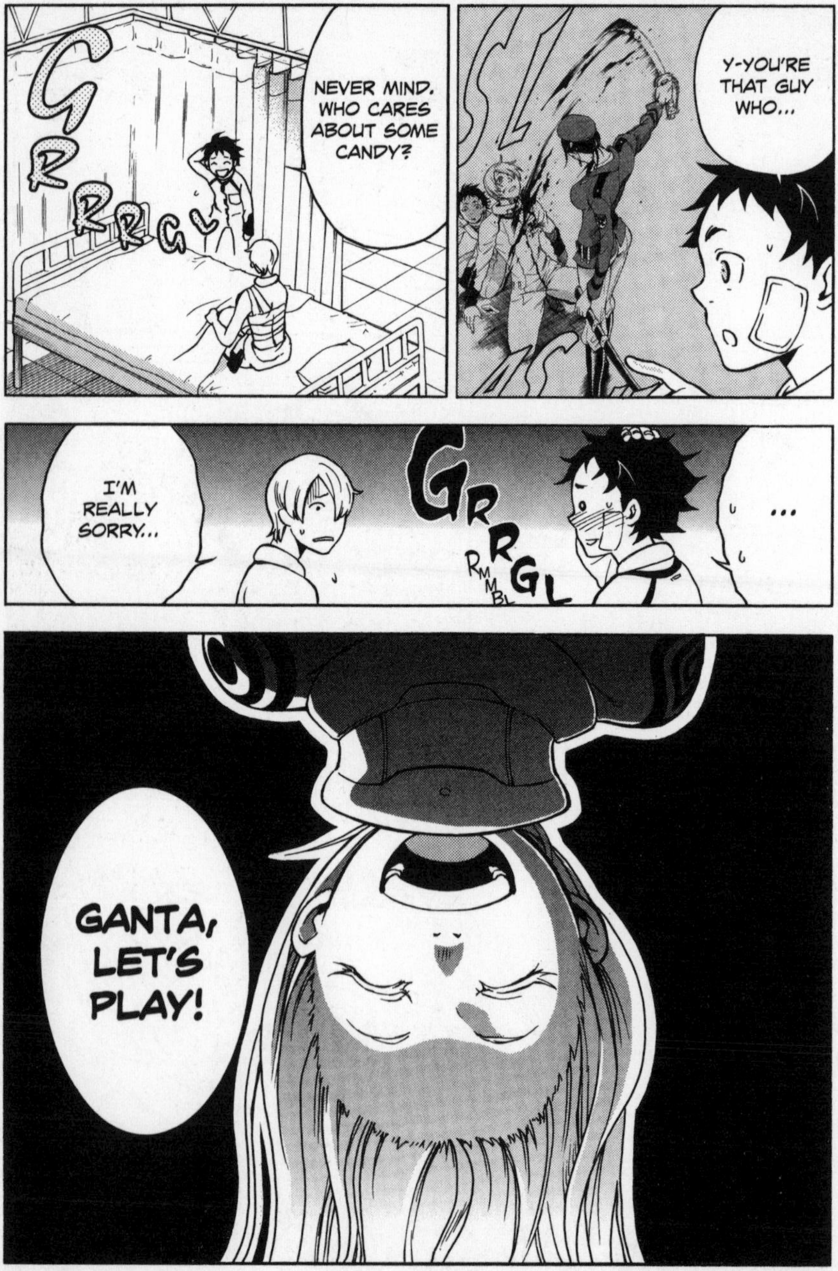
Y-YOU'RE THAT GUY WHO...
NEVER MIND. WHO CARES ABOUT SOME CANDY?
GRRRRGL
...
GRRRGL
RMMBL
I'M REALLY SORRY...
GANTA, LET'S PLAY!

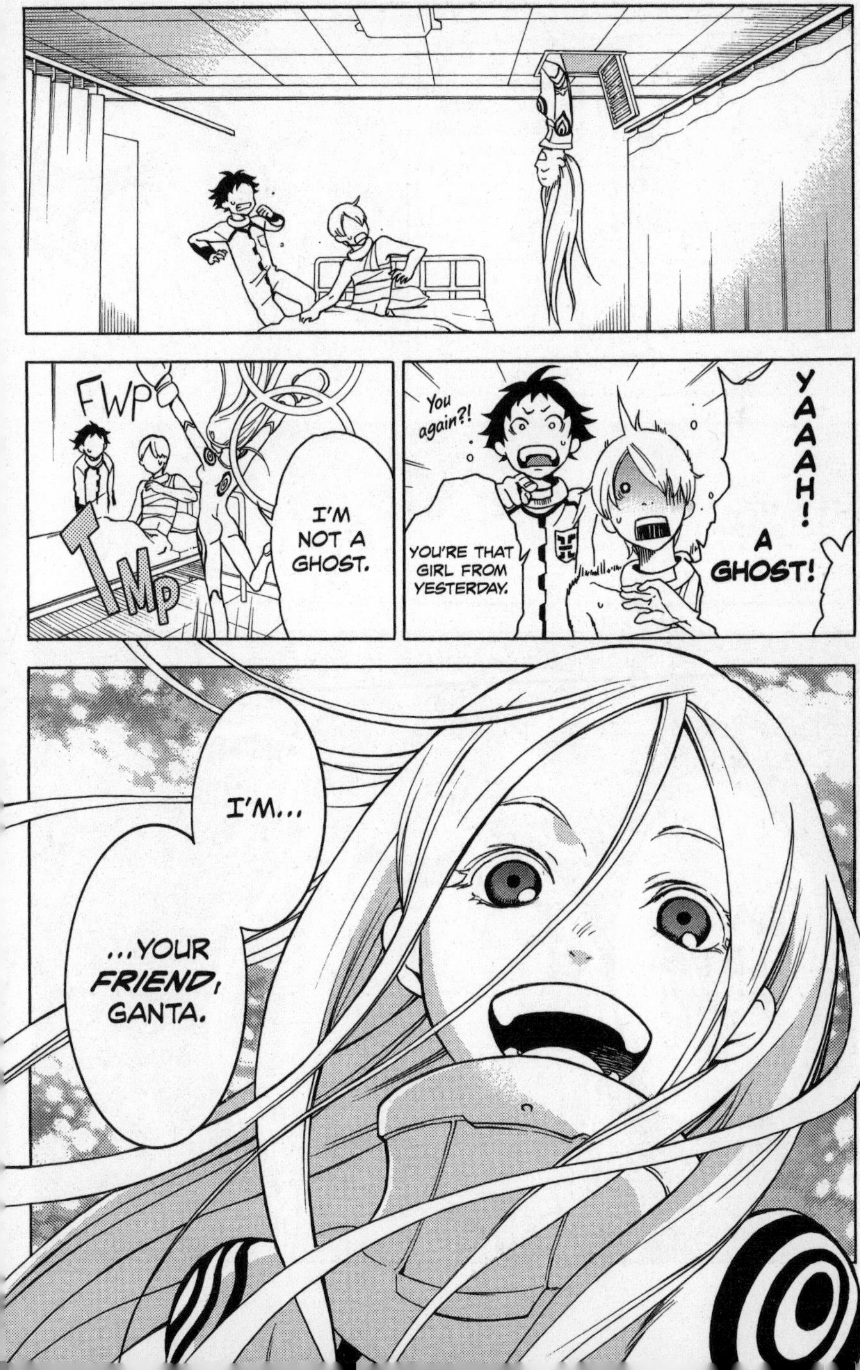
YAAAH! A GHOST!
You again?!
YOU'RE THAT GIRL FROM YESTERDAY.
FWP
I'M NOT A GHOST.
TMP
I'M...
...YOUR FRIEND, GANTA.

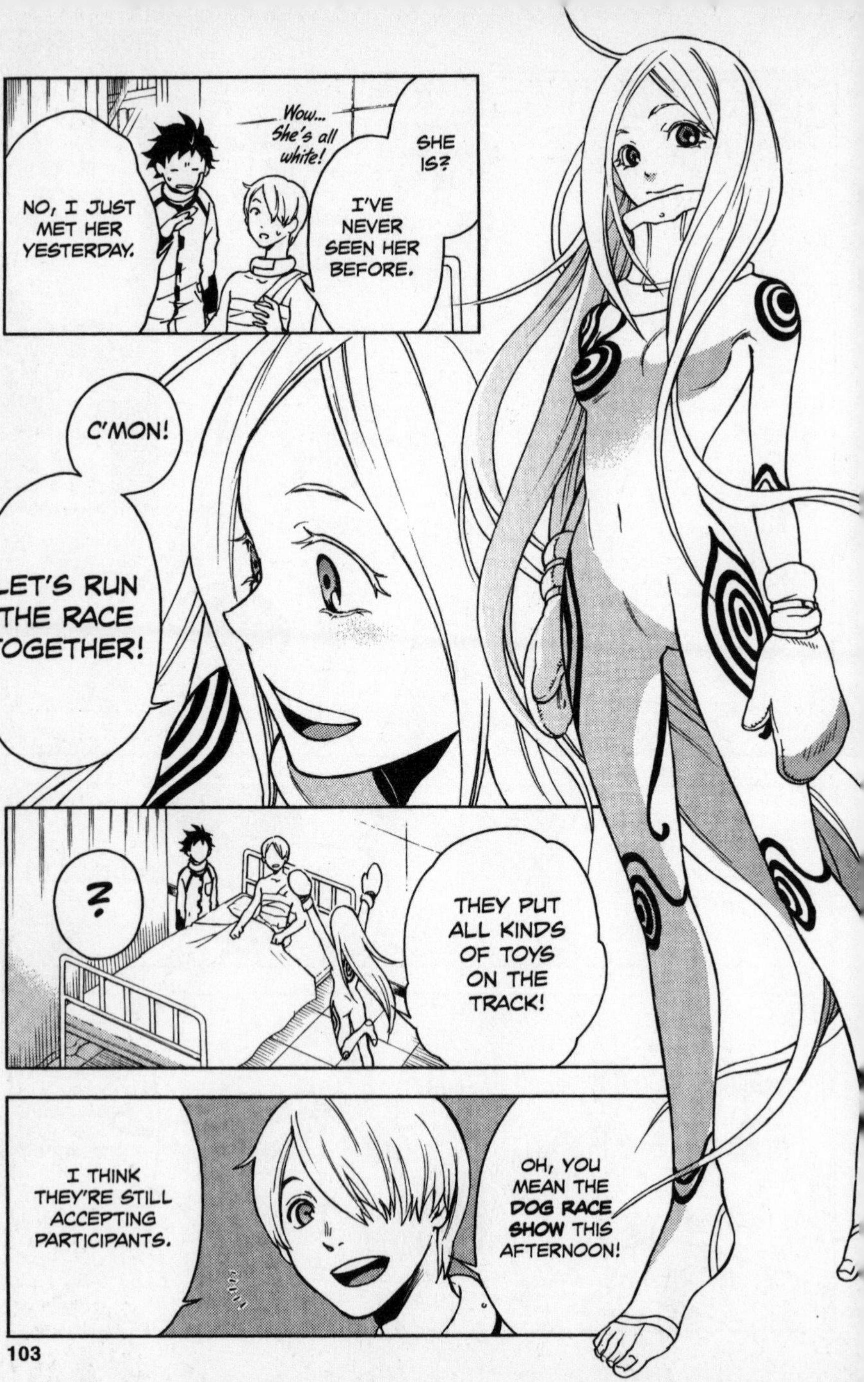
SHE IS?
I'VE NEVER SEEN HER BEFORE.
Wow... She's all white!
NO, I JUST MET HER YESTERDAY.
C'MON!
LET'S RUN THE RACE TOGETHER!
THEY PUT ALL KINDS OF TOYS ON THE TRACK!
?
OH, YOU MEAN THE **DOG RACE SHOW** THIS AFTERNOON!
I THINK THEY'RE STILL ACCEPTING PARTICIPANTS.

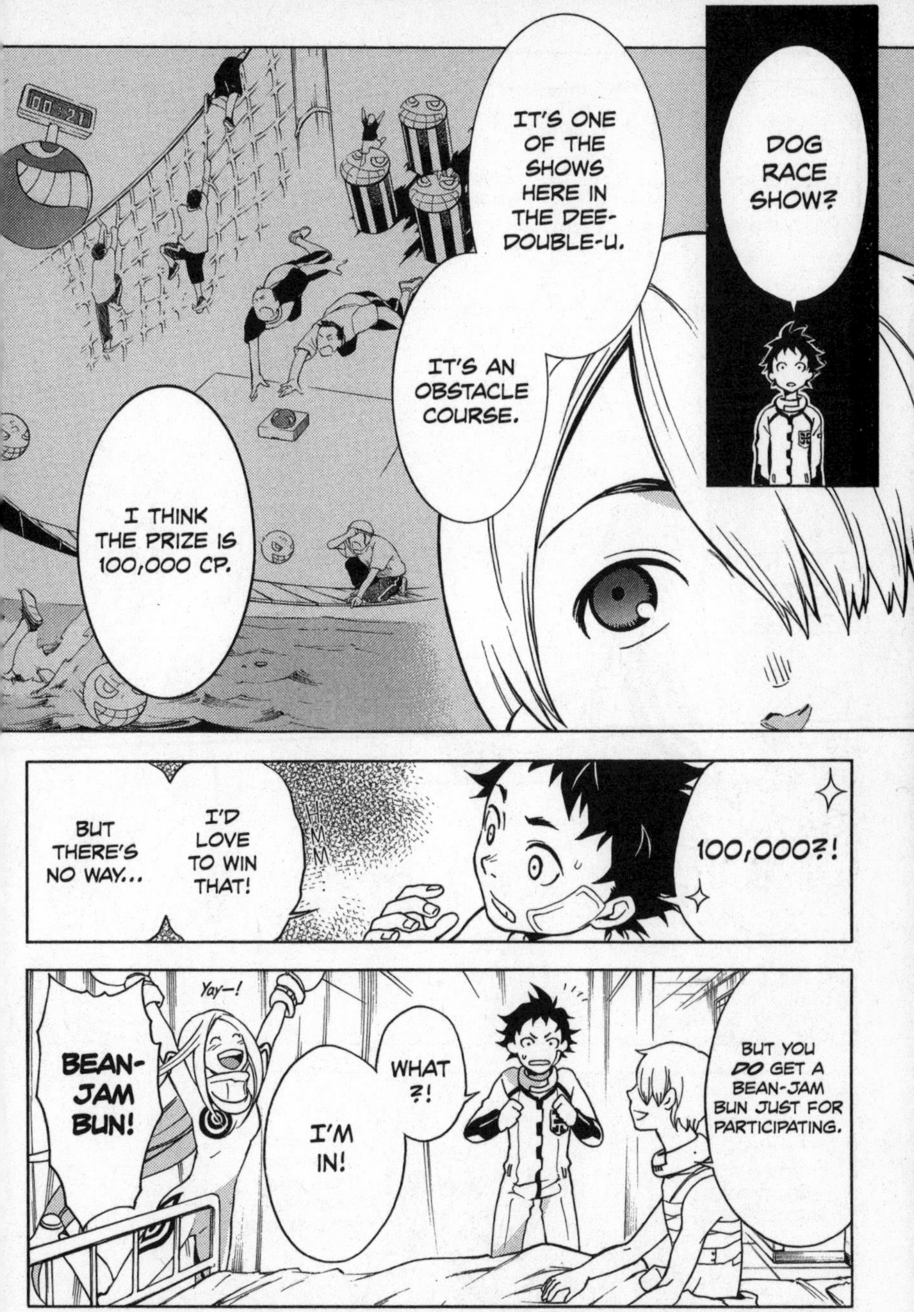
DOG RACE SHOW?
IT'S ONE OF THE SHOWS HERE IN THE DEE-DOUBLE-U.
IT'S AN OBSTACLE COURSE.
I THINK THE PRIZE IS 100,000 CP.
100,000?!
HMM
I'D LOVE TO WIN THAT!
BUT THERE'S NO WAY...
BUT YOU *DO* GET A BEAN-JAM BUN JUST FOR PARTICIPATING.
WHAT?!
I'M IN!
Yay—!
BEAN-JAM BUN!

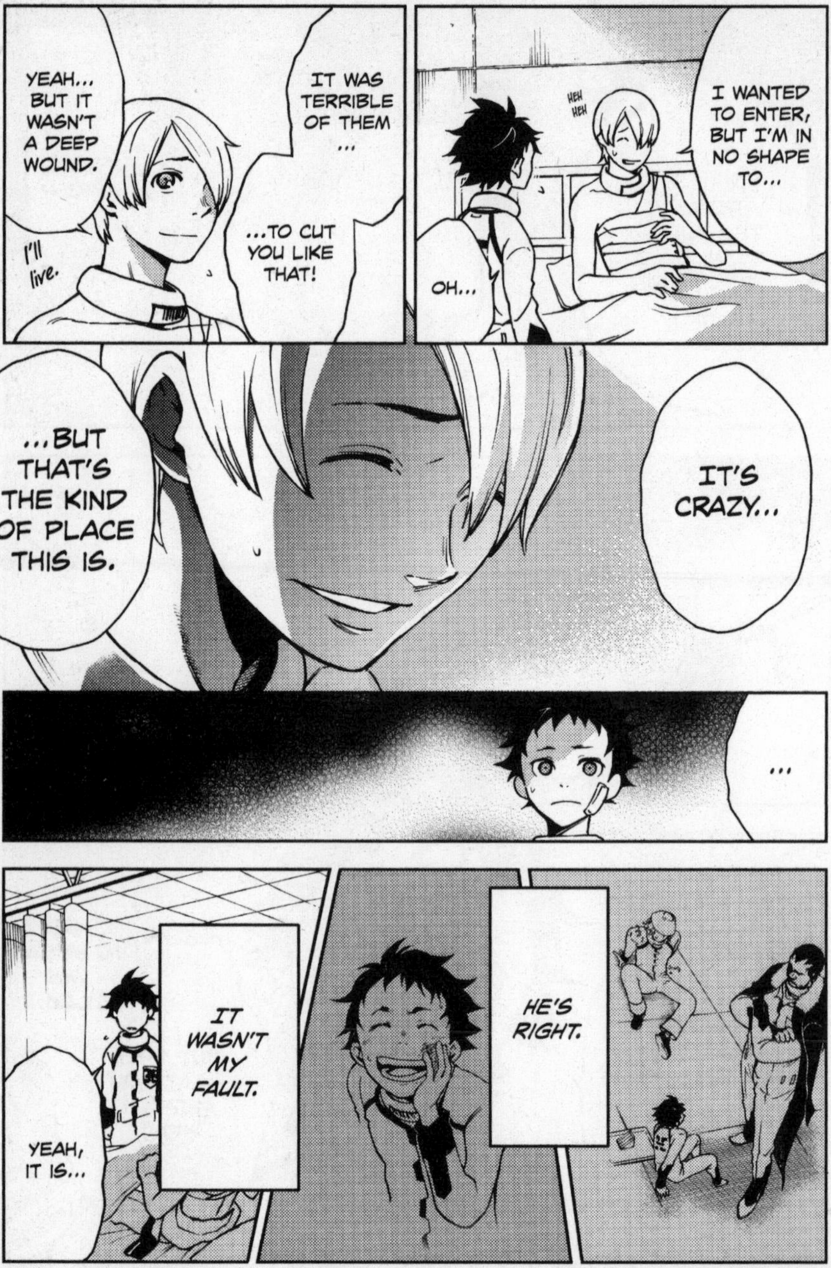
I WANTED TO ENTER, BUT I'M IN NO SHAPE TO...
HEH HEH
OH...
IT WAS TERRIBLE OF THEM ...
...TO CUT YOU LIKE THAT!
YEAH... BUT IT WASN'T A DEEP WOUND.
I'll live.
IT'S CRAZY...
...BUT THAT'S THE KIND OF PLACE THIS IS.
...
HE'S RIGHT.
IT WASN'T MY FAULT.
YEAH, IT IS...

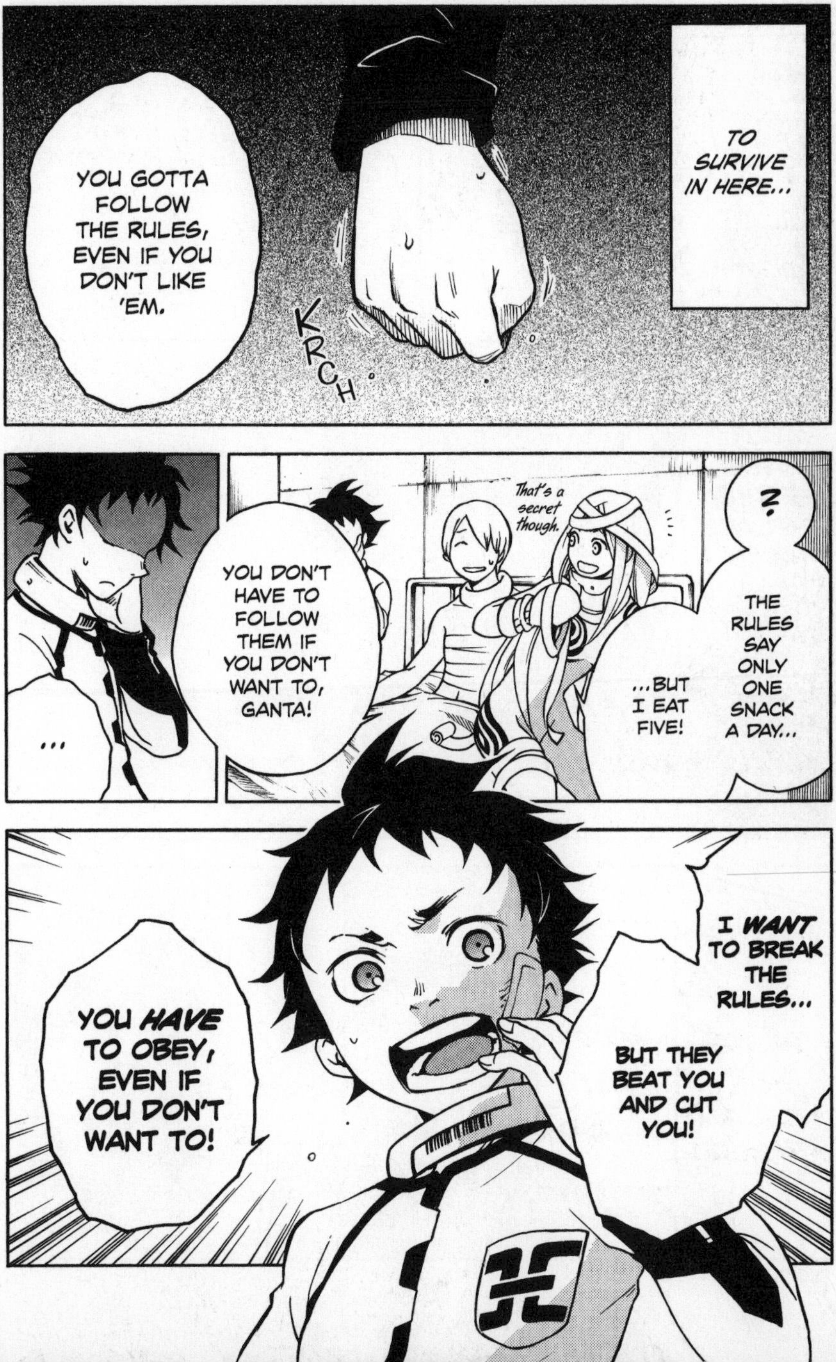
TO SURVIVE IN HERE...
YOU GOTTA FOLLOW THE RULES, EVEN IF YOU DON'T LIKE 'EM.
KRCH
?
THE RULES SAY ONLY ONE SNACK A DAY...
...BUT I EAT FIVE!
That's a secret though.
YOU DON'T HAVE TO FOLLOW THEM IF YOU DON'T WANT TO, GANTA!
...
I *WANT* TO BREAK THE RULES...
BUT THEY BEAT YOU AND CUT YOU!
YOU *HAVE* TO OBEY, EVEN IF YOU DON'T WANT TO!

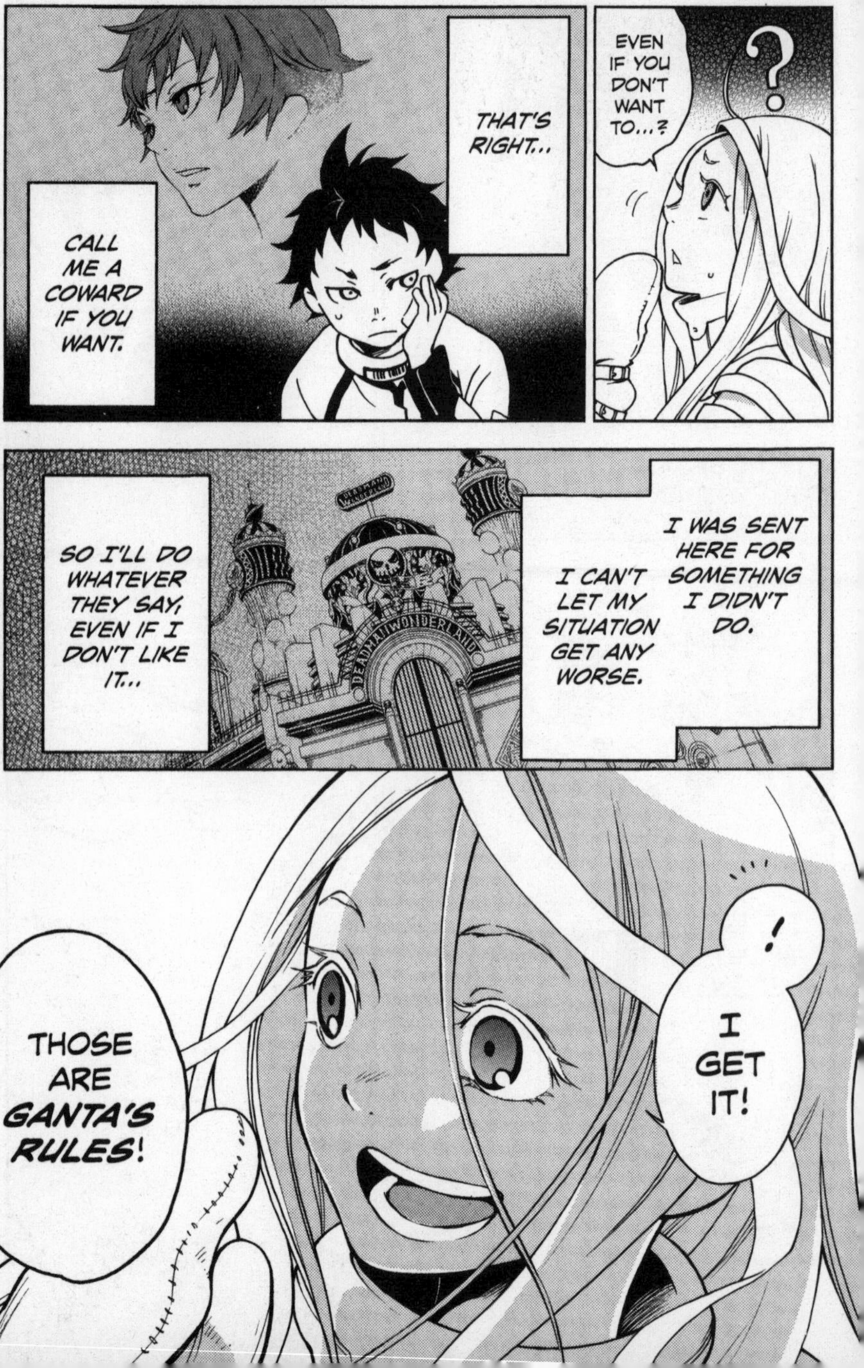
EVEN IF YOU DON'T WANT TO...?
THAT'S RIGHT...
CALL ME A COWARD IF YOU WANT.
I WAS SENT HERE FOR SOMETHING I DIDN'T DO.
I CAN'T LET MY SITUATION GET ANY WORSE.
SO I'LL DO WHATEVER THEY SAY, EVEN IF I DON'T LIKE IT...
DEADMAN WONDERLAND
!
I GET IT!
THOSE ARE GANTA'S RULES!

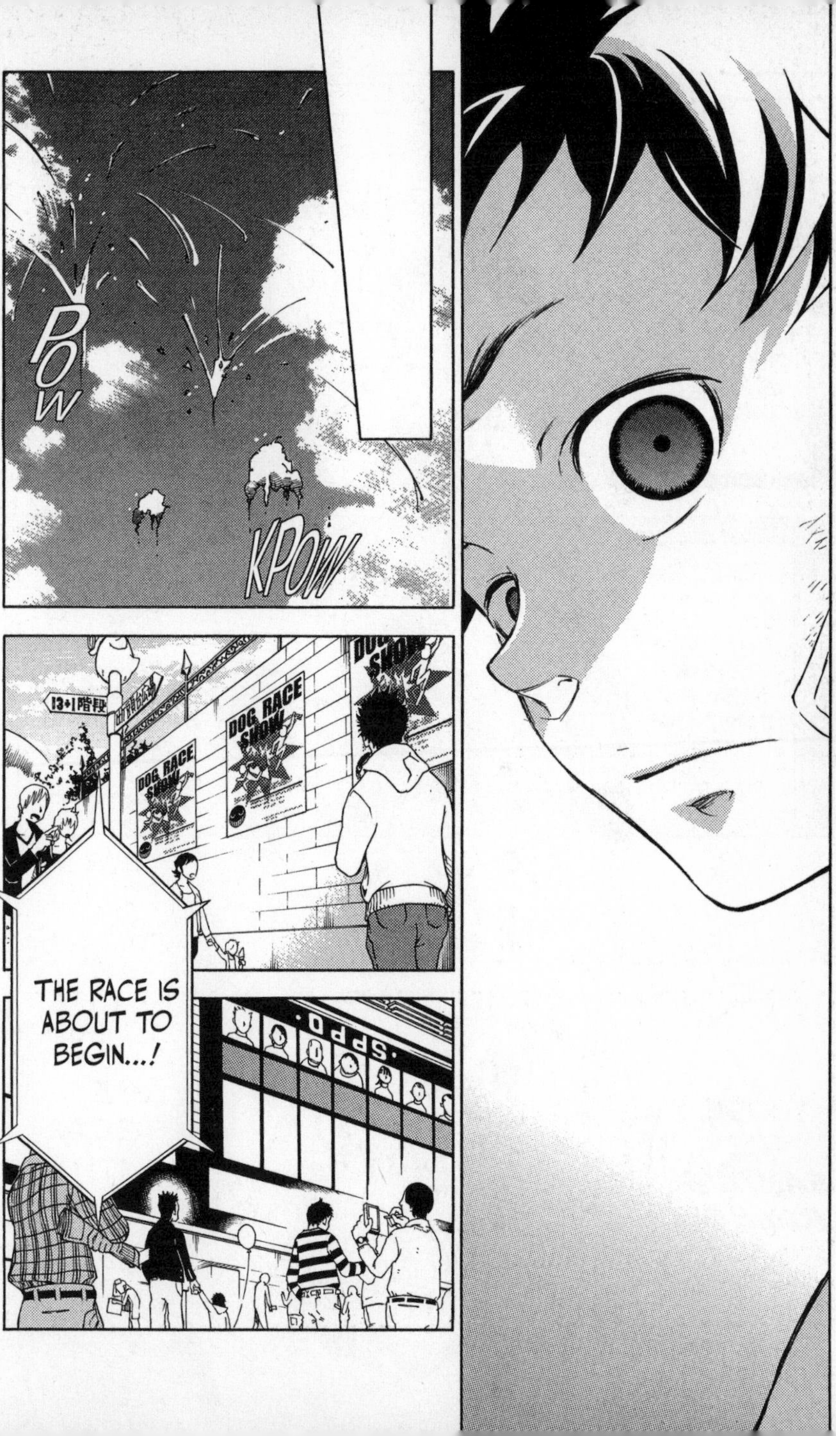
POW
KPOW
13+1階段
DOG RACE SHOW
DOG RACE SHOW
THE RACE IS ABOUT TO BEGIN...!
SPPO

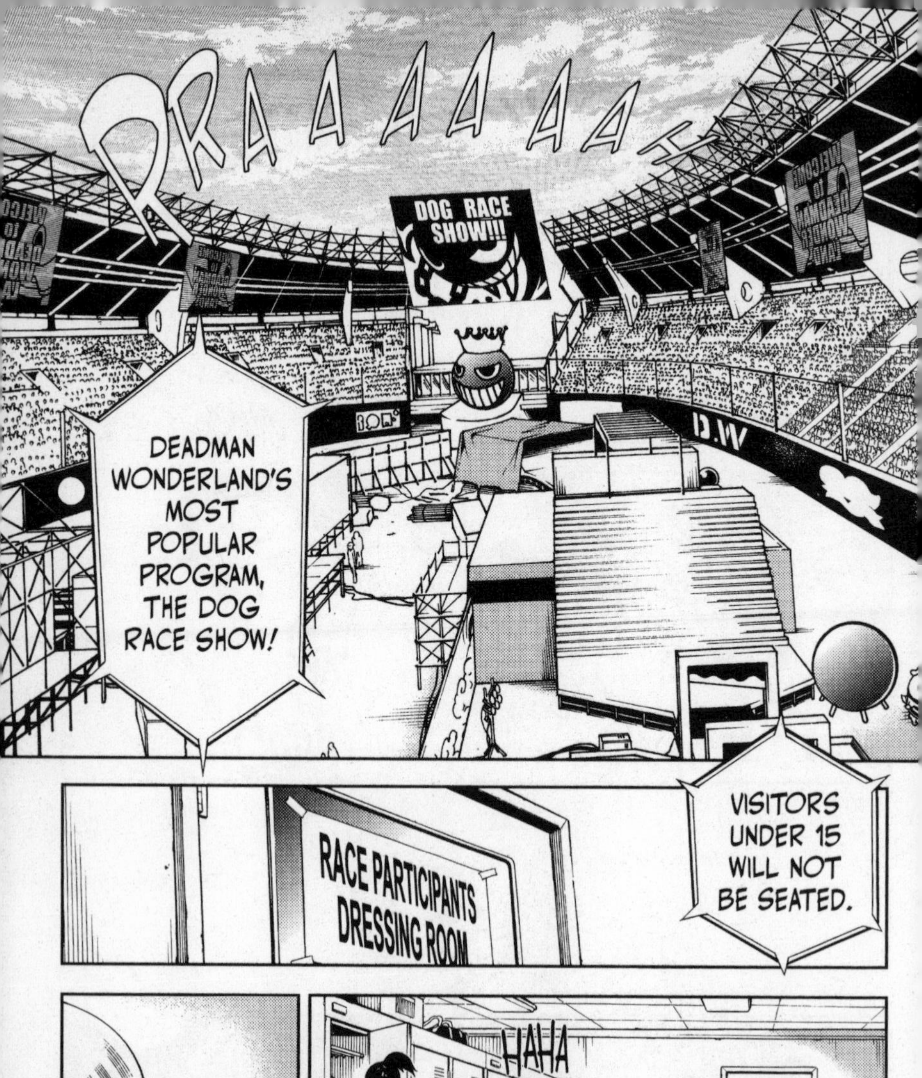
RAAAAAAH
DOG RACE SHOW!!!
DEADMAN WONDERLAND'S MOST POPULAR PROGRAM, THE DOG RACE SHOW!
VISITORS UNDER 15 WILL NOT BE SEATED.
RACE PARTICIPANTS DRESSING ROOM
HAHA
MMPH
RULES Chapter 3
What are Cast Points?
1CP=1Yen

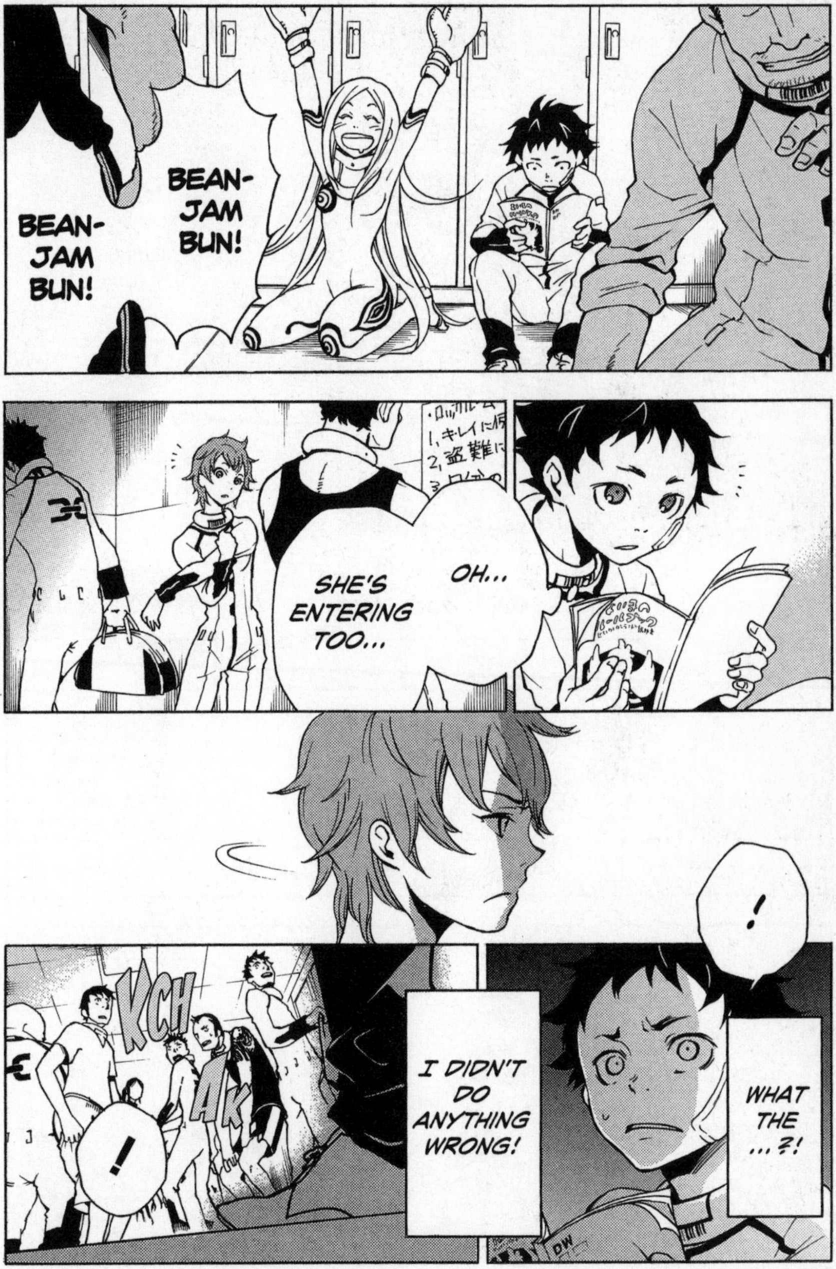
BEAN-JAM BUN!
BEAN-JAM BUN!
OH...
SHE'S ENTERING TOO...
!
!
WHAT THE ...?!
I DIDN'T DO ANYTHING WRONG!
KCHAK
!

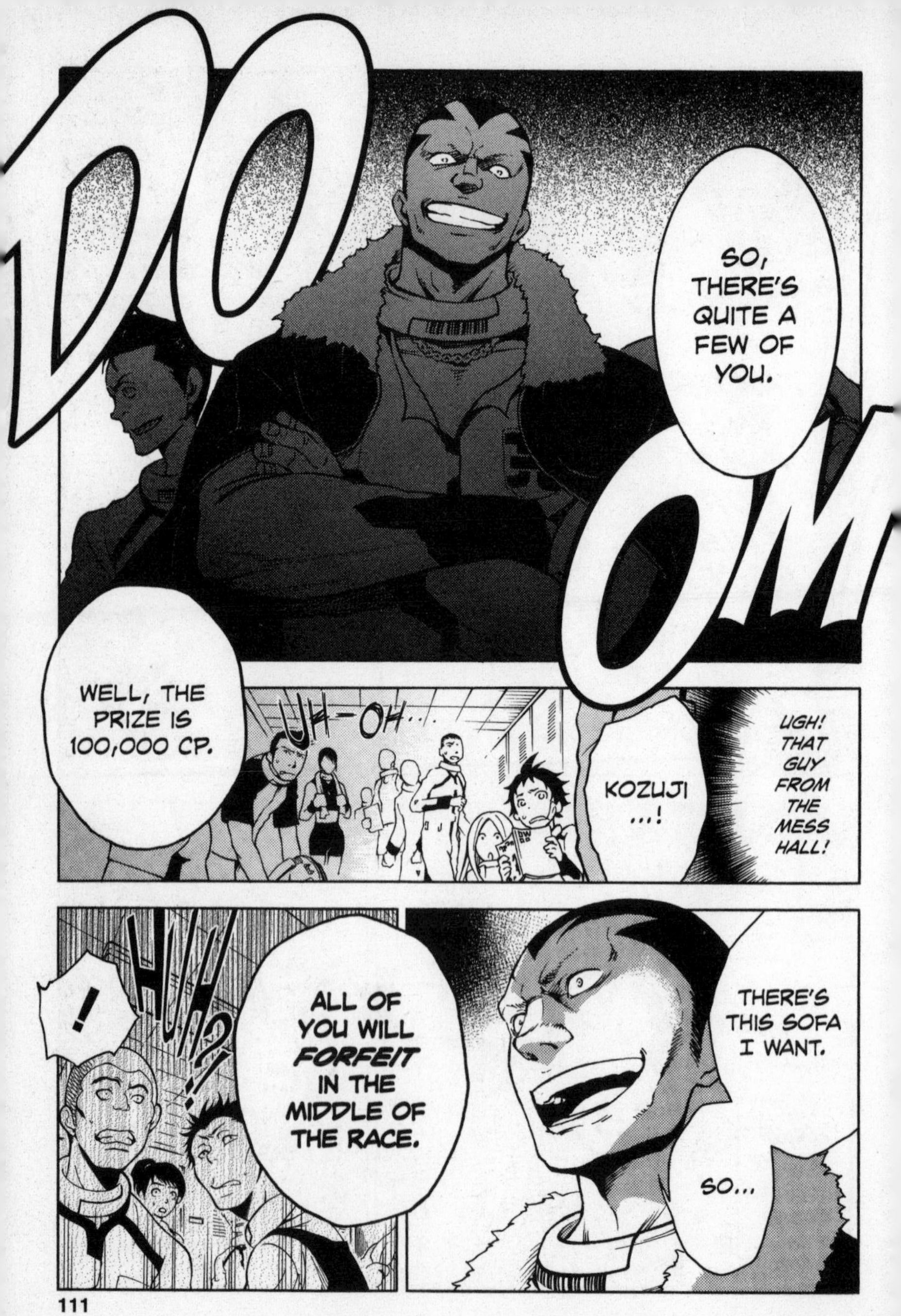
DOOM
SO, THERE'S QUITE A FEW OF YOU.
WELL, THE PRIZE IS 100,000 CP.
UGH! THAT GUY FROM THE MESS HALL!
KOZUJI ...!
UH-OH...
THERE'S THIS SOFA I WANT.
SO...
ALL OF YOU WILL *FORFEIT* IN THE MIDDLE OF THE RACE.
HUH?!
!

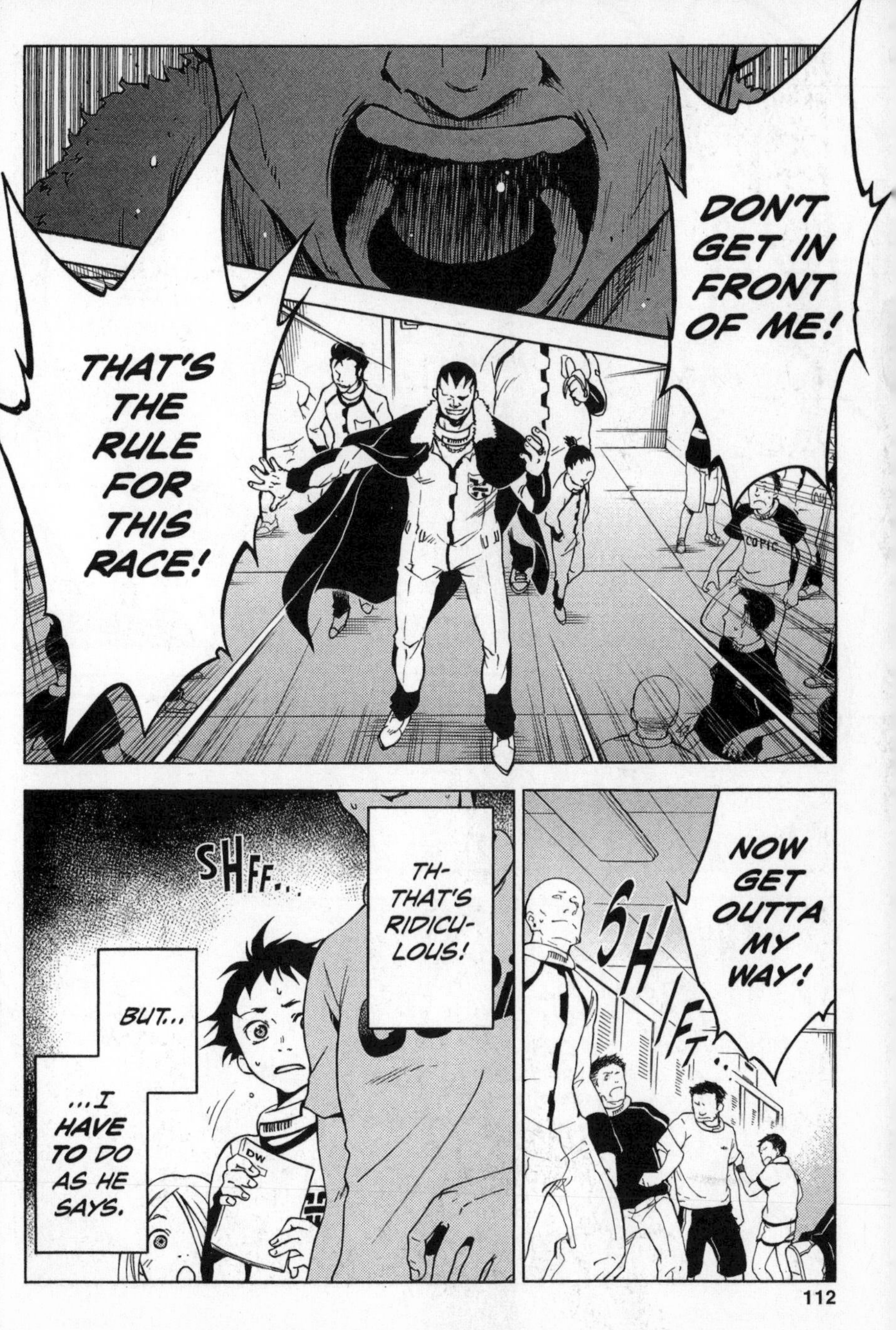
DON'T GET IN FRONT OF ME!
THAT'S THE RULE FOR THIS RACE!
NOW GET OUTTA MY WAY!
SHIFT...
SHFF...
TH- THAT'S RIDICULOUS!
BUT...
...I HAVE TO DO AS HE SAYS.

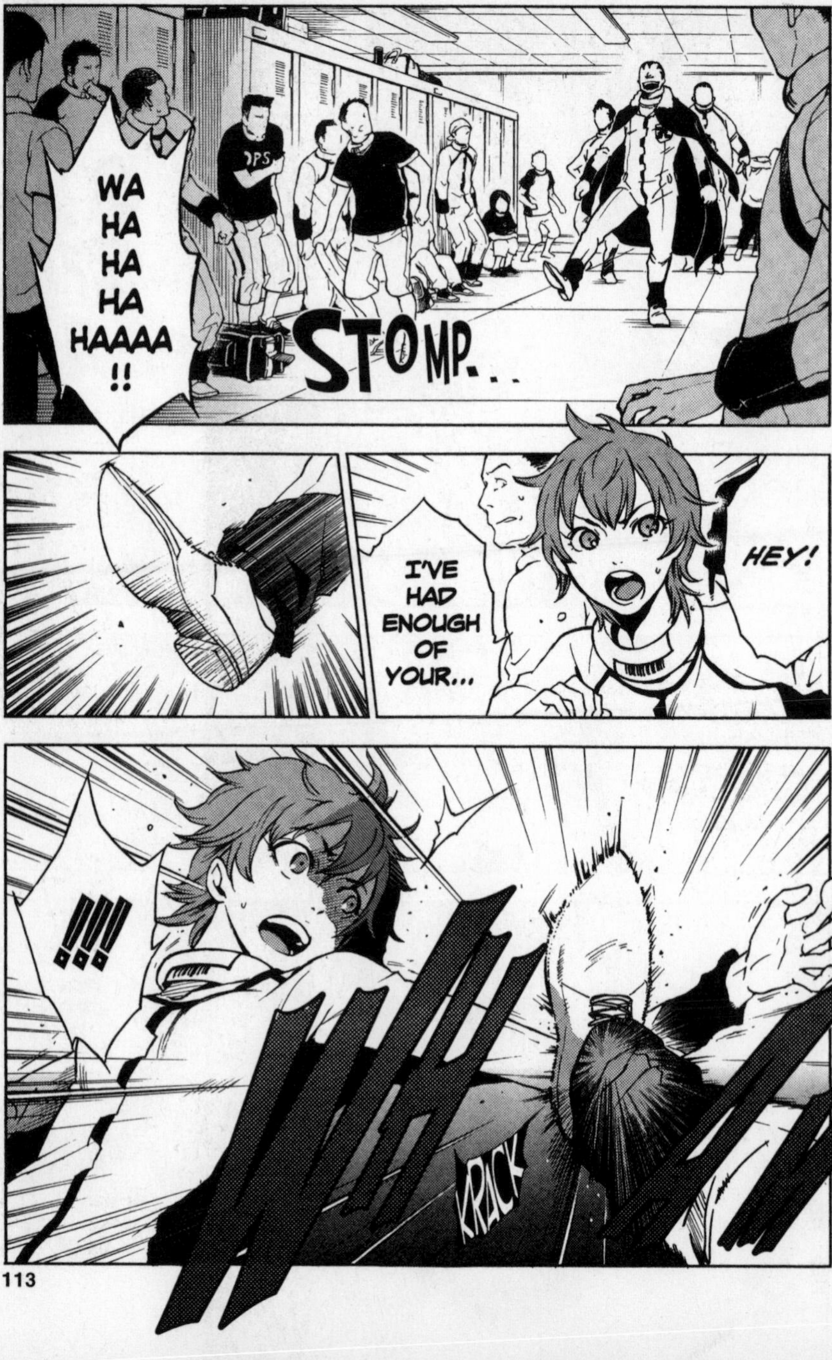
WA HA HA HA HAAAA !!
STOMP...
HEY!
I'VE HAD ENOUGH OF YOUR...
!!!!
KRACK

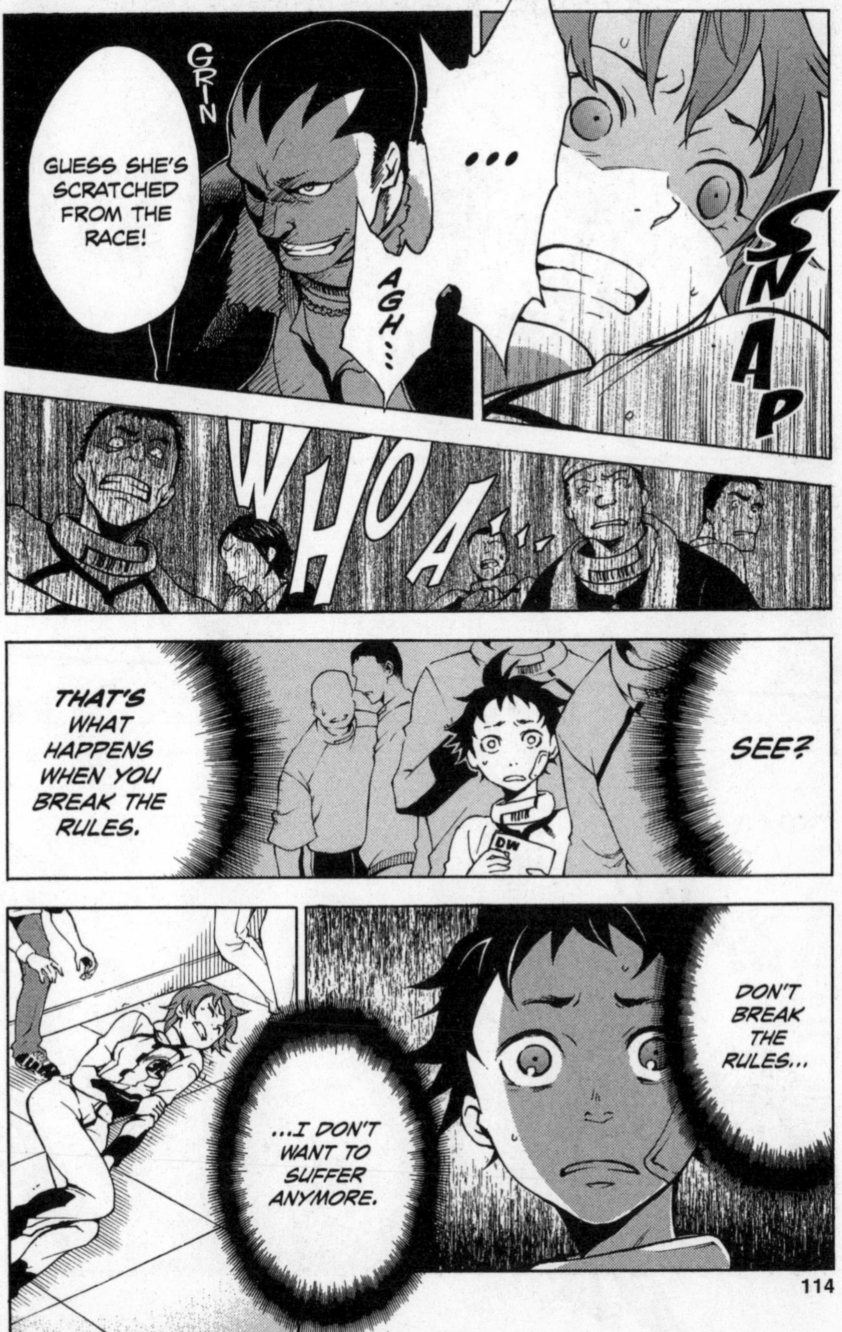
...
SNAP
AGH...
GRIN
GUESS SHE'S SCRATCHED FROM THE RACE!
WHOA!
SEE?
THAT'S WHAT HAPPENS WHEN YOU BREAK THE RULES.
DON'T BREAK THE RULES...
...I DON'T WANT TO SUFFER ANYMORE.

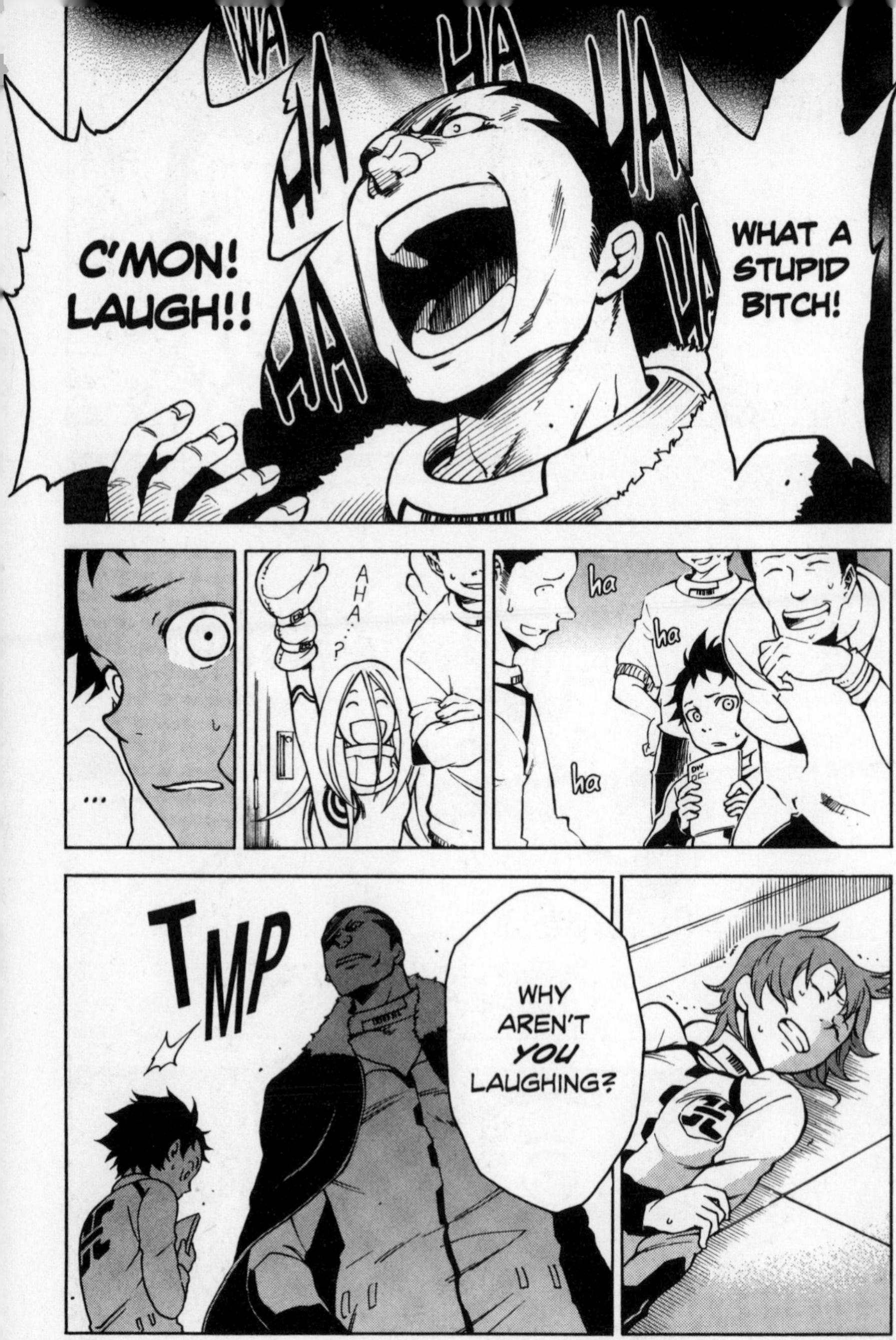
WHAT A STUPID BITCH!
WA HA HA HA HA HA HA
C'MON! LAUGH!!
ha
ha
ha
AHA...?
...
WHY AREN'T *YOU* LAUGHING?
TMP

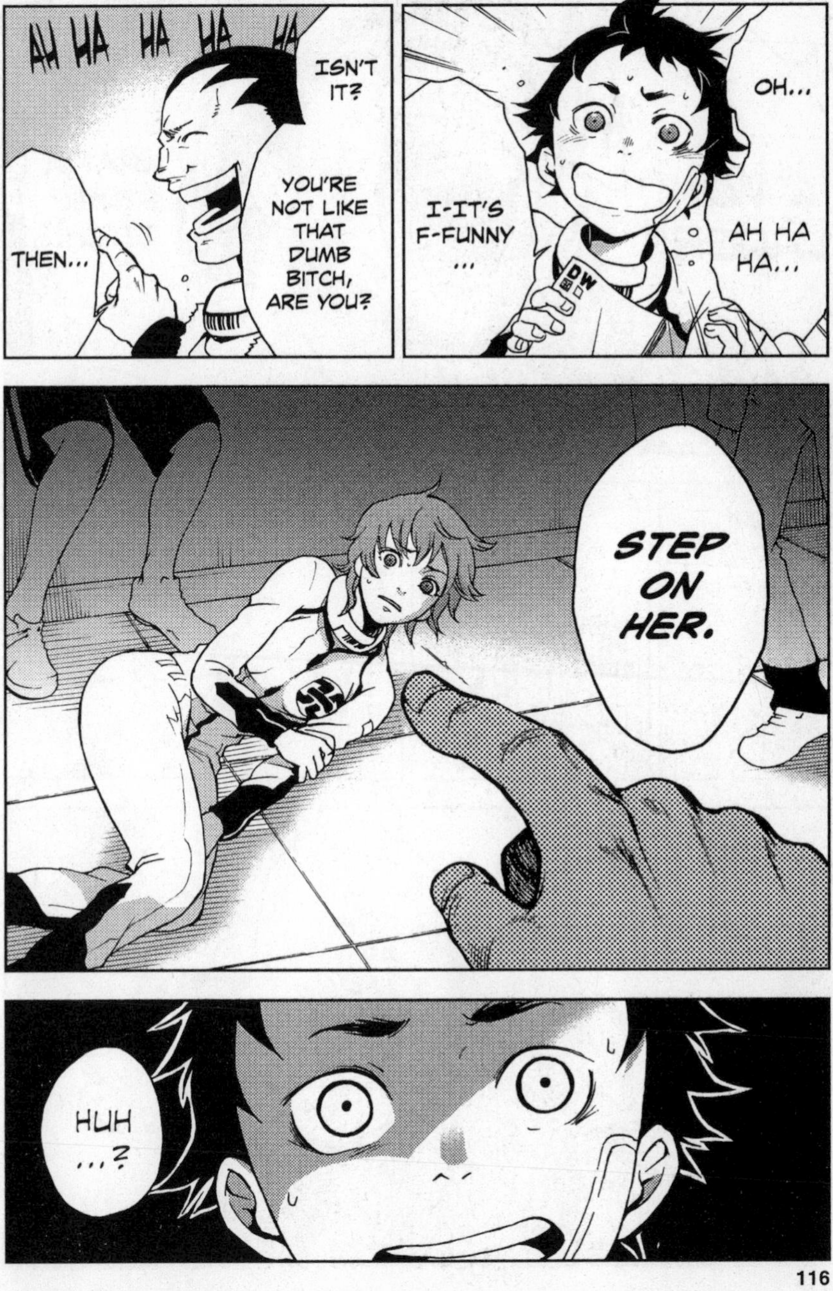
OH...
AH HA HA...
I-IT'S F-FUNNY ...
AH HA HA HA HA
ISN'T IT?
YOU'RE NOT LIKE THAT DUMB BITCH, ARE YOU?
THEN...
STEP ON HER.
HUH ...?

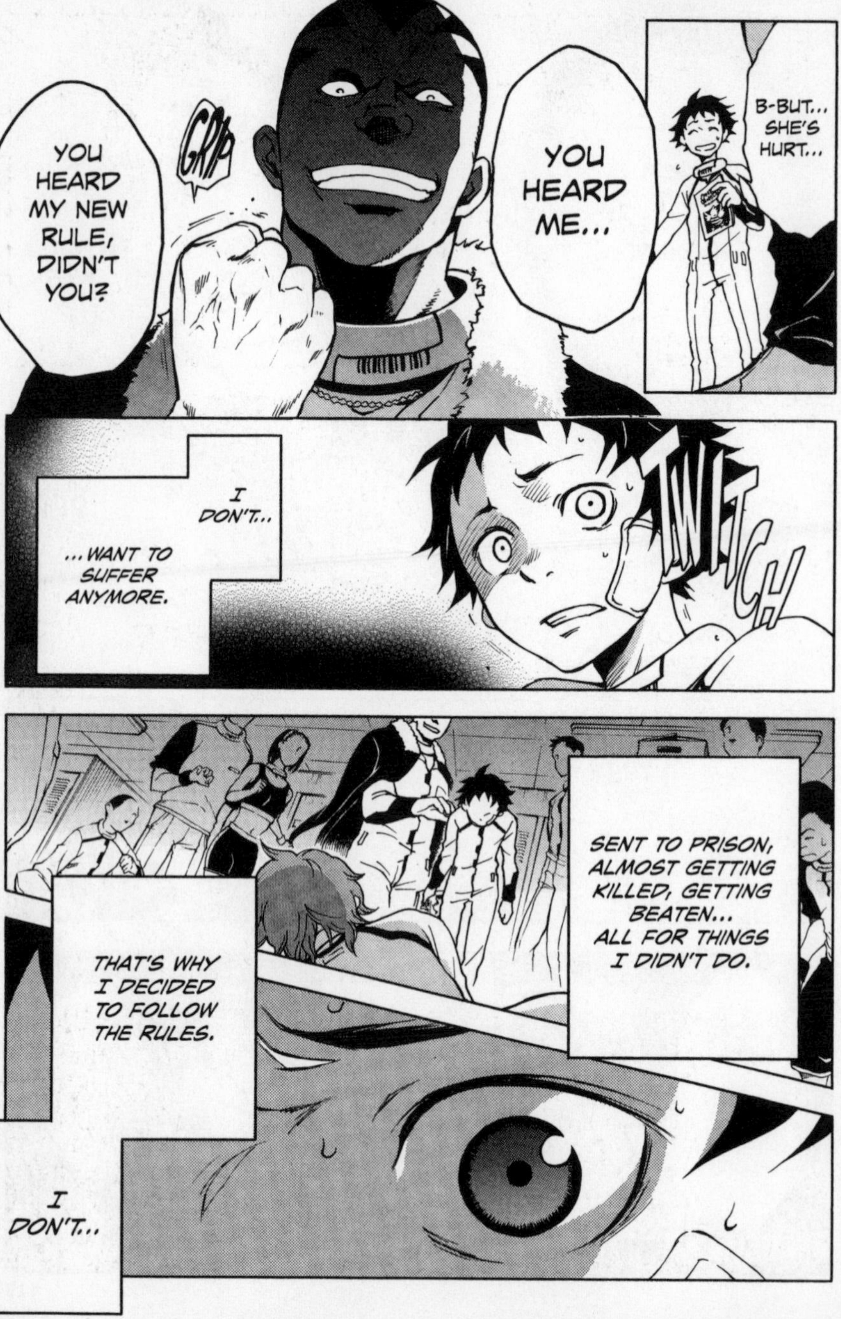
B-BUT... SHE'S HURT...
YOU HEARD ME...
GRIP
YOU HEARD MY NEW RULE, DIDN'T YOU?
TWITCH
I DON'T...
...WANT TO SUFFER ANYMORE.
SENT TO PRISON, ALMOST GETTING KILLED, GETTING BEATEN... ALL FOR THINGS I DIDN'T DO.
THAT'S WHY I DECIDED TO FOLLOW THE RULES.
I DON'T...

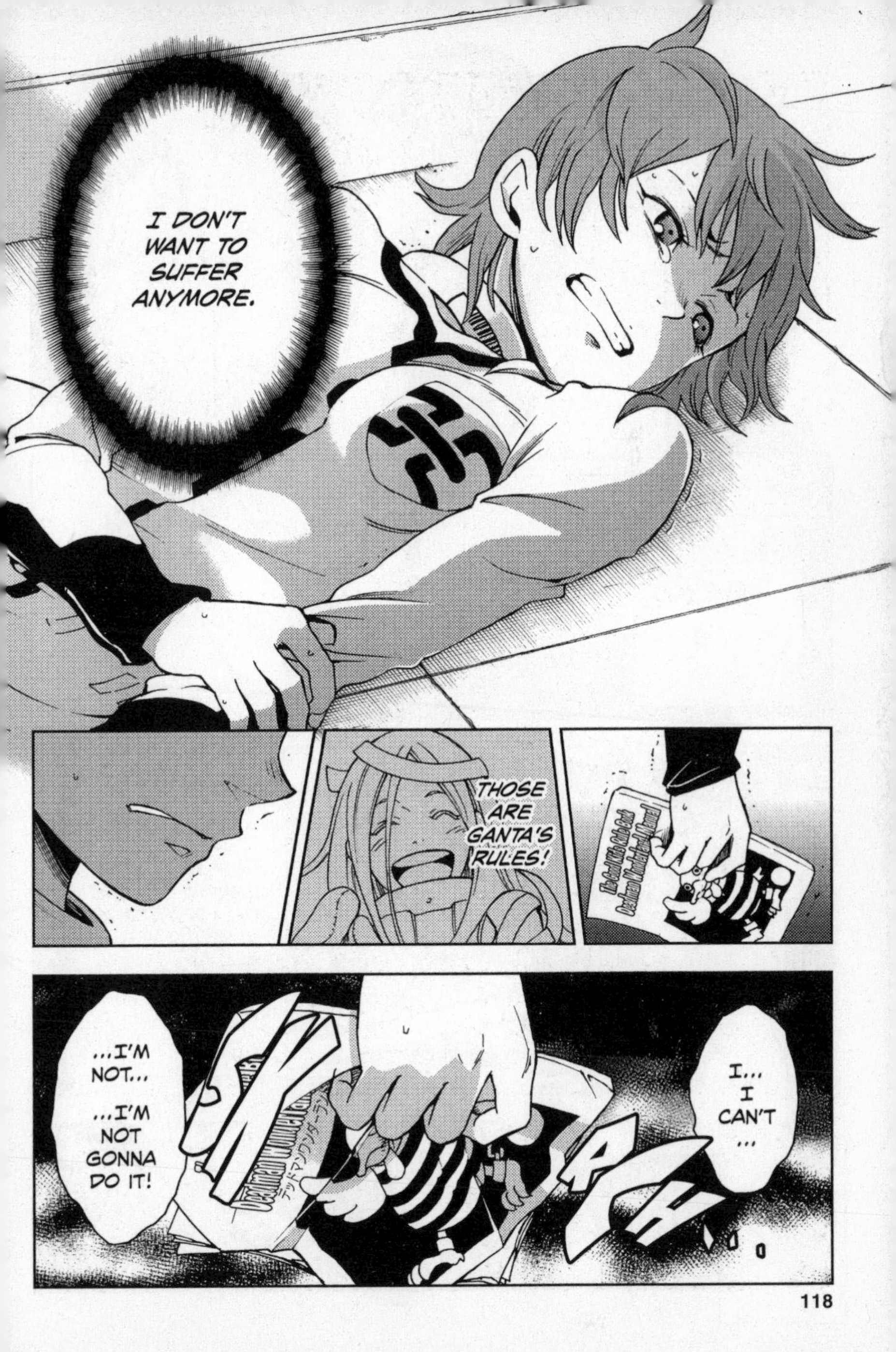
I DON'T WANT TO SUFFER ANYMORE.
THOSE ARE GANTA'S RULES!
I... I CAN'T ...
...I'M NOT...
...I'M NOT GONNA DO IT!

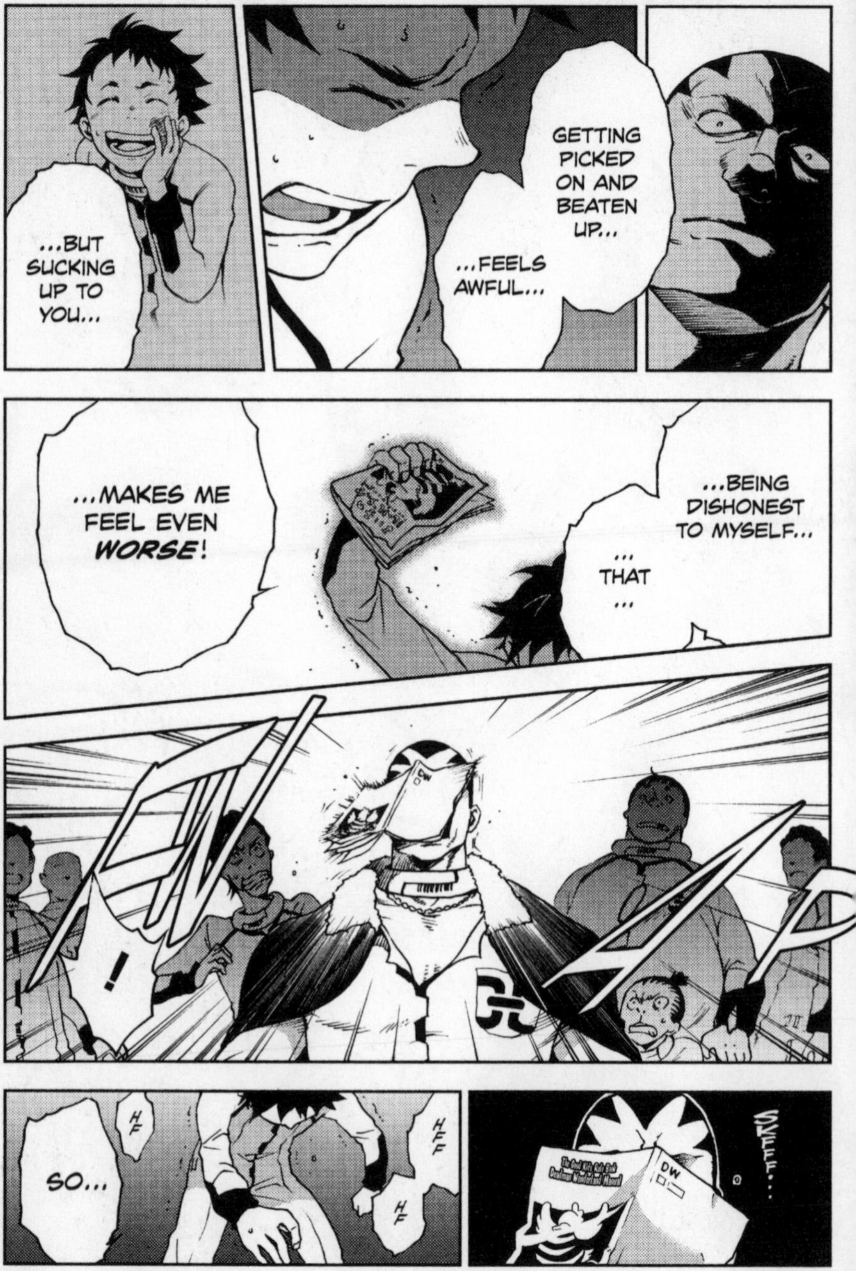
GETTING PICKED ON AND BEATEN UP...
...FEELS AWFUL...
...BUT SUCKING UP TO YOU...
...BEING DISHONEST TO MYSELF...
... THAT ...
...MAKES ME FEEL EVEN *WORSE*!
!
SNFFF...
DW
The Good Kids Rule Book Deadman Wonderland Manual
HFF
HF
HF
SO...

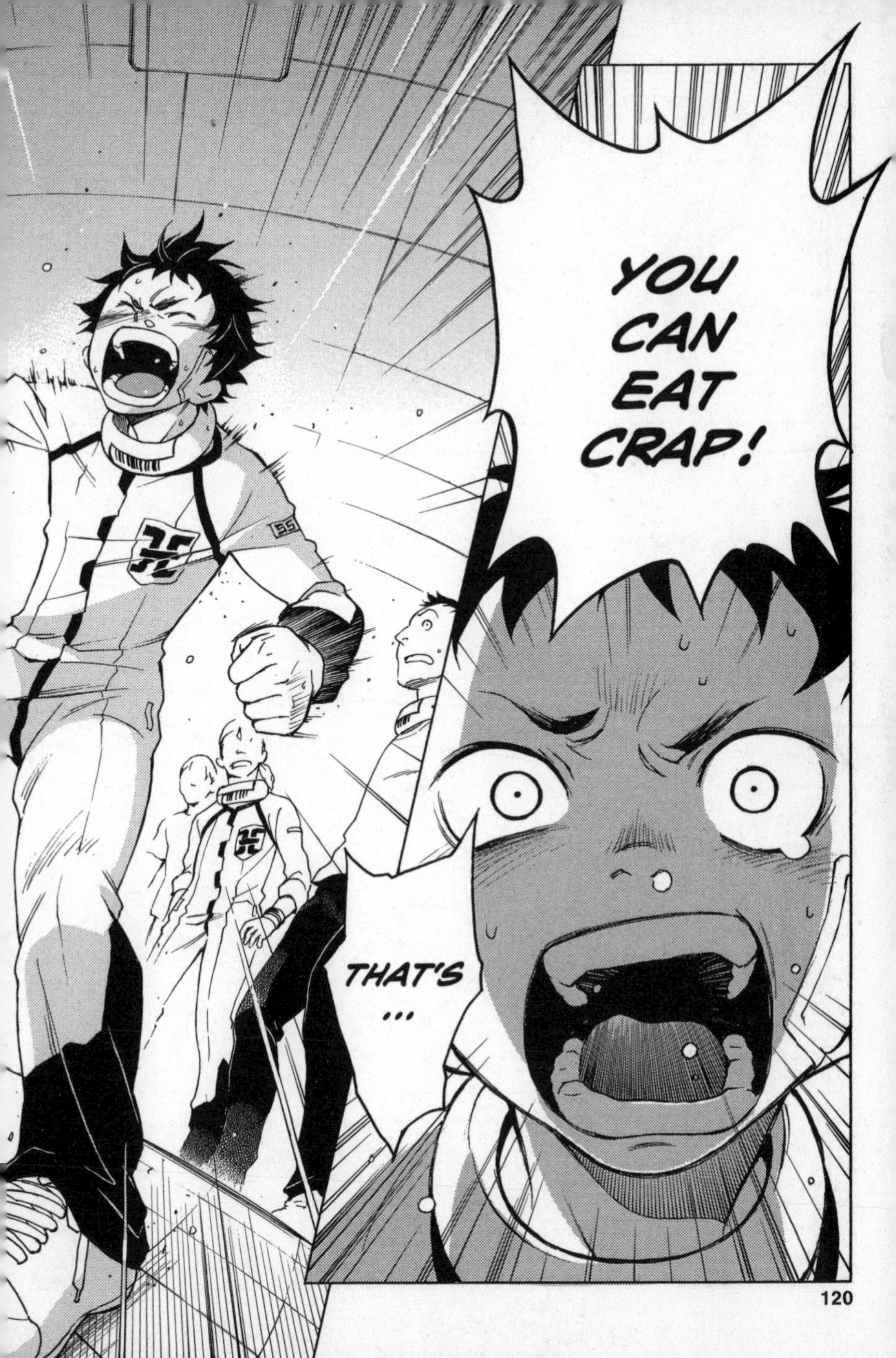
YOU CAN EAT CRAP!
THAT'S ...

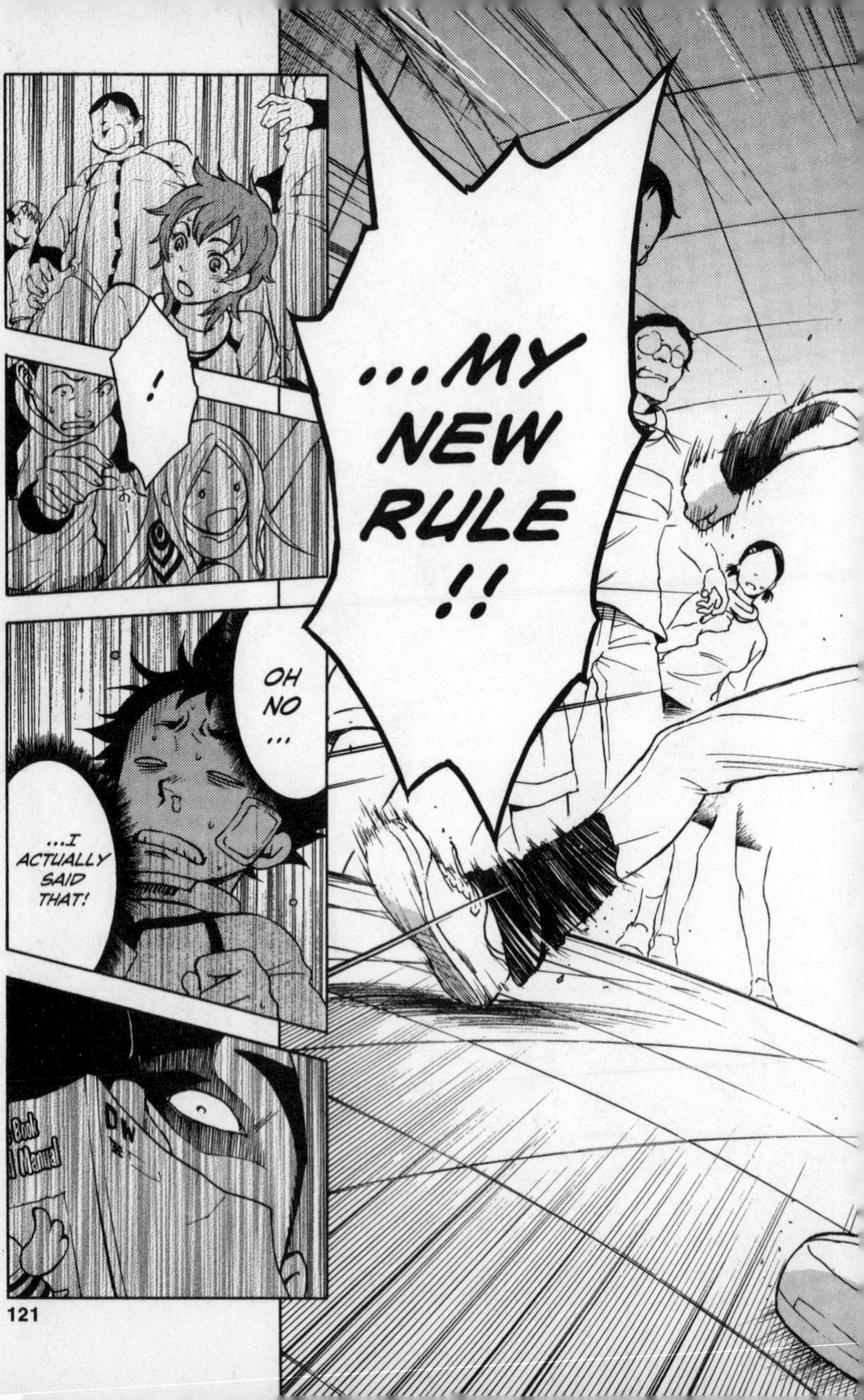
...MY NEW RULE !!
!
OH NO ...
...I ACTUALLY SAID THAT!

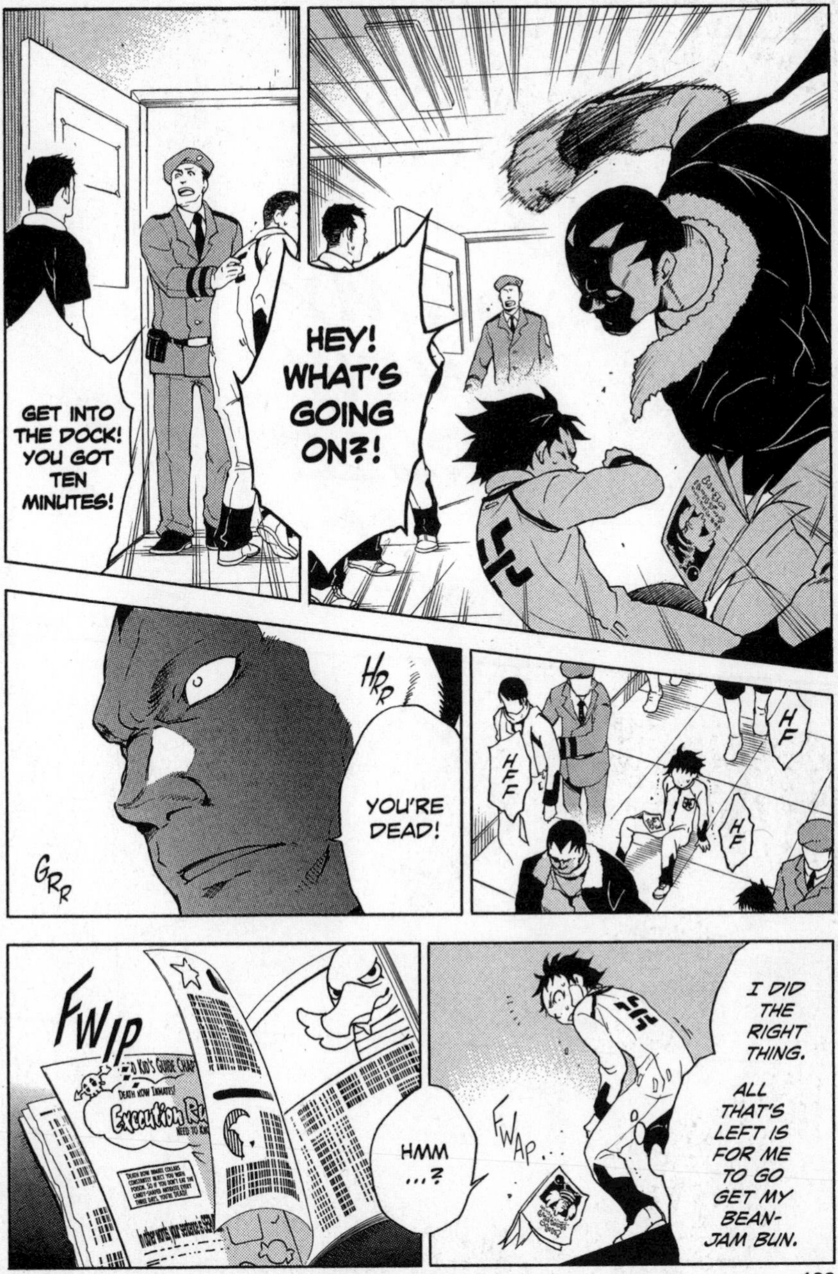
HEY! WHAT'S GOING ON?!
GET INTO THE DOCK! YOU GOT TEN MINUTES!
HF
HEF
HF
HRR
YOU'RE DEAD!
GRR
I DID THE RIGHT THING.
ALL THAT'S LEFT IS FOR ME TO GO GET MY BEAN-JAM BUN.
FWAP...
FWIP
HMM ...?

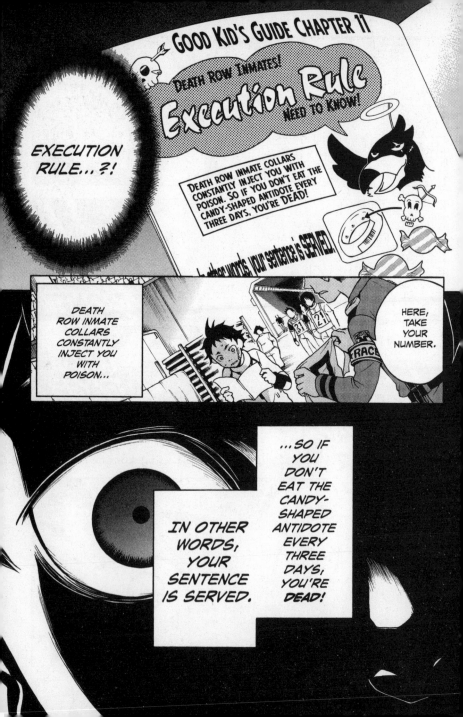

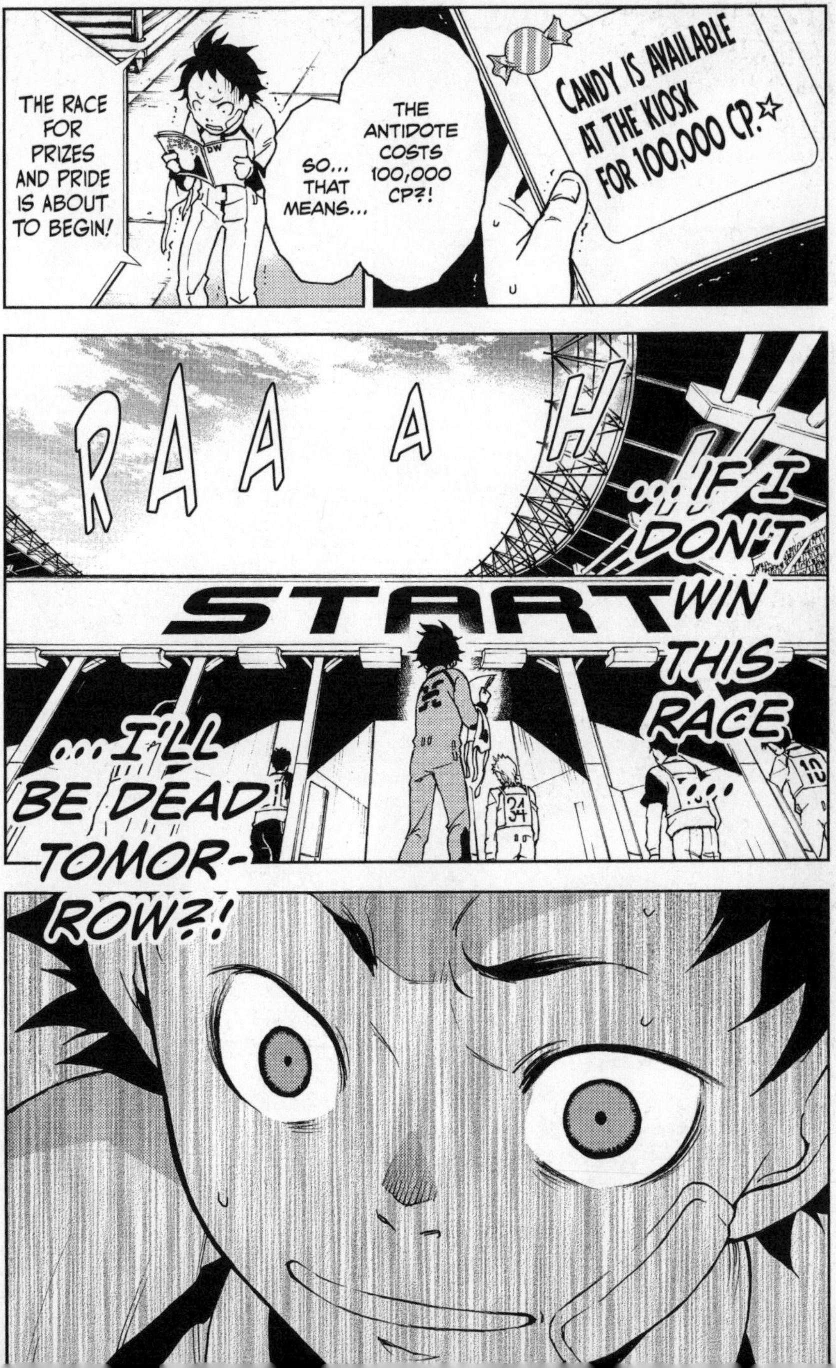
CANDY IS AVAILABLE AT THE KIOSK FOR 100,000 CP.☆
THE ANTIDOTE COSTS 100,000 CP?!
SO... THAT MEANS...
THE RACE FOR PRIZES AND PRIDE IS ABOUT TO BEGIN!
RAAAH
START
...IF I DON'T WIN THIS RACE...
...I'LL BE DEAD TOMOR-ROW?!

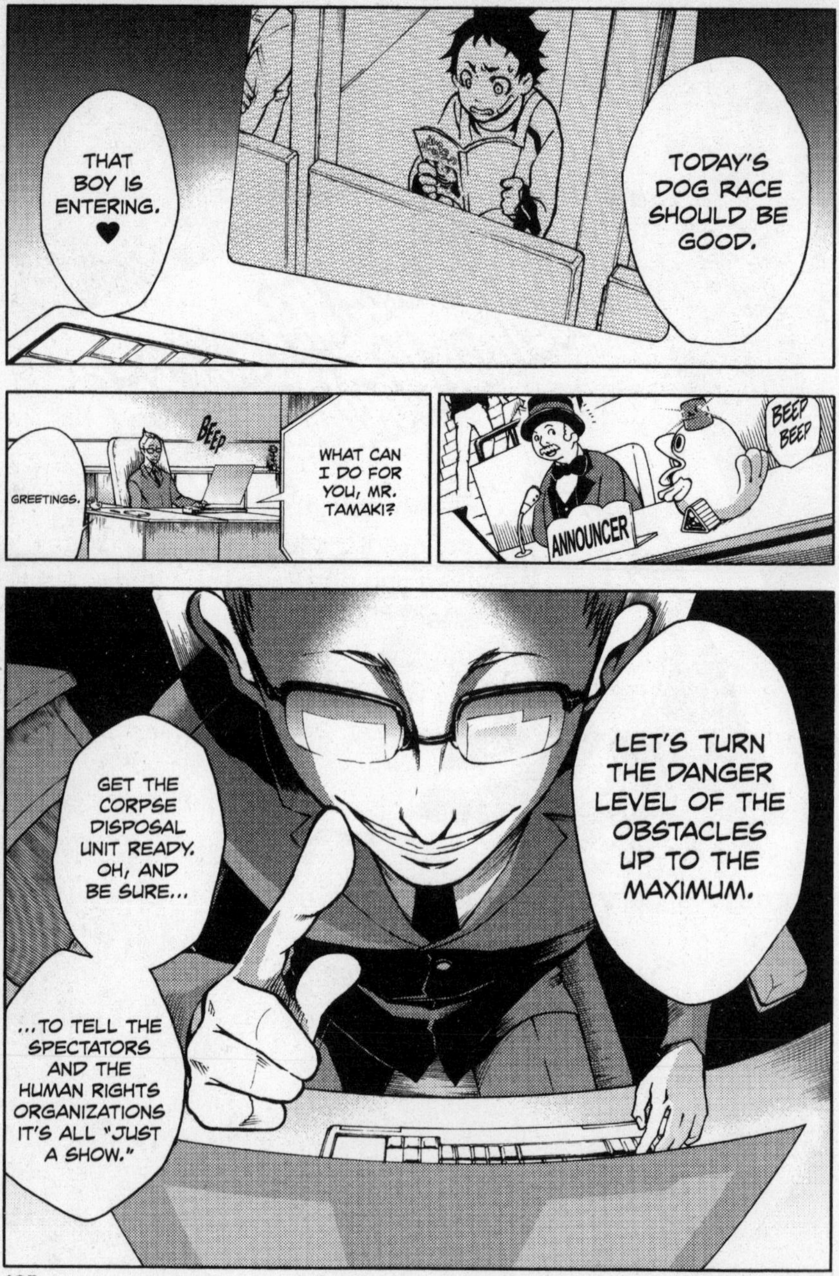
TODAY'S DOG RACE SHOULD BE GOOD.
THAT BOY IS ENTERING. ♥
BEEP BEEP
ANNOUNCER
WHAT CAN I DO FOR YOU, MR. TAMAKI?
BEEP
GREETINGS.
LET'S TURN THE DANGER LEVEL OF THE OBSTACLES UP TO THE MAXIMUM.
GET THE CORPSE DISPOSAL UNIT READY. OH, AND BE SURE...
...TO TELL THE SPECTATORS AND THE HUMAN RIGHTS ORGANIZATIONS IT'S ALL "JUST A SHOW."

## The Execution Rule

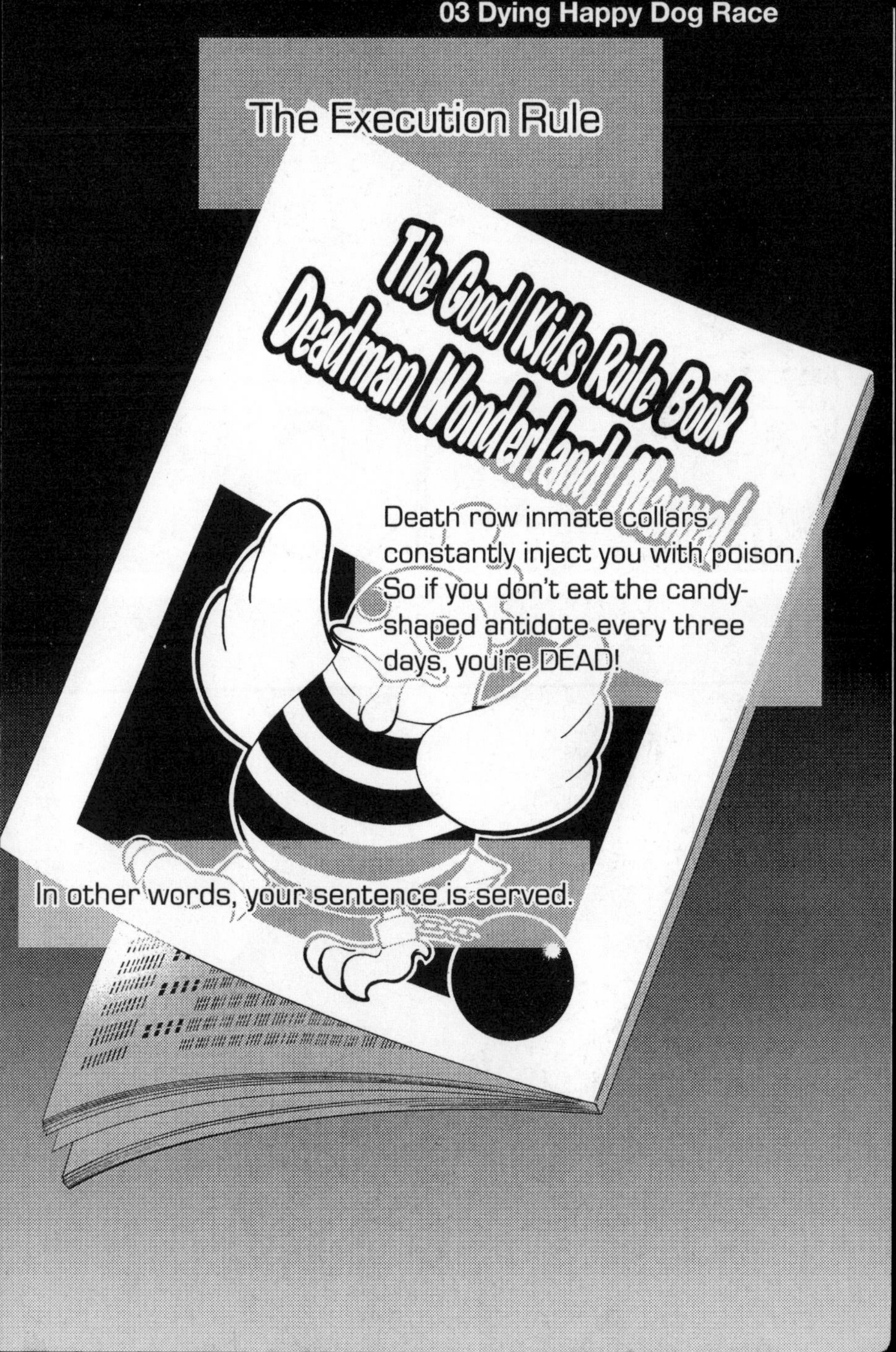
The Good Kids Rule Book
Deadman Wonderland

Death row inmate collars constantly inject you with poison. So if you don't eat the candy-shaped antidote every three days, you're DEAD!

In other words, your sentence is served.

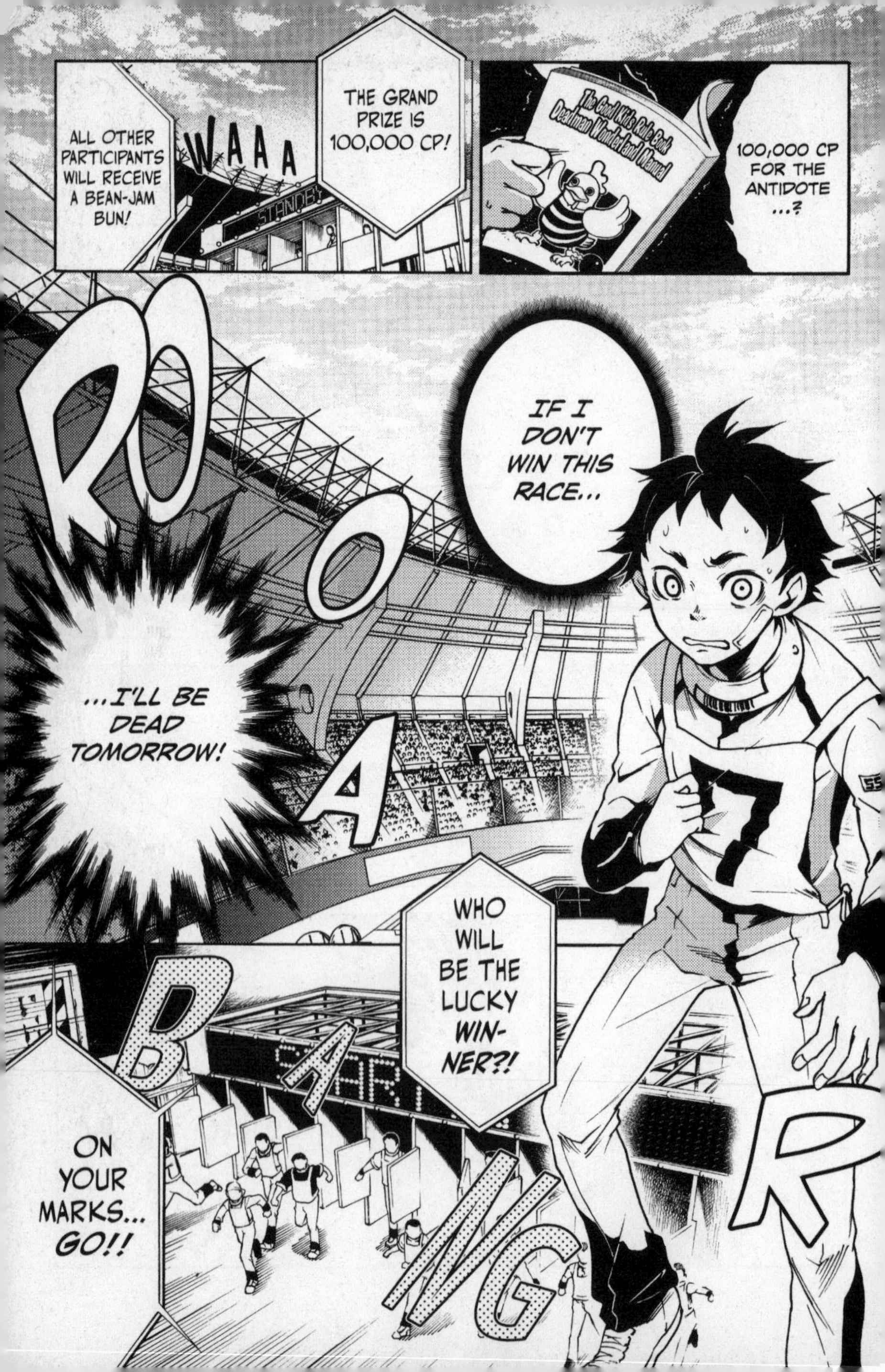
The Good Kids Rule Book
Deadman Wonderland Manual
100,000 CP FOR THE ANTIDOTE ...?
THE GRAND PRIZE IS 100,000 CP!
WAAA
STANDBY
ALL OTHER PARTICIPANTS WILL RECEIVE A BEAN-JAM BUN!
IF I DON'T WIN THIS RACE...
...I'LL BE DEAD TOMORROW!
ROOAR
WHO WILL BE THE LUCKY WIN-NER?!
ON YOUR MARKS... GO!!
BANG

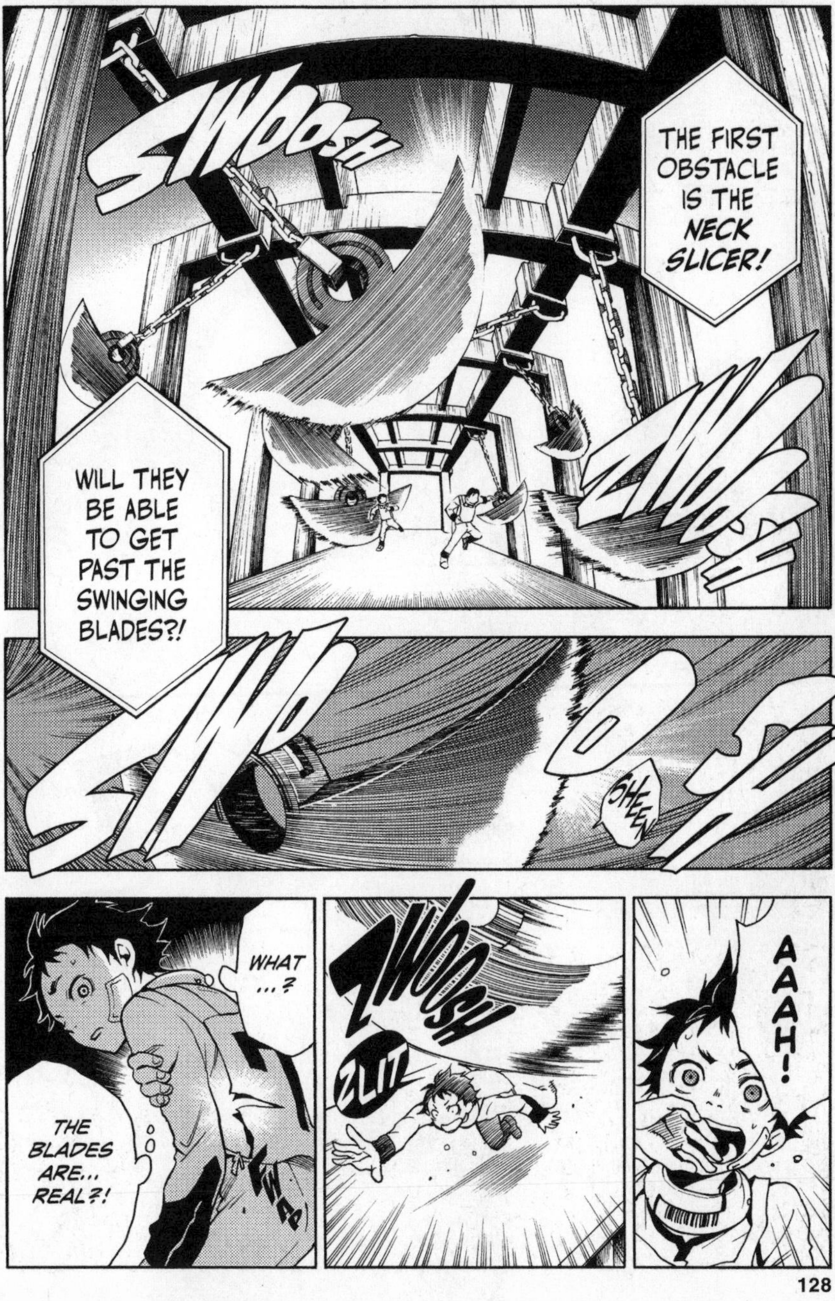
THE FIRST OBSTACLE IS THE NECK SLICER!
SWOOSH
ZWOOSH
WILL THEY BE ABLE TO GET PAST THE SWINGING BLADES?!
SWOOSH
SHEEN
AAAH!
ZWOOSH
ZLIT
WHAT ...?
THE BLADES ARE... REAL?!

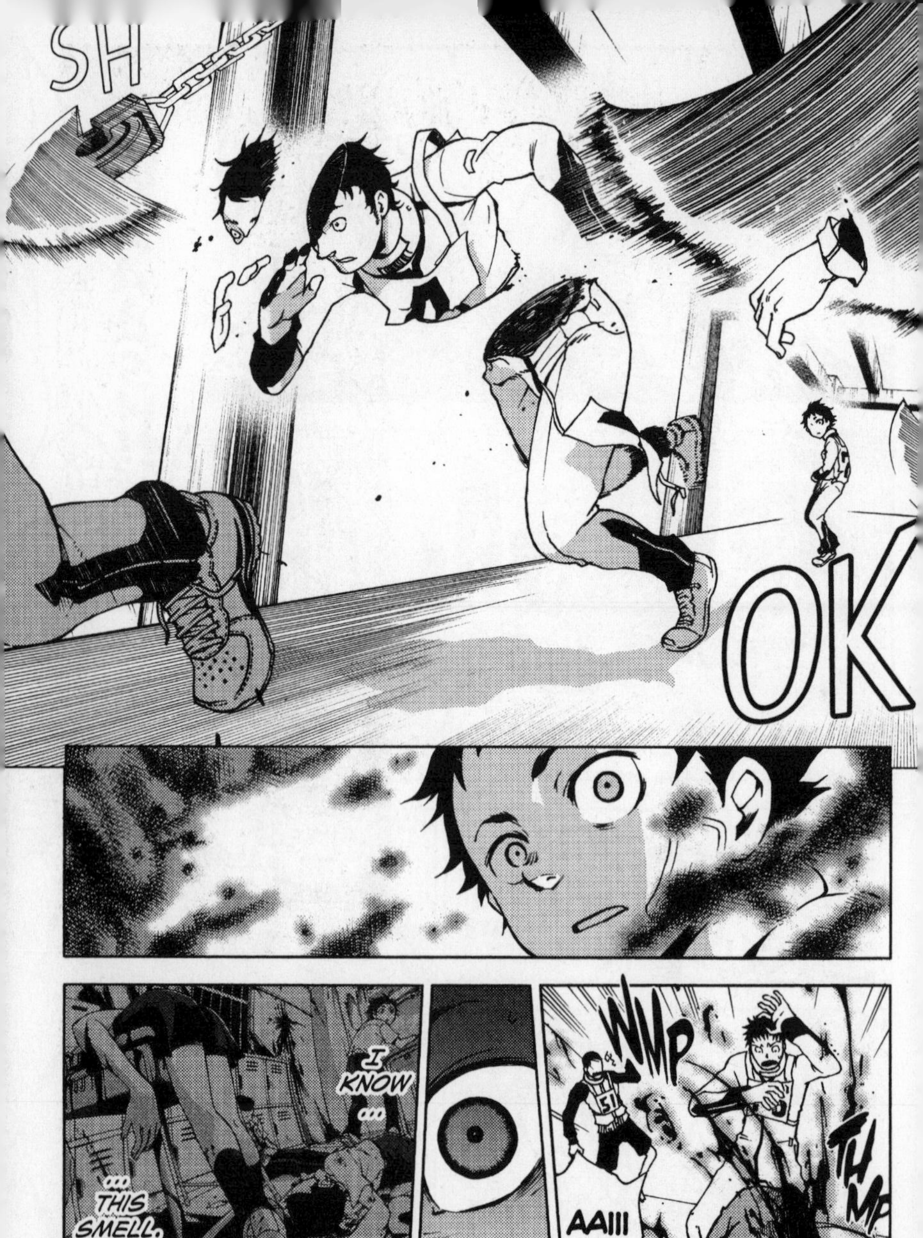
SH
OK
WMP
THMP
AAIII !!
I KNOW ...
... THIS SMELL.

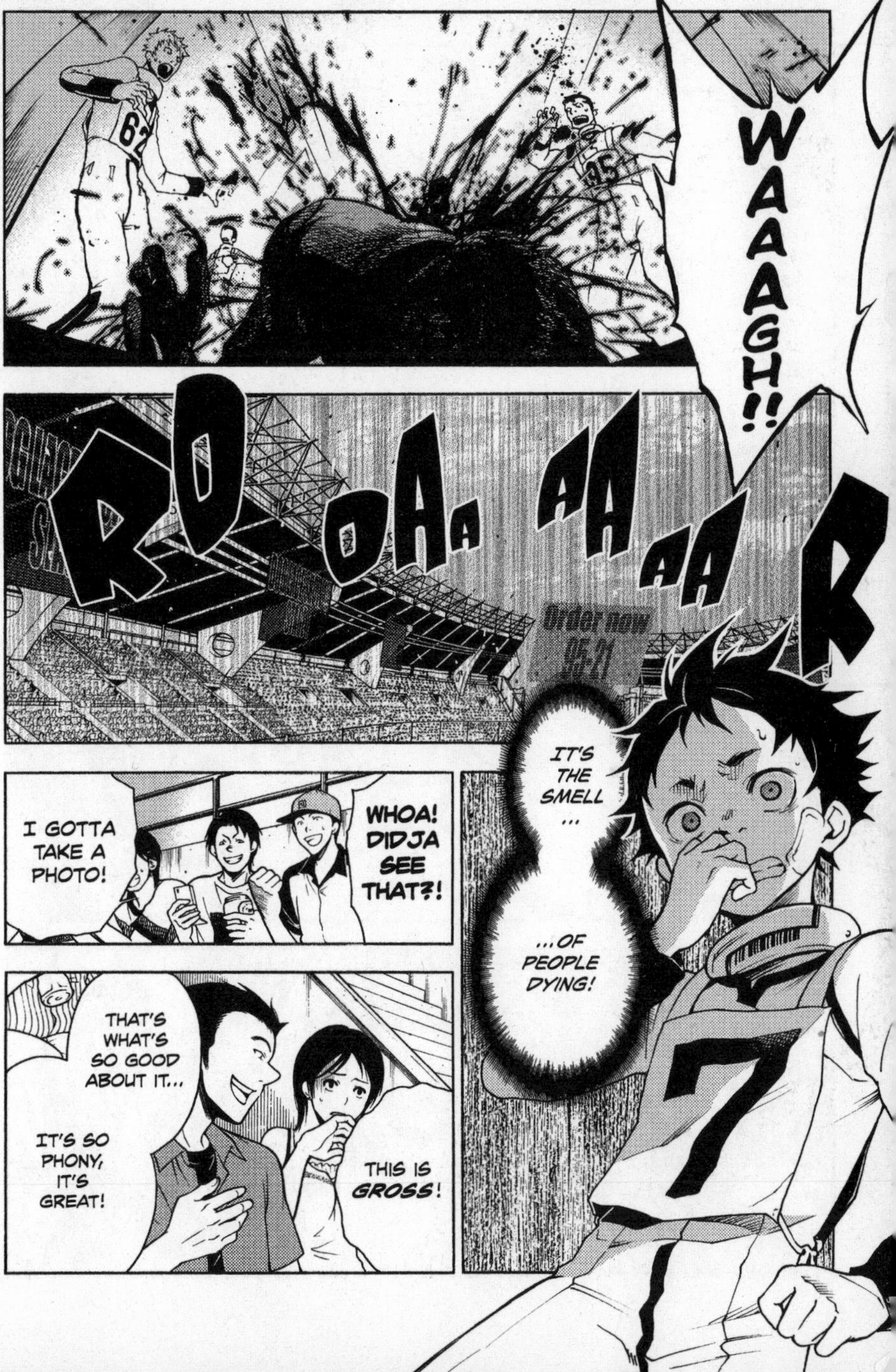
WAAAAGH!!
ROOAAAAAAR
IT'S THE SMELL ...
...OF PEOPLE DYING!
WHOA! DIDJA SEE THAT?!
I GOTTA TAKE A PHOTO!
THIS IS GROSS!
THAT'S WHAT'S SO GOOD ABOUT IT...
IT'S SO PHONY, IT'S GREAT!

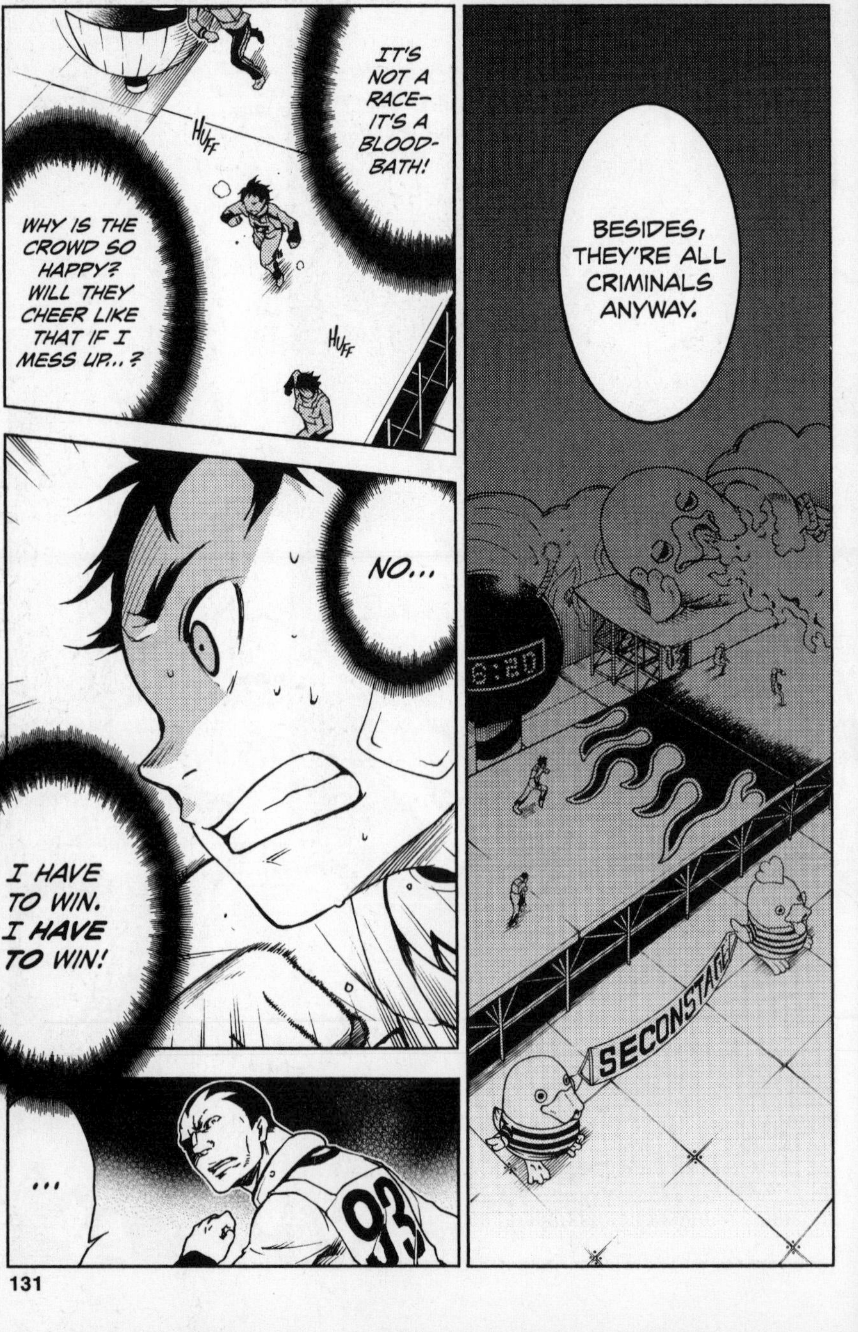
BESIDES, THEY'RE ALL CRIMINALS ANYWAY.
SECONSTAGE
IT'S NOT A RACE—IT'S A BLOOD-BATH!
HUFF
WHY IS THE CROWD SO HAPPY? WILL THEY CHEER LIKE THAT IF I MESS UP...?
HUFF
NO...
I HAVE TO WIN. I HAVE TO WIN!
...

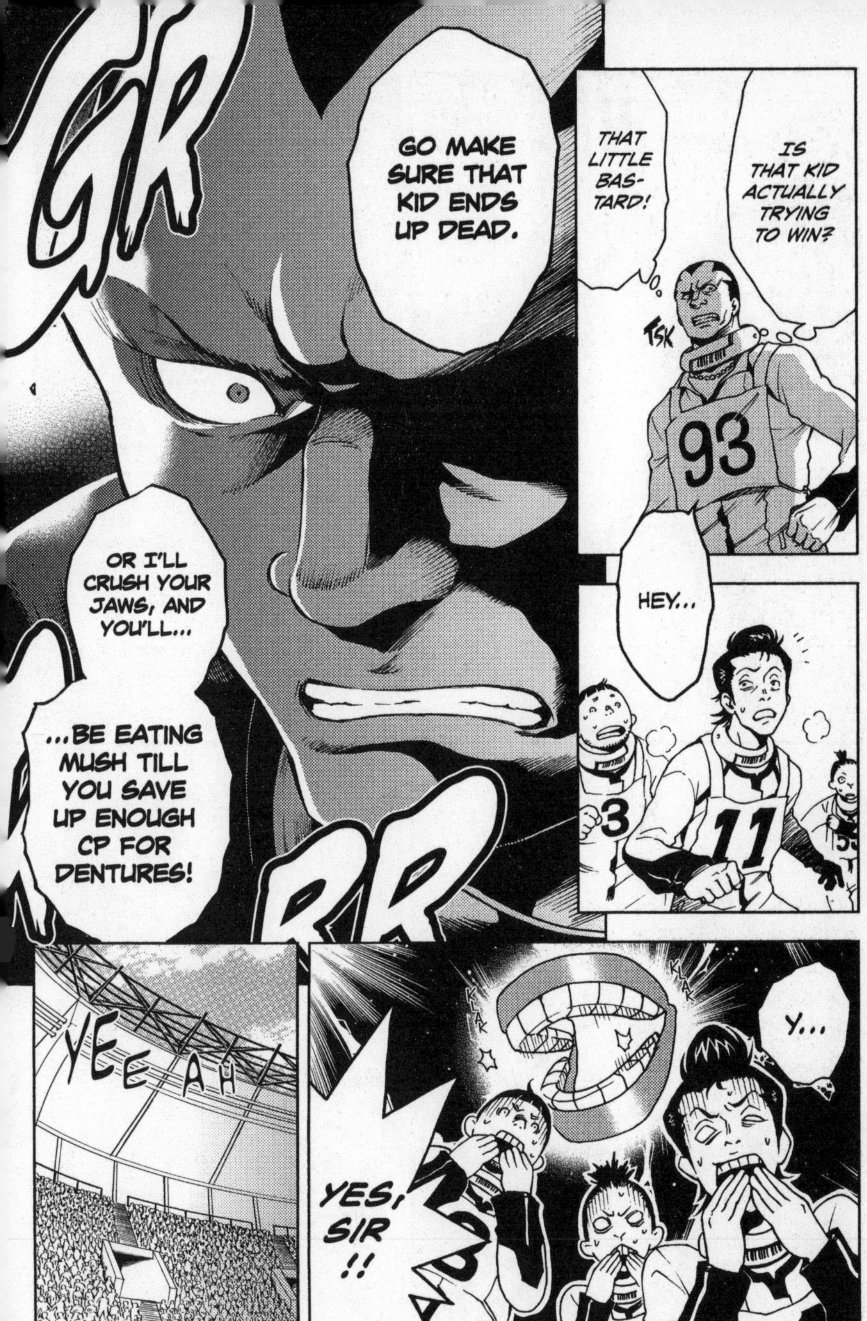
IS THAT KID ACTUALLY TRYING TO WIN?
THAT LITTLE BAS-TARD!
TSK
HEY...
GO MAKE SURE THAT KID ENDS UP DEAD.
GR
OR I'LL CRUSH YOUR JAWS, AND YOU'LL...
...BE EATING MUSH TILL YOU SAVE UP ENOUGH CP FOR DENTURES!
RR
Y...
KLAK
KLAK
YES, SIR !!
YEEAH

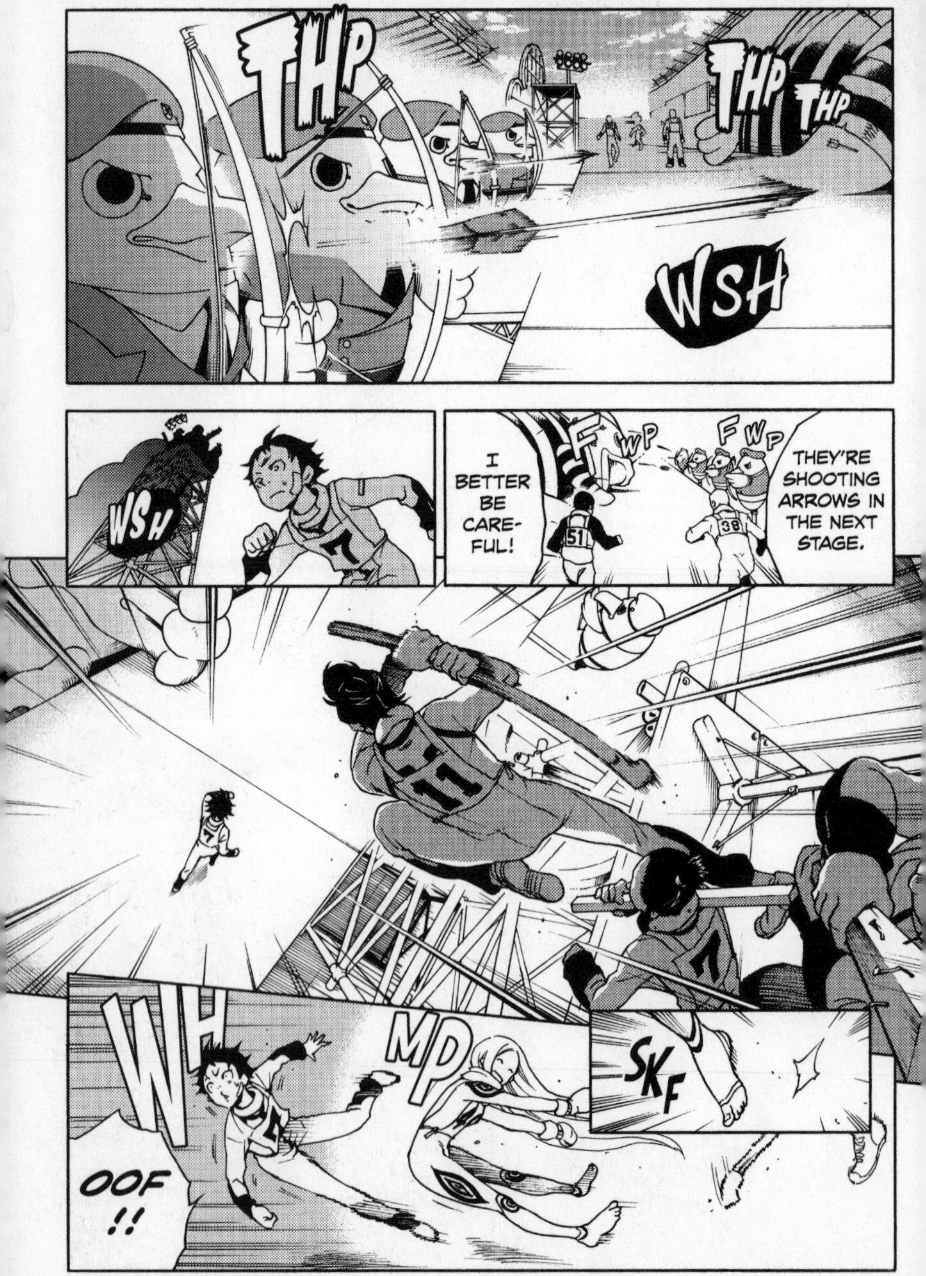
THP THP
THP
WSH
THEY'RE SHOOTING ARROWS IN THE NEXT STAGE.
FWP
FWP
I BETTER BE CARE-FUL!
WSH
SKF
MP
WH
OOF !!

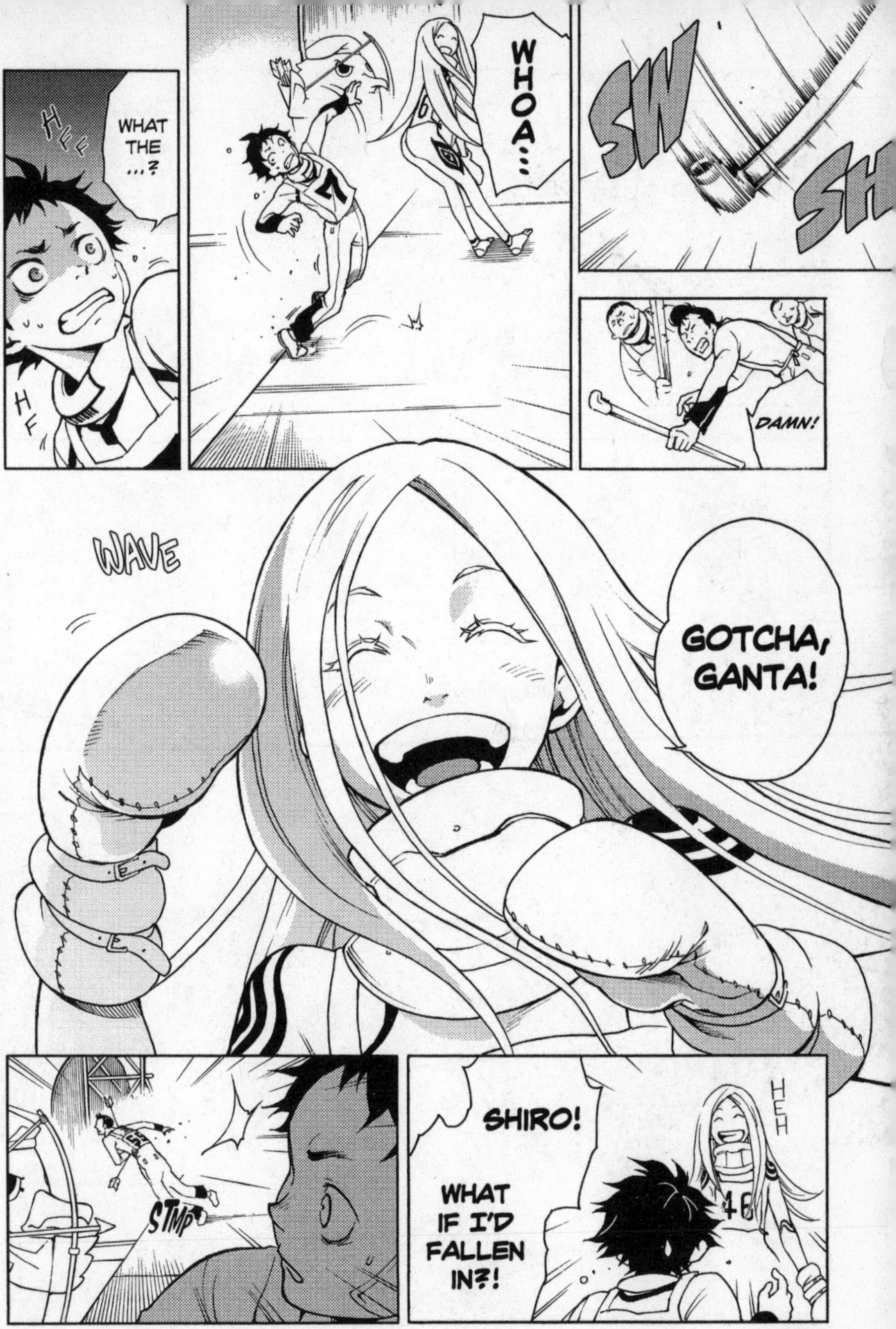
SW
SH
DAMN!
WHOA...
WHAT THE ...?
HFF
HF
GOTCHA, GANTA!
WAVE
HEH
SHIRO!
WHAT IF I'D FALLEN IN?!
STMP

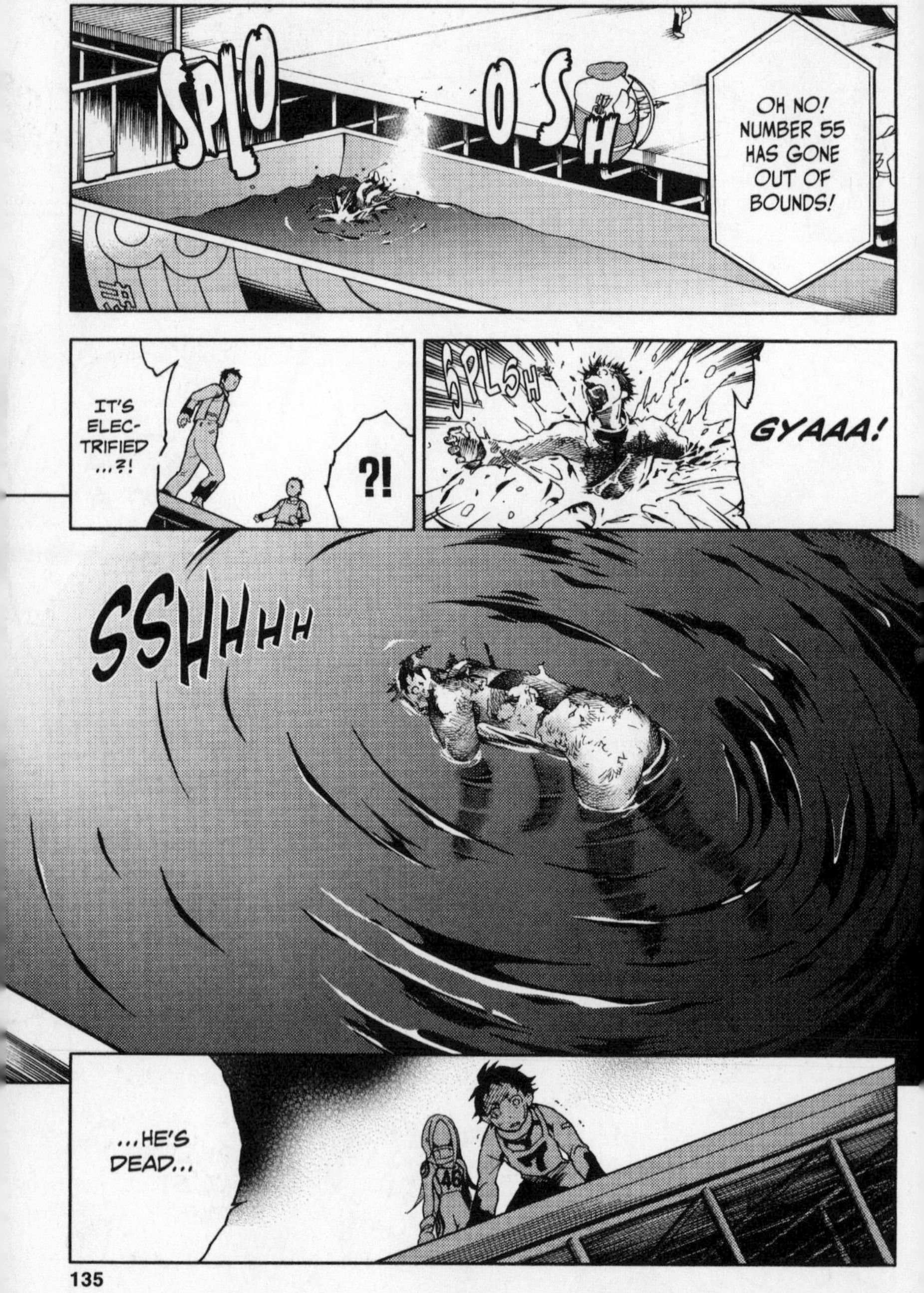
OH NO! NUMBER 55 HAS GONE OUT OF BOUNDS!
SPLOOSH
SPLSH
GYAAA!
?!
IT'S ELECTRIFIED ...?!
SSHHHHH
...HE'S DEAD...

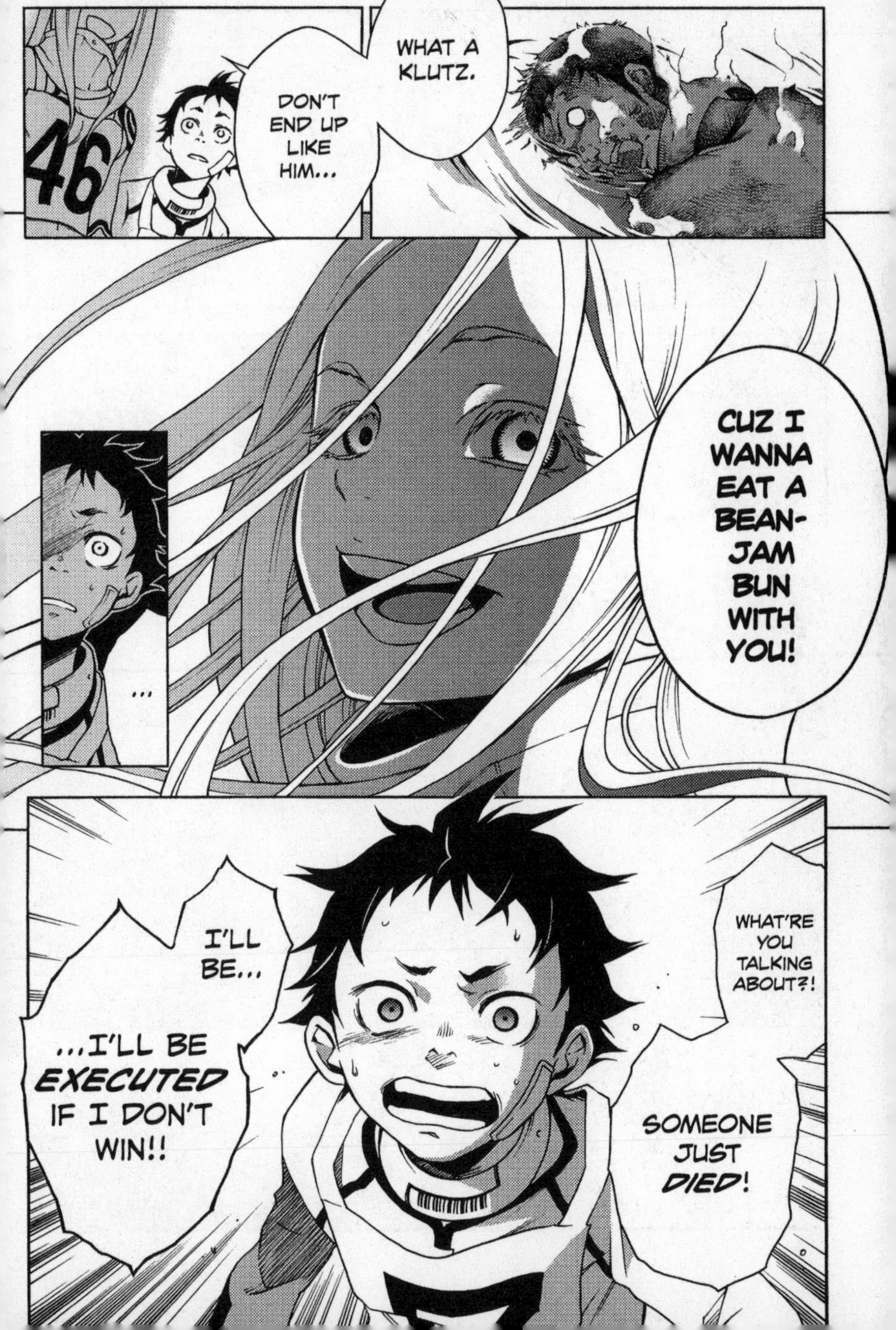
WHAT A KLUTZ.
DON'T END UP LIKE HIM...
46
CUZ I WANNA EAT A BEAN-JAM BUN WITH YOU!
...
WHAT'RE YOU TALKING ABOUT?!
SOMEONE JUST *DIED*!
I'LL BE...
...I'LL BE *EXECUTED* IF I DON'T WIN!!

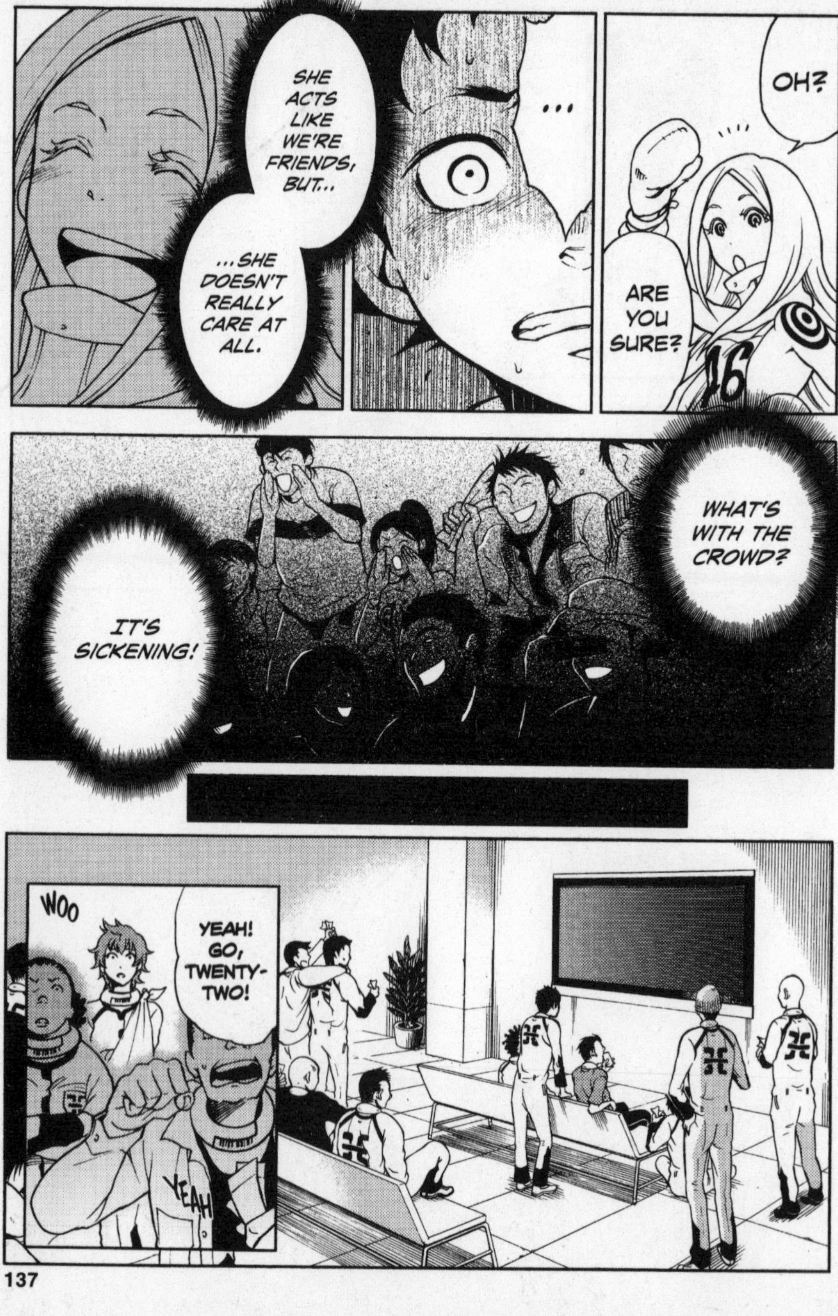
OH?
ARE YOU SURE?
...
SHE ACTS LIKE WE'RE FRIENDS, BUT...
...SHE DOESN'T REALLY CARE AT ALL.
WHAT'S WITH THE CROWD?
IT'S SICKENING!
YEAH! GO, TWENTY-TWO!
WOO
YEAH

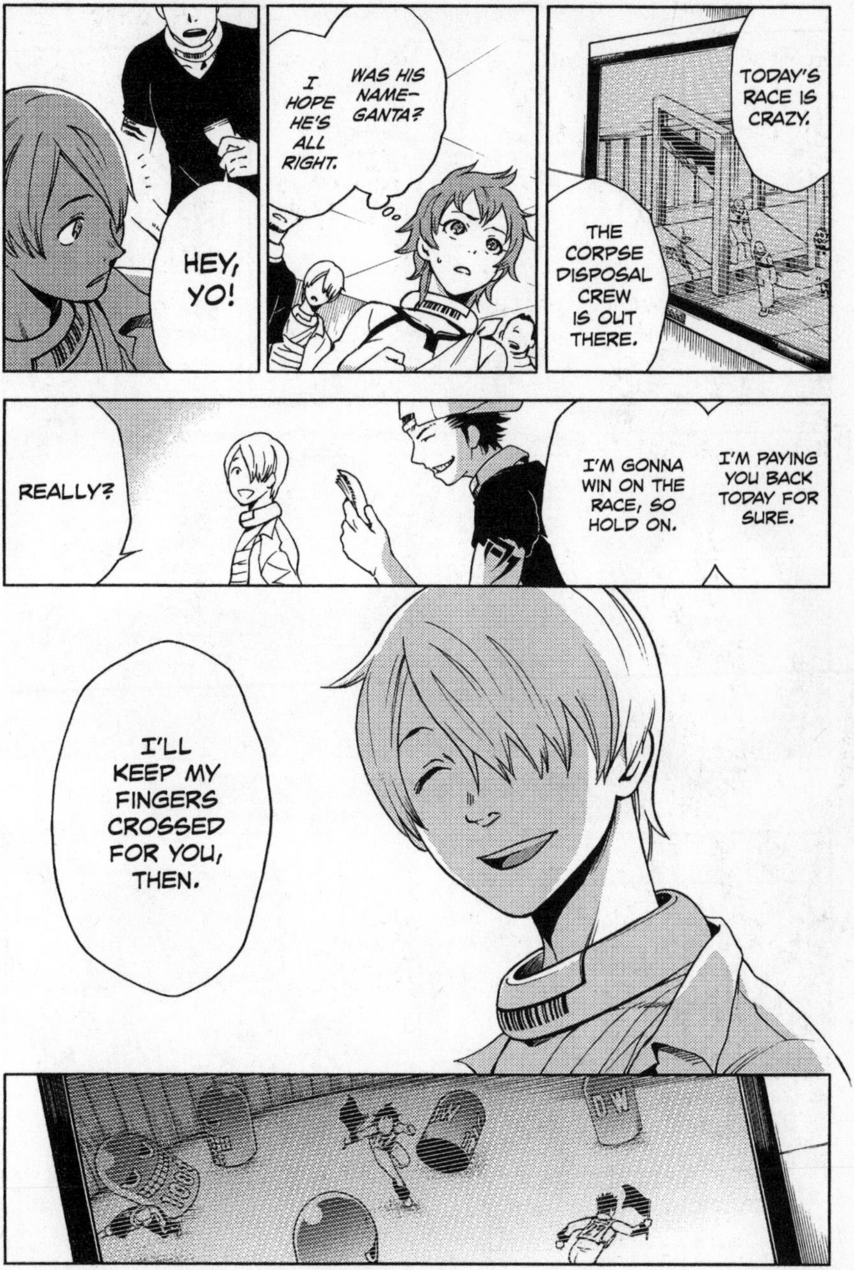
TODAY'S RACE IS CRAZY.
THE CORPSE DISPOSAL CREW IS OUT THERE.
WAS HIS NAME—GANTA?
I HOPE HE'S ALL RIGHT.
HEY, YO!
I'M PAYING YOU BACK TODAY FOR SURE.
I'M GONNA WIN ON THE RACE, SO HOLD ON.
REALLY?
I'LL KEEP MY FINGERS CROSSED FOR YOU, THEN.

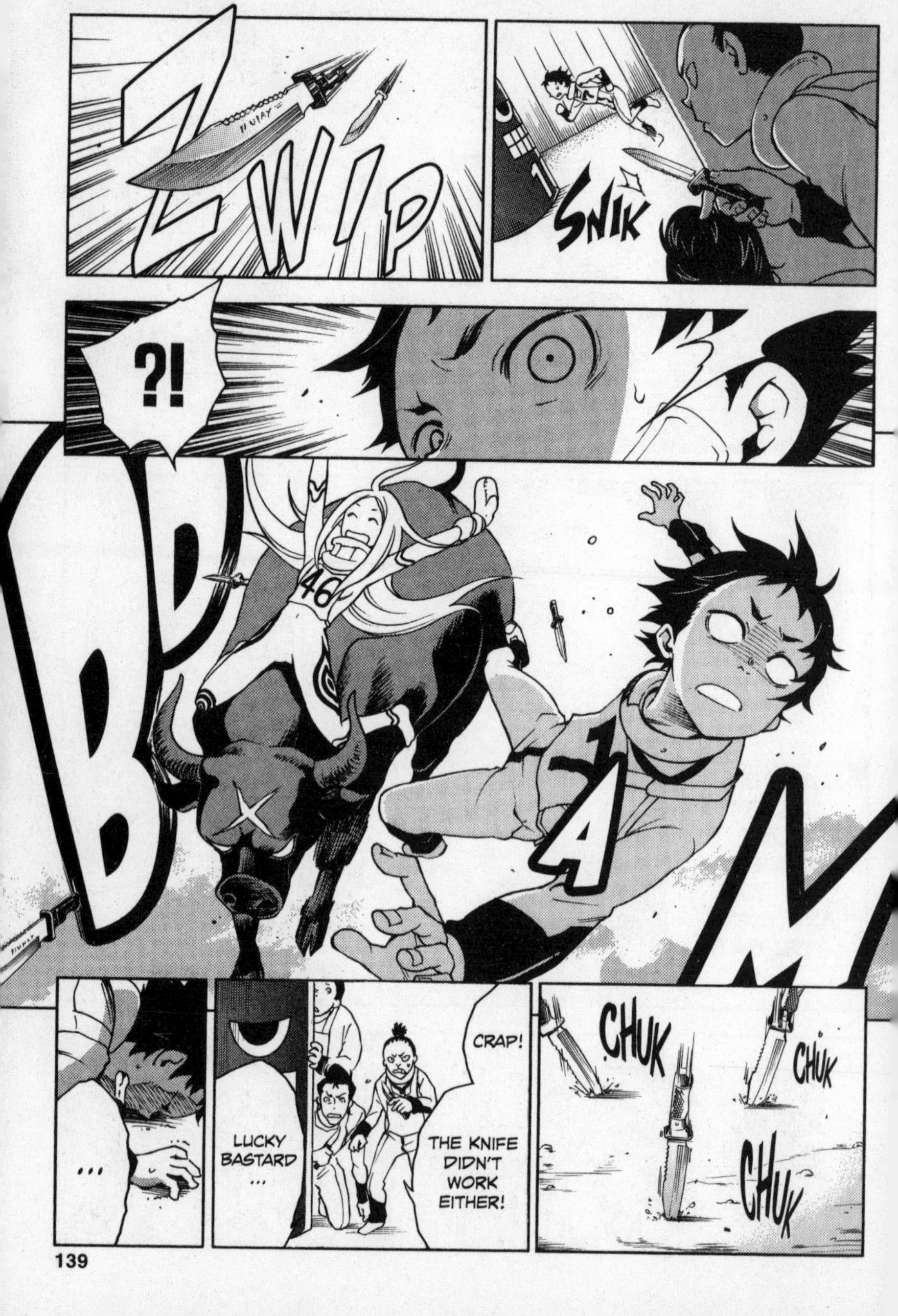
SNIK
ZWIP
?!
BAM
CHUK
CHUK
CHUK
CRAP!
THE KNIFE DIDN'T WORK EITHER!
LUCKY BASTARD ...
...

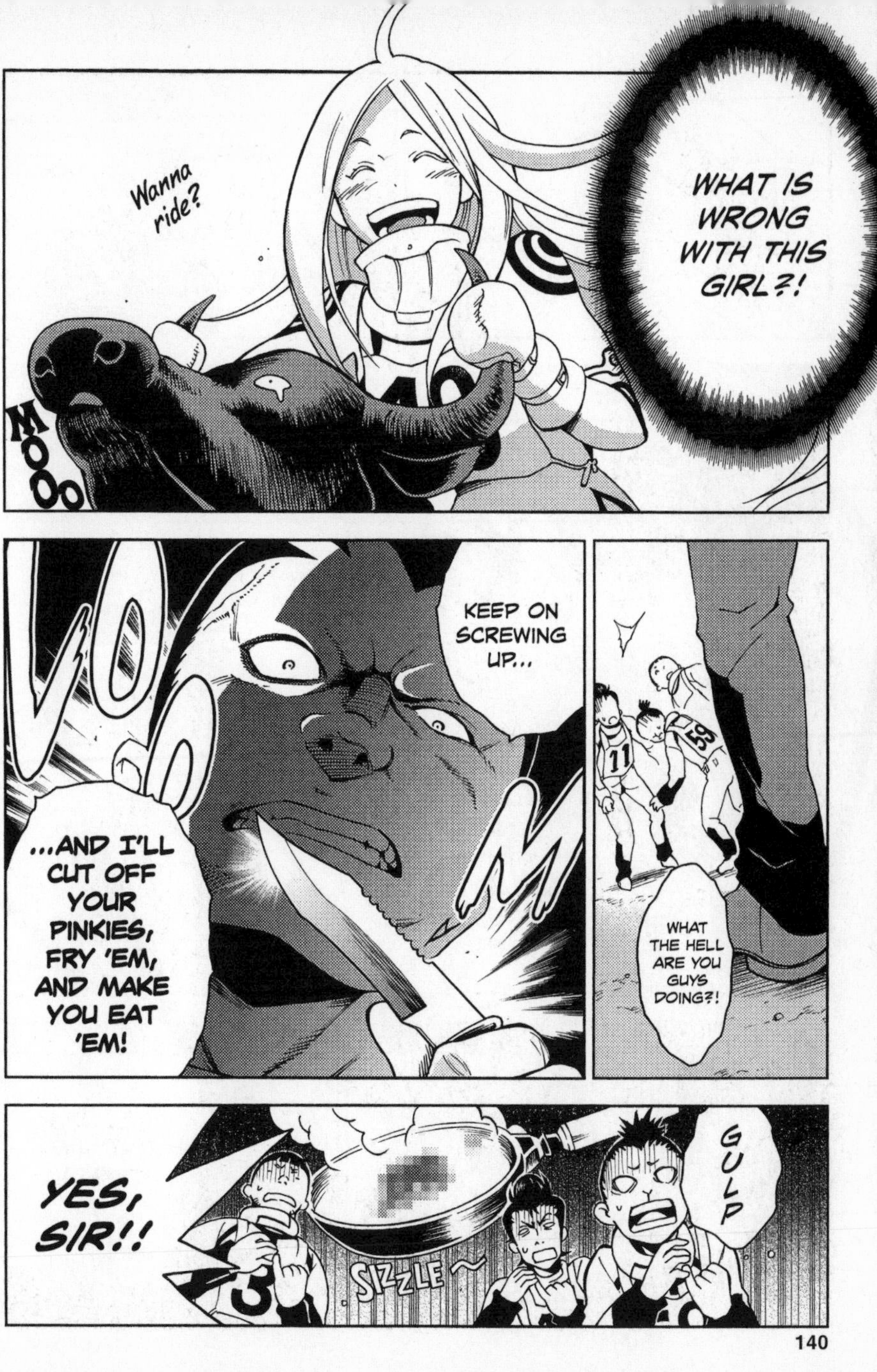
WHAT IS WRONG WITH THIS GIRL?!
Wanna ride?
MOOO
WHAT THE HELL ARE YOU GUYS DOING?!
KEEP ON SCREWING UP...
...AND I'LL CUT OFF YOUR PINKIES, FRY 'EM, AND MAKE YOU EAT 'EM!
GULP
YES, SIR!!
SIZZLE~

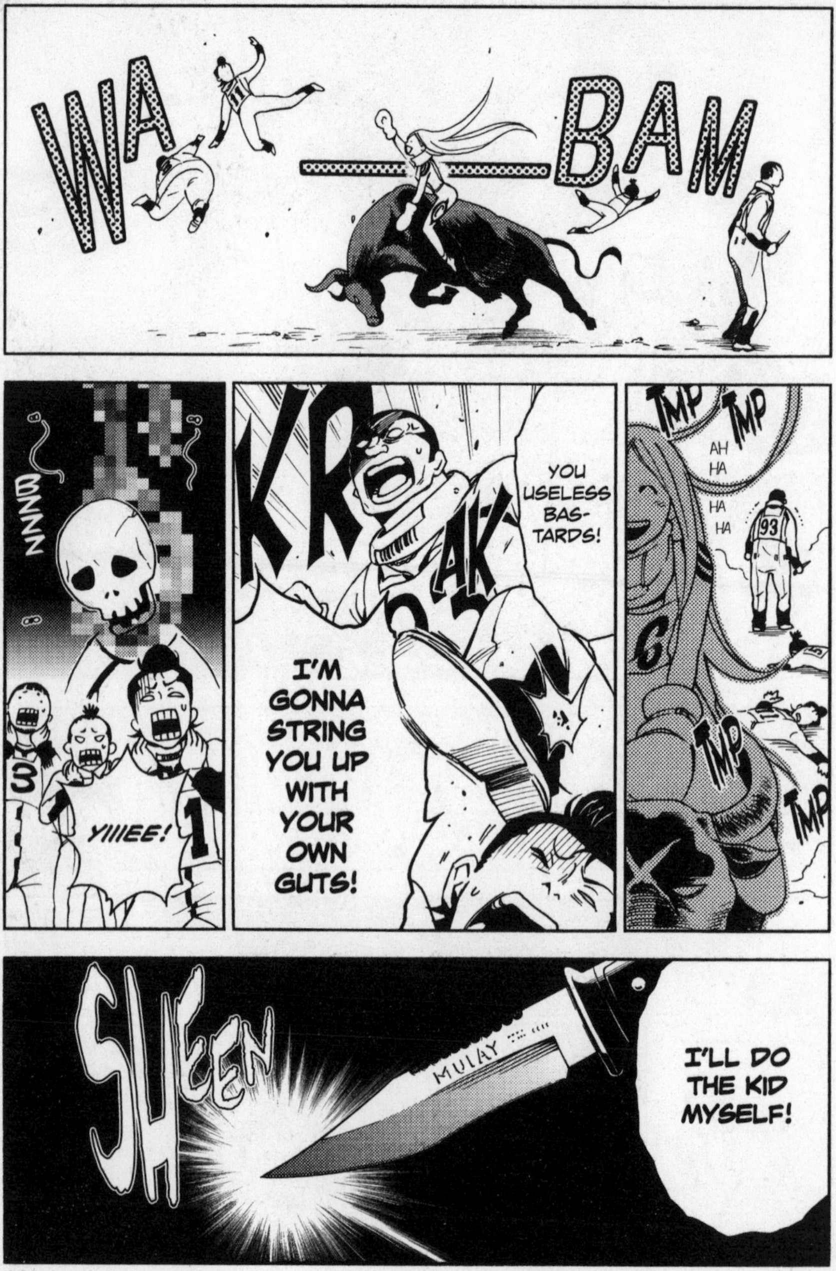
WA—BAM
TMP TMP
AH HA HA HA
TMP TMP
KRAK
YOU USELESS BAS-TARDS!
I'M GONNA STRING YOU UP WITH YOUR OWN GUTS!
BZZZ
YIIIEE!
I'LL DO THE KID MYSELF!
SHEEN

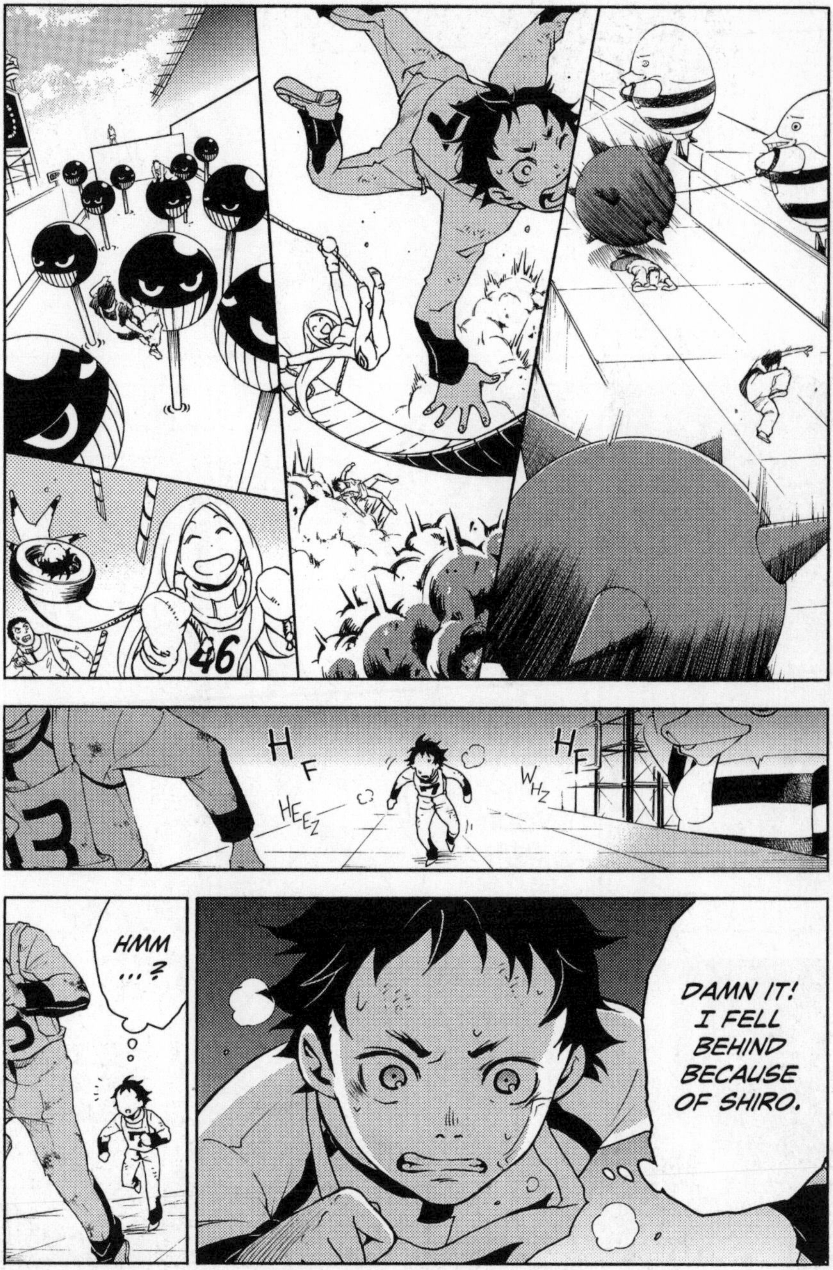
HF
WHZ
HF
HEEZ
DAMN IT! I FELL BEHIND BECAUSE OF SHIRO.
HMM ...?

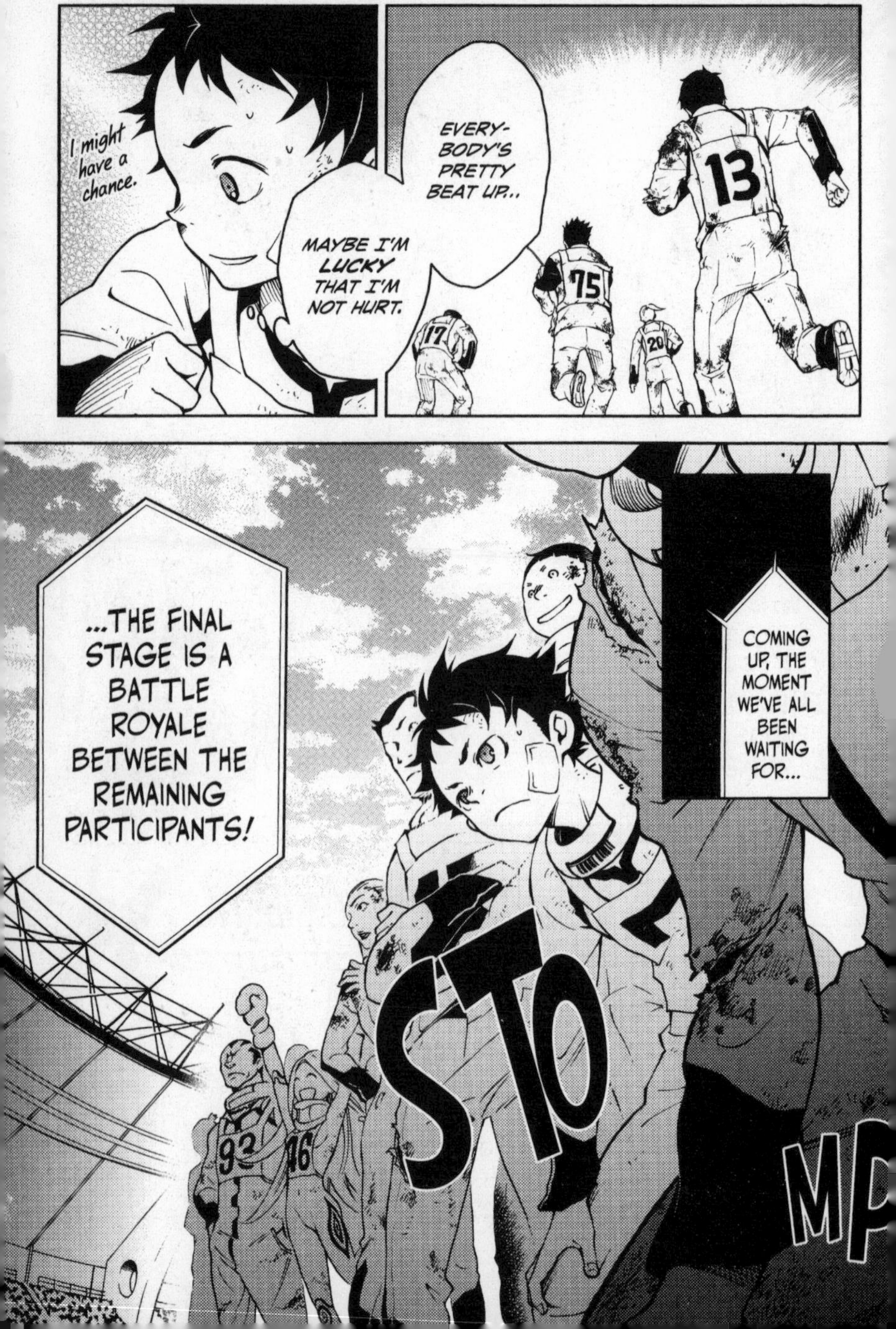
EVERY-BODY'S PRETTY BEAT UP...
MAYBE I'M **LUCKY** THAT I'M NOT HURT.
I might have a chance.
COMING UP, THE MOMENT WE'VE ALL BEEN WAITING FOR...
...THE FINAL STAGE IS A BATTLE ROYALE BETWEEN THE REMAINING PARTICIPANTS!
STO
MP

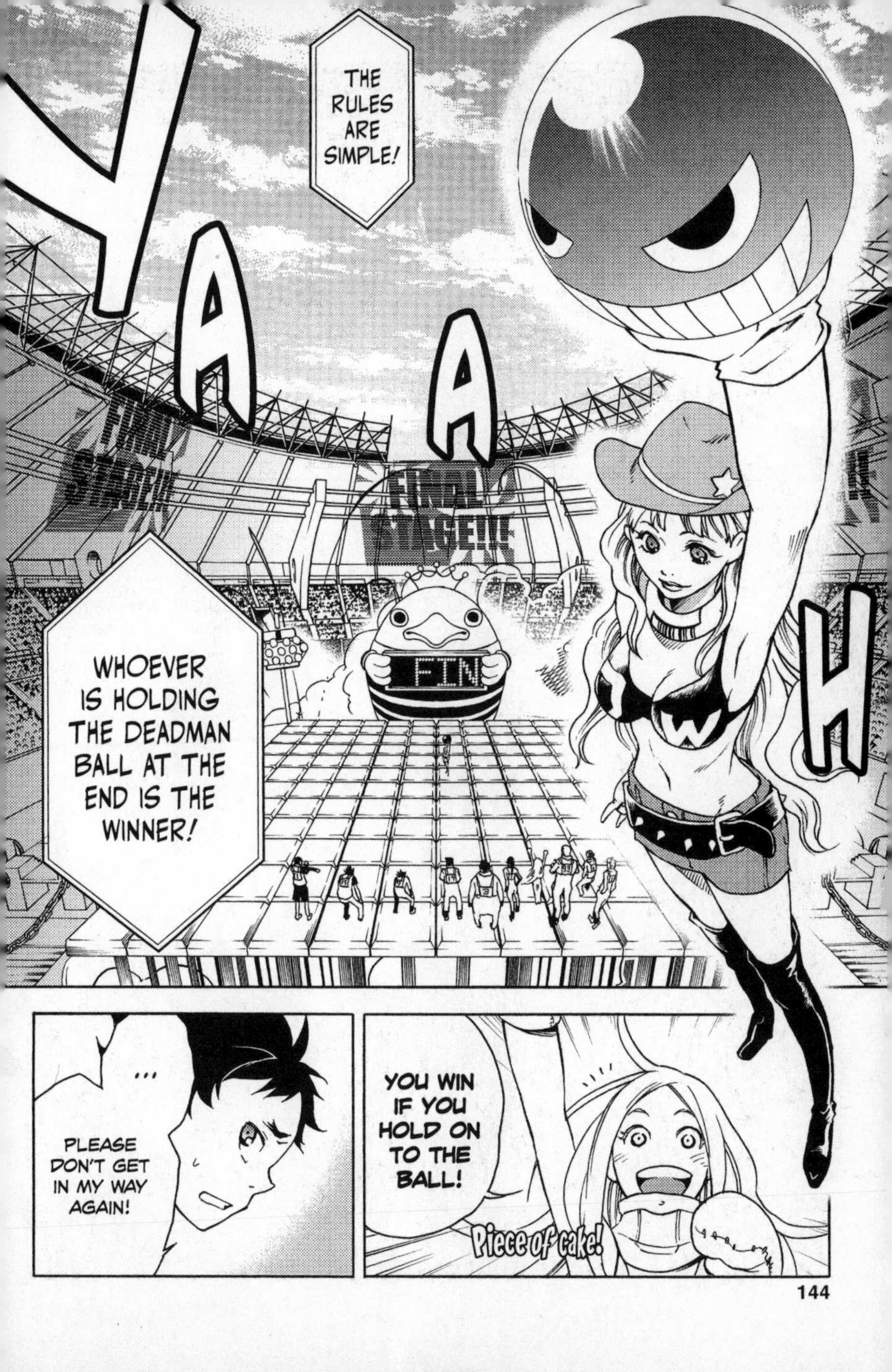
THE FINAL RULES ARE SIMPLE!
YAAAH
FINAL STAGE!!
FIN
WHOEVER IS HOLDING THE DEADMAN BALL AT THE END IS THE WINNER!
YOU WIN IF YOU HOLD ON TO THE BALL!
Piece of cake!
...
PLEASE DON'T GET IN MY WAY AGAIN!

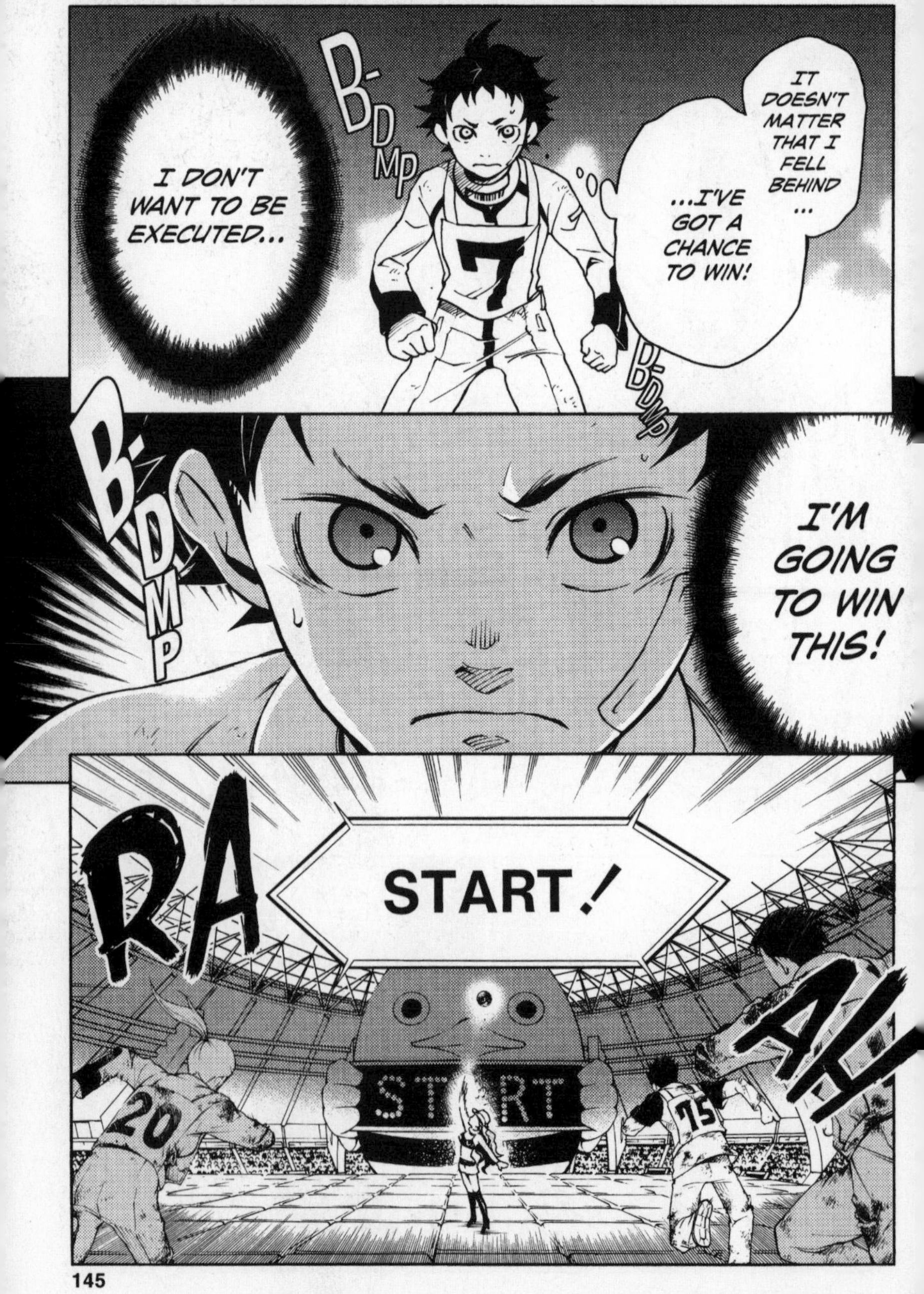
IT DOESN'T MATTER THAT I FELL BEHIND...
...I'VE GOT A CHANCE TO WIN!
B-DMP
I DON'T WANT TO BE EXECUTED...
B-DMP
I'M GOING TO WIN THIS!
B-DMP
START!
RA
AH

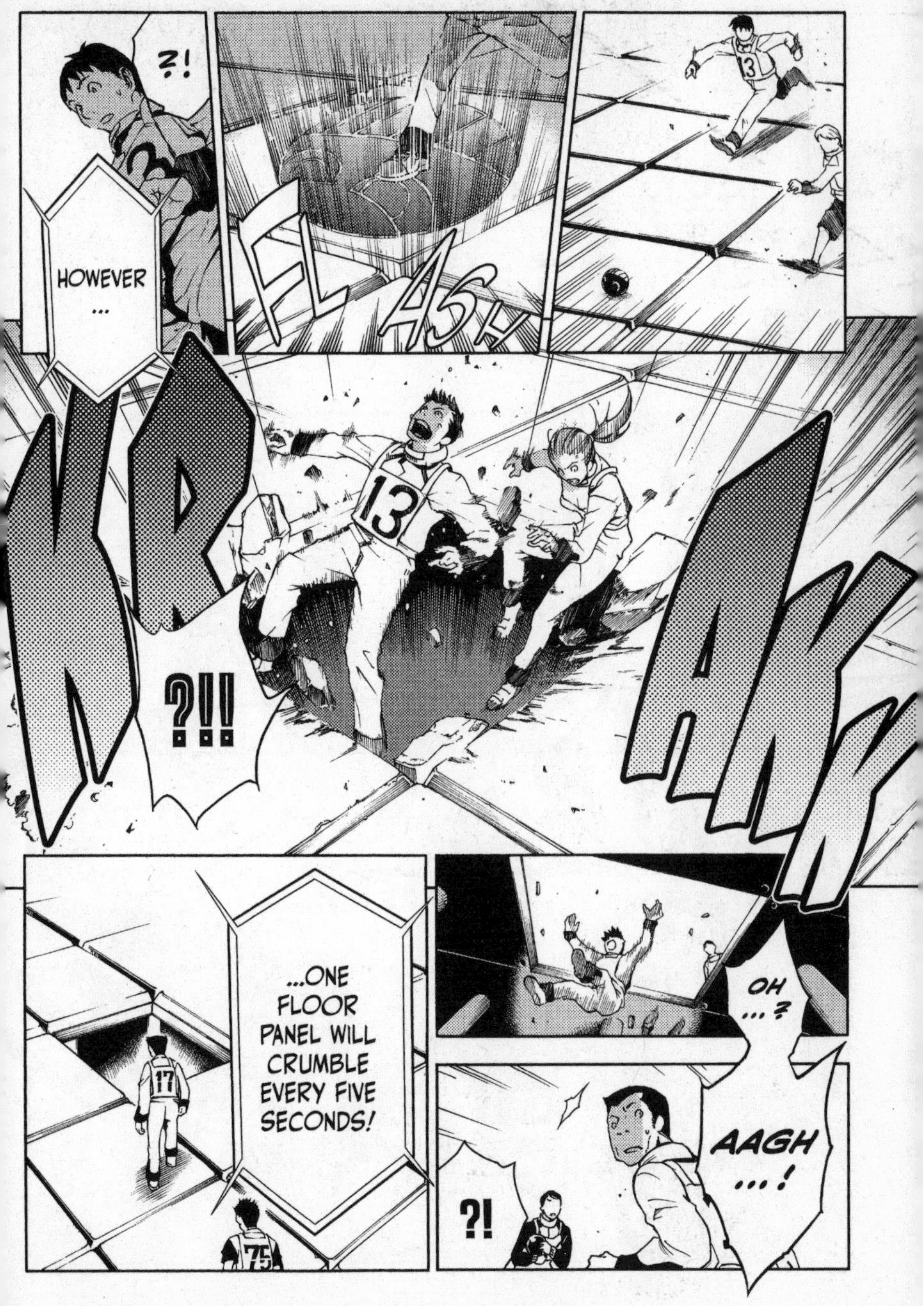
FLASH
?!
HOWEVER ...
KR
AAK
?!!
OH ...?
AAGH ...!
?!
...ONE FLOOR PANEL WILL CRUMBLE EVERY FIVE SECONDS!

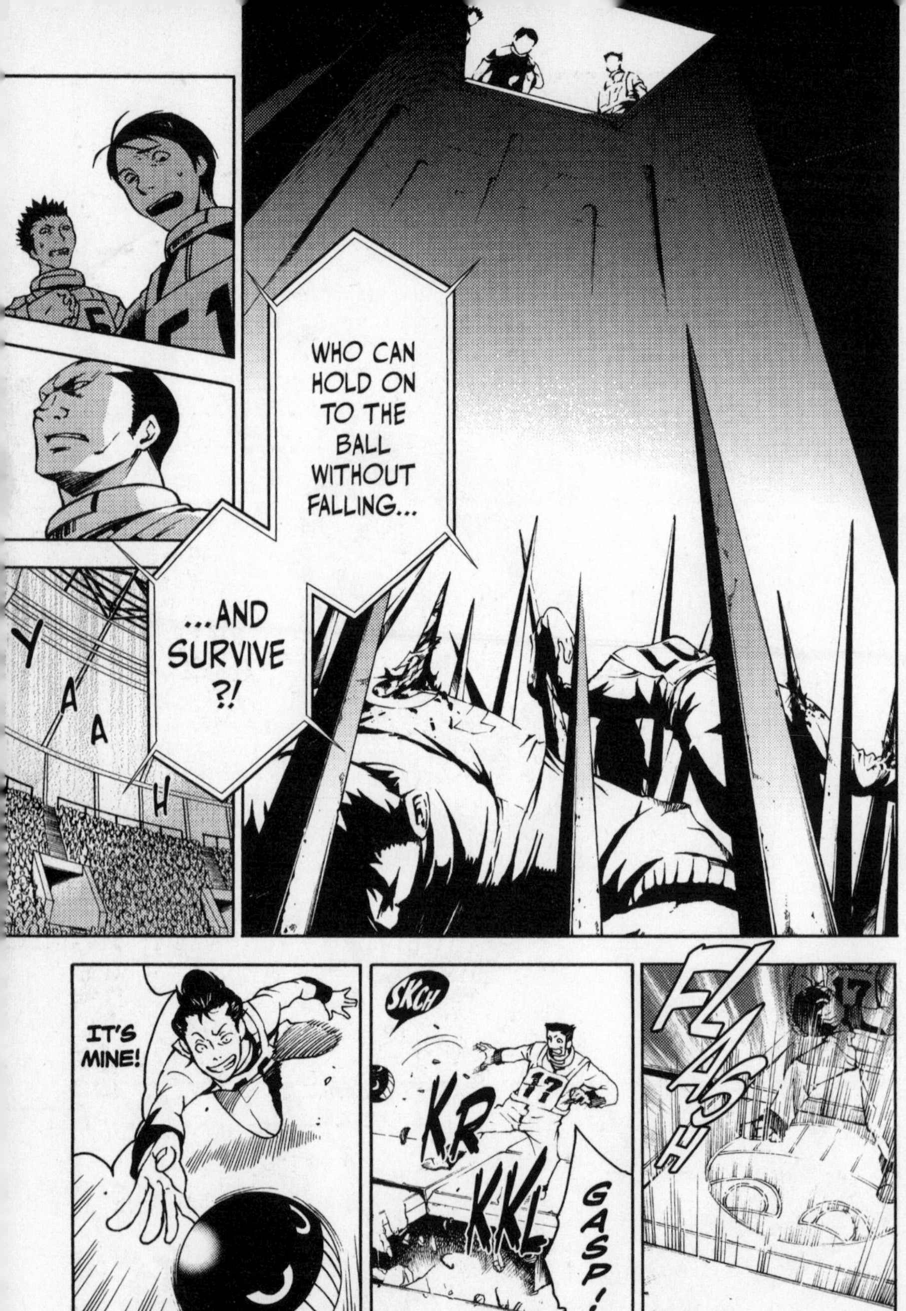
WHO CAN HOLD ON TO THE BALL WITHOUT FALLING...
...AND SURVIVE ?!
YAAAH
FLASHH
SKCH
KRKKL
GASP!
IT'S MINE!

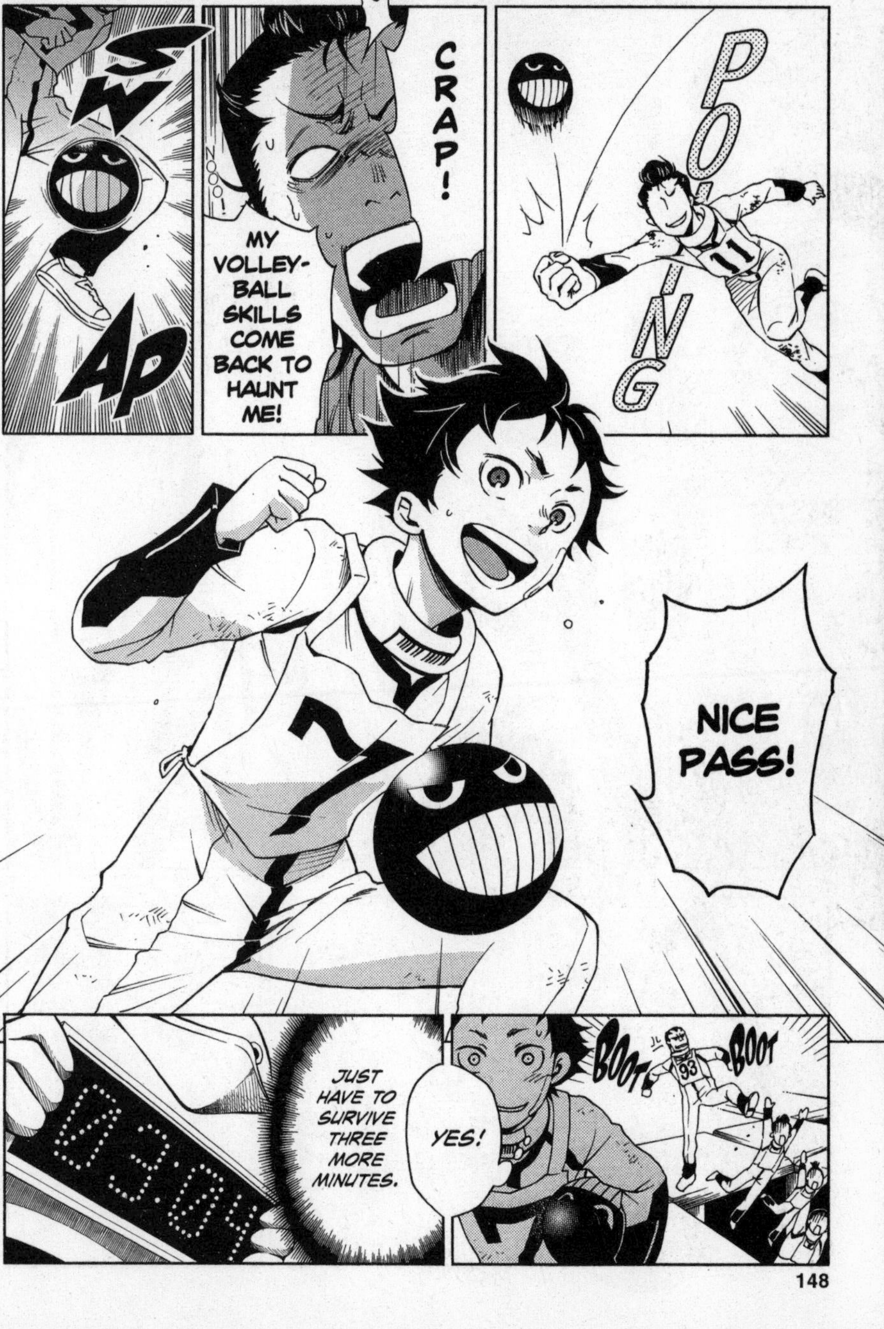
POING
CRAP!
NOOO!
MY VOLLEY-BALL SKILLS COME BACK TO HAUNT ME!
SWAP
NICE PASS!
BOOT BOOT
YES!
JUST HAVE TO SURVIVE THREE MORE MINUTES.

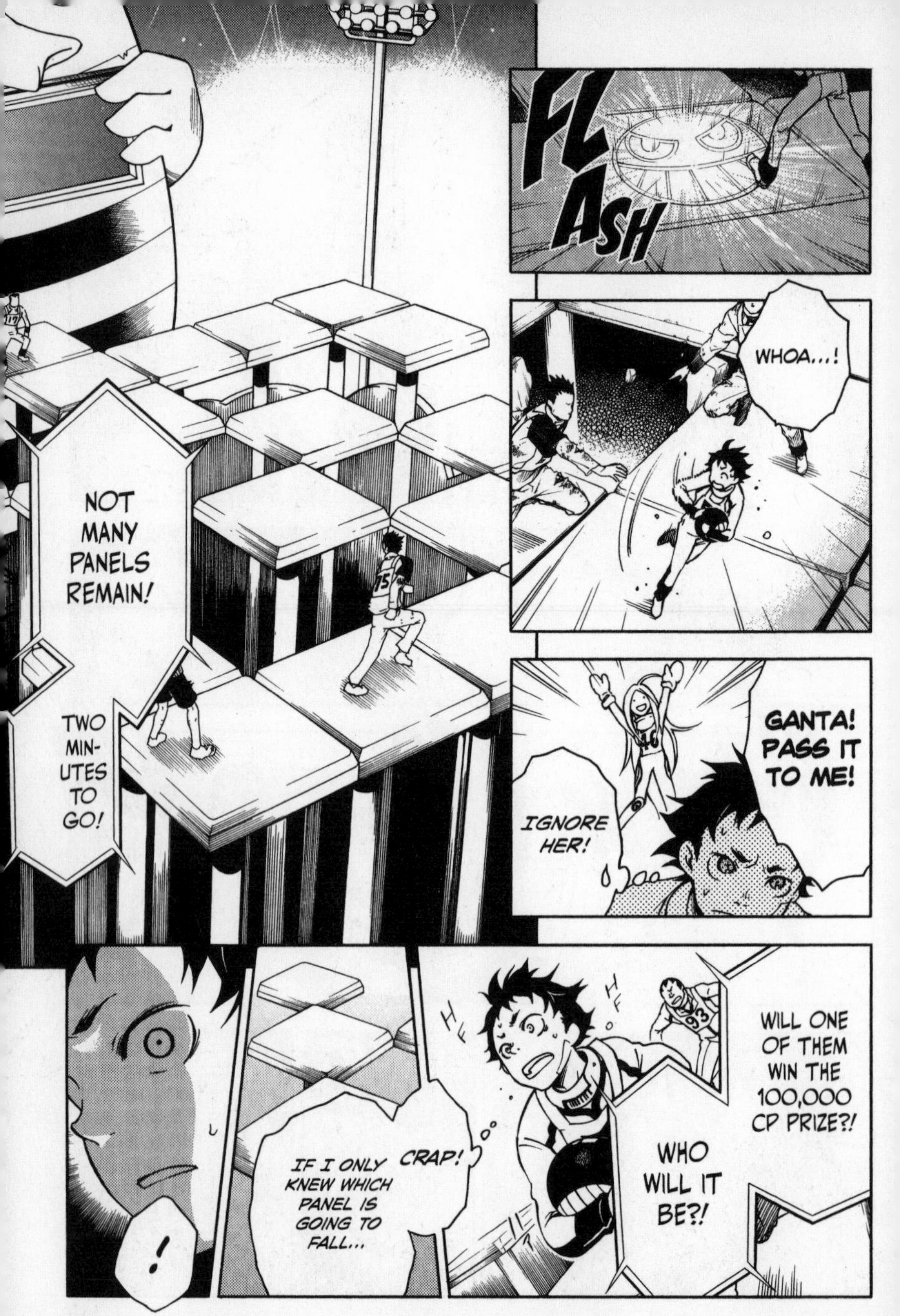
FLASH
WHOA...!
GANTA! PASS IT TO ME!
IGNORE HER!
NOT MANY PANELS REMAIN!
TWO MINUTES TO GO!
WILL ONE OF THEM WIN THE 100,000 CP PRIZE?!
WHO WILL IT BE?!
CRAP!
IF I ONLY KNEW WHICH PANEL IS GOING TO FALL...
!

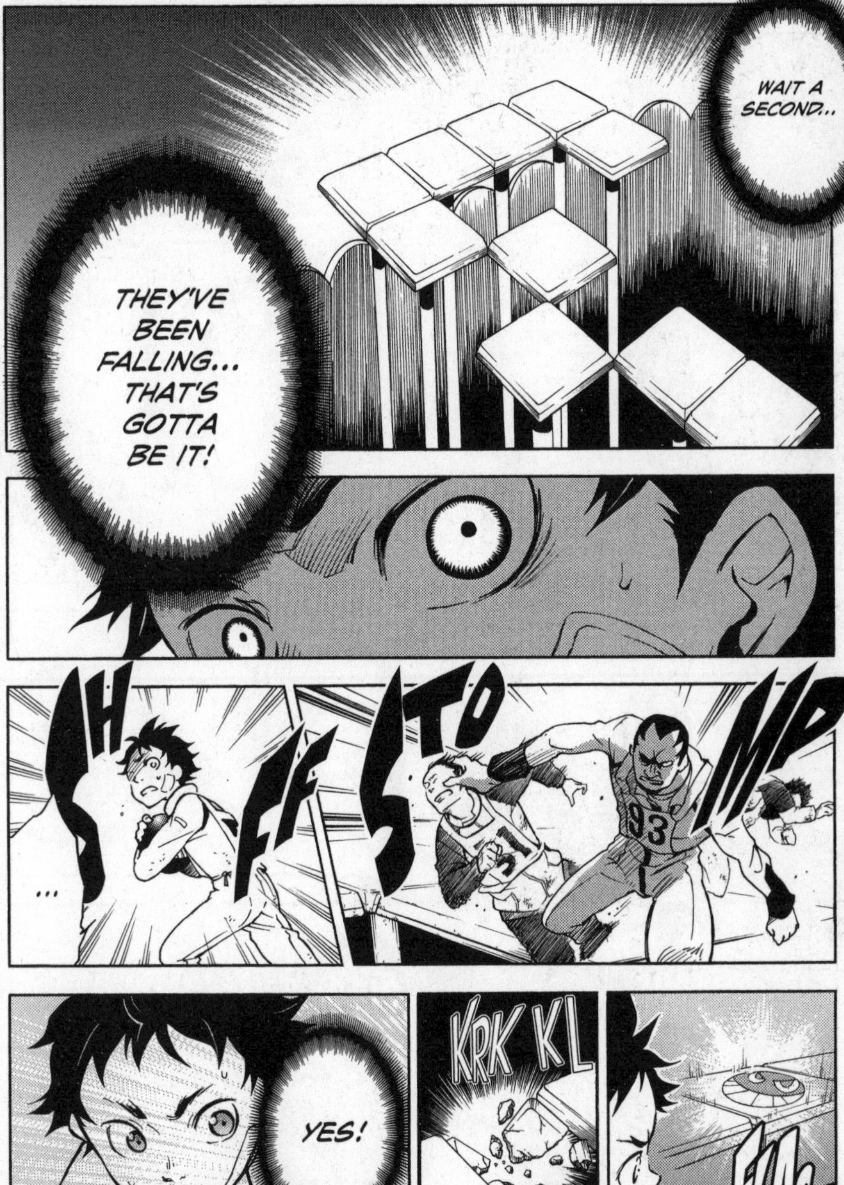
WAIT A SECOND...
THEY'VE BEEN FALLING... THAT'S GOTTA BE IT!
...
FLASH
KRK KL
YES!

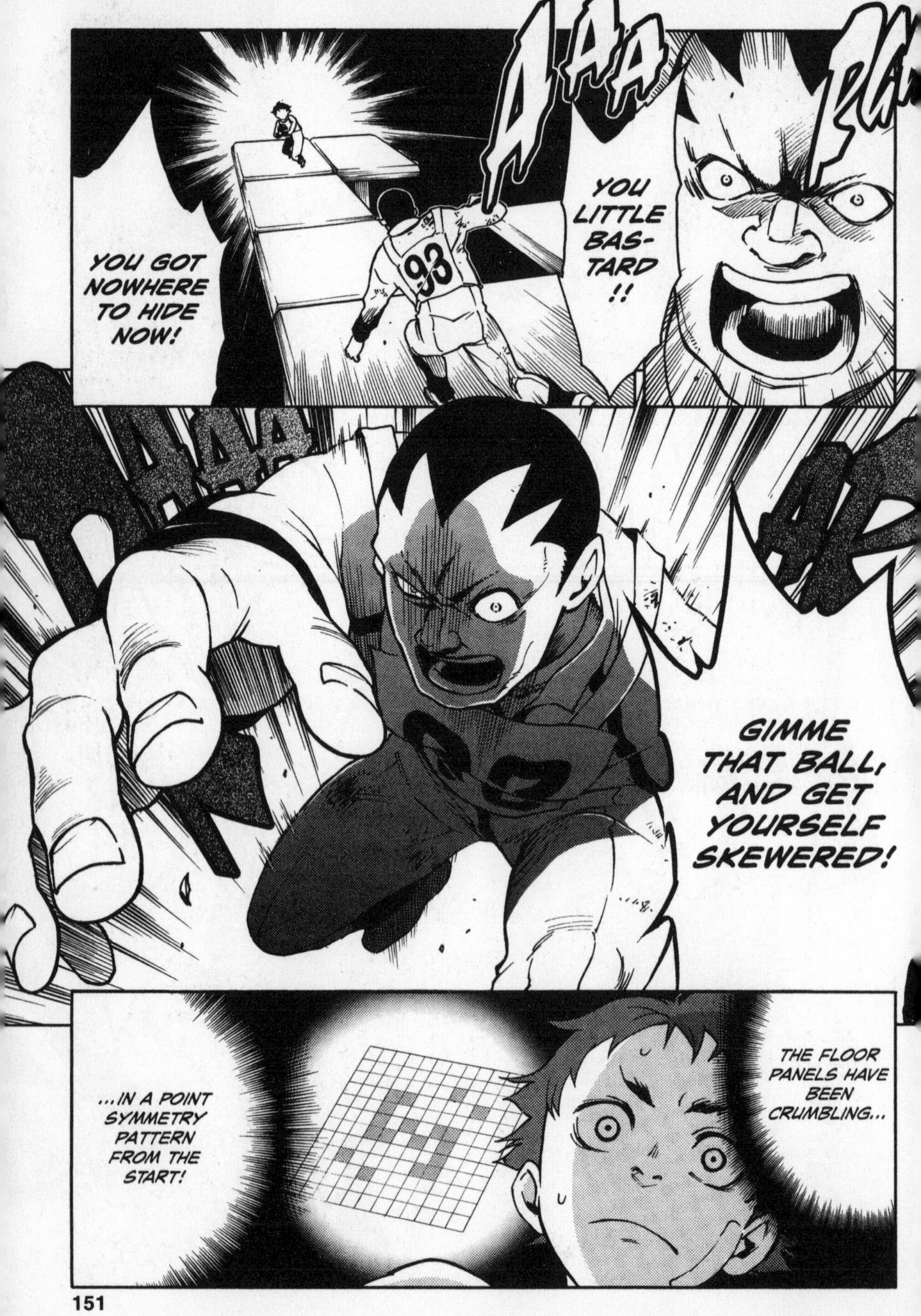
YOU LITTLE BAS-TARD!!
YOU GOT NOWHERE TO HIDE NOW!
GIMME THAT BALL, AND GET YOURSELF SKEWERED!
THE FLOOR PANELS HAVE BEEN CRUMBLING...
...IN A POINT SYMMETRY PATTERN FROM THE START!

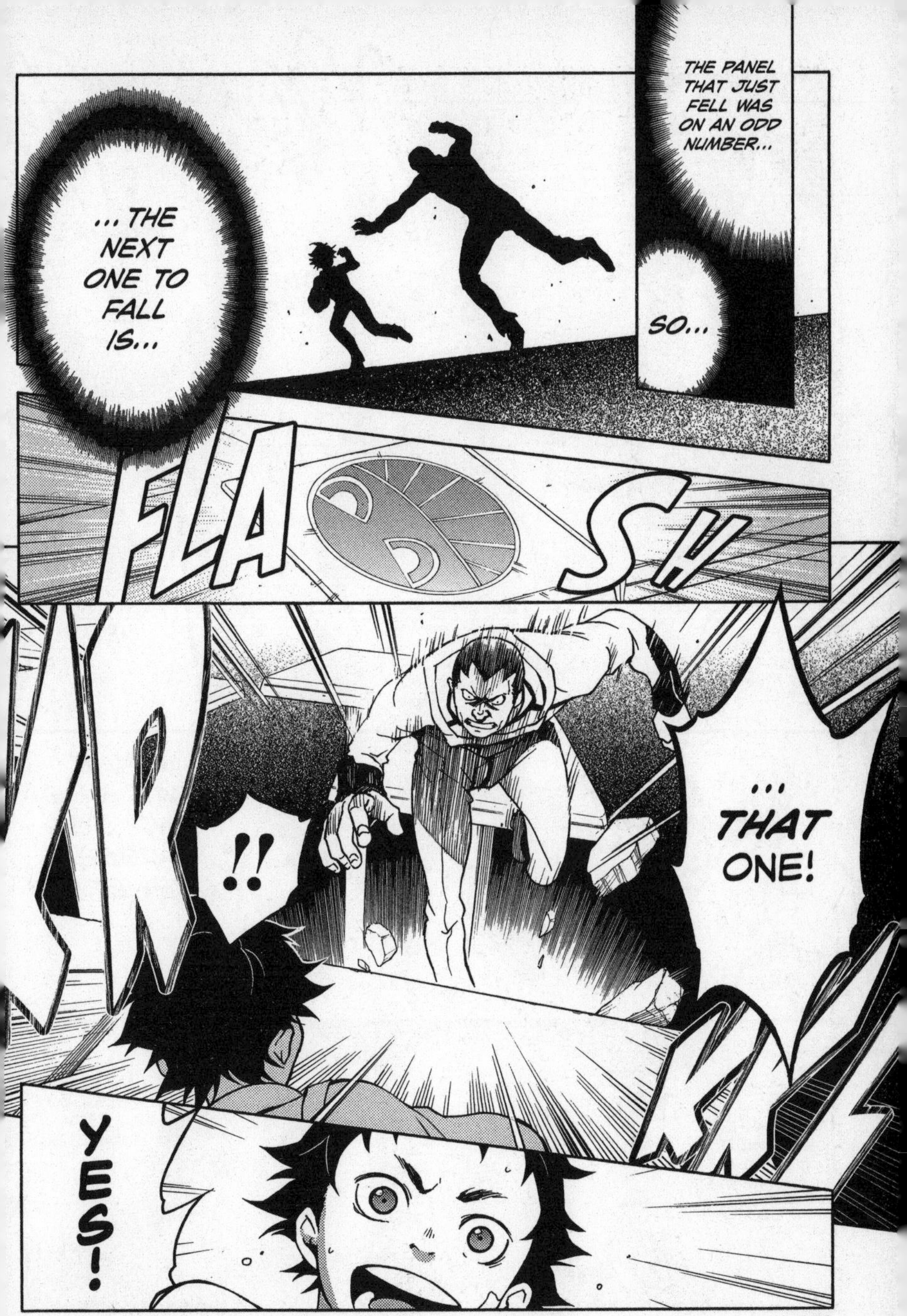
THE PANEL THAT JUST FELL WAS ON AN ODD NUMBER...
SO...
...THE NEXT ONE TO FALL IS...
FLASH
...THAT ONE!
!!
YES!

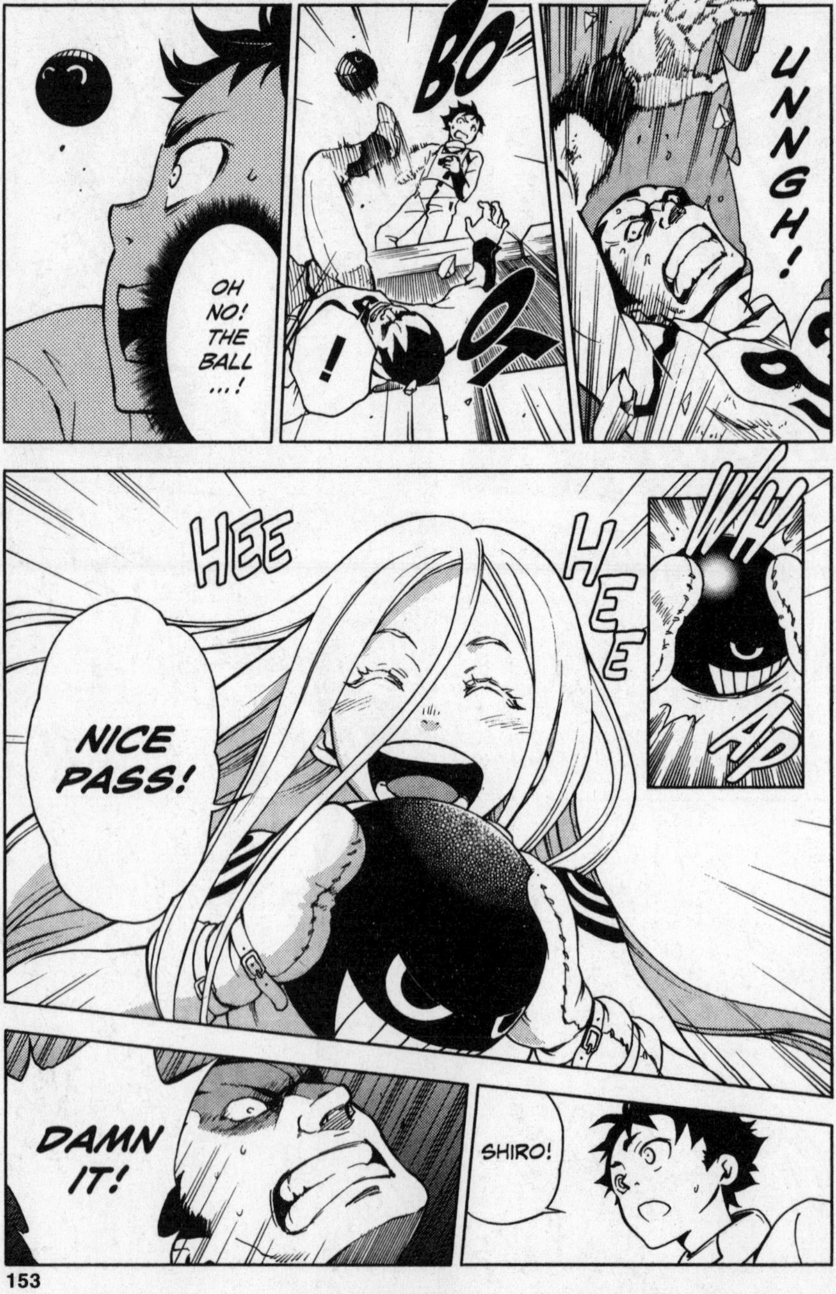
UNNNGH!
BO
OT
!
OH NO! THE BALL ...!
WH
AP
HEE
HEE
NICE PASS!
SHIRO!
DAMN IT!

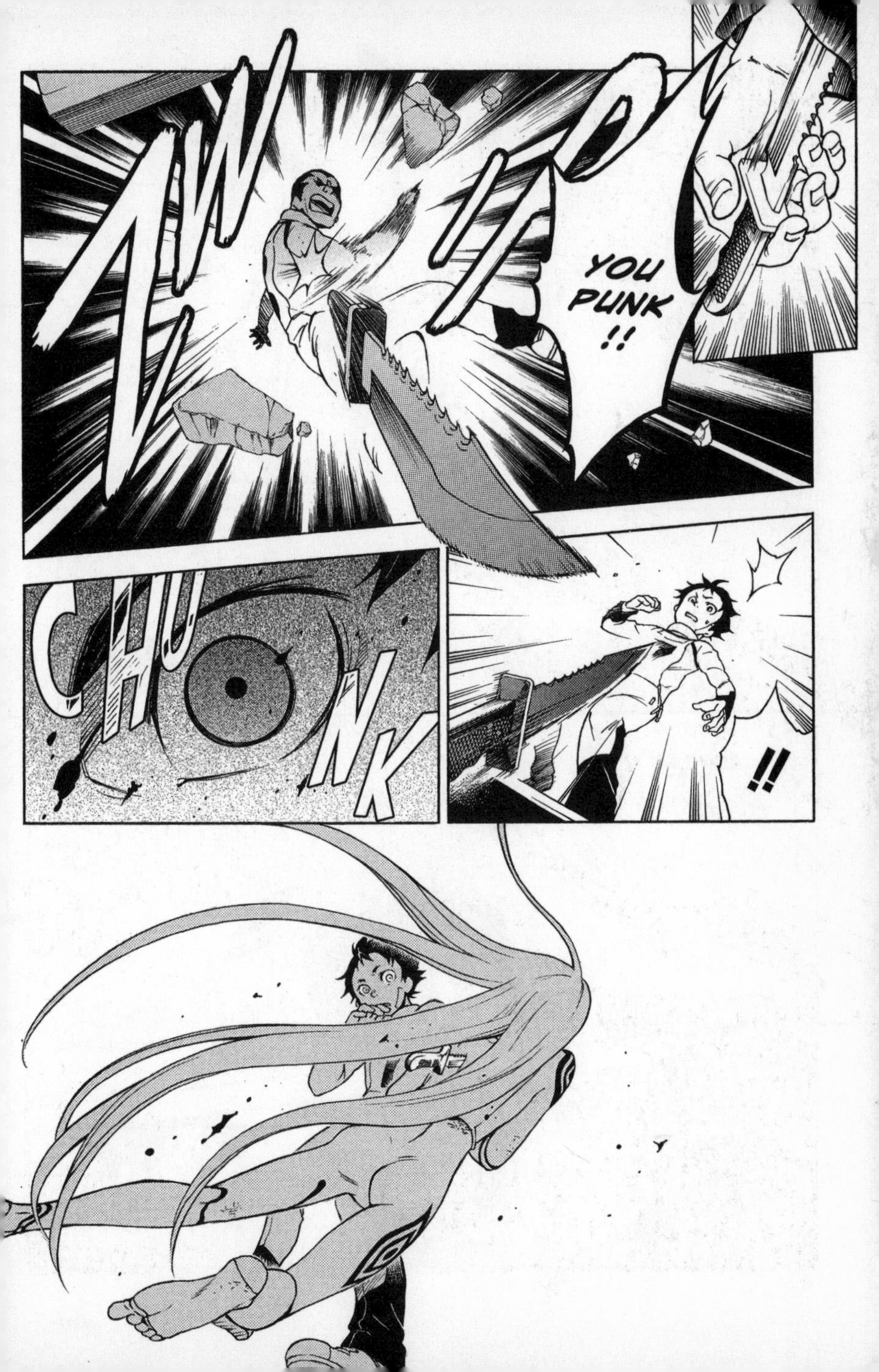
YOU PUNK !!
!!
CHUNK

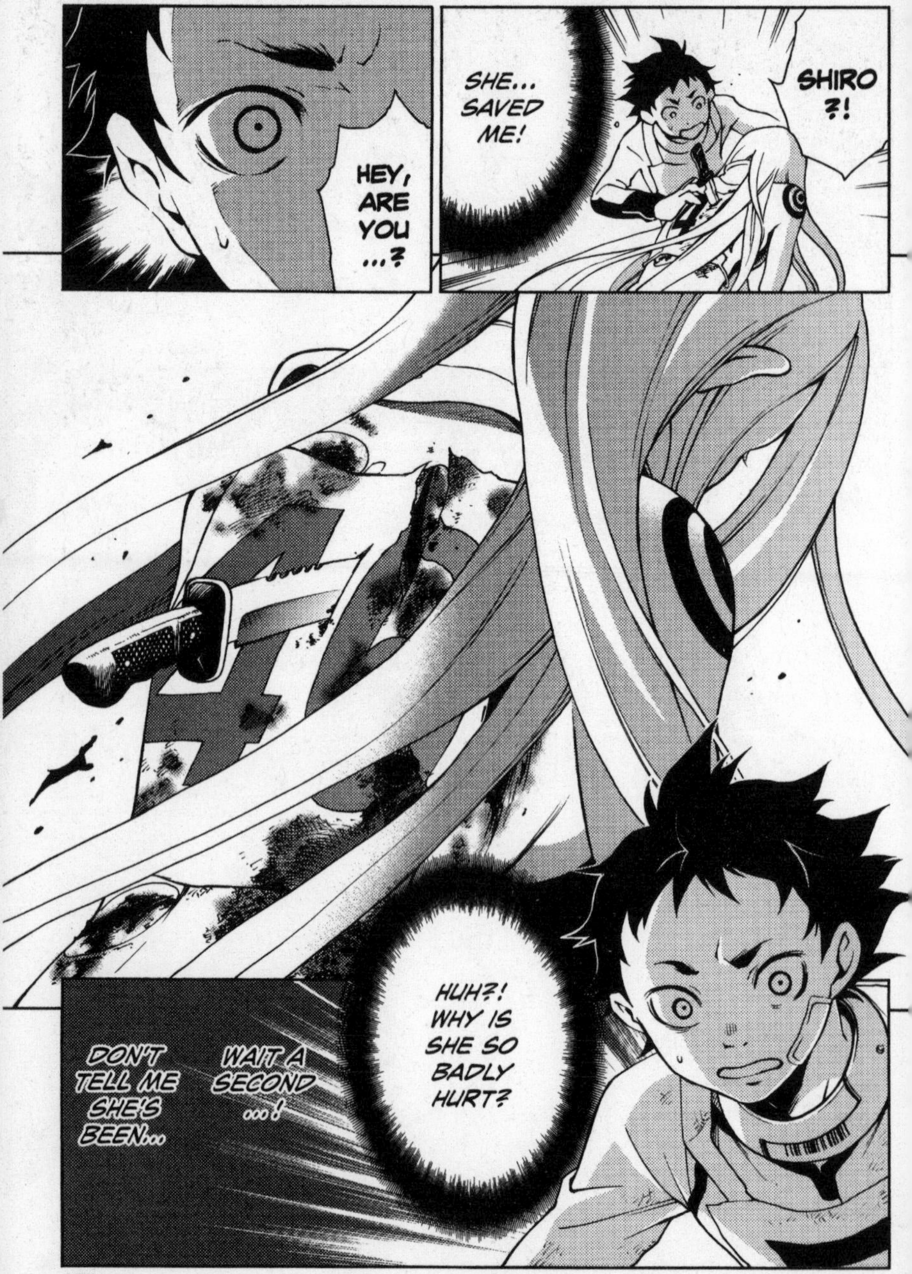
SHIRO?!
SHE... SAVED ME!
HEY, ARE YOU...?
HUH?! WHY IS SHE SO BADLY HURT?
WAIT A SECOND...!
DON'T TELL ME SHE'S BEEN...

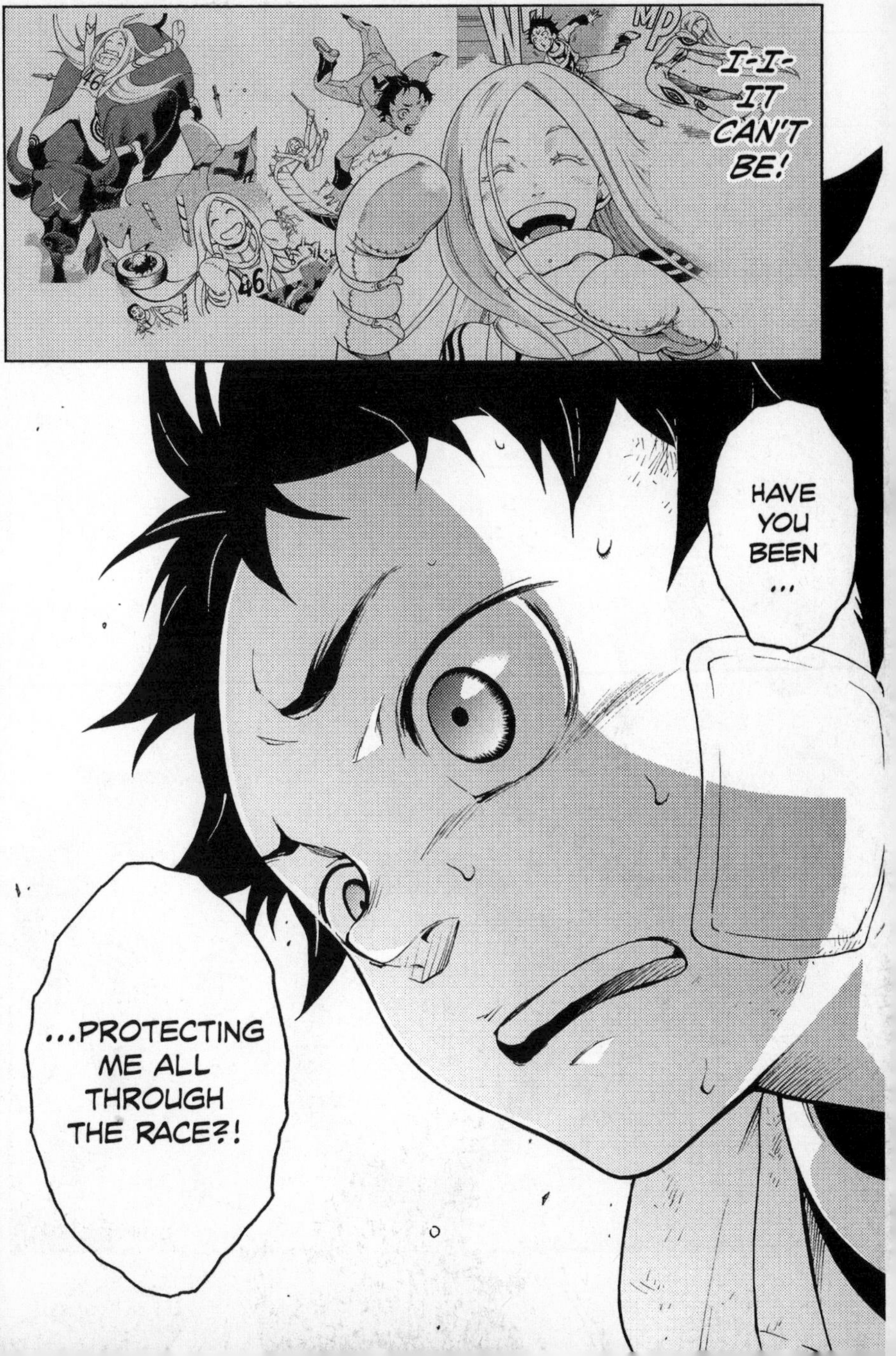
I-I-IT CAN'T BE!
HAVE YOU BEEN...
...PROTECTING ME ALL THROUGH THE RACE?!

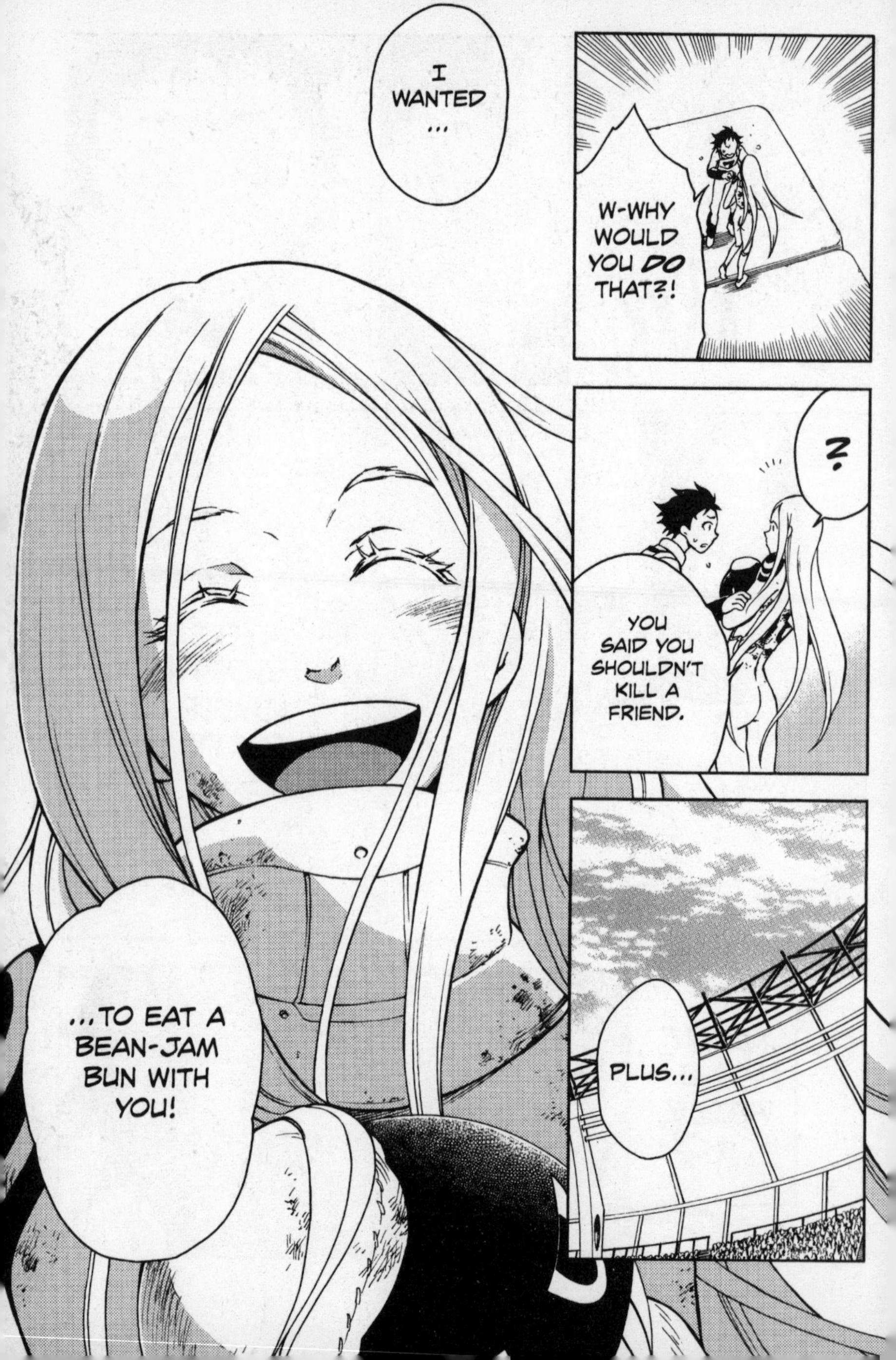
W-WHY WOULD YOU *DO* THAT?!
?
YOU SAID YOU SHOULDN'T KILL A FRIEND.
PLUS...
I WANTED ...
...TO EAT A BEAN-JAM BUN WITH YOU!

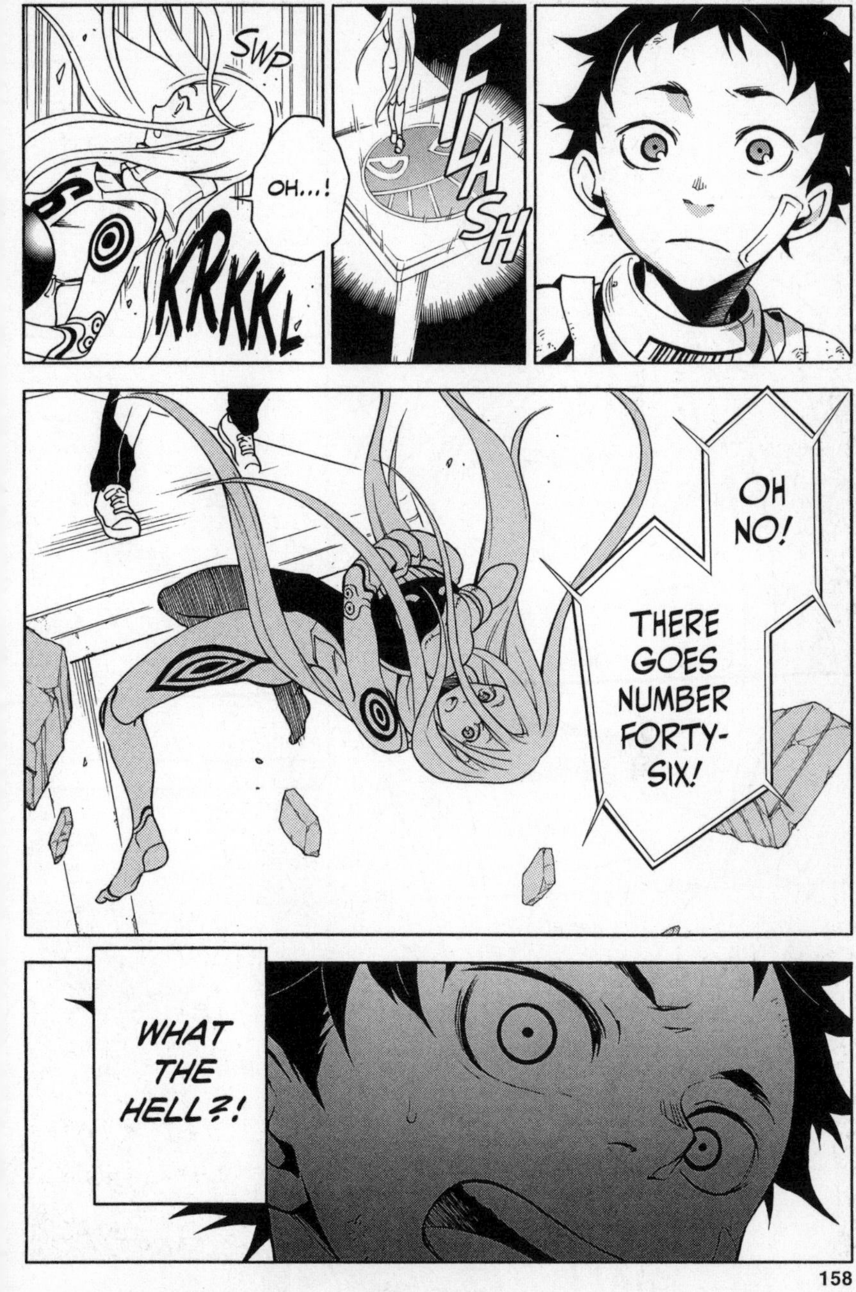
FLASH
SWP
OH...!
KRKKL
OH NO!
THERE GOES NUMBER FORTY-SIX!
WHAT THE HELL?!

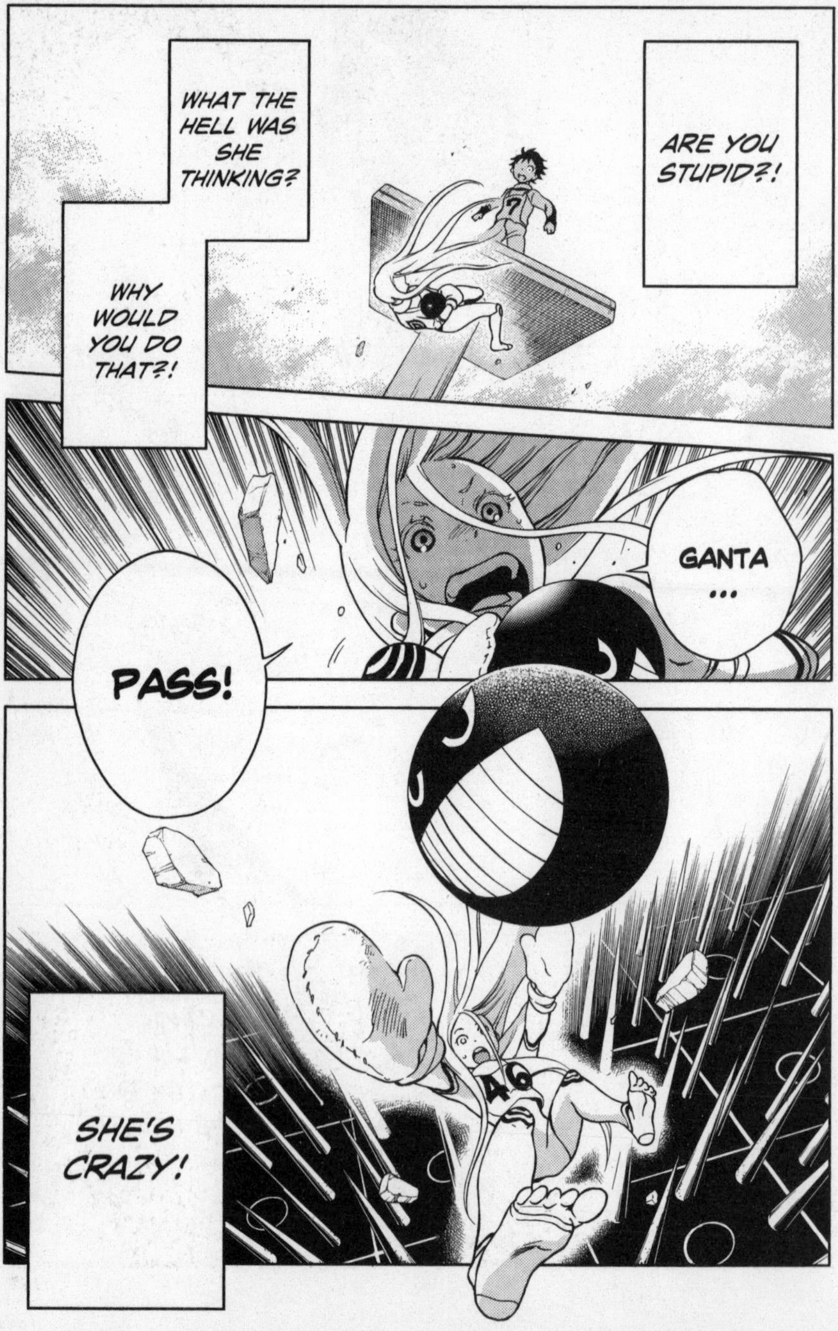
ARE YOU STUPID?!
WHAT THE HELL WAS SHE THINKING?
WHY WOULD YOU DO THAT?!
GANTA...
PASS!
SHE'S CRAZY!

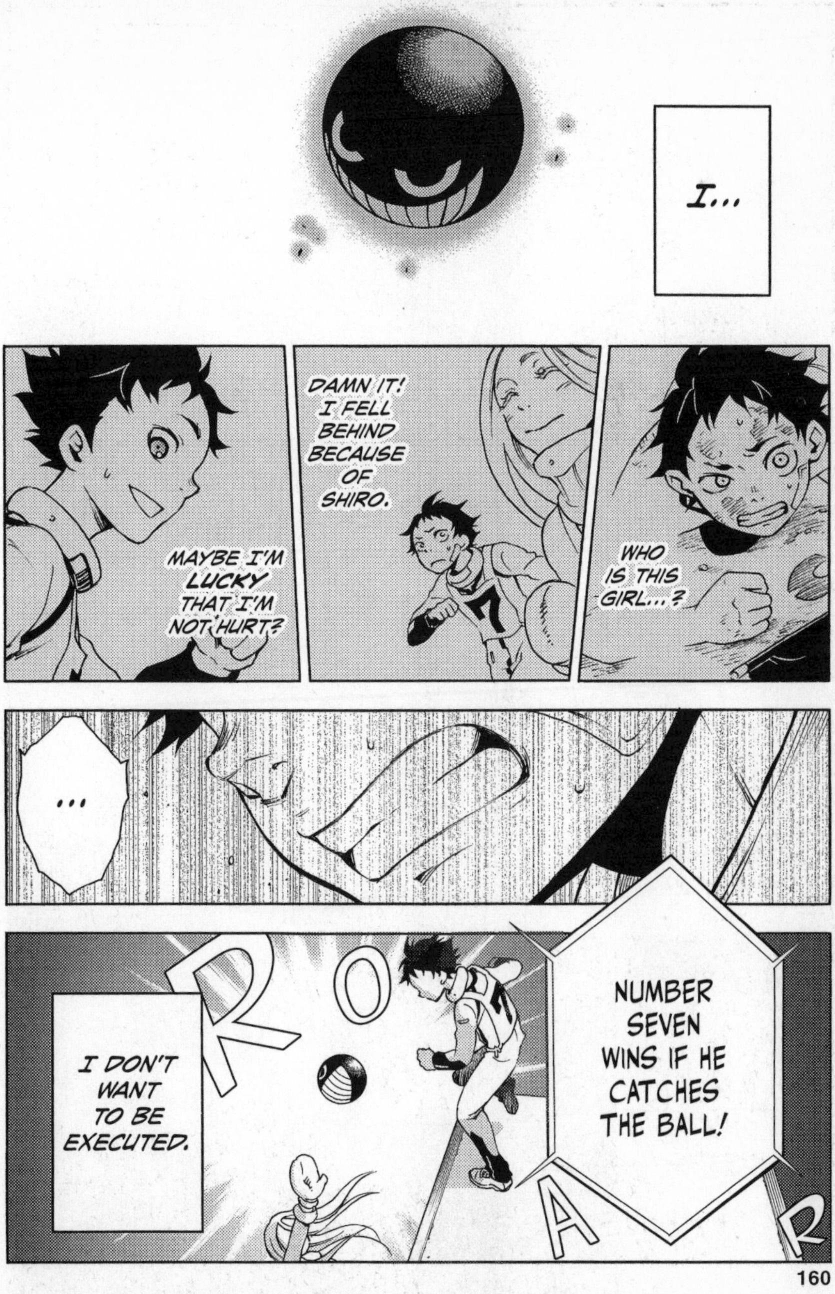
I...
WHO IS THIS GIRL...?
DAMN IT! I FELL BEHIND BECAUSE OF SHIRO.
MAYBE I'M **LUCKY** THAT I'M NOT HURT?
...
NUMBER SEVEN WINS IF HE CATCHES THE BALL!
ROAR
I DON'T WANT TO BE EXECUTED.

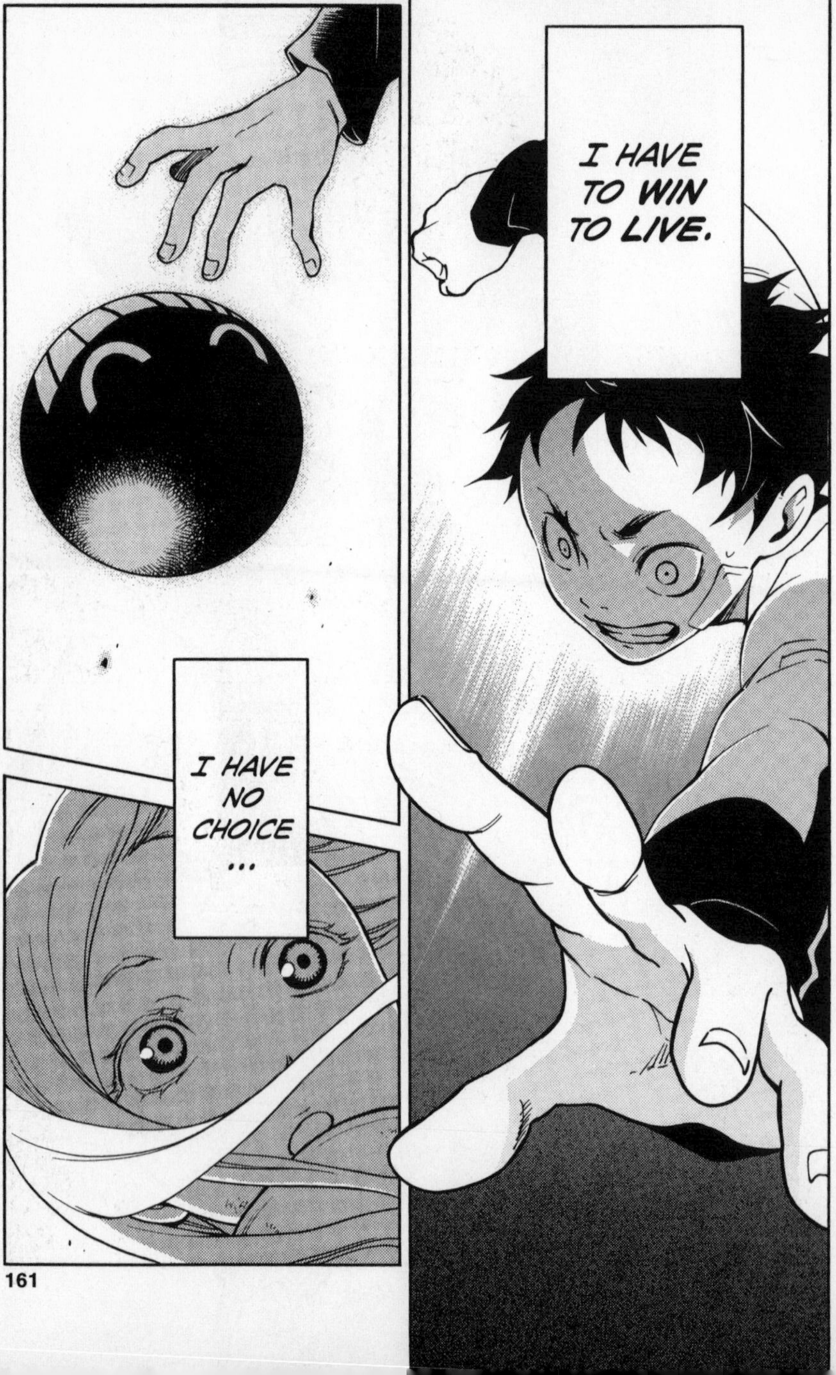
I HAVE TO WIN TO LIVE.
I HAVE NO CHOICE ...

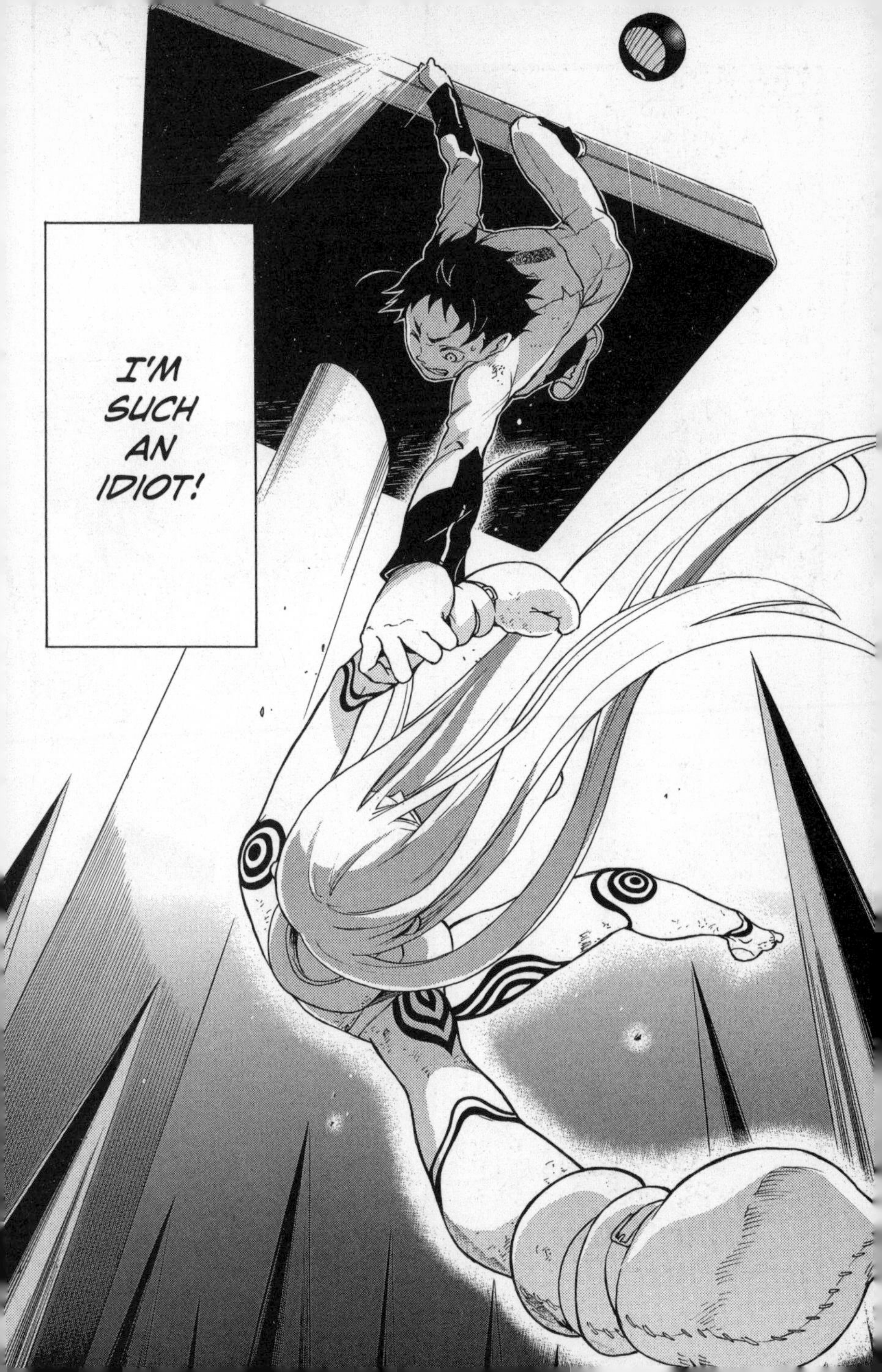
I'M SUCH AN IDIOT!

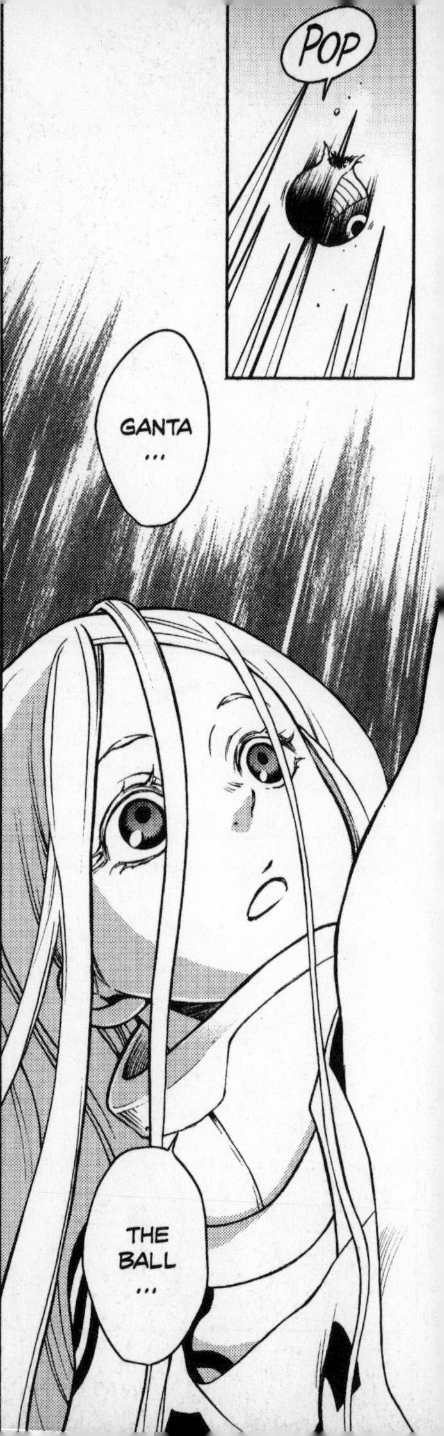
POP
GANTA ...
THE BALL ...

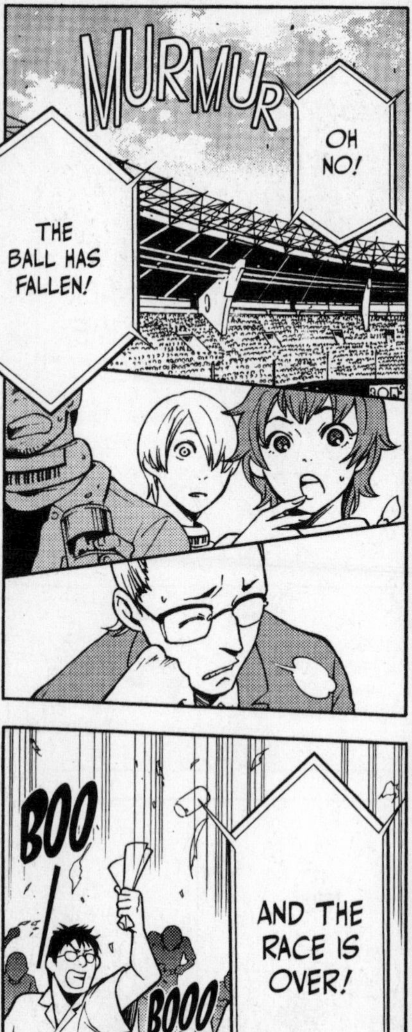
OH NO!
MURMUR
THE BALL HAS FALLEN!
AND THE RACE IS OVER!
BOO
BOOO

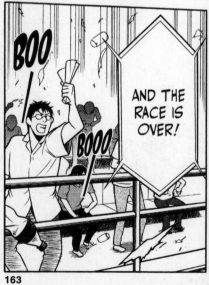

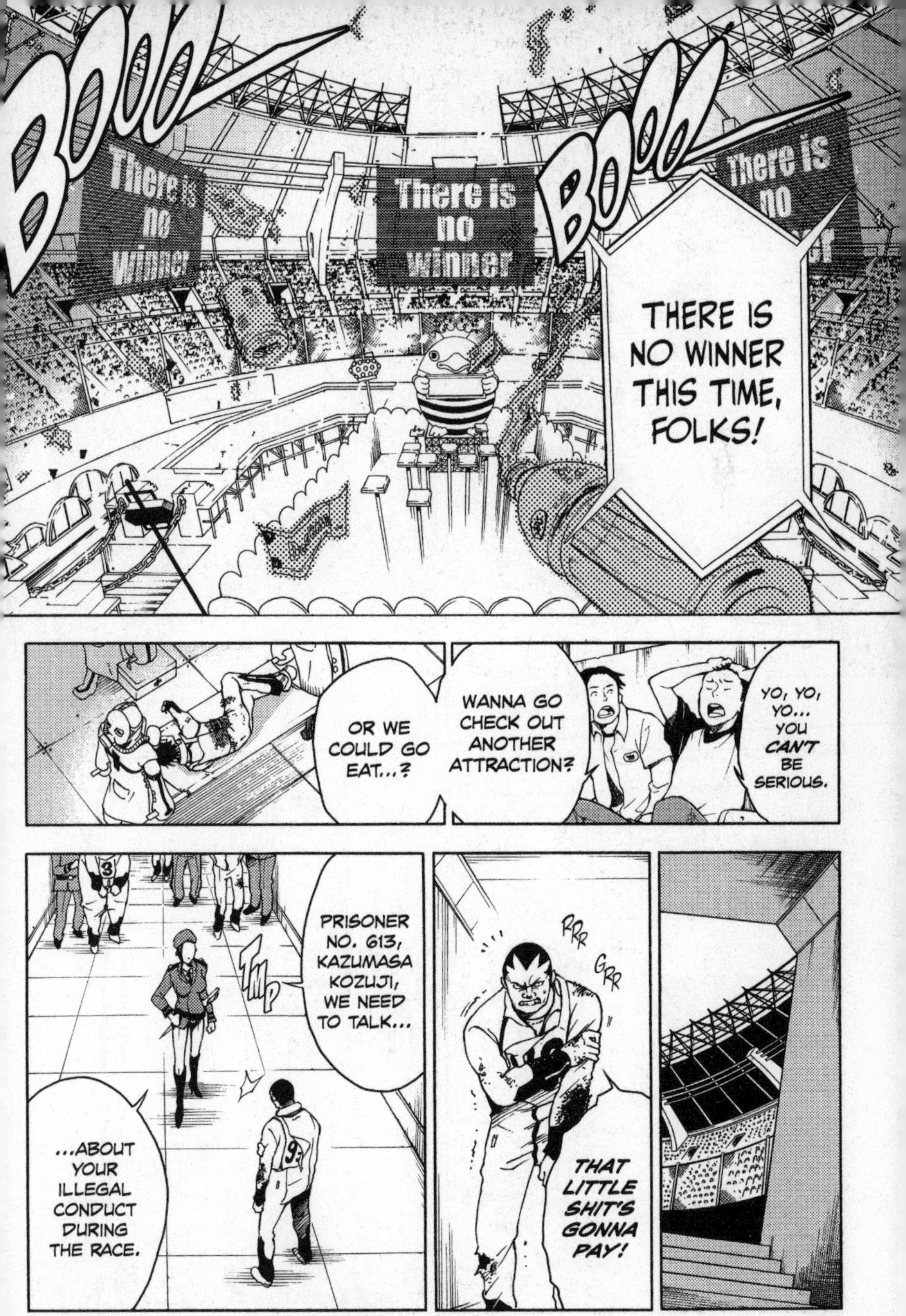
There is no
Boo
THERE IS NO WINNER THIS TIME, FOLKS!
There is no winner
Boo
There is no winner
YO, YO, YO... YOU *CAN'T* BE SERIOUS.
WANNA GO CHECK OUT ANOTHER ATTRACTION?
OR WE COULD GO EAT...?
RRR
GRR
*THAT LITTLE SHIT'S GONNA PAY!*
TMP
PRISONER NO. 613, KAZUMASA KOZUJI, WE NEED TO TALK...
...ABOUT YOUR ILLEGAL CONDUCT DURING THE RACE.

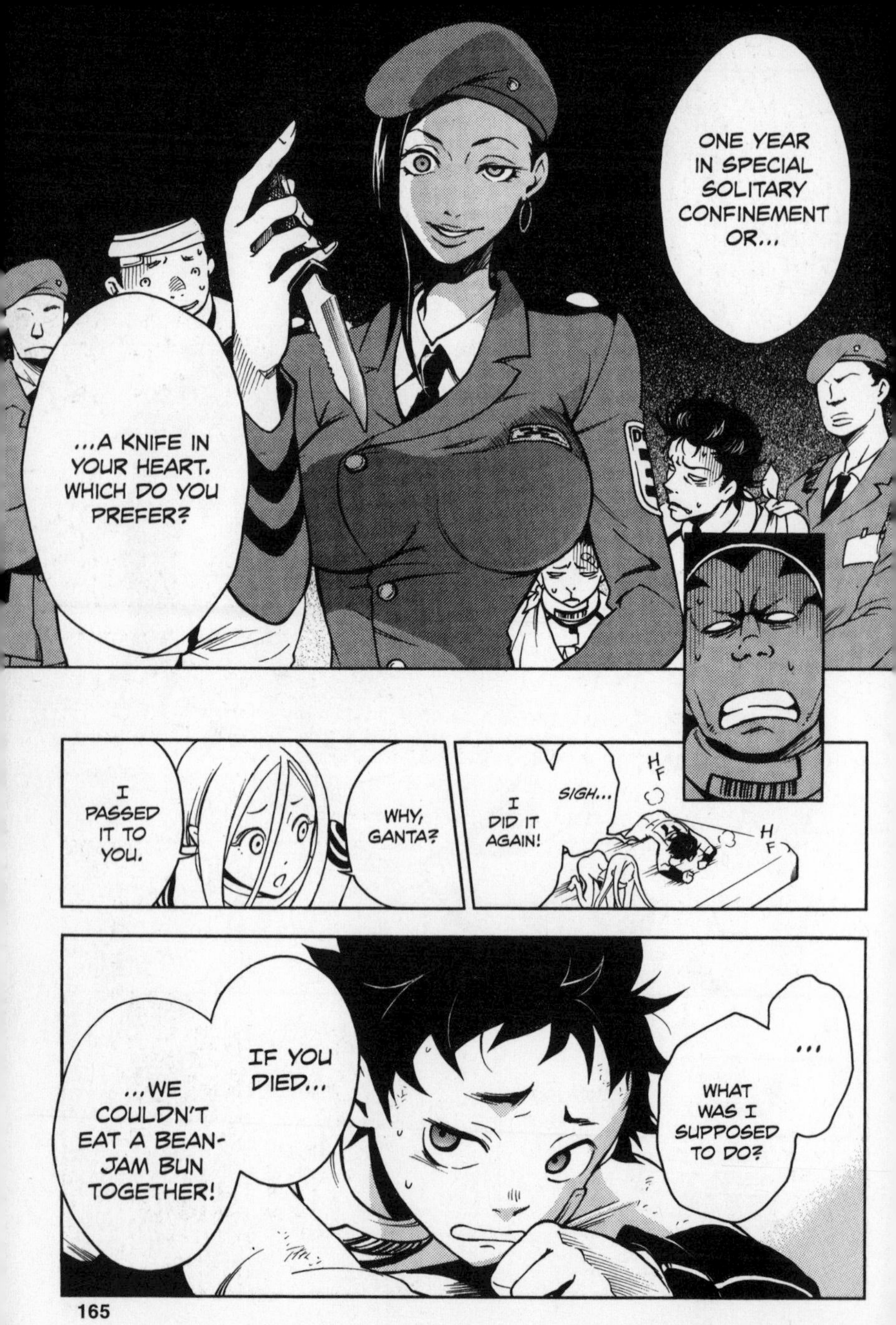
ONE YEAR IN SPECIAL SOLITARY CONFINEMENT OR...
...A KNIFE IN YOUR HEART. WHICH DO YOU PREFER?
SIGH...
I DID IT AGAIN!
HF
HF
WHY, GANTA?
I PASSED IT TO YOU.
...
WHAT WAS I SUPPOSED TO DO?
IF YOU DIED...
...WE COULDN'T EAT A BEAN-JAM BUN TOGETHER!

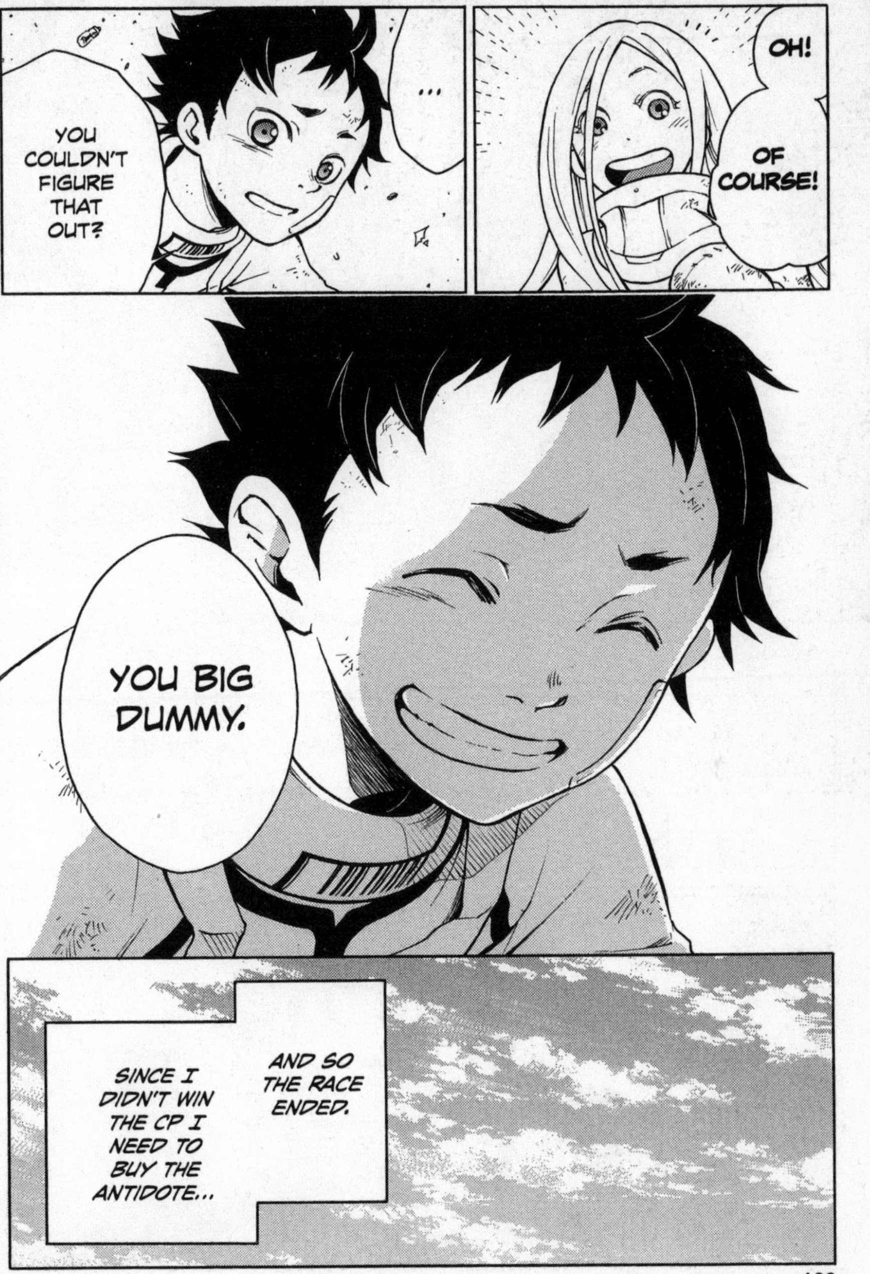
OH! OF COURSE!
...
YOU COULDN'T FIGURE THAT OUT?
YOU BIG DUMMY.
AND SO THE RACE ENDED.
SINCE I DIDN'T WIN THE CP I NEED TO BUY THE ANTIDOTE...

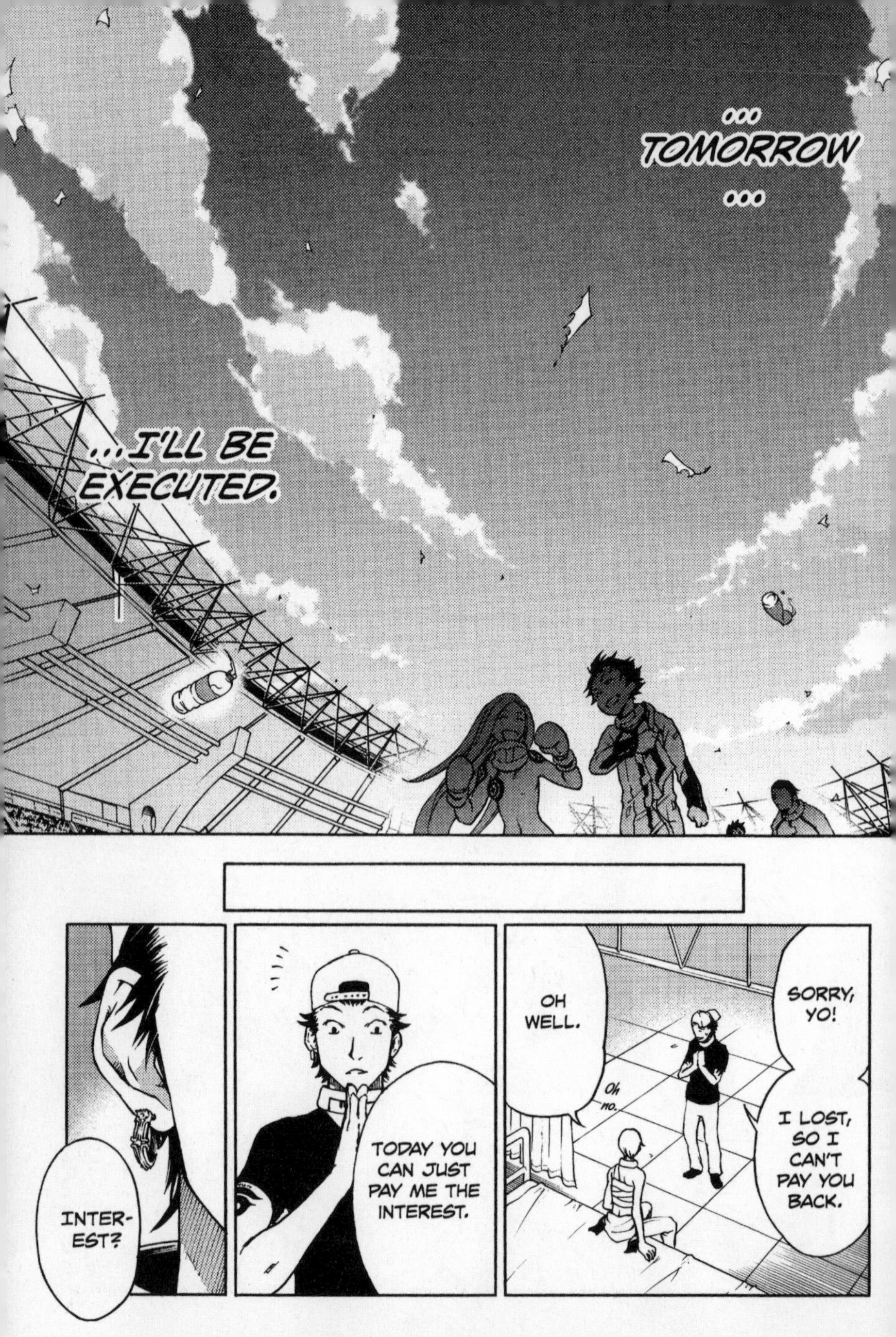
...TOMORROW...
...I'LL BE EXECUTED.
SORRY, YO!
I LOST, SO I CAN'T PAY YOU BACK.
OH WELL.
Oh no.
TODAY YOU CAN JUST PAY ME THE INTEREST.
INTER-EST?

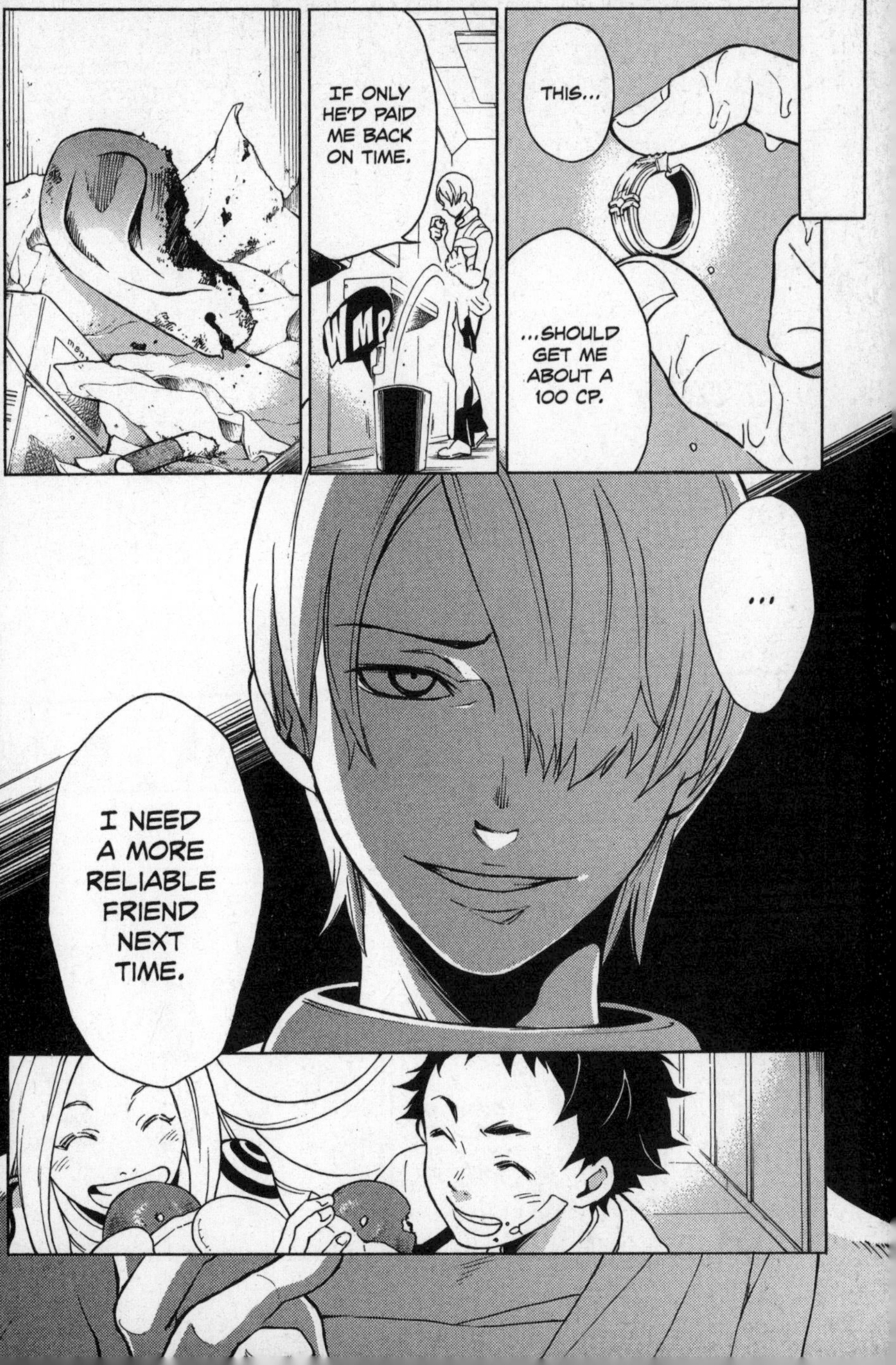
THIS...
...SHOULD GET ME ABOUT A 100 CP.
IF ONLY HE'D PAID ME BACK ON TIME.
WMP
...
I NEED A MORE RELIABLE FRIEND NEXT TIME.

# DEADMAN WONDERLAND

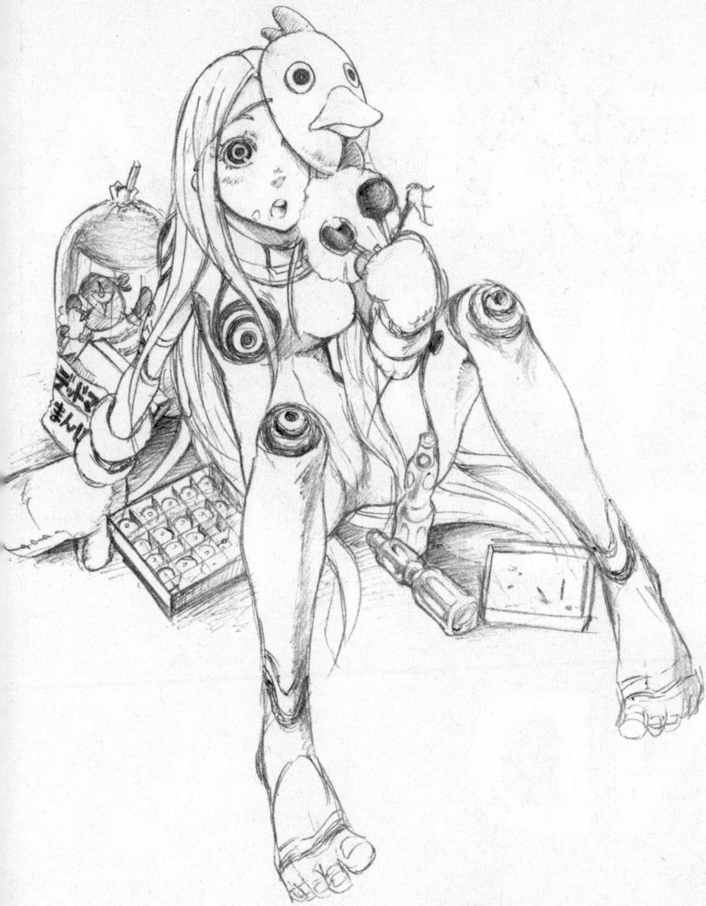
デッドマ
まんじ

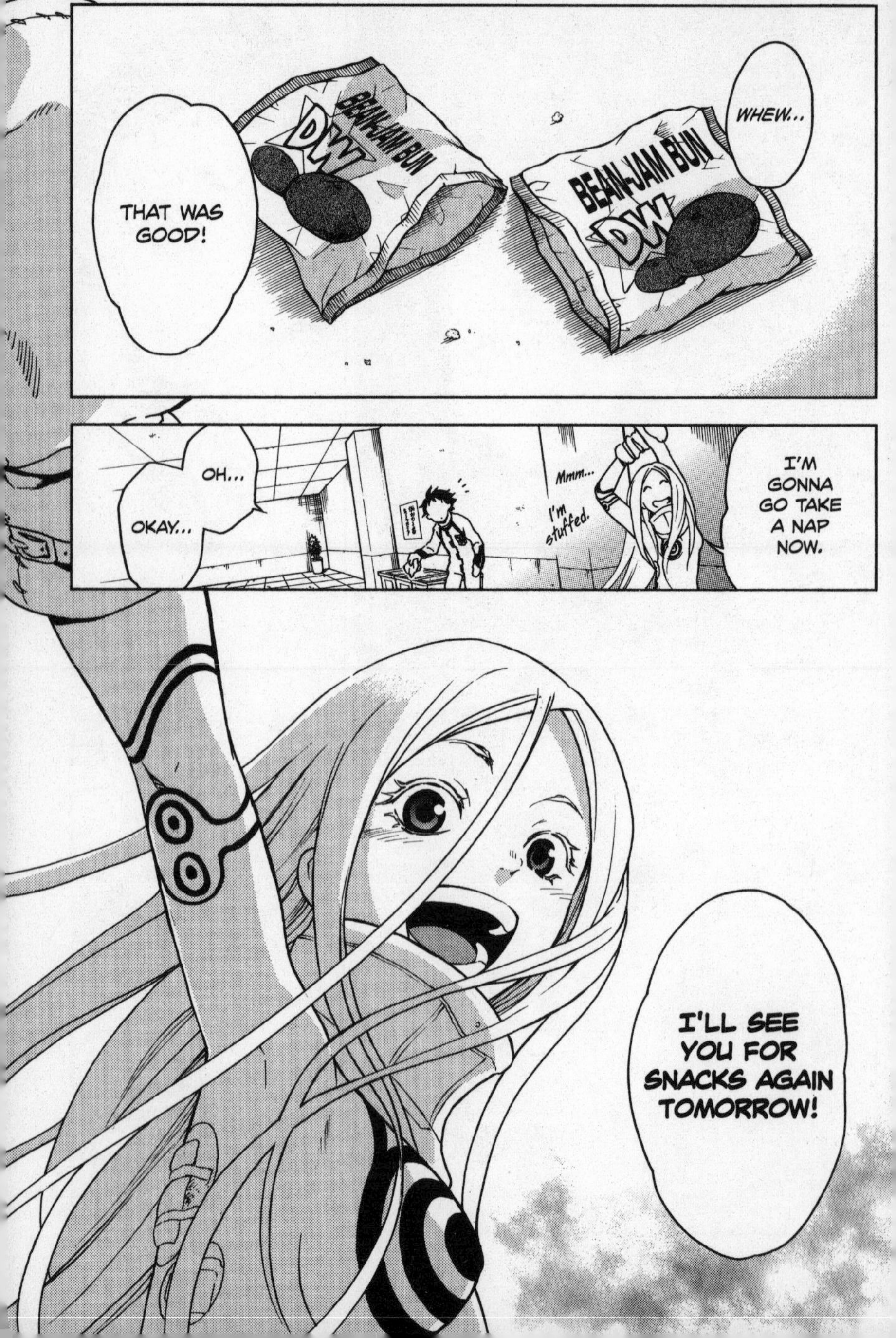
BEAN-JAM BUN
DW
WHEW...
BEAN-JAM BUN
DW
THAT WAS GOOD!
I'M GONNA GO TAKE A NAP NOW.
Mmm... I'm stuffed.
OH... OKAY...
I'LL SEE YOU FOR SNACKS AGAIN TOMORROW!

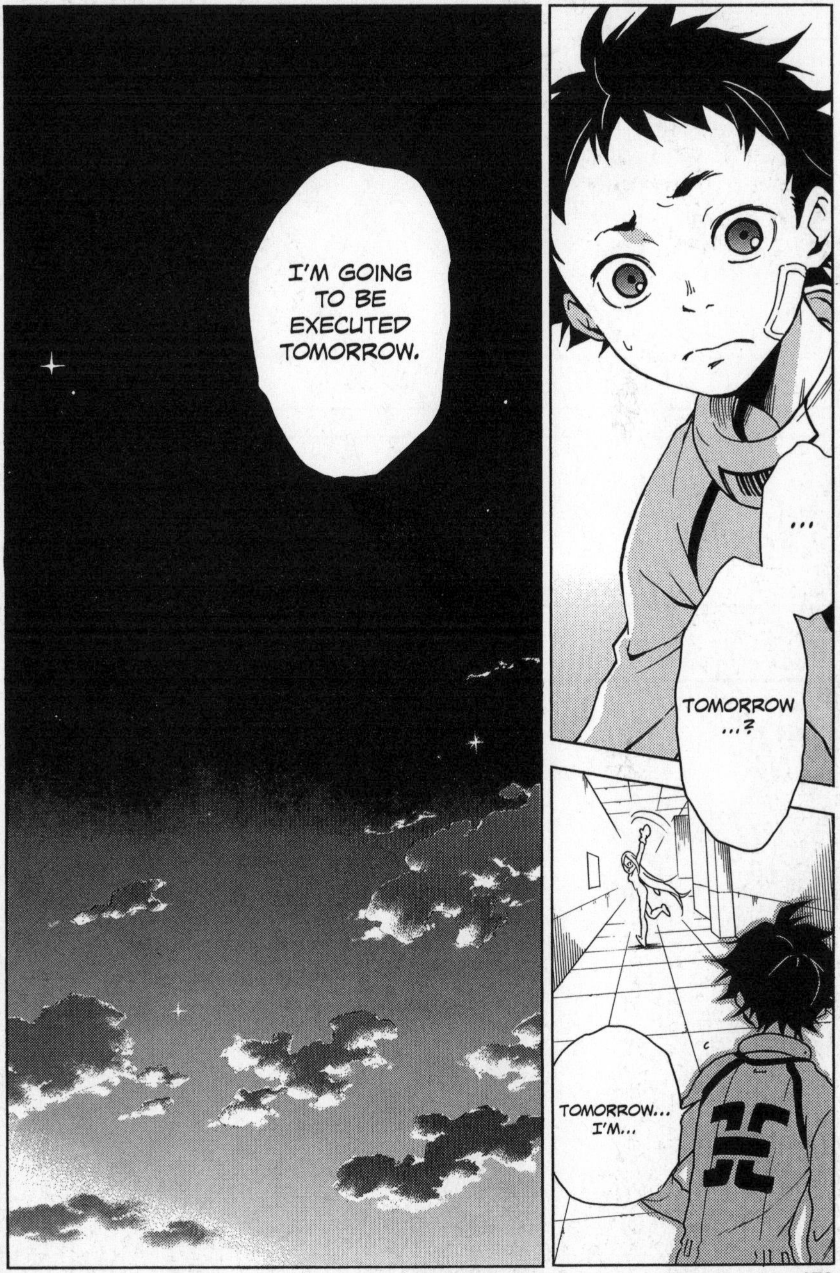
...
TOMORROW ...?
TOMORROW... I'M...
I'M GOING TO BE EXECUTED TOMORROW.

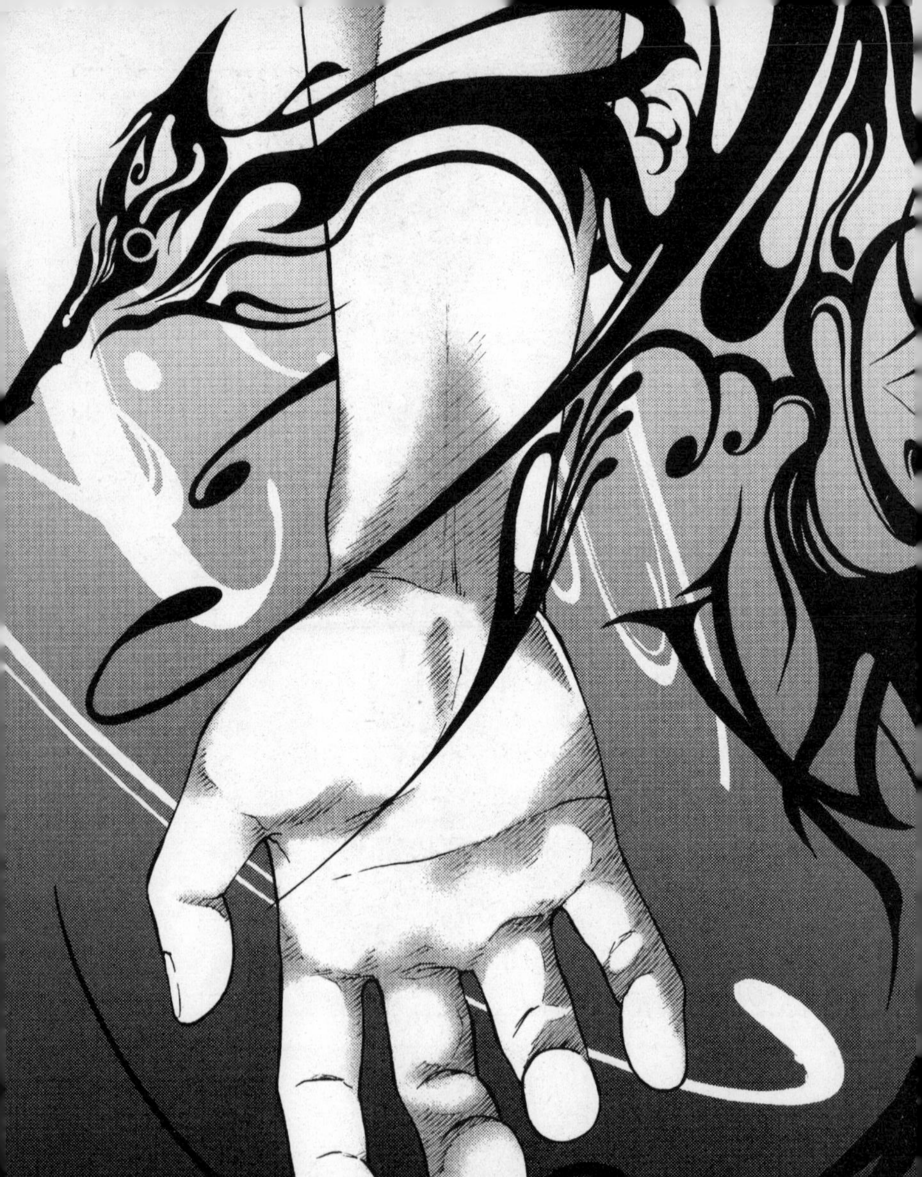

# 04 SLAYER'S SLAVE

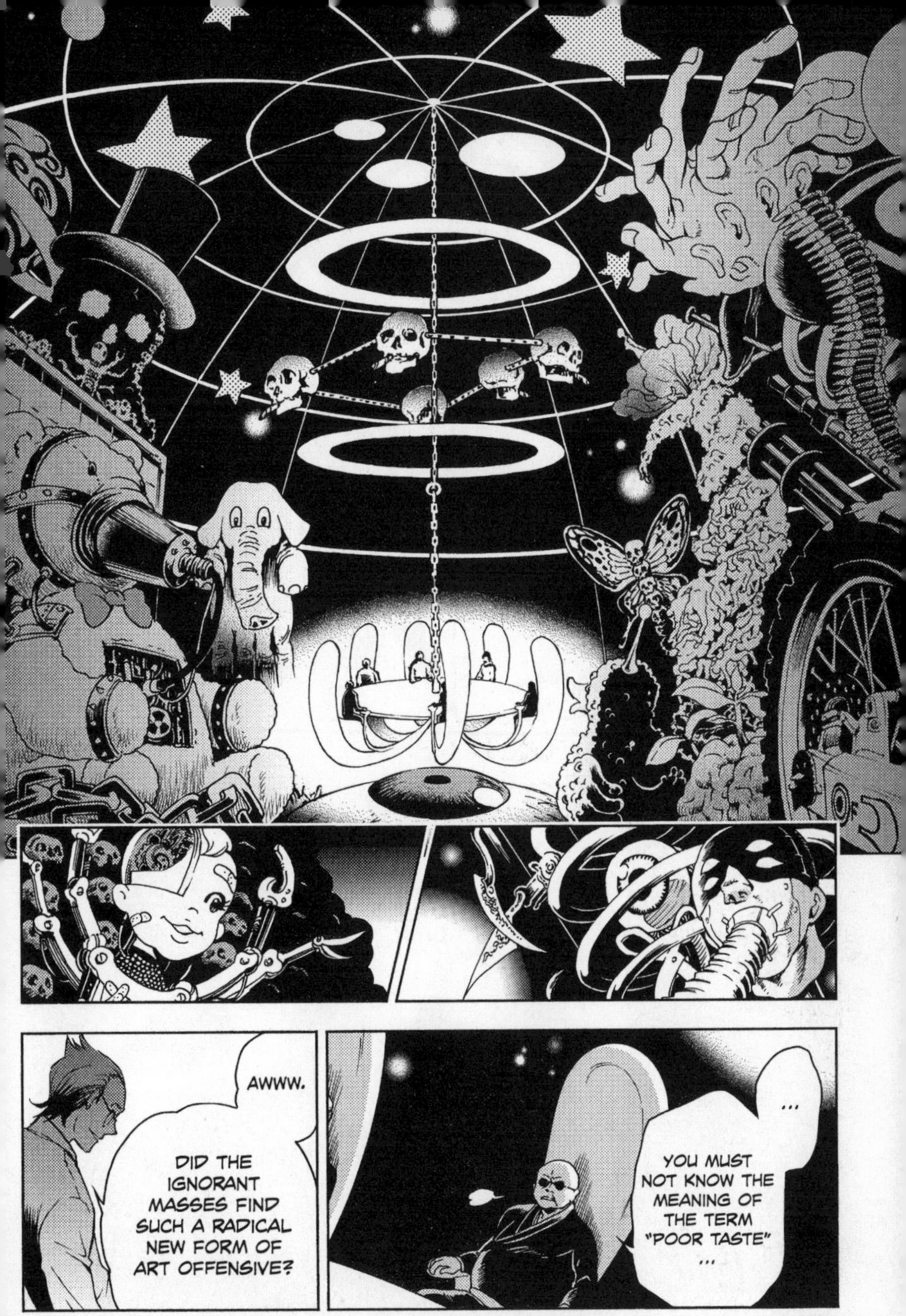
...
YOU MUST NOT KNOW THE MEANING OF THE TERM "POOR TASTE" ...
AWWW.
DID THE IGNORANT MASSES FIND SUCH A RADICAL NEW FORM OF ART OFFENSIVE?

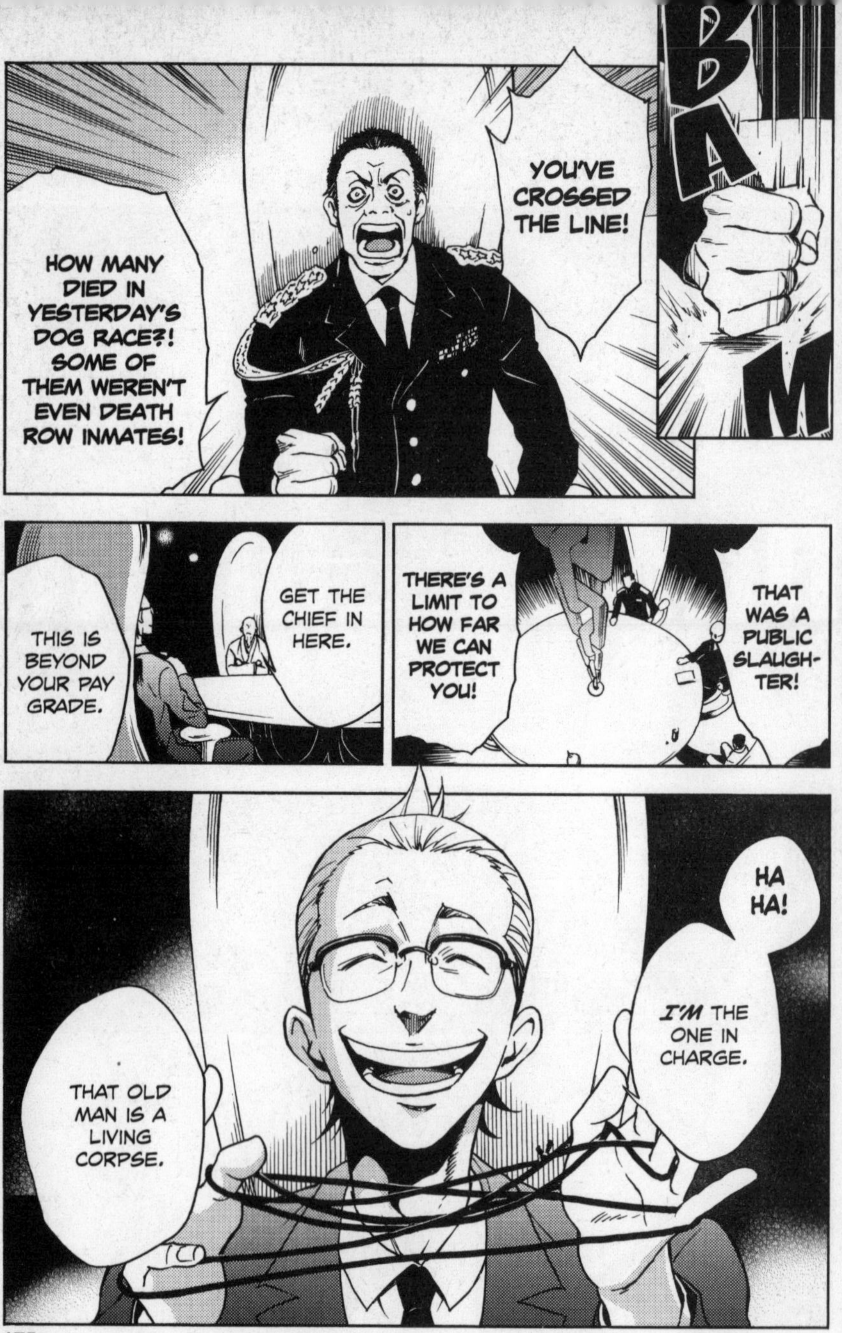
BAM
YOU'VE CROSSED THE LINE!
HOW MANY DIED IN YESTERDAY'S DOG RACE?! SOME OF THEM WEREN'T EVEN DEATH ROW INMATES!
THAT WAS A PUBLIC SLAUGHTER!
THERE'S A LIMIT TO HOW FAR WE CAN PROTECT YOU!
GET THE CHIEF IN HERE.
THIS IS BEYOND YOUR PAY GRADE.
HA HA!
*I'M* THE ONE IN CHARGE.
THAT OLD MAN IS A LIVING CORPSE.

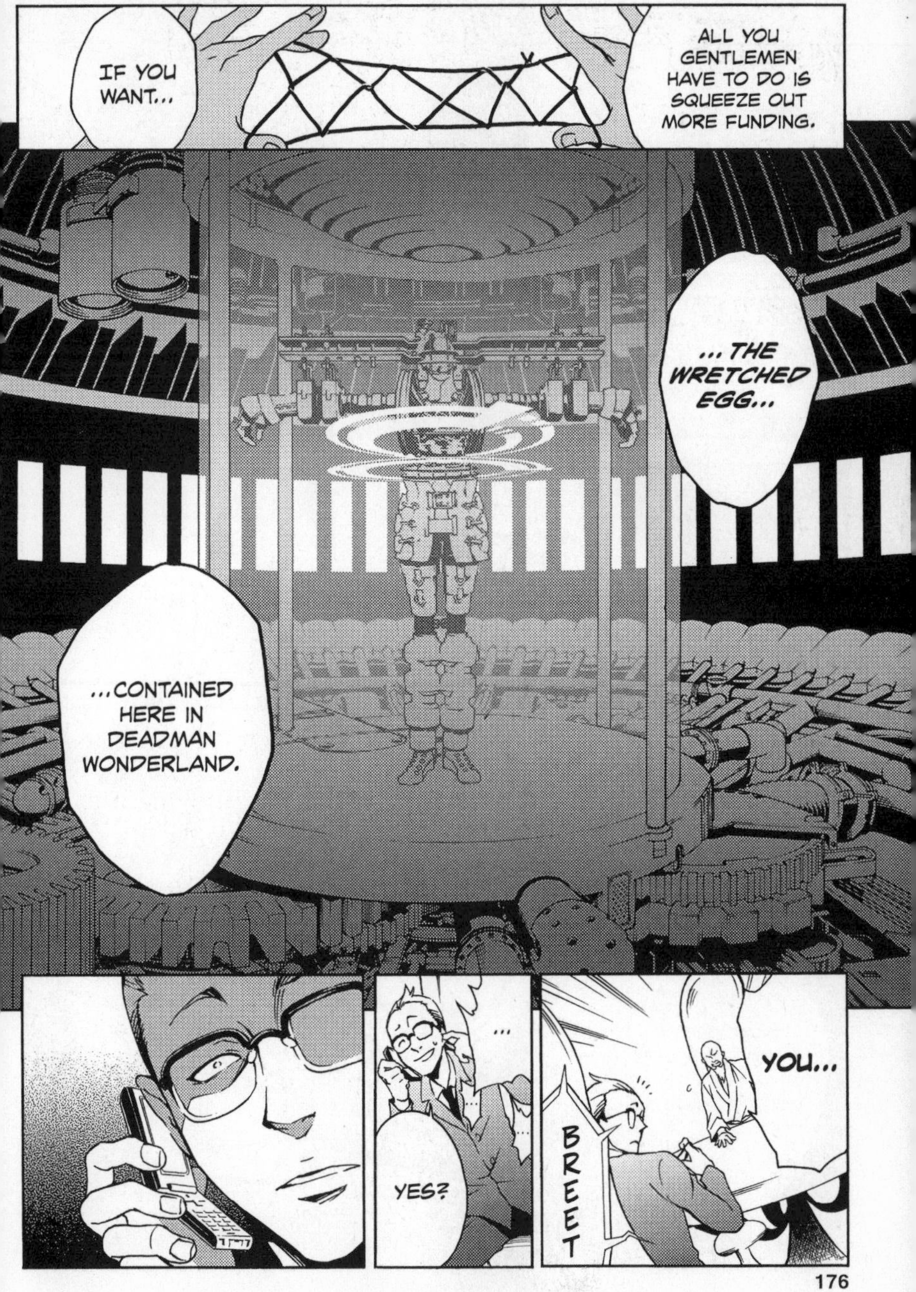
ALL YOU GENTLEMEN HAVE TO DO IS SQUEEZE OUT MORE FUNDING.
IF YOU WANT...
...THE WRETCHED EGG...
...CONTAINED HERE IN DEADMAN WONDERLAND.
YOU...
BREET
...
YES?

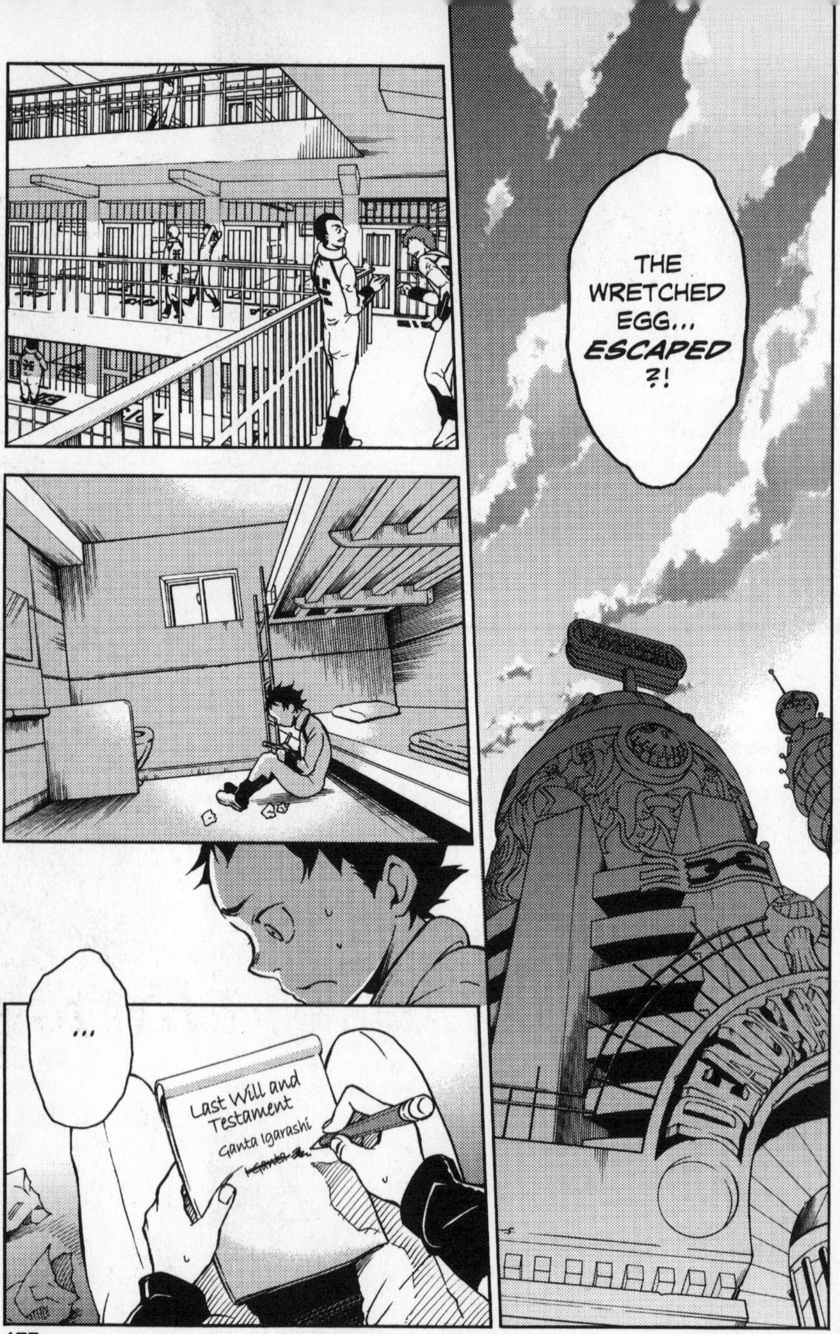
THE WRETCHED EGG... ESCAPED?!
...
Last Will and Testament
Ganta Igarashi

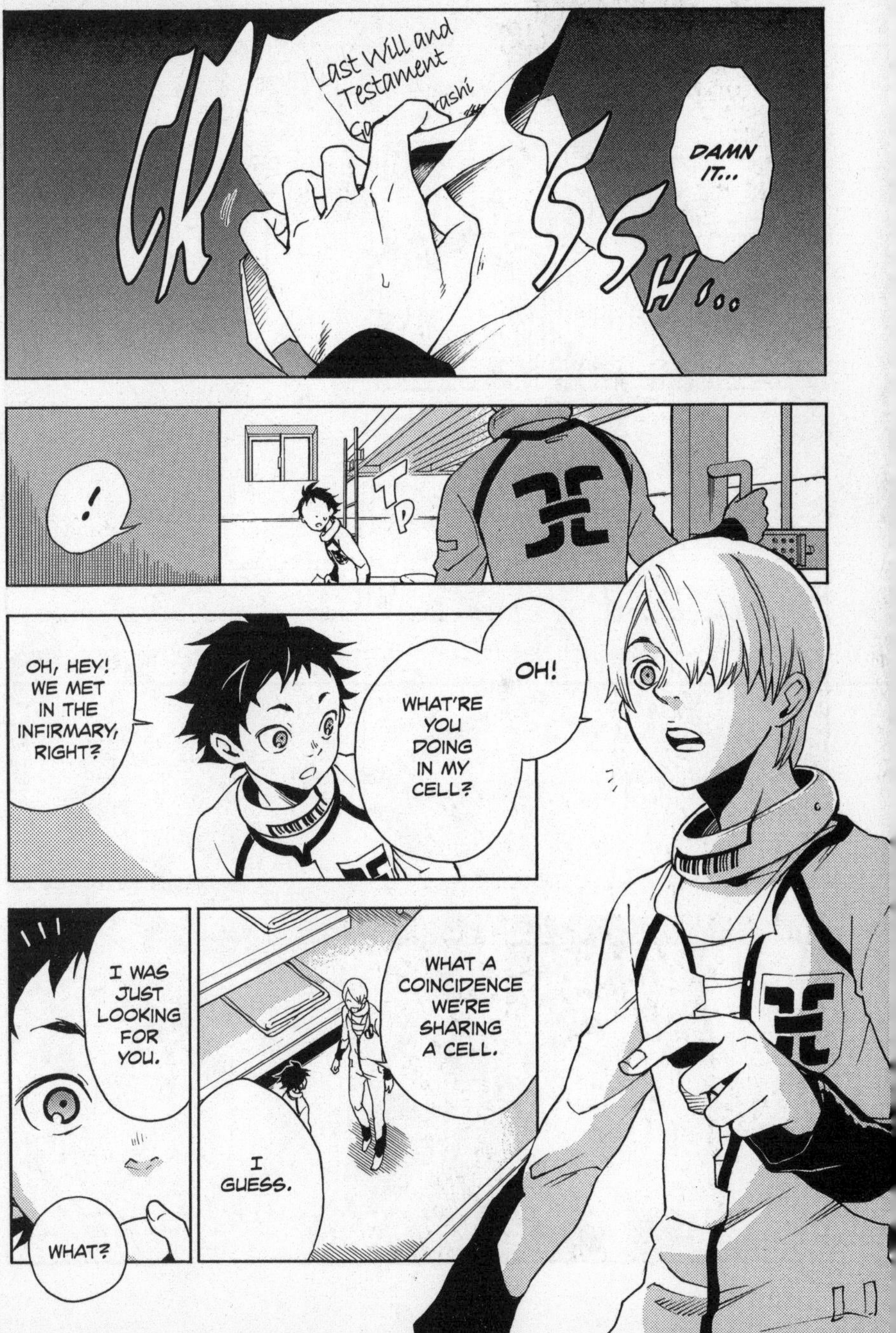
Last Will and Testament
DAMN IT...
CRSSSH...
TP
!
OH!
WHAT'RE YOU DOING IN MY CELL?
OH, HEY! WE MET IN THE INFIRMARY, RIGHT?
WHAT A COINCIDENCE WE'RE SHARING A CELL.
I GUESS.
I WAS JUST LOOKING FOR YOU.
WHAT?

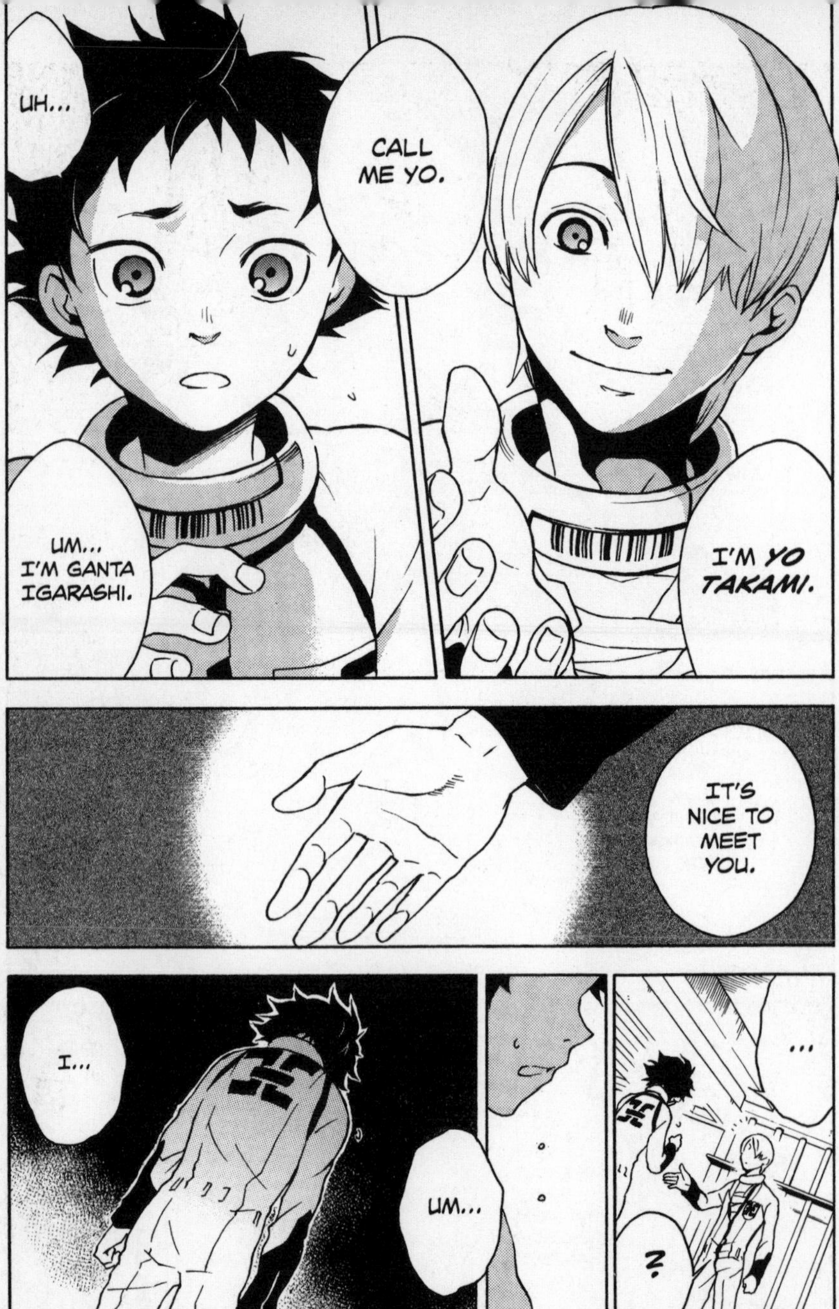
I'M YO TAKAMI.
CALL ME YO.
UH...
UM... I'M GANTA IGARASHI.
IT'S NICE TO MEET YOU.
...
?
UM...
I...

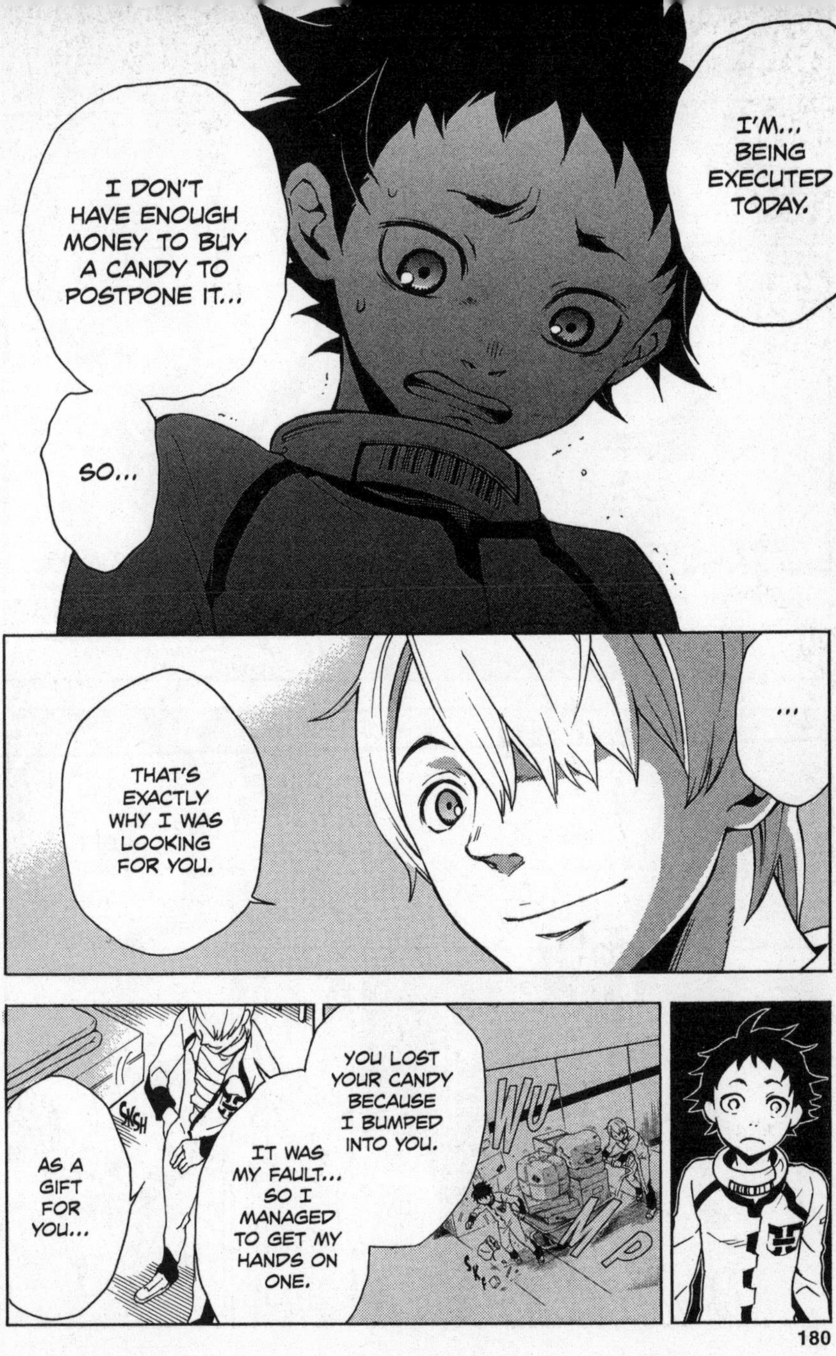
I'M... BEING EXECUTED TODAY.
I DON'T HAVE ENOUGH MONEY TO BUY A CANDY TO POSTPONE IT...
SO...
...
THAT'S EXACTLY WHY I WAS LOOKING FOR YOU.
YOU LOST YOUR CANDY BECAUSE I BUMPED INTO YOU.
WUMP
IT WAS MY FAULT... SO I MANAGED TO GET MY HANDS ON ONE.
SKSH
AS A GIFT FOR YOU...

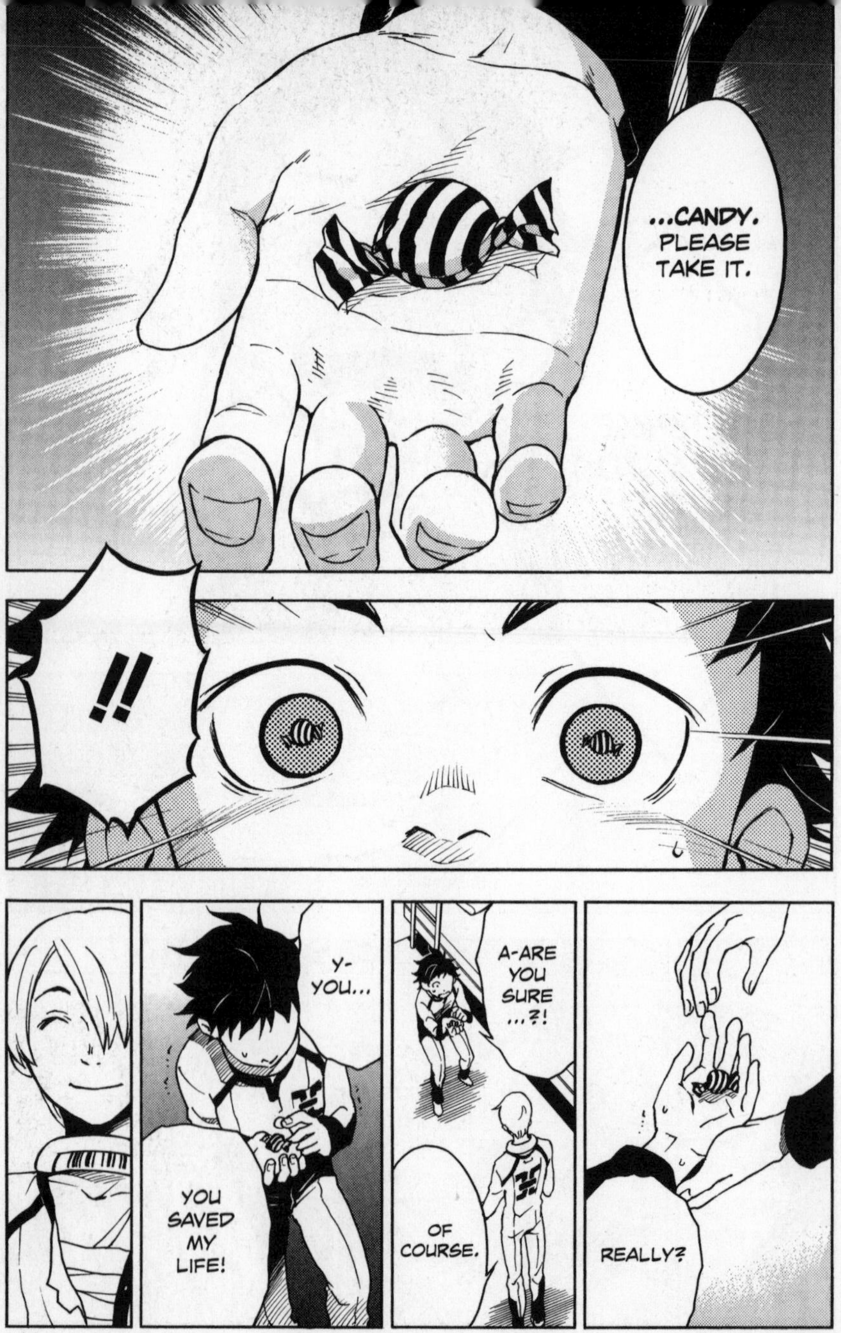
...CANDY. PLEASE TAKE IT.
!!
REALLY?
A-ARE YOU SURE ...?!
OF COURSE.
Y-YOU...
YOU SAVED MY LIFE!

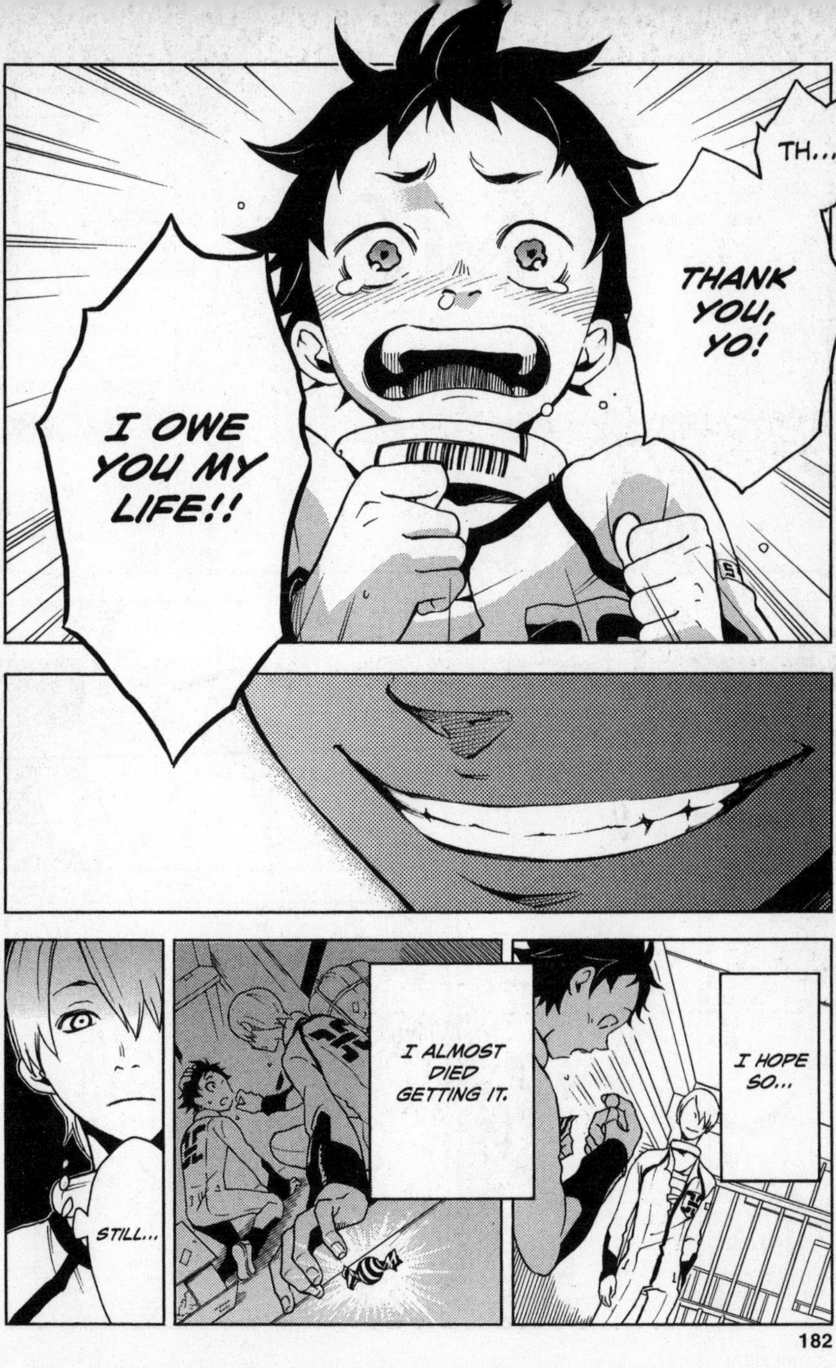
TH...
THANK YOU, YO!
I OWE YOU MY LIFE!!
I HOPE SO...
I ALMOST DIED GETTING IT.
STILL...

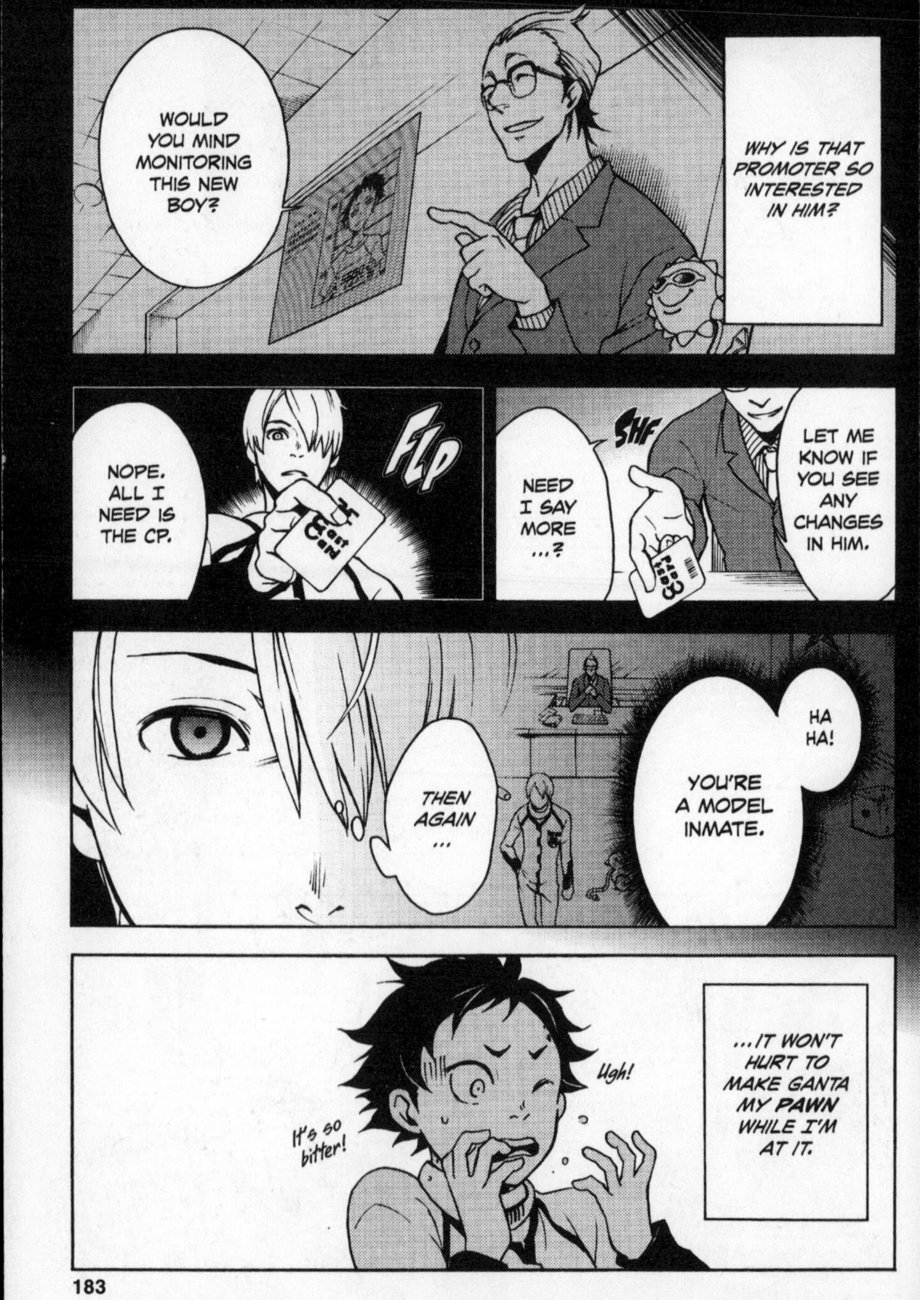
WHY IS THAT PROMOTER SO INTERESTED IN HIM?
WOULD YOU MIND MONITORING THIS NEW BOY?
LET ME KNOW IF YOU SEE ANY CHANGES IN HIM.
SHF
NEED I SAY MORE ...?
FLP
NOPE. ALL I NEED IS THE CP.
HA HA!
YOU'RE A MODEL INMATE.
THEN AGAIN ...
...IT WON'T HURT TO MAKE GANTA MY PAWN WHILE I'M AT IT.
Ugh!
It's so bitter!

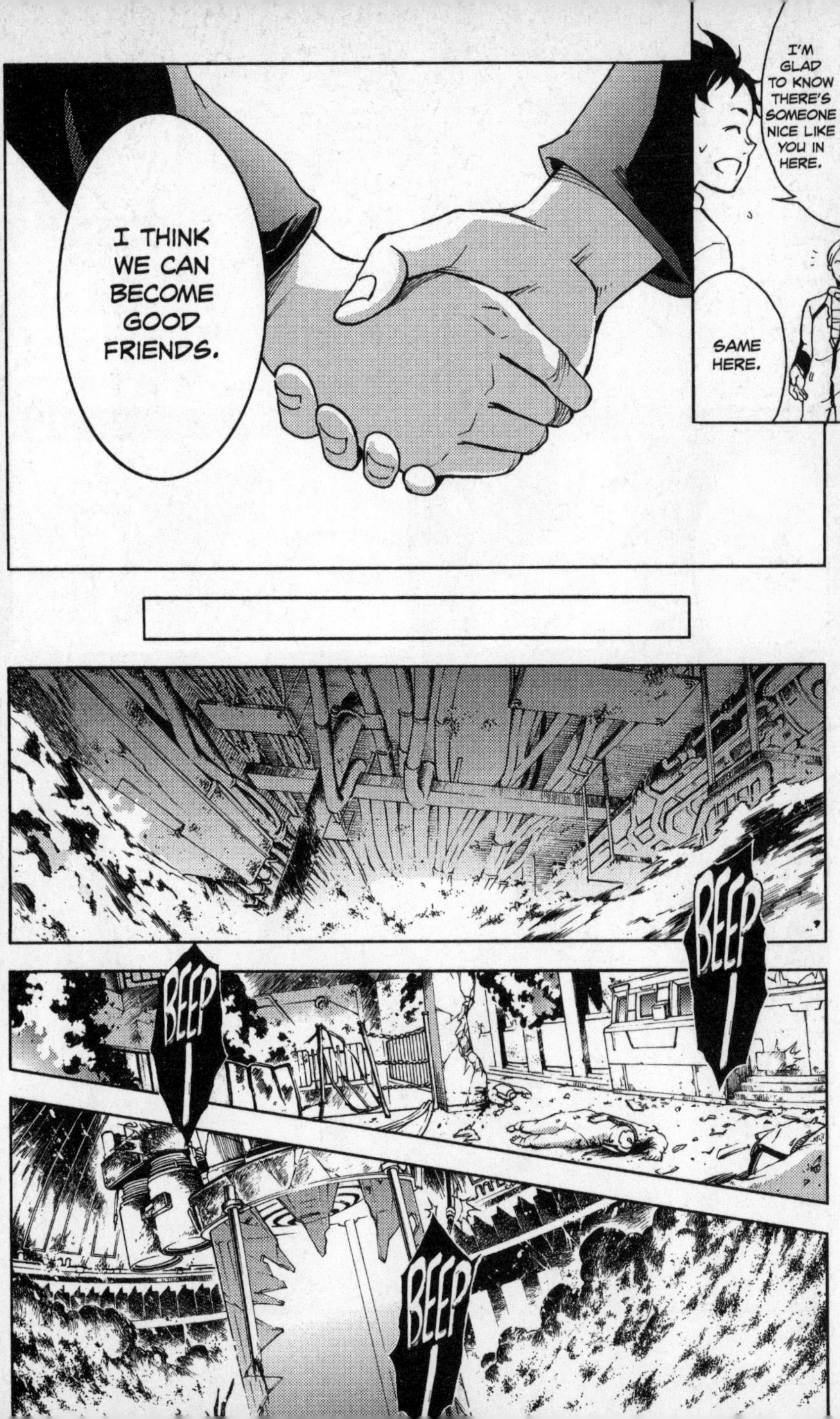
I'M GLAD TO KNOW THERE'S SOMEONE NICE LIKE YOU IN HERE.
SAME HERE.
I THINK WE CAN BECOME GOOD FRIENDS.
BEEP
BEEP
BEEP

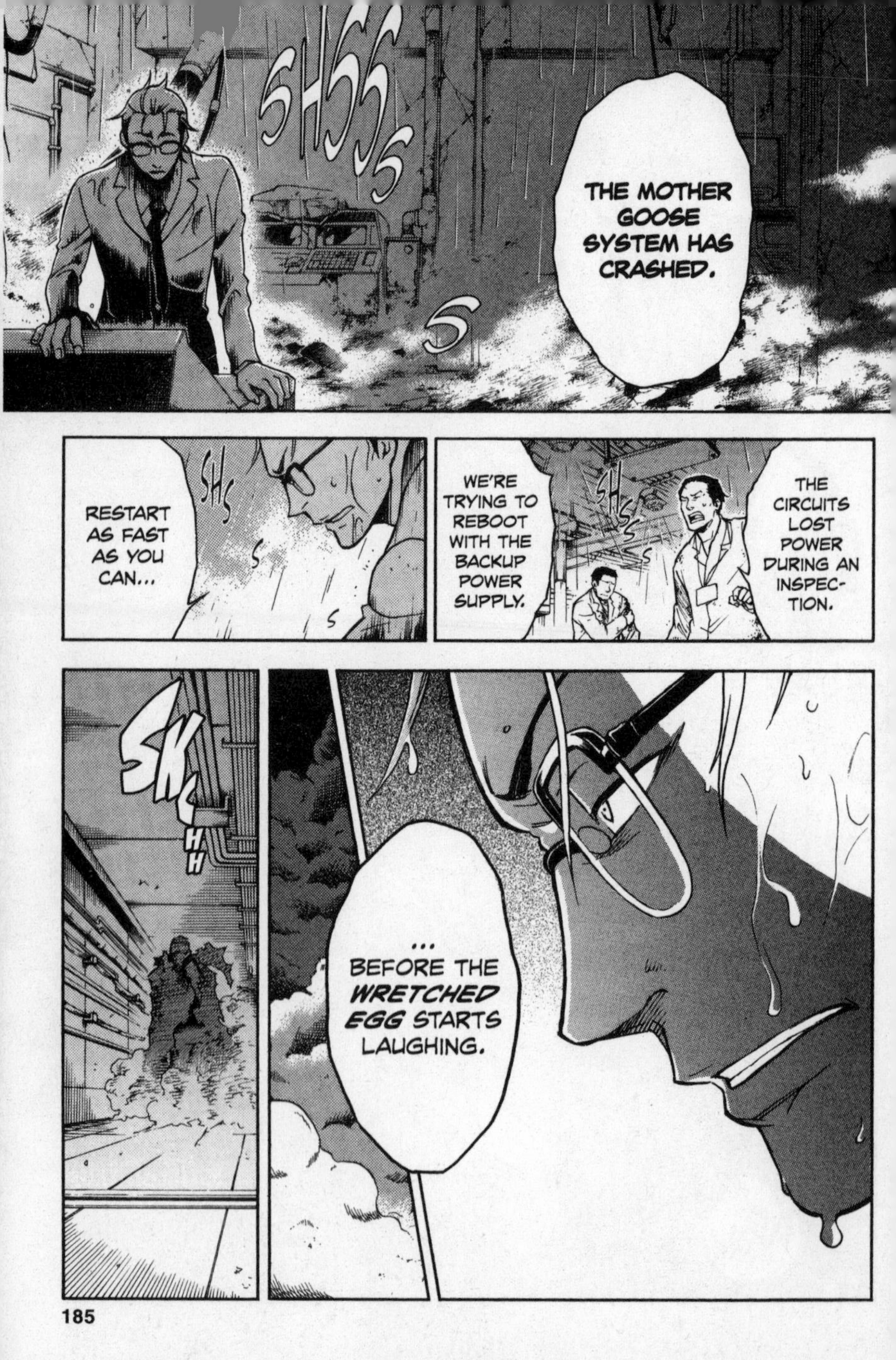
SHSSS
S
THE MOTHER GOOSE SYSTEM HAS CRASHED.
THE CIRCUITS LOST POWER DURING AN INSPECTION.
WE'RE TRYING TO REBOOT WITH THE BACKUP POWER SUPPLY.
SHSS
RESTART AS FAST AS YOU CAN...
SHSS
...BEFORE THE *WRETCHED EGG* STARTS LAUGHING.
SKCHH

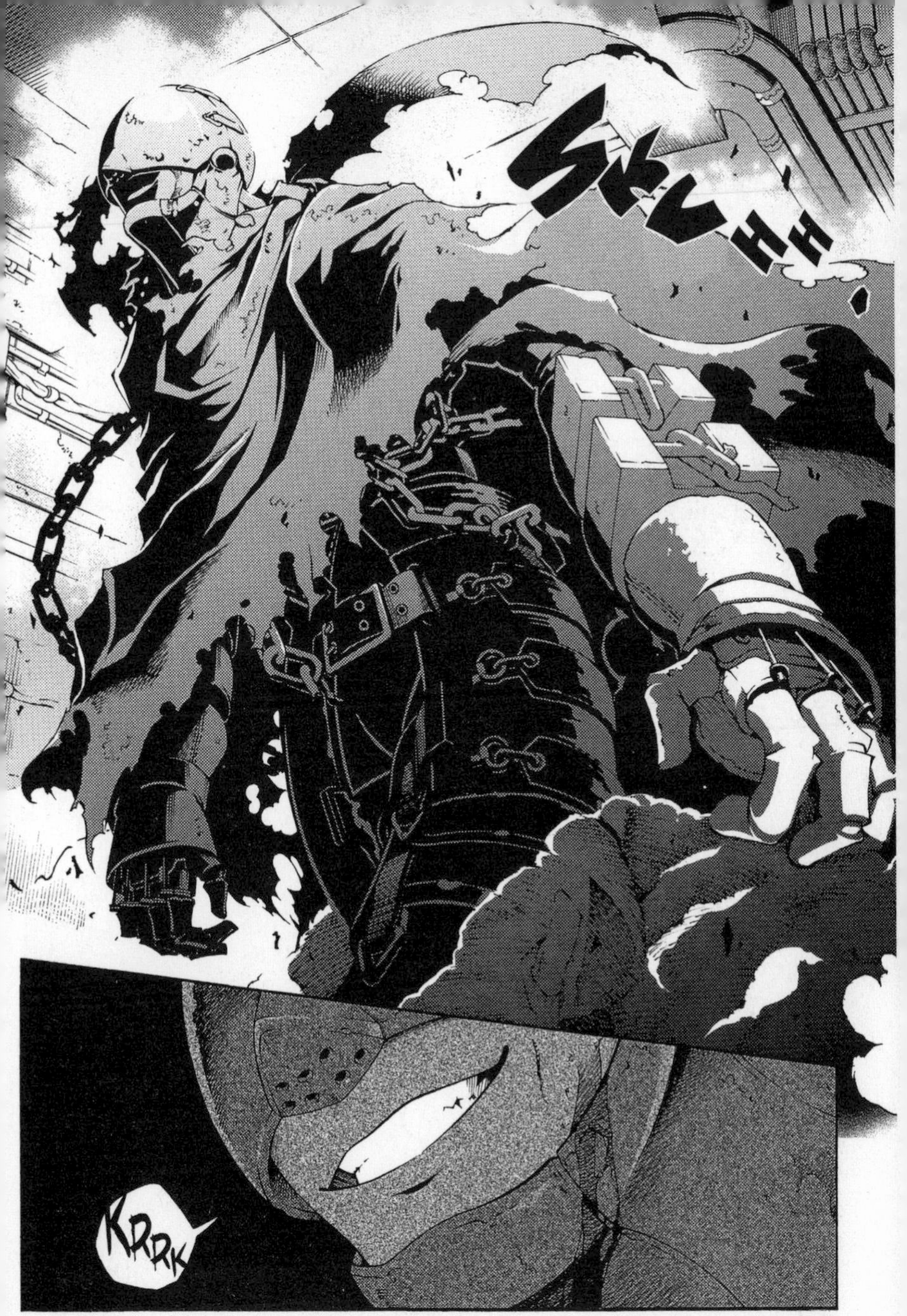
SKLUHH
KRRK

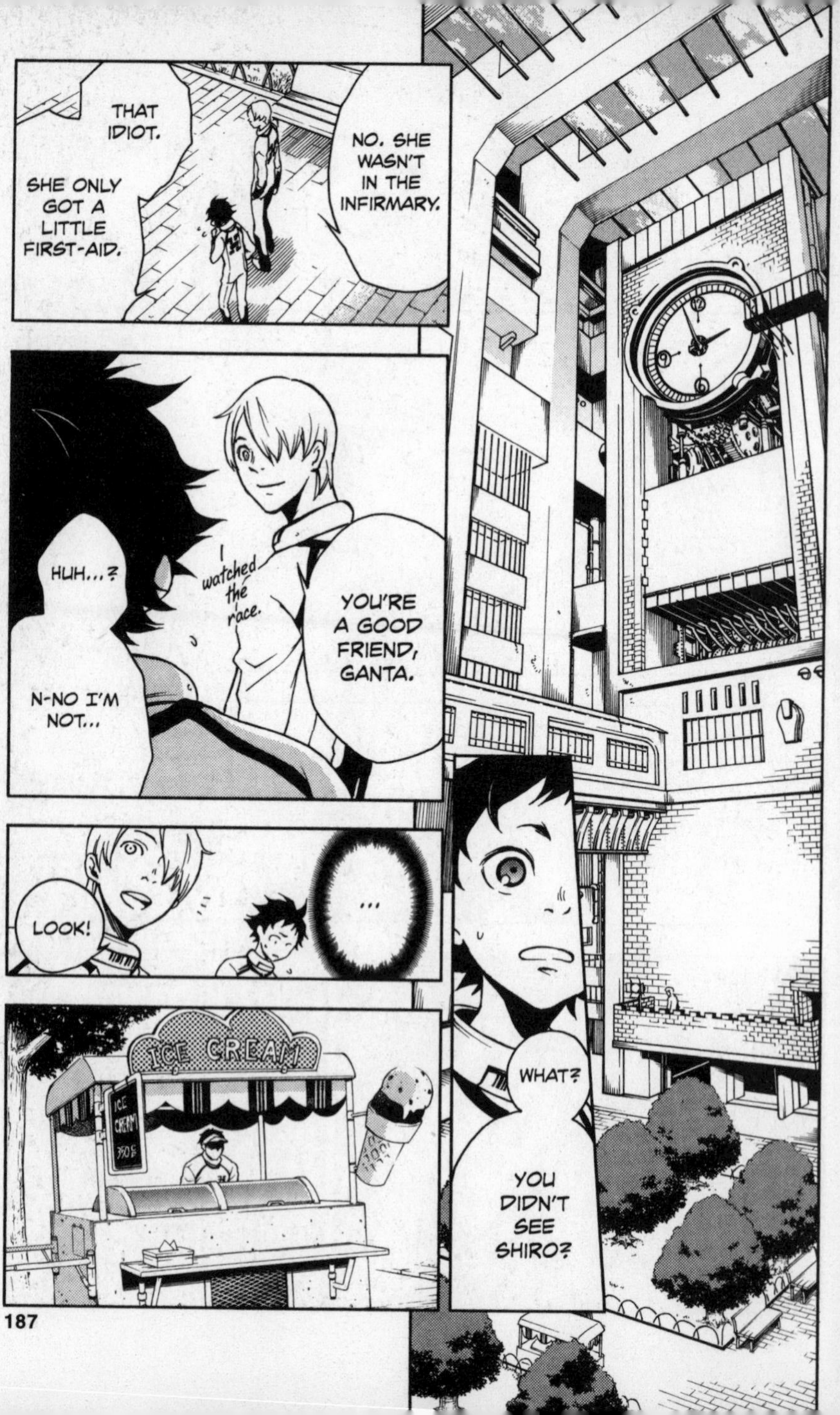
WHAT?
YOU DIDN'T SEE SHIRO?
NO. SHE WASN'T IN THE INFIRMARY.
THAT IDIOT.
SHE ONLY GOT A LITTLE FIRST-AID.
YOU'RE A GOOD FRIEND, GANTA.
I watched the race.
HUH...?
N-NO I'M NOT...
...
LOOK!
ICE CREAM
ICE CREAM

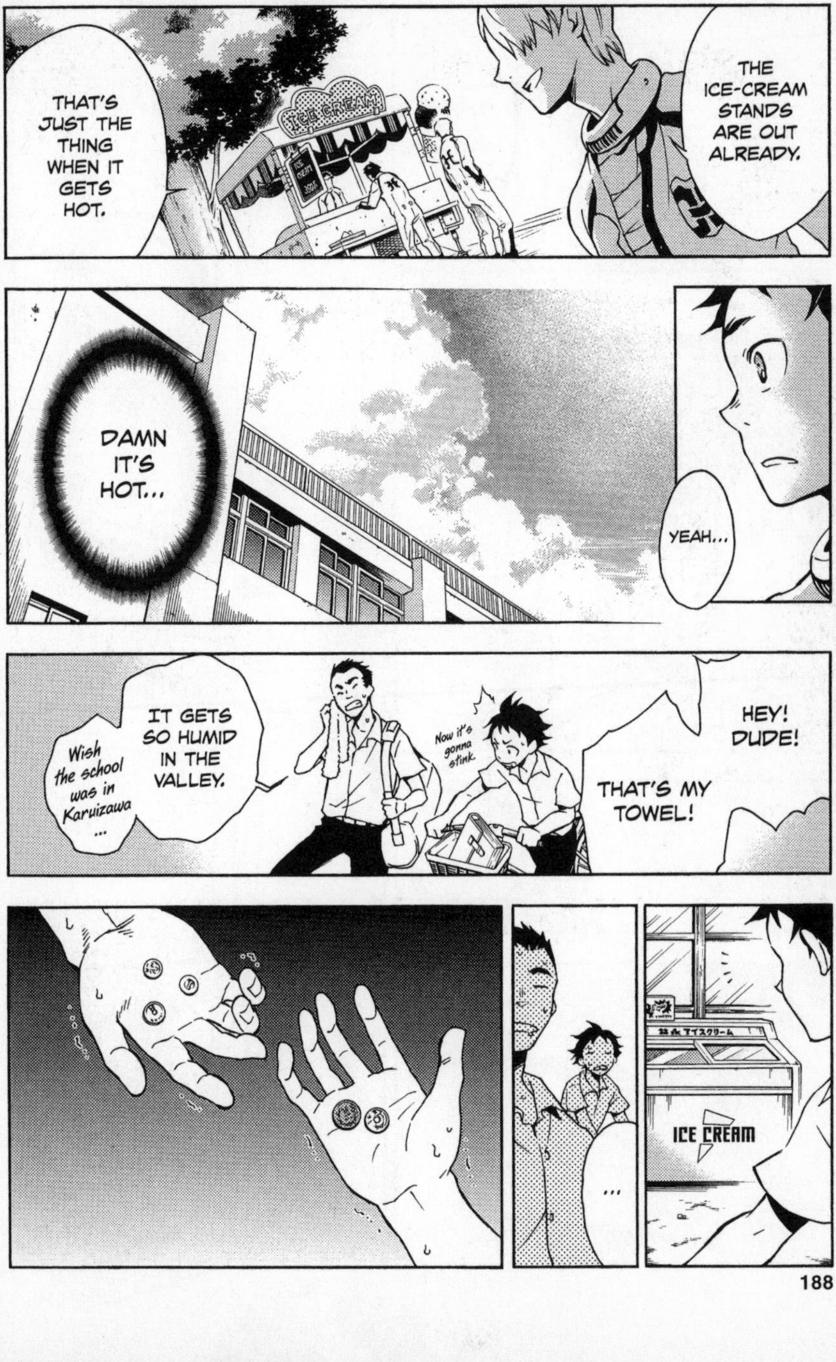
THE ICE-CREAM STANDS ARE OUT ALREADY.
THAT'S JUST THE THING WHEN IT GETS HOT.
YEAH...
DAMN IT'S HOT...
HEY! DUDE!
THAT'S MY TOWEL!
Now it's gonna stink.
IT GETS SO HUMID IN THE VALLEY.
Wish the school was in Karuizawa ...
ICE CREAM
...

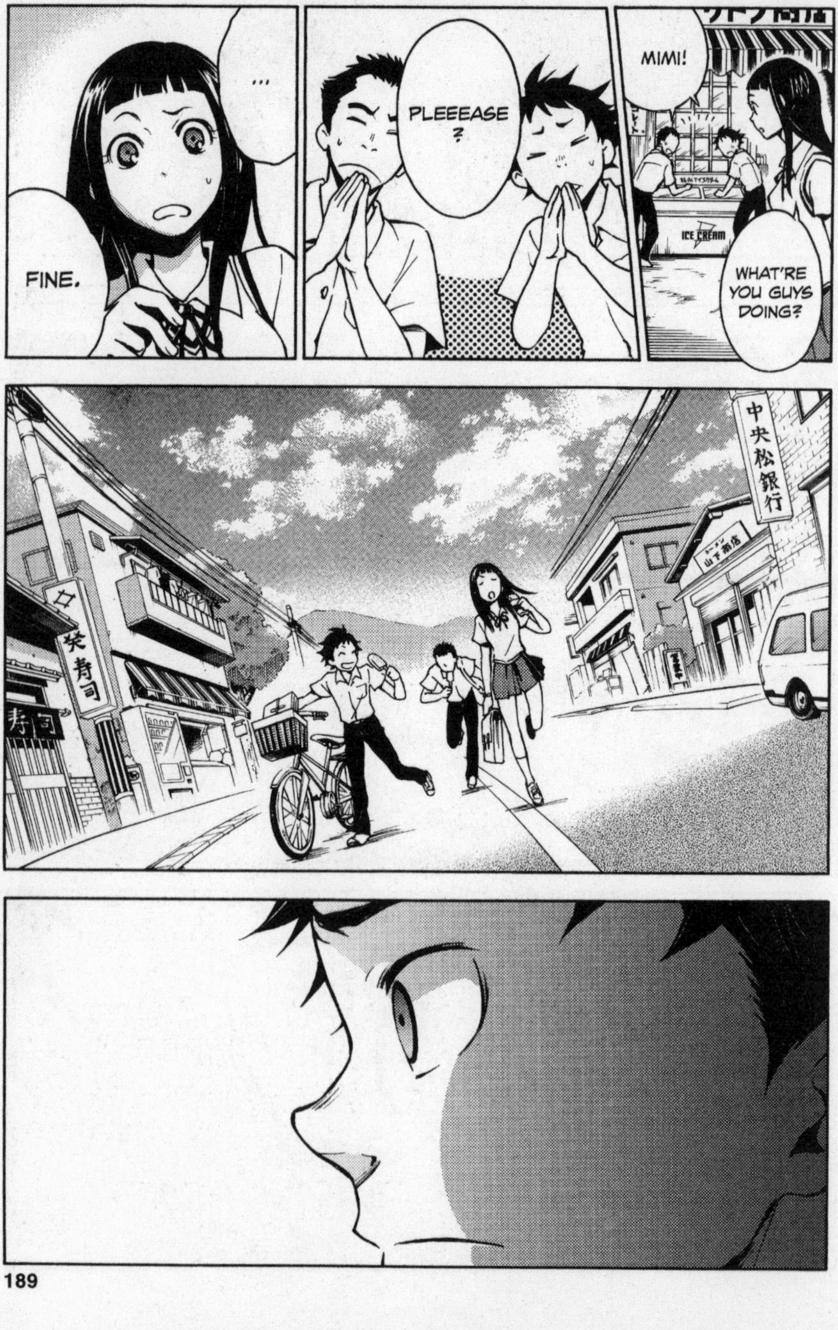
MIMI!
ICE CREAM
WHAT'RE YOU GUYS DOING?
PLEEEASE?
...
FINE.
中央松銀行
寿司

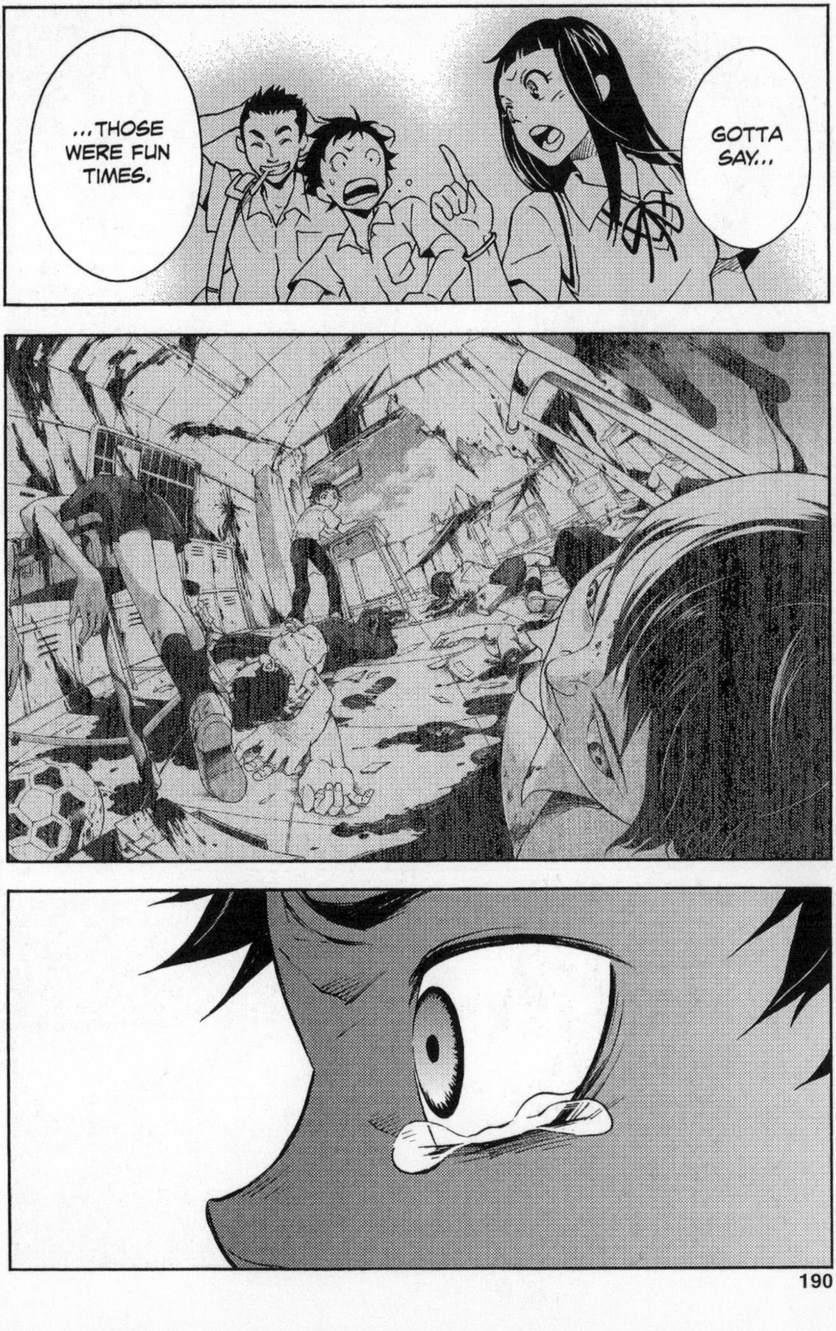
GOTTA SAY...
...THOSE WERE FUN TIMES.

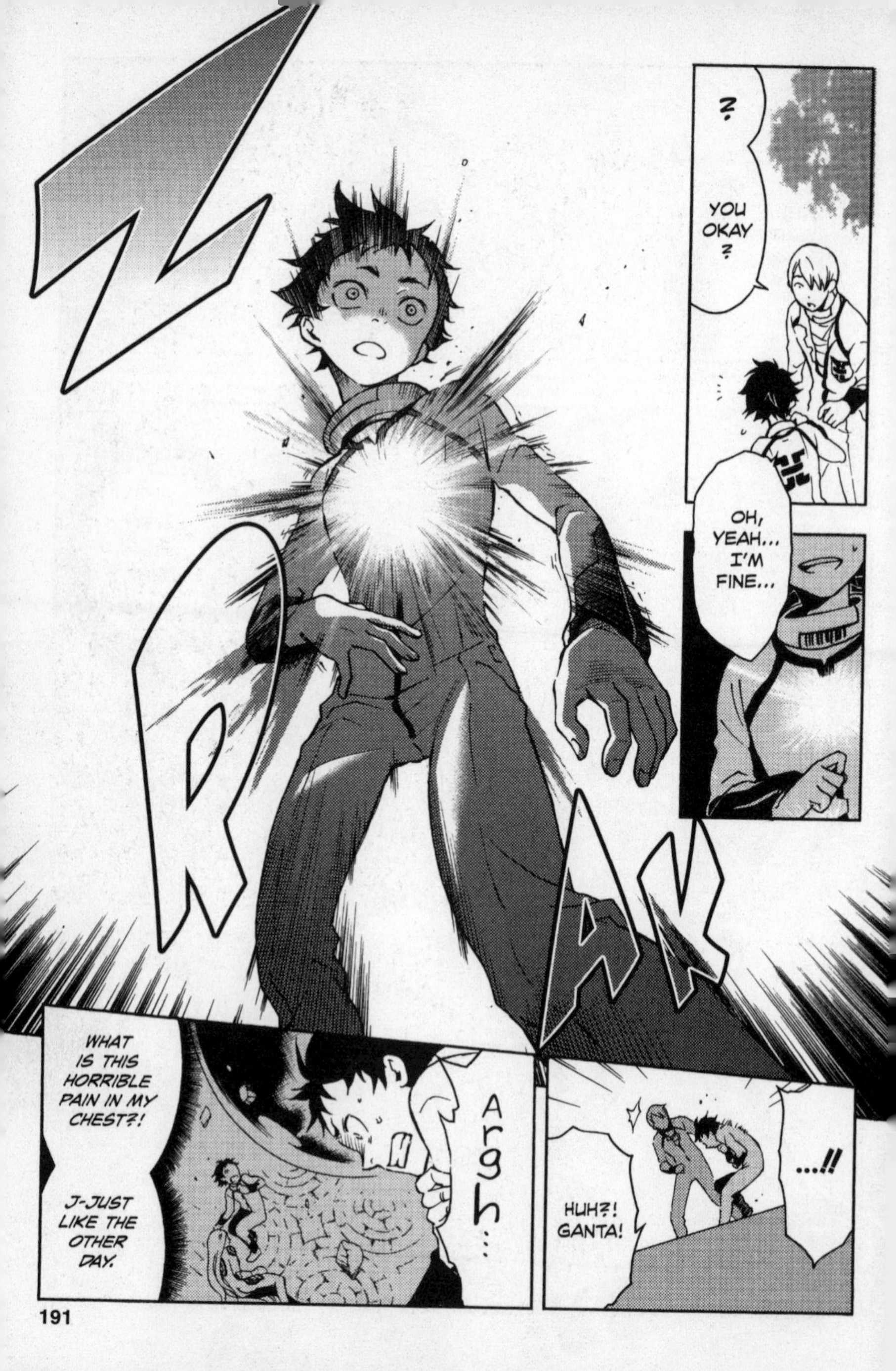
?
YOU OKAY?
...
OH, YEAH... I'M FINE...
ZRAK
...!!
HUH?! GANTA!
WHAT IS THIS HORRIBLE PAIN IN MY CHEST?!
Argh...
J-JUST LIKE THE OTHER DAY.

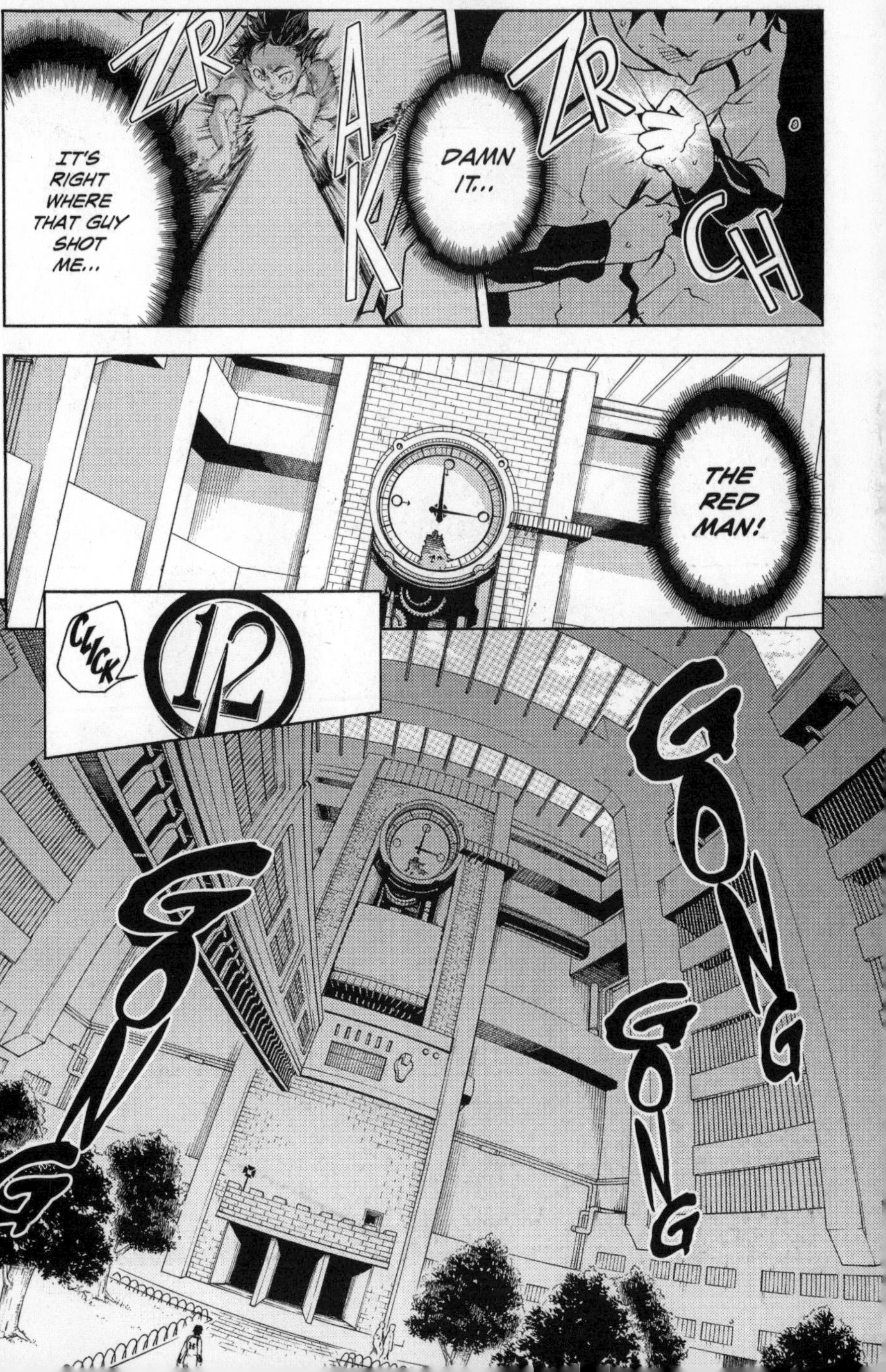
ZRCH
DAMN IT...
ZRAK
IT'S RIGHT WHERE THAT GUY SHOT ME...
THE RED MAN!
CLICK
12
GONG
GONG
GONG
GONG

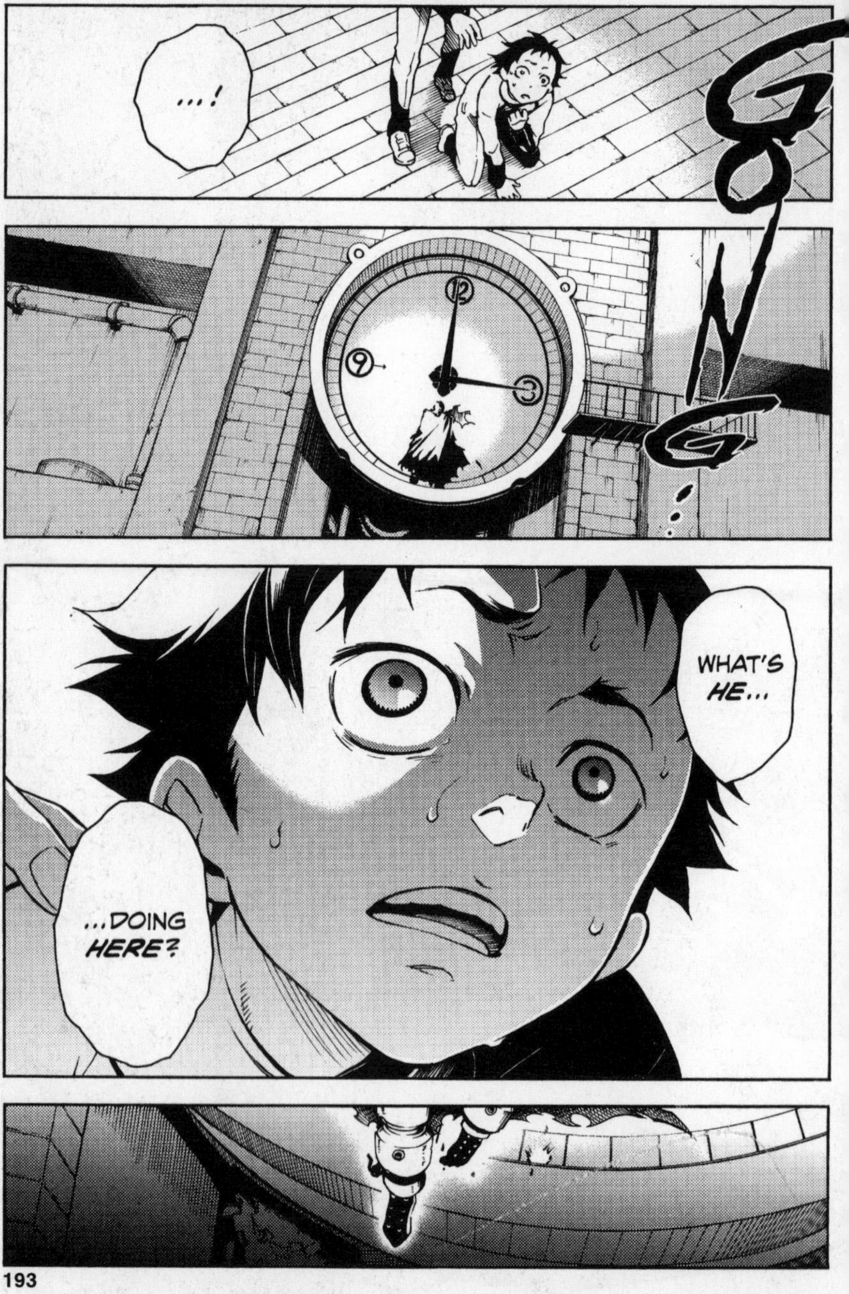
...!
GONG...
WHAT'S HE...
...DOING HERE?

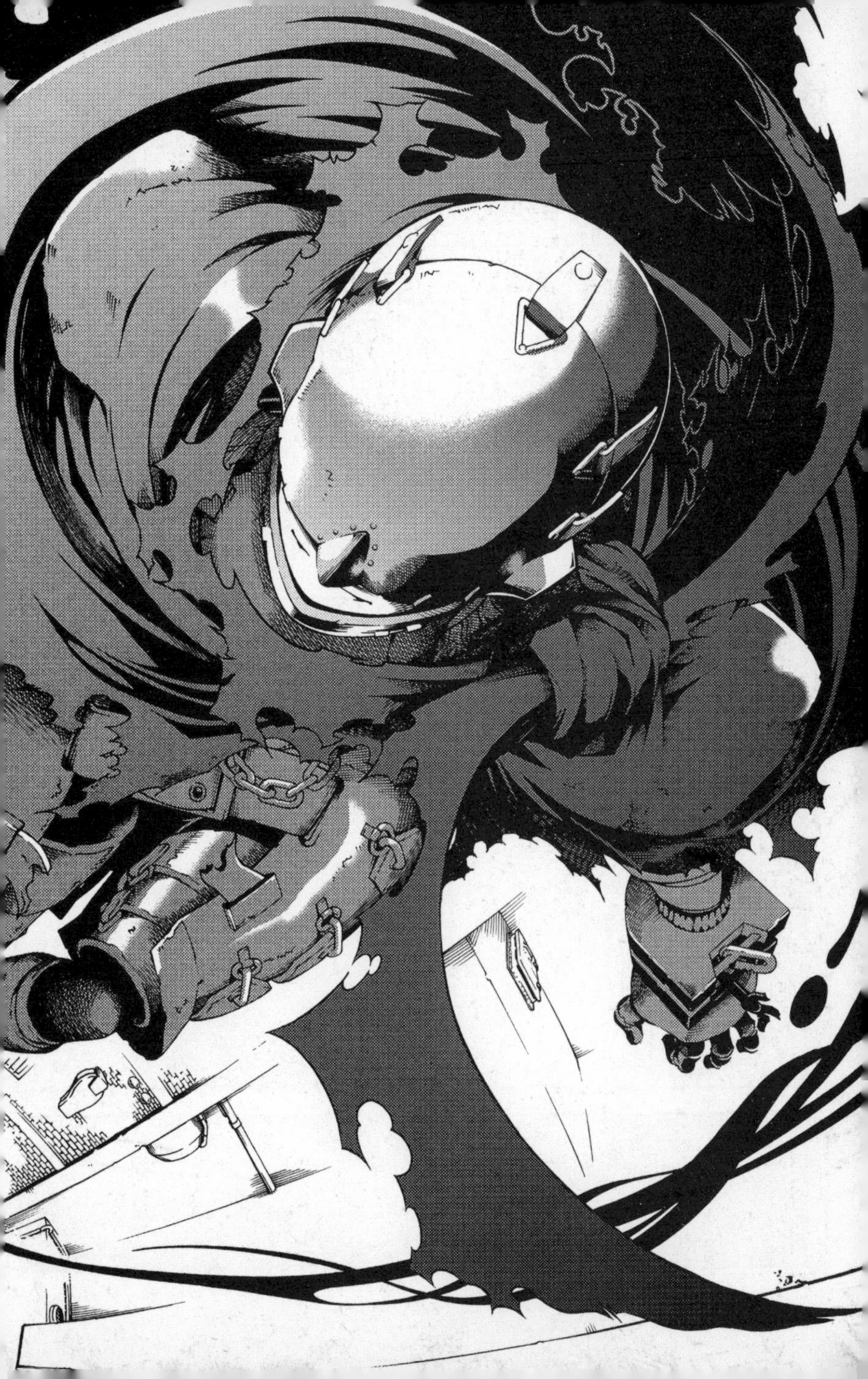

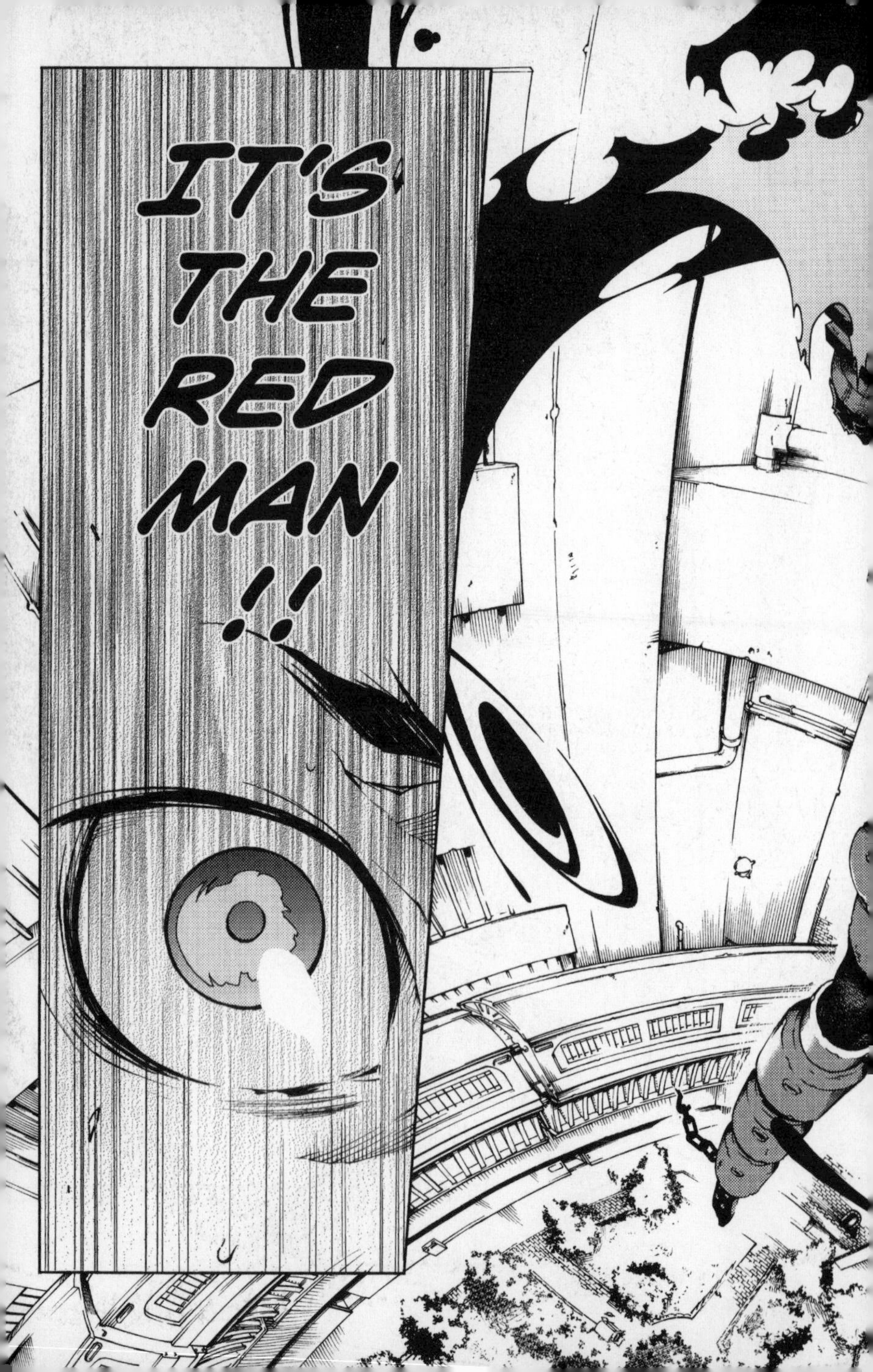
IT'S THE RED MAN!!

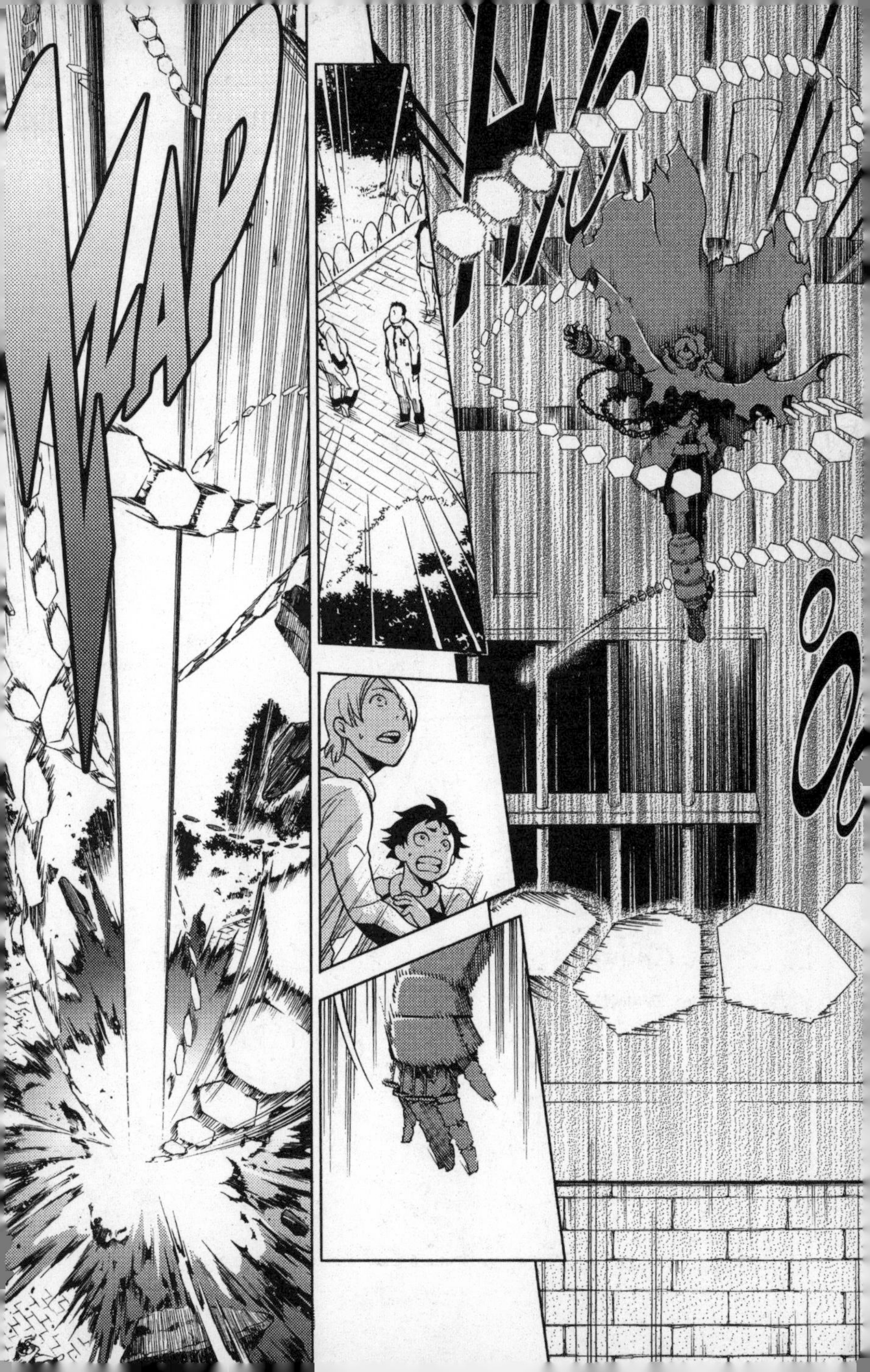
WAP

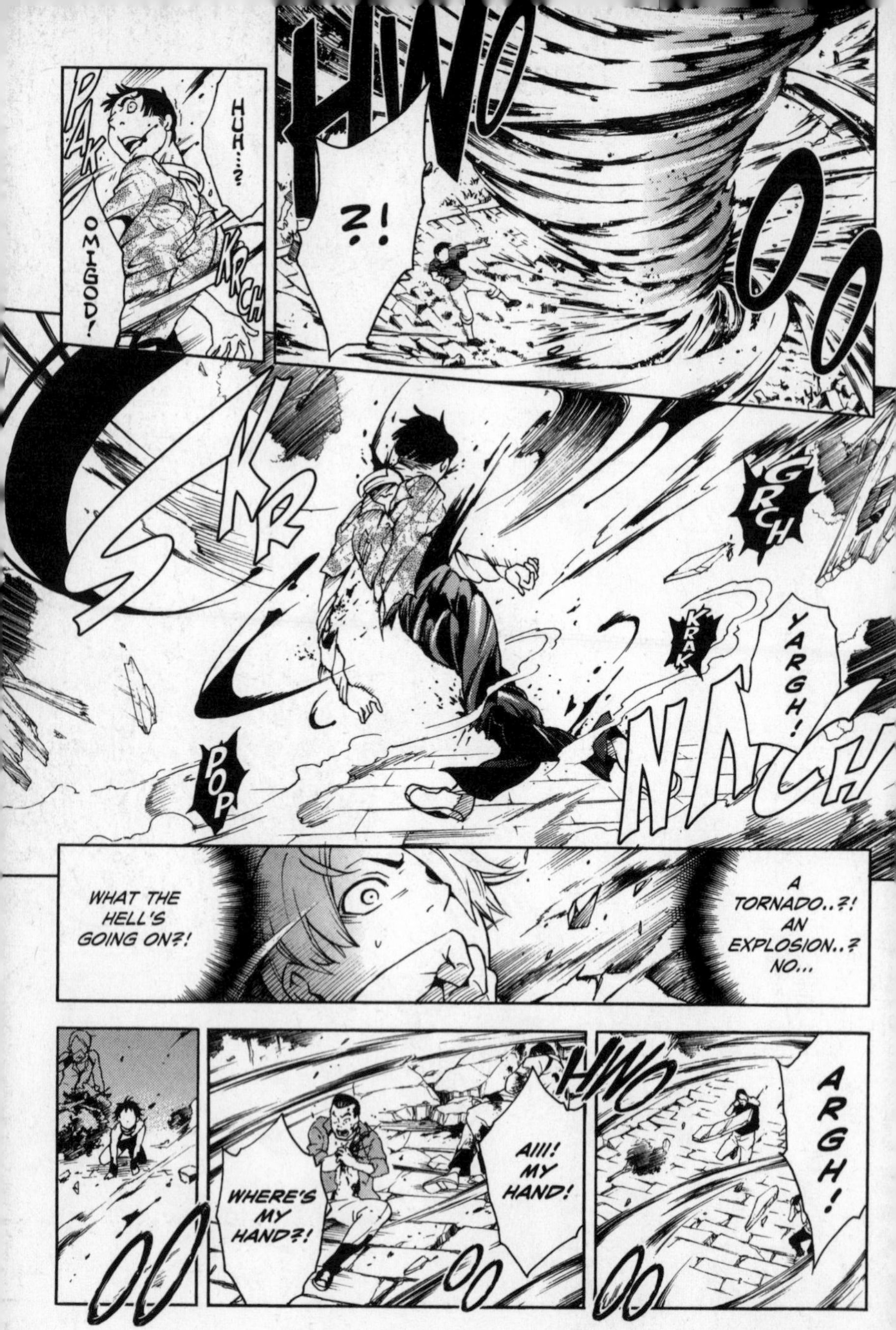
HWOOOO
?!
HUH...?
PAK
KRCH
OMIGOD!
GRCH
YARGH!
KRAK
SKR
NACH
POP
A TORNADO..?! AN EXPLOSION..?! NO...
WHAT THE HELL'S GOING ON?!
ARGH!
HWO
OO
AIII! MY HAND!
WHERE'S MY HAND?!
OO
OO

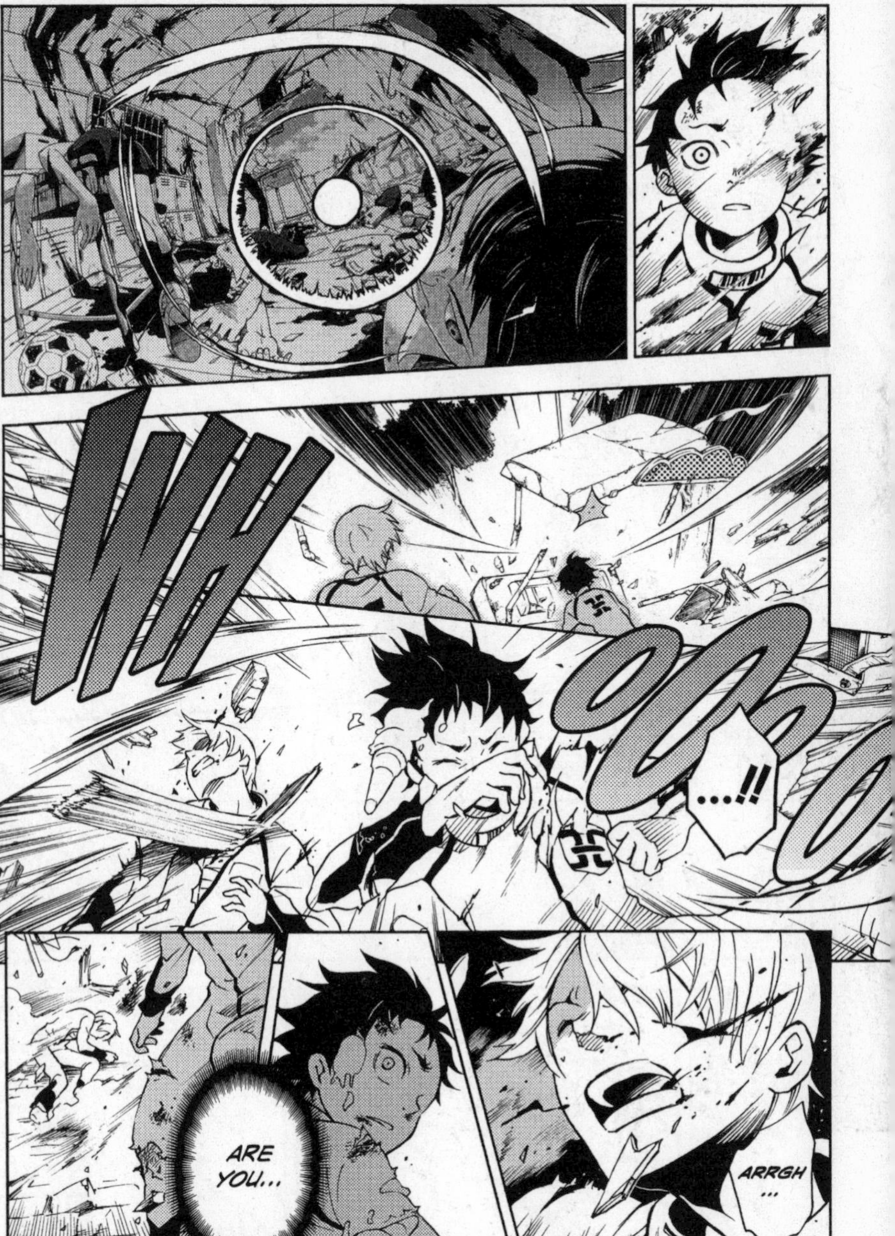
WHOOOO
...!!
ARRGH
...
ARE
YOU...

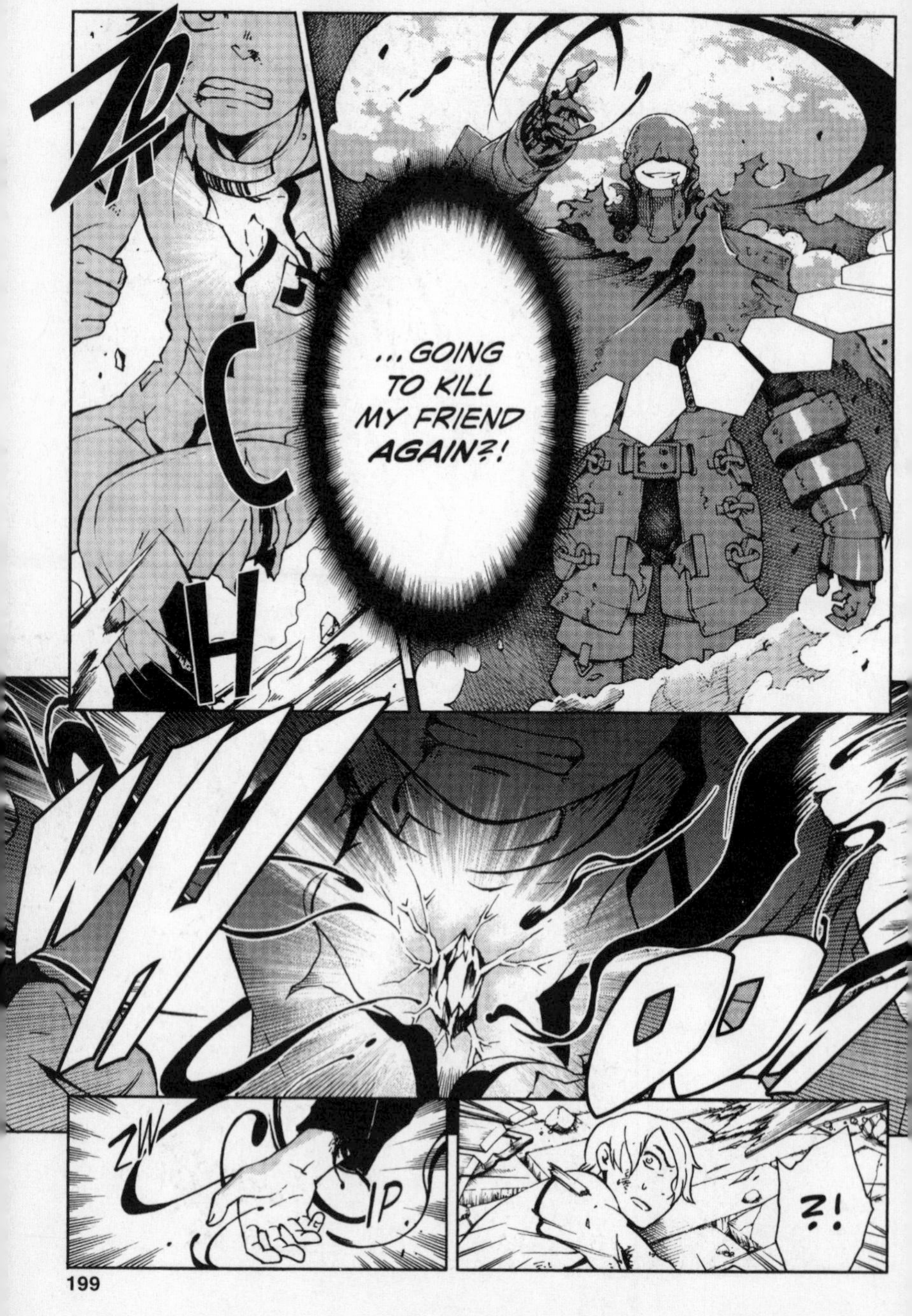
...GOING TO KILL MY FRIEND AGAIN?!
?!

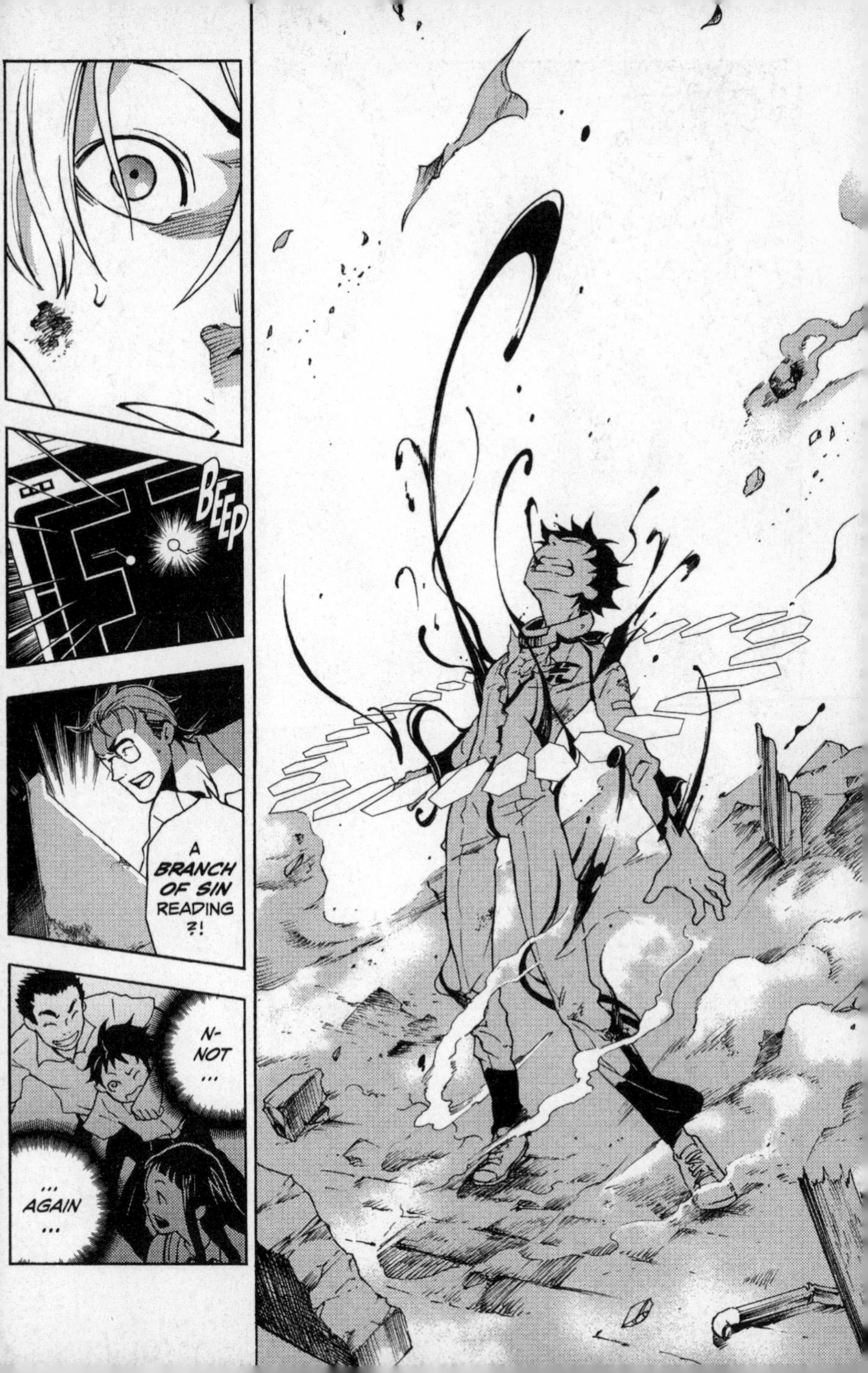
BEEP
A BRANCH OF SIN READING ?!
N-NOT ...
... AGAIN ...

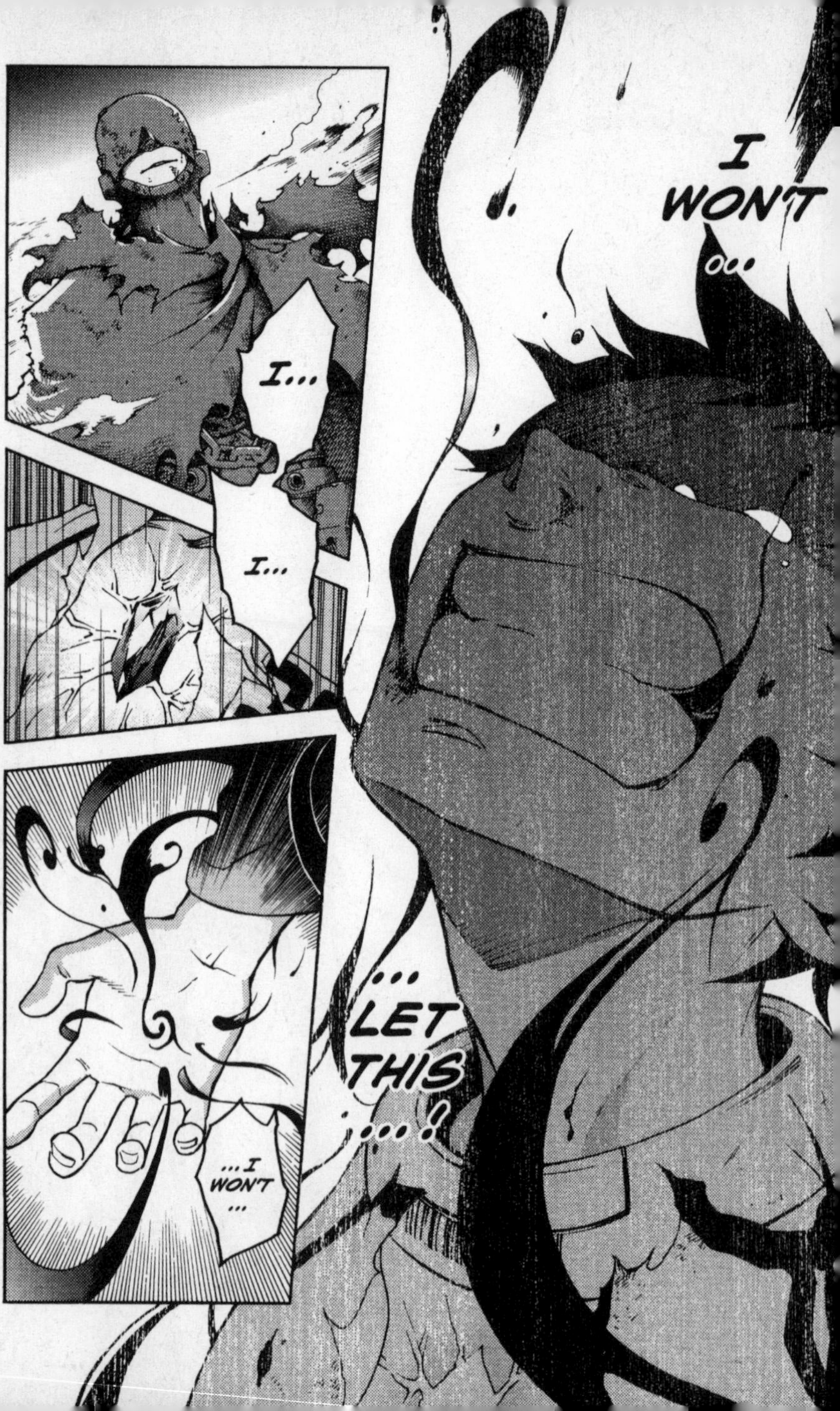
I WON'T ...
...LET THIS ...!
I...
I...
...I WON'T ...

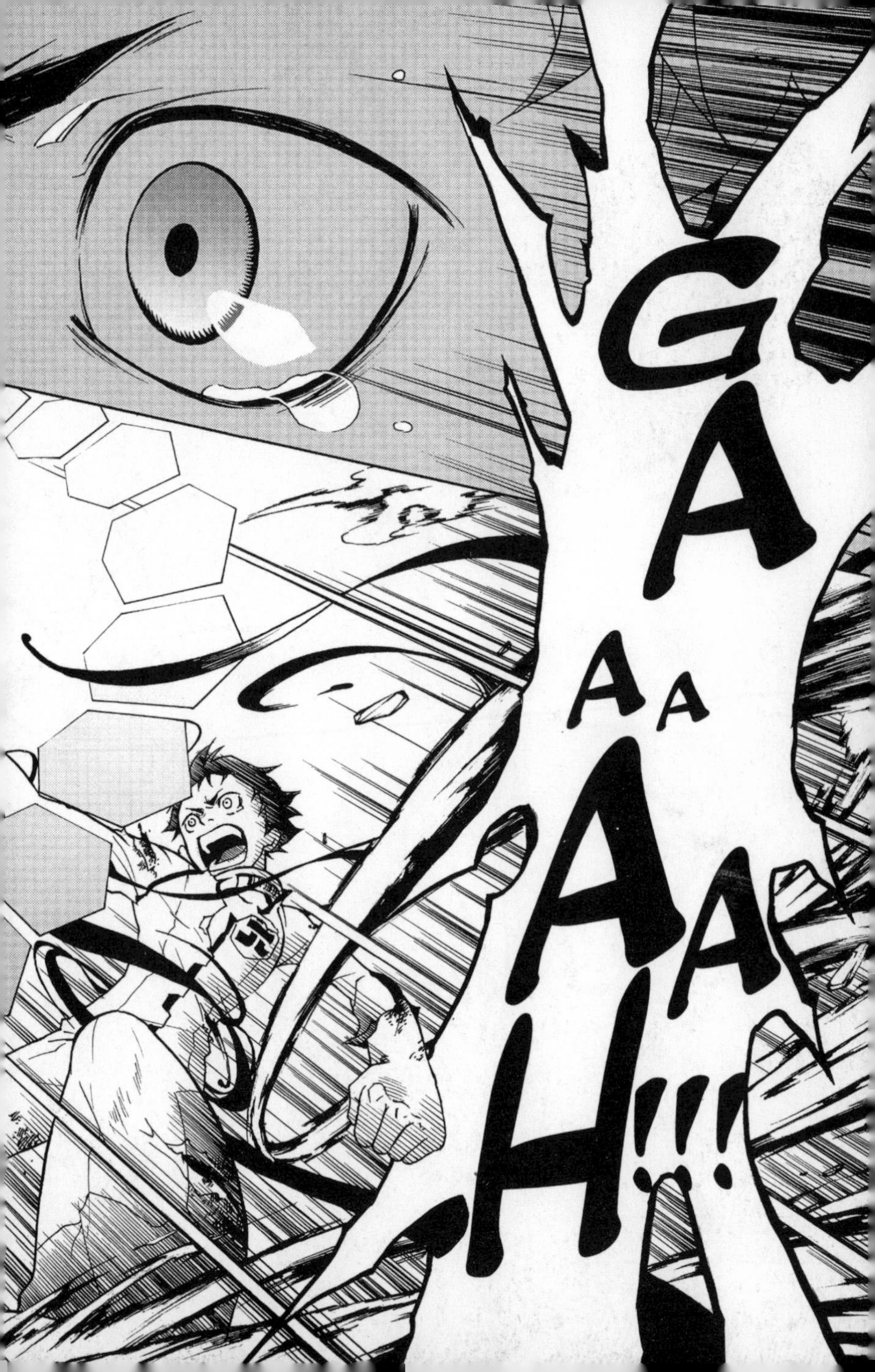
GAAAAAH!!!

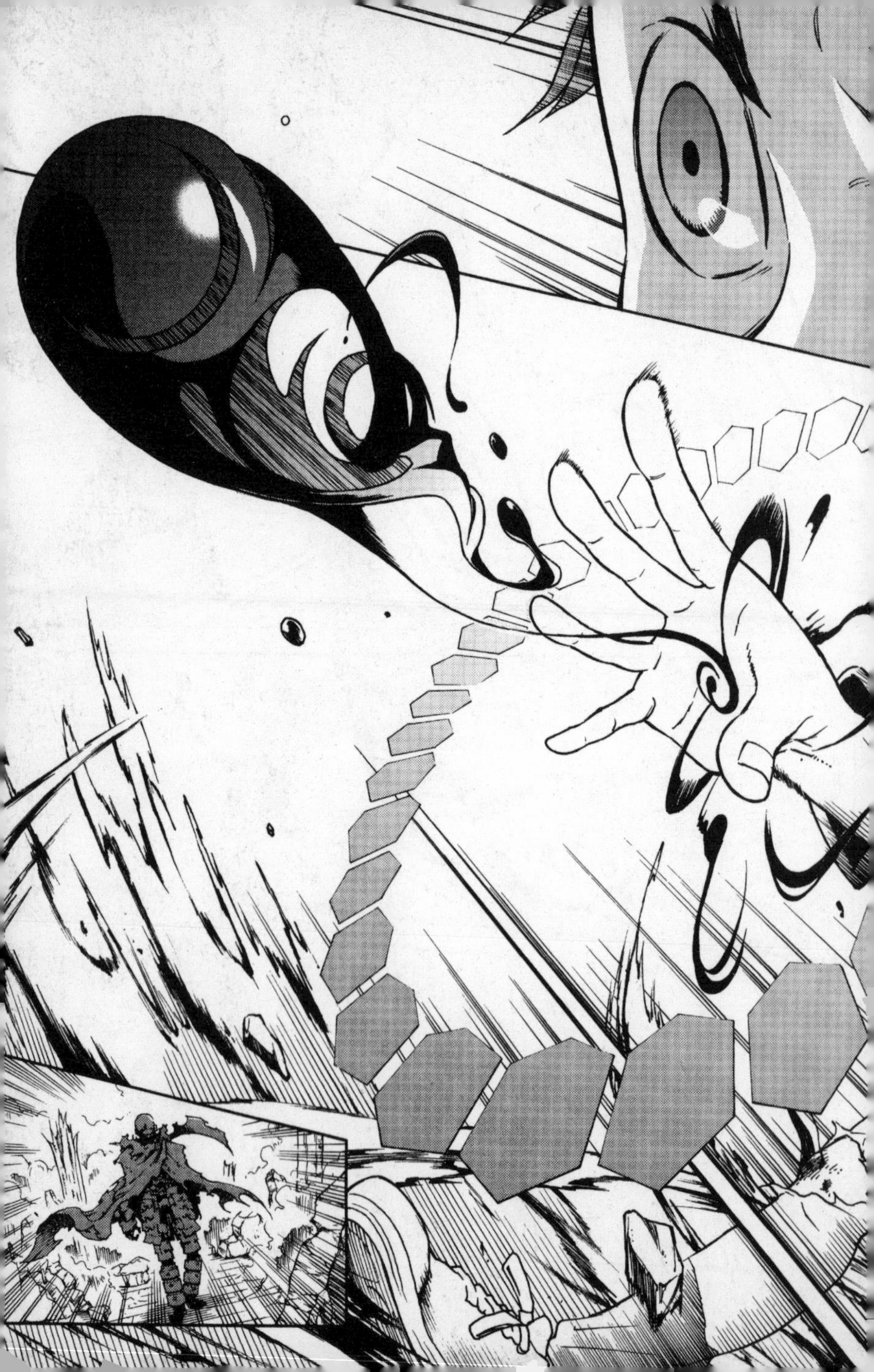

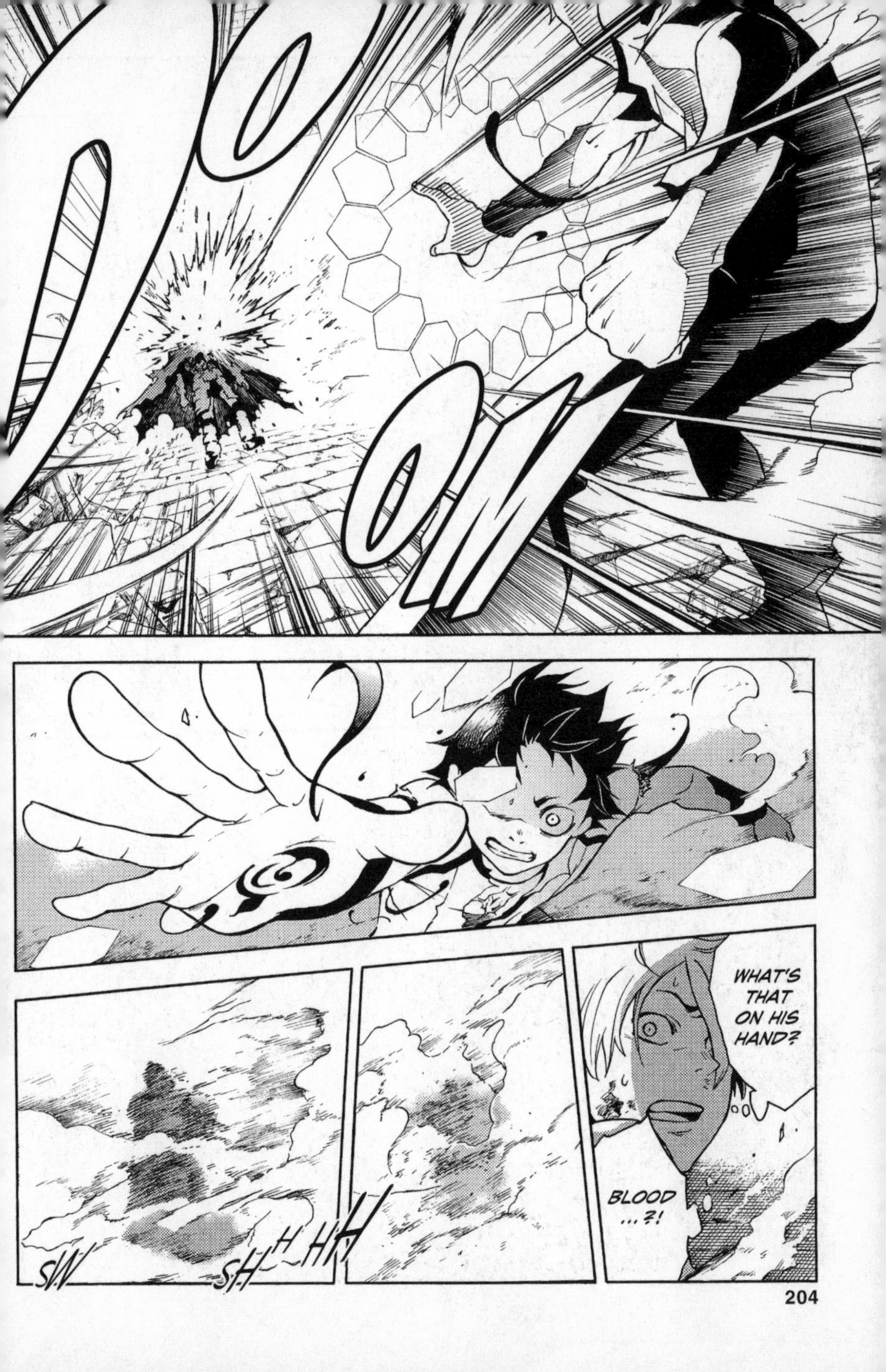
WHAT'S THAT ON HIS HAND?
BLOOD ...?!

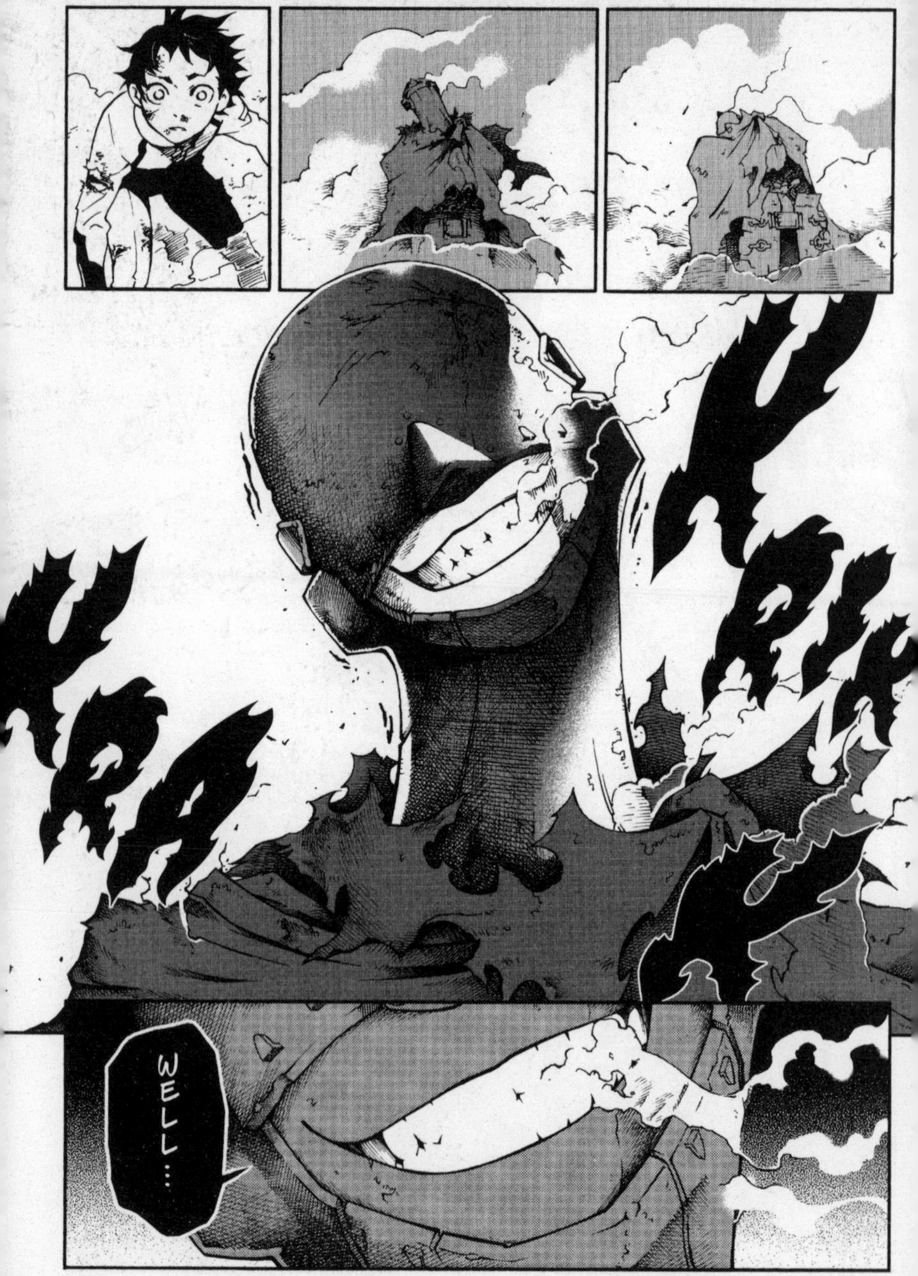
WELL...

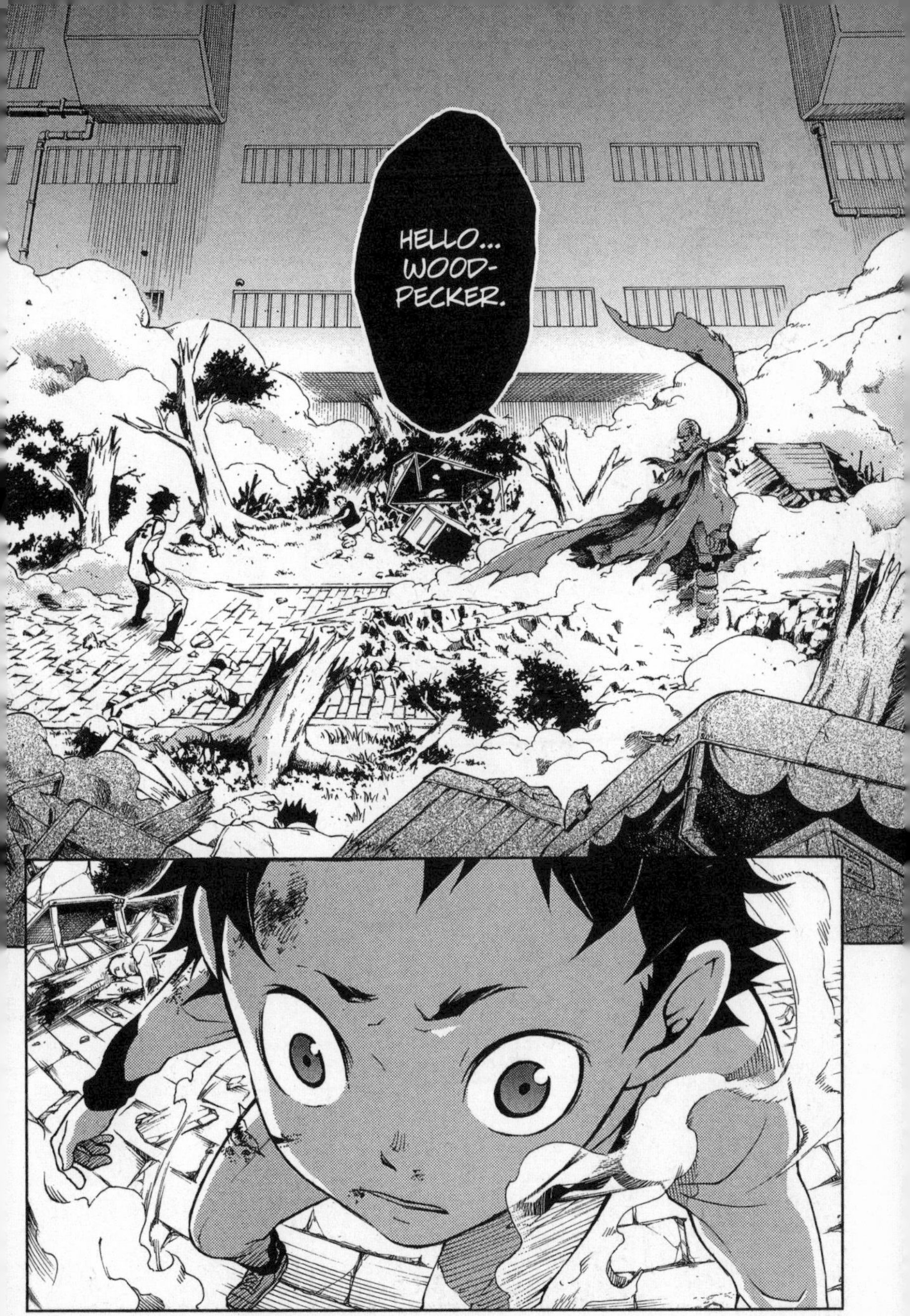
HELLO... WOOD-PECKER.

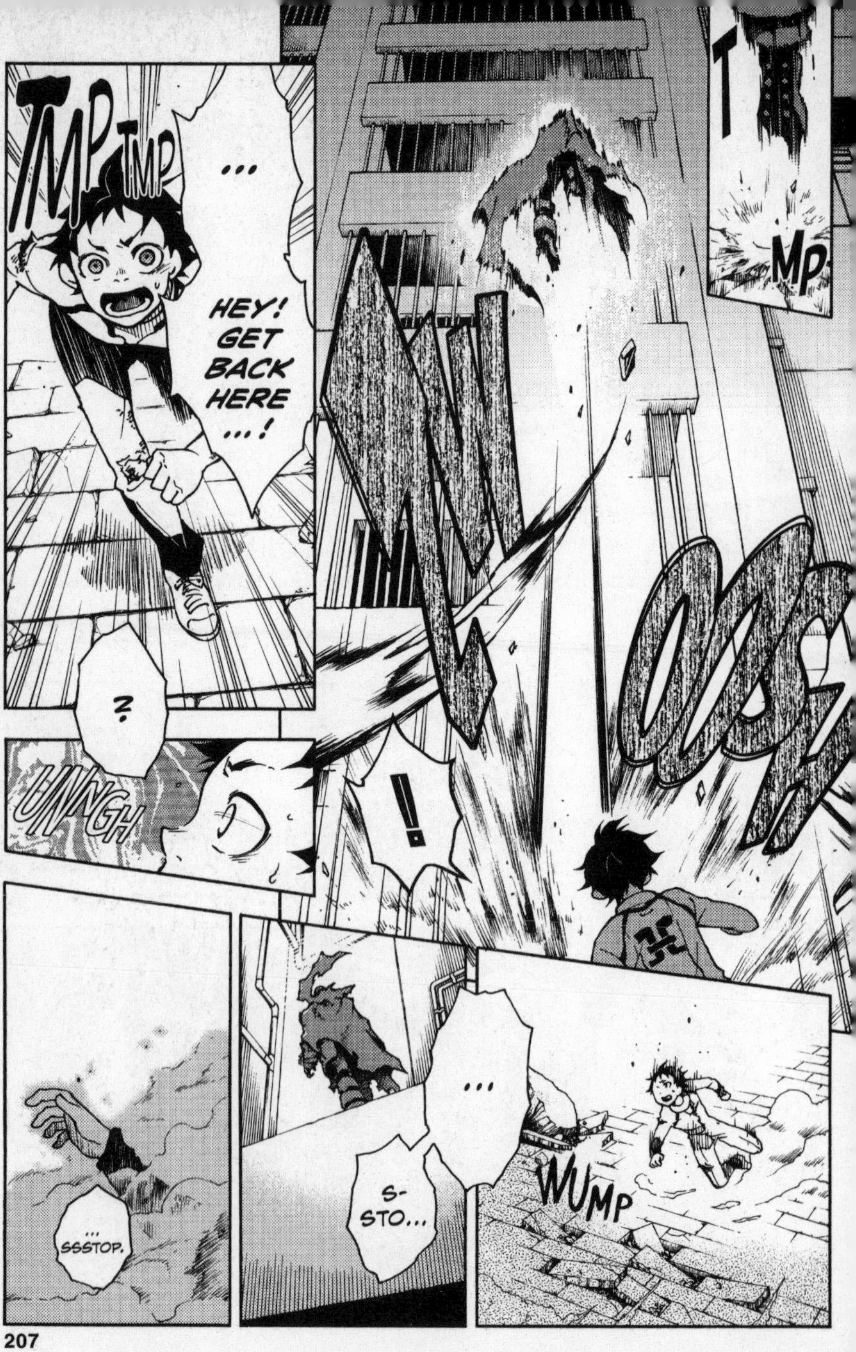
TMP TMP
...
HEY! GET BACK HERE ...!
?
!
UNNGH
...
WUMP
S- STO...
... SSSTOP.

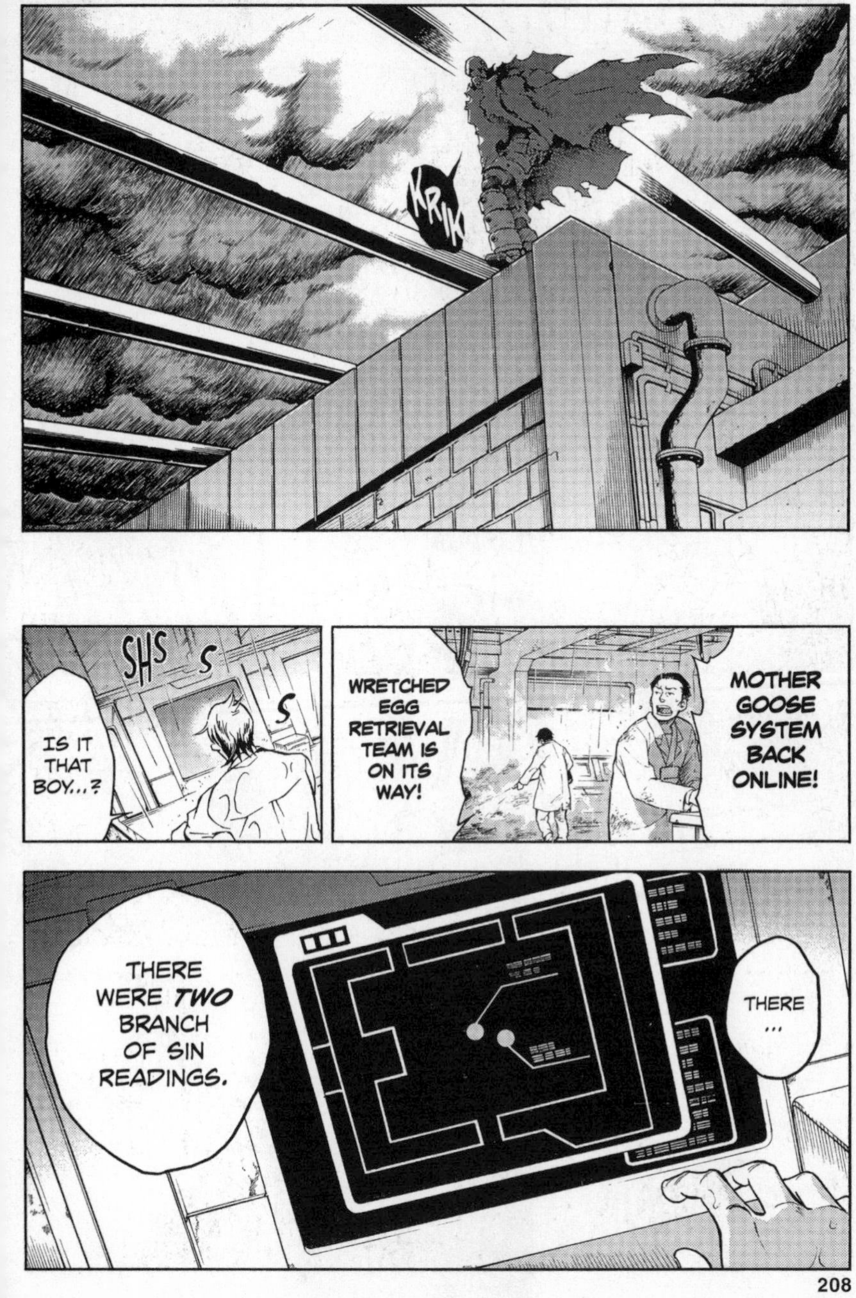
KRIK
MOTHER GOOSE SYSTEM BACK ONLINE!
WRETCHED EGG RETRIEVAL TEAM IS ON ITS WAY!
SHS S S
IS IT THAT BOY...?
THERE ...
THERE WERE TWO BRANCH OF SIN READINGS.

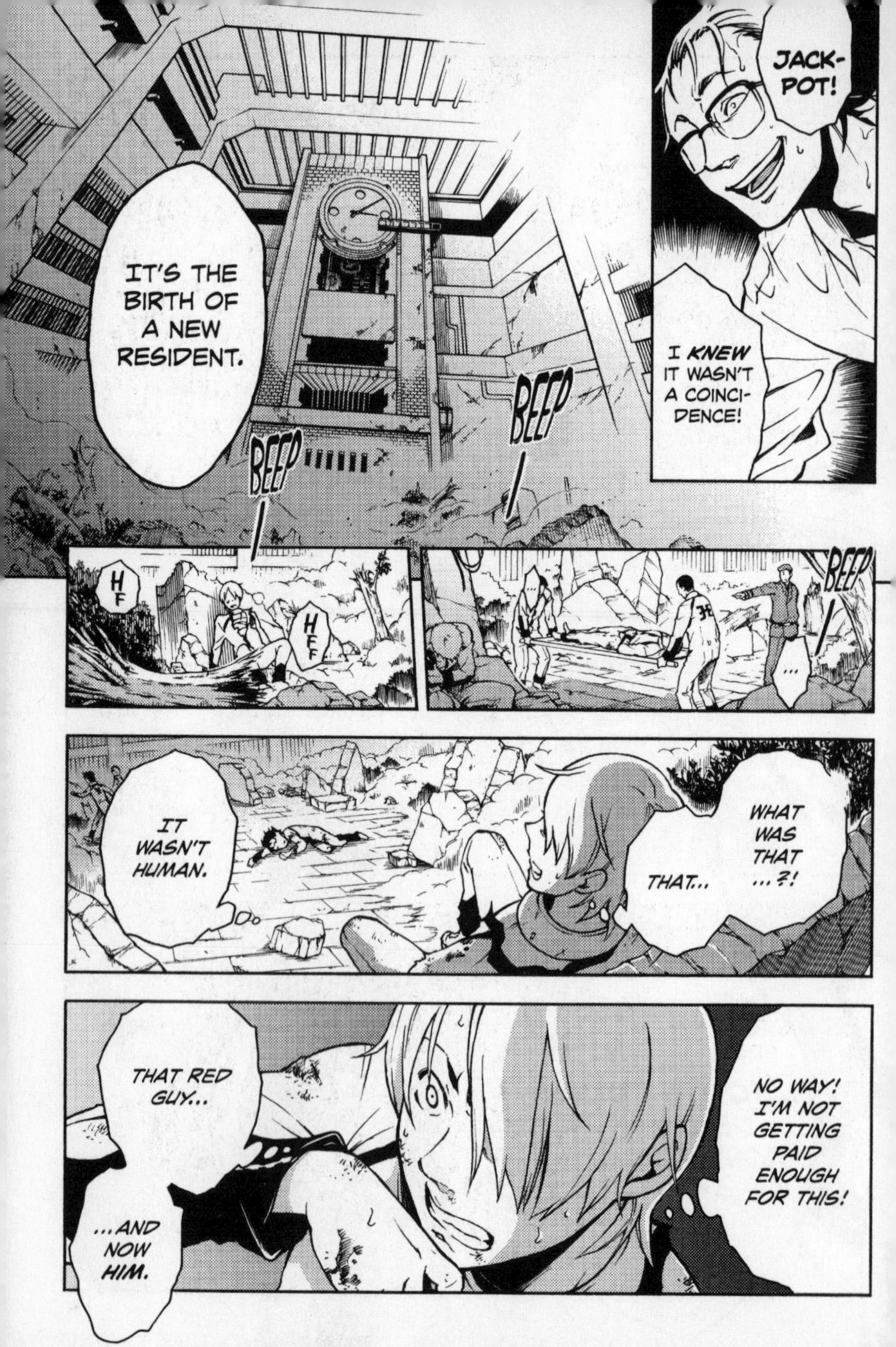
JACK-POT!
I KNEW IT WASN'T A COINCIDENCE!
IT'S THE BIRTH OF A NEW RESIDENT.
BEEP
BEEP
BEEP
...
HF
HF
WHAT WAS THAT ...?!
THAT...
IT WASN'T HUMAN.
NO WAY! I'M NOT GETTING PAID ENOUGH FOR THIS!
THAT RED GUY...
...AND NOW HIM.

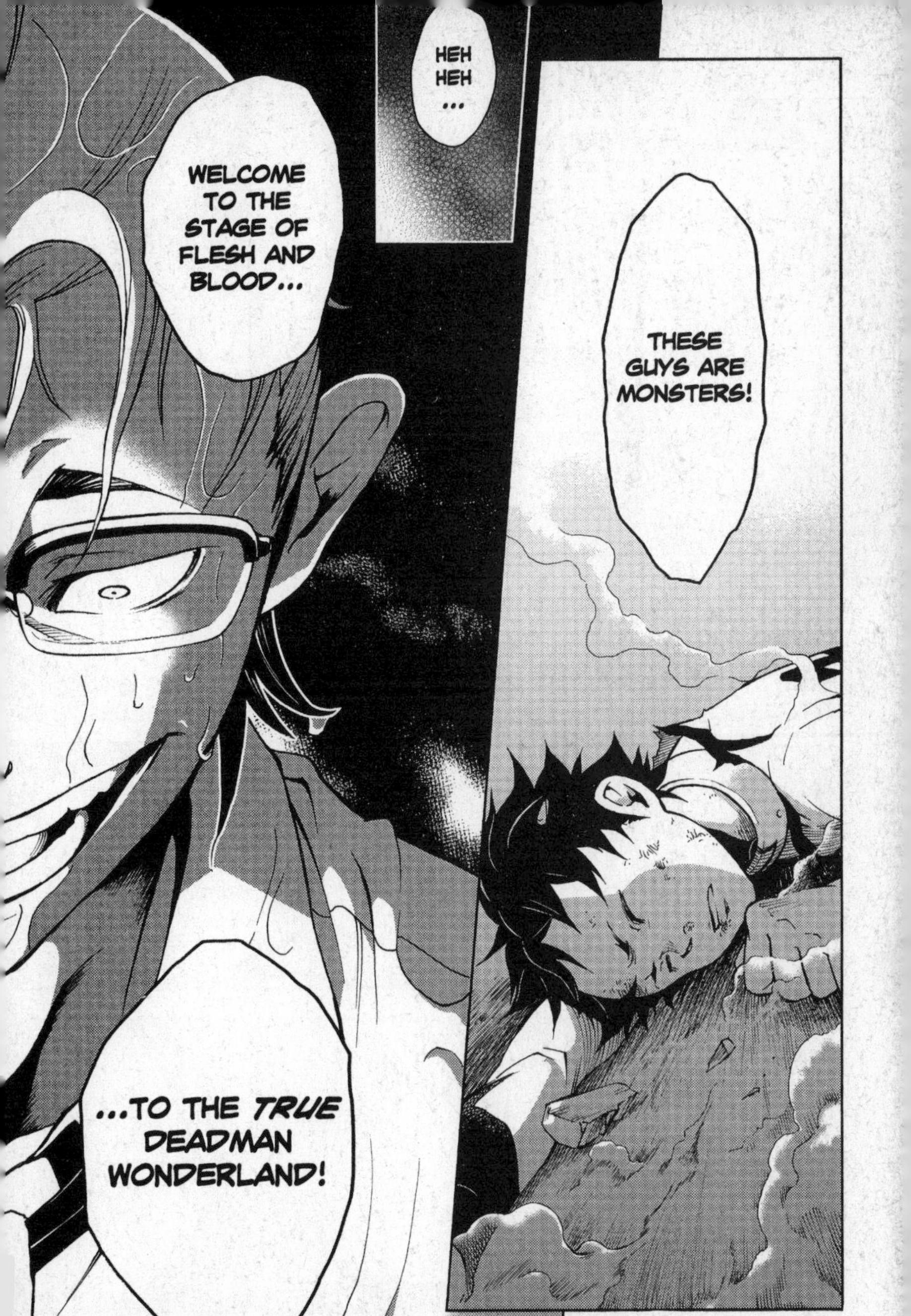
THESE GUYS ARE MONSTERS!
HEH HEH ...
WELCOME TO THE STAGE OF FLESH AND BLOOD...
...TO THE *TRUE* DEADMAN WONDERLAND!

DEADMAN WONDERLAND - VOLUME 1 - END

# DEADMAN
# WONDERLAND
# 1

## Jinsei Kataoka
## Kazuma Kondou

STAFF

Uta Ekaki

Hazuki Kanno

Narumi Kino

Ryuichi Saitaniya

Toshihiro Noguchi

Takako Nobe

Akihiko Higuchi

# CONTINUED
# IN VOLUME
# 2

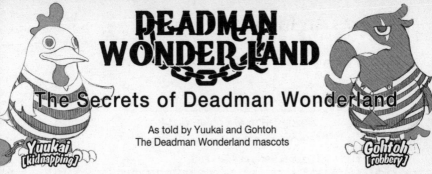

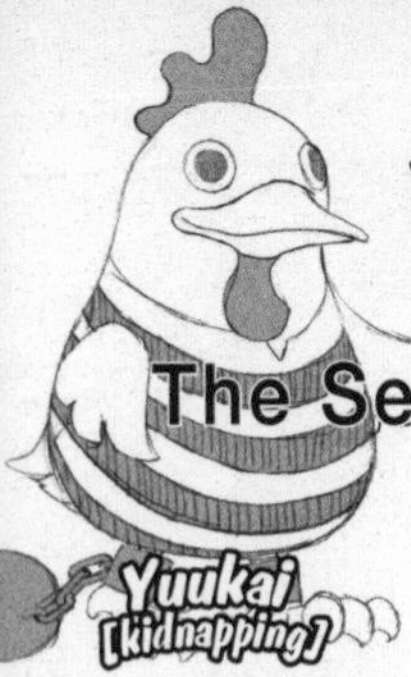
Yuukai
[kidnapping]

# DEADMAN WONDERLAND

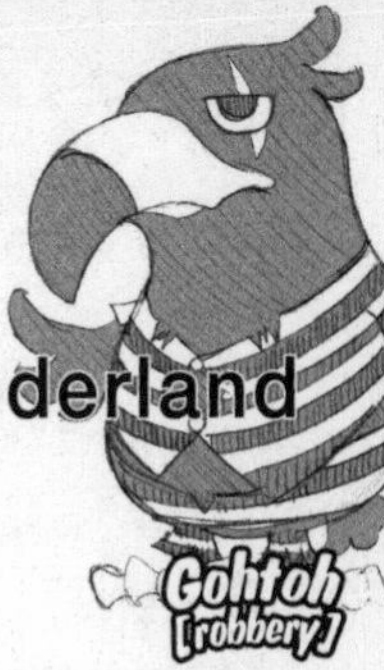
Gohtoh
[robbery]

## The Secrets of Deadman Wonderland

As told by Yuukai and Gohtoh
The Deadman Wonderland mascots

Deadman Wonderland is one of Japan's most popular tourist spots in the wake of the Great Tokyo Earthquake.

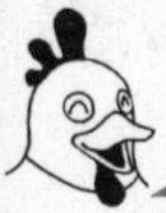

Many people are confused because there aren't many rats. Why is that?

I ate 'em!

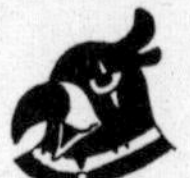

Deadman Wonderland is an Amusement Prison.

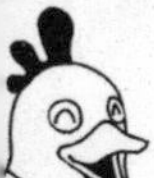

Shows and performances by the prisoners are popular.
It's part of their voluntary social service. Never mind their scary looks!
They've got lots of cool pictures on their skin!

Some of the shows are violent, and we encourage betting on races—but only if you're old enough, so watch for the age restrictions.

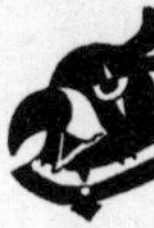

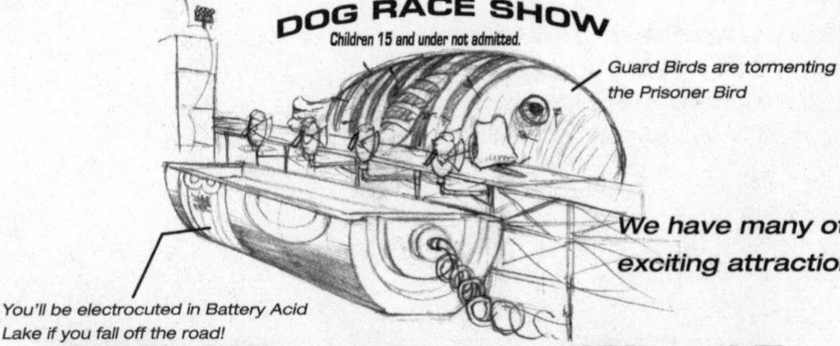
DOG RACE SHOW
Children 15 and under not admitted.
Guard Birds are tormenting the Prisoner Bird
You'll be electrocuted in Battery Acid Lake if you fall off the road!

***We have many other exciting attractions!***

We also have an exclusive broadcast TV channel, so check that out as well!

Nothing's censored on Pay-per-view!
*Female Ex-Model's Secret Room *Murder Mystery—Why I Killed___
*Mafia Boss's Daily Prison Recipes
And many other great programs. Sign up here:

Our heartwarming romantic-comedy "13 Stairs" and other webcomics are available online/mobile.

# Life as an Inmate

★ Prisoners live by earning 'Cast Points' (CP) that they can spend like money.

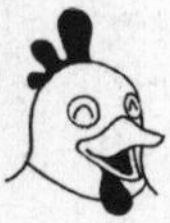

They can eat steak or sashimi with CP.

The harder they work, the better they live,

unlike in other private prisons!

On the other hand, those that don't work don't deserve to live!

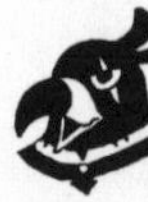

## ★Q & A Segment

Q: Isn't it dangerous to have the visitors so close to the prisoners?
A: We make sure they are separated by a security wall. So you won't be attacked, no matter how much you make fun of them!

Q: Is it true you imprison death row inmates?
A: Yes. In normal prisons, death row inmates, while waiting for their sentences to be carried out, are separated from other prisoners who are serving a limited time in prison.
However, in Deadman Wonderland we have a system of "ongoing execution," so they can be treated the same as other prisoners.

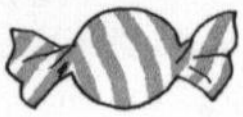

Q: What are their quarters like?
A: The cell block is designed in a panopticon shape. The health and behavior of the prisoners are monitored through collars worn by all inmates.

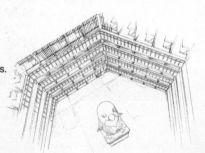

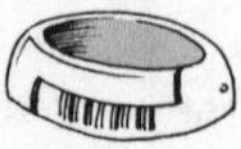

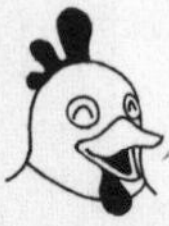

What did you think? Deadman Wonderland sounds like a safe and fun place, right? Come visit us!

Come serve some time here!

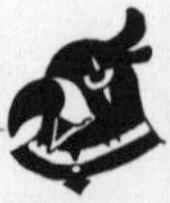

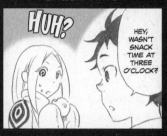

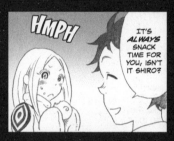

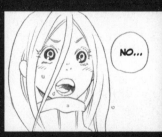

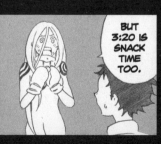

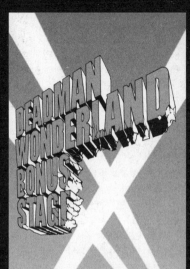

DEADMAN WONDERLAND BONUS STAGE
Jinsei Kataoka
Kazuma Kondou

Snack Time

HUH?
HEY, WASN'T SNACK TIME AT THREE O'CLOCK?
HMPH
IT'S ALWAYS SNACK TIME FOR YOU, ISN'T IT SHIRO?
NO...
BUT 3:20 IS SNACK TIME TOO.

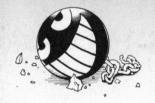

## Unreasonable Demand

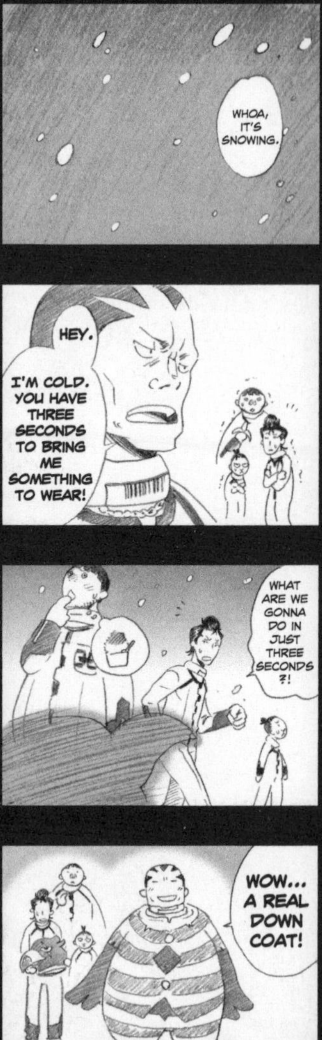
WHOA, IT'S SNOWING.
HEY.
I'M COLD. YOU HAVE THREE SECONDS TO BRING ME SOMETHING TO WEAR!
WHAT ARE WE GONNA DO IN JUST THREE SECONDS?!
WOW... A REAL DOWN COAT!

## Puzzle Ring

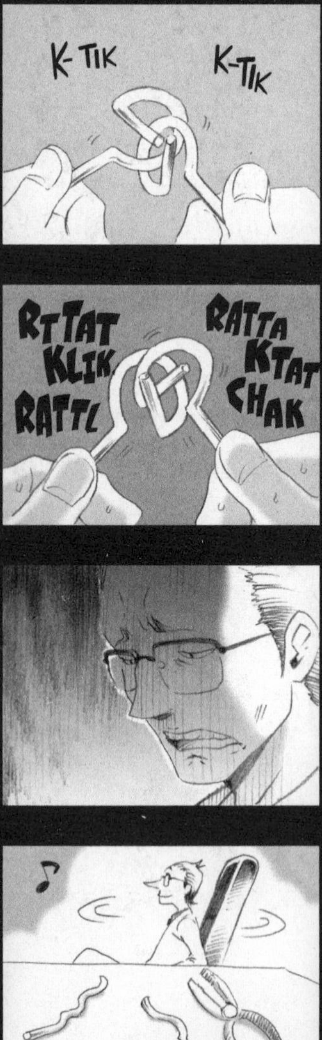
K-TIK
K-TIK
RATTA KTAT CHAK
RTTAT KLIK RATTL

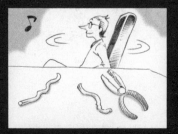

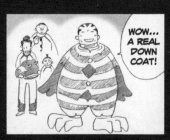

DEADMAN WONDERLAND

EDITED BY KADOKAWA SHOTEN
FIRST PUBLISHED IN JAPAN IN 2007 BY KADOKAWA CORPORATION, TOKYO.
ENGLISH TRANSLATION RIGHTS ARRANGED WITH KADOKAWA CORPORATION, TOKYO.

TRANSLATION/JOE YAMAZAKI
ENGLISH ADAPTATION/STAN!
TOUCH-UP ART & LETTERING/JAMES GAUBATZ
DESIGN/SAM ELZWAY
EDITOR/MIKE MONTESA

THE STORIES, CHARACTERS AND INCIDENTS MENTIONED
IN THIS PUBLICATION ARE ENTIRELY FICTIONAL.

PRINTED IN THE U.S.A.

PUBLISHED BY VIZ MEDIA, LLC
P.O. BOX 77010
SAN FRANCISCO, CA 94107

10 9 8 7 6 5 4 3 2 1
FIRST PRINTING, FEBRUARY 2014

VIZ
MEDIA

www.viz.com

**PARENTAL ADVISORY**
DEADMAN WONDERLAND is rated T+ and is
recommended for older teens. This volume
contains scenes of supernatural horror and
violence, and suggestive themes.
ratings.viz.com